BlackBerry Curve Made Simple

For the BlackBerry Curve 8520, 8530 and 8500 Series

Martin Trautschold
and
Gary Mazo

Apress®

Blackberry Curve Made Simple

ISBN-13 (pbk): 978-1-4302-3123-3

ISBN-13 (electronic): 978-1-4302-3124-0

President and Publisher: Paul Manning
Lead Editor: Steve Anglin
Development Editor: James Markham
Editorial Board: Clay Andres, Steve Anglin, Mark Beckner, Ewan Buckingham, Gary Cornell, Jonathan Gennick, Jonathan Hassell, Michelle Lowman, Matthew Moodie, Duncan Parkes, Jeffrey Pepper, Frank Pohlmann, Douglas Pundick, Ben Renow-Clarke, Dominic Shakeshaft, Matt Wade, Tom Welsh
Coordinating Editor: Laurin Becker
Copy Editor: Mary Ann Fugate, Chris Marcheso, Patrick Meador, Ralph Moore, Katie Stence
Compositor: MacPS, LLC
Indexer: BIM Indexing & Proofreading Services
Cover Designer: Anna Ishchenko

Distributed to the book trade worldwide by Springer Science+Business Media, LLC., 233 Spring Street, 6th Floor, New York, NY 10013. Phone 1-800-SPRINGER, fax (201) 348-4505, e-mail orders-ny@springer-sbm.com, or visit www.springeronline.com.

For information on translations, please e-mail rights@apress.com, or visit www.apress.com.

Apress and friends of ED books may be purchased in bulk for academic, corporate, or promotional use. eBook versions and licenses are also available for most titles. For more information, reference our Special Bulk Sales–eBook Licensing web page at www.apress.com/info/bulksales.

Contents at a Glance

Contents

■ Chapter 11: Advanced Phone 229

■ Chapter 12: E-mail Like a Pro... 239

About the Authors

Martin Trautschold is the founder and CEO of Made Simple Learning, a leading provider of Apple iPad, iPhone, iPod touch, BlackBerry, and Palm webOS books and video tutorials. He has been a successful entrepreneur in the mobile device training and software business since 2001. With Made Simple Learning, he helped to train thousands of BlackBerry Smartphone users with short, to-the-point video tutorials. Martin has now co-authored fifteen "Made Simple" guide books. He also co-founded, ran for 3 years, and then sold a mobile device software company. Prior to this, Martin spent 15 years in technology and business consulting in the US and Japan. He holds an engineering degree from Princeton University and an MBA from the Kellogg School at Northwestern University. Martin and his wife, Julia, have three daughters. He enjoys rowing and cycling. Martin can be reached at martin@madesimplelearning.com.

Gary Mazo is Vice President of Made Simple Learning and is a writer, a college professor, a gadget nut, and an ordained rabbi. Gary joined Made Simple Learning in 2007 and has co-authored the last thirteen books in the Made Simple series. Along with Martin, and Kevin Michaluk from CrackBerry.com, Gary co-wrote *CrackBerry: True Tales of BlackBerry Use and Abuse*—a book about BlackBerry addiction and how to get a grip on one's BlackBerry use. Gary also teaches writing, philosophy, technical writing, and more at the University of Phoenix. Gary is a regular contributor to CrackBerry.com—writing product reviews and adding editorial content. He holds a BA in anthropology from Brandeis University. Gary earned his M.A.H.L (Masters in Hebrew Letters) as well as ordination as Rabbi from the Hebrew Union College-Jewish Institute of Religion in Cincinnati, Ohio. He has served congregations in Dayton, Ohio, Cherry Hill, New Jersey and Cape Cod, Massachusetts. Gary is married to Gloria Schwartz Mazo; they have six children. Gary can be reached at: gary@madesimplelearning.com.

Acknowledgments

A book like this takes many people to put together. We would like to thank Apress for believing in us and our unique style of writing.

We would like to thank our editors, Jim and Laurin, and the entire editorial team at Apress.

We would like to thank our families for their patience and support in allowing us to pursue projects such as this one.

Part I

Quick Start Guide

In your hands is one of the most capable devices to hit the market in quite some time: the BlackBerry Curve. This Quick Start Guide will help get you and your new Curve up and running in a hurry. You'll learn all about the buttons, switches, and ports, and how to use the responsive Trackpad to help you get around. Our App Reference Tables introduce you to the apps on your Curve—and serve as a quick way to find out how to accomplish a task.

Getting Around Quickly

This Quick Start Guide is meant to be just that—a tool that can help you jump right in and find information in this book—and learn the basics of how to get around and enjoy your Curve right away.

We start with the nuts and bolts in our "Learning Your Way Around" section—what all the keys, buttons, switches, and symbols mean and do on your Curve. You will learn how to get inside the back of your Curve to remove and replace the battery, SIM card and media card. You will also learn how to use the **Menu** key, **Escape** key, **Trackpad** and other important buttons. We show you some great time-saving tips for menus and setting dates and times as well as how to multitask.

In the section "Working With the Wireless Network," we help you understand when the letters, numbers, and symbols at the top of your Curve screen tell you and which help you make phone calls, send SMS text messages, send and receive e-mail, or browse the web. We also show you how to handle your Curve on an airplane when you might need to turn off the wireless network, Wi-Fi and Bluetooth radios.

In the "App Reference Tables," section, we've organized the app icons into general categories so that you can quickly browse the icons and jump to a section in the book to learn more about the app a particular icon represents. The following are the tables:

- Getting Set Up (Table 2)
- Staying In Touch (Table 3)
- Staying Organized (Table 4)
- Being Productive (Table 5)
- Being Entertained (Table 6)
- Networking Socially (Table 7)
- Personalize Your Curve (Table 8)
- Add and Remove Software (Table 9)

Learning Your Way Around

To help you get comfortable with your Curve, we start with the basics—what the keys, buttons, ports and trackpad do and how to open up the back cover to get at your battery, media, and SIM card. Then, we move into how you start apps and navigate the menus. We end this section with a number of very useful time-saving tips and tricks about getting around the menus, setting dates and times, and many great ways to use the **Space** key.

Keys, Buttons, and Ports

Figure 1 shows all the things you can do with the buttons, keys, switches, and ports on your Curve. Go ahead and try out a few things to see what happens. Try pressing the **Menu** key for 2 seconds, press and hold the **1** key, press the side **Convenience** keys, click on an icon, then press the **Escape** key. Have some fun getting acquainted with your device.

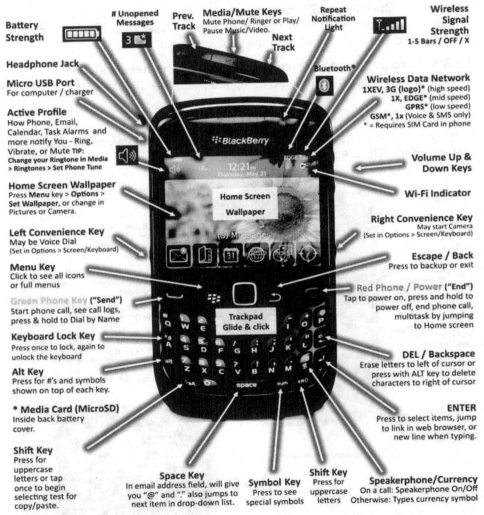

Battery Strength

 # Unopened Messages

Prev. Track

Media/Mute Keys Mute Phone/ Ringer or Play/ Pause Music/Video.

Next Track

Repeat Notification Light

Wireless Signal Strength 1-5 Bars / OFF / X

Headphone Jack

Micro USB Port For computer / charger

Bluetooth®

Wireless Data Network 1XEV, 3G (logo)* (high speed) 1X, EDGE* (mid speed) GPRS* (low speed) GSM*, 1x (Voice & SMS only) * = Requires SIM Card in phone

Active Profile How Phone, Email, Calendar, Task Alarms and more notify You - Ring, Vibrate, or Mute TIP: Change your Ringtone in Media > Ringtones > Set Phone Tune

Volume Up & Down Keys

Home Screen Wallpaper Press Menu key > Options > Set Wallpaper, or change in Pictures or Camera.

Wi-Fi Indicator

Right Convenience Key May start Camera (Set in Options > Screen/Keyboard)

Left Convenience Key May be Voice Dial (Set in Options > Screen/Keyboard)

Escape / Back Press to backup or exit

Menu Key Click to see all icons or full menus

Red Phone / Power ("End") Tap to power on, press and hold to power off, end phone call, multitask by jumping to Home screen

Green Phone Key ("Send") Start phone call, see call logs, press & hold to Dial by Name

Keyboard Lock Key Press once to lock, again to unlock the keyboard

DEL / Backspace Erase letters to left of cursor or press with ALT key to delete characters to right of cursor

Alt Key Press for #'s and symbols shown on top of each key.

ENTER Press to select items, jump to link in web browser, or new line when typing.

* Media Card (MicroSD) Inside back battery cover.

Shift Key Press for uppercase letters or tap once to begin selecting test for copy/paste.

Space Key In email address field, will give you "@" and "." also jumps to next item in drop-down list.

Symbol Key Press to see special symbols

Shift Key Press for uppercase letters

Speakerphone/Currency On a call: Speakerphone On/Off Otherwise: Types currency symbol

Trackpad Glide & click

Home Screen Wallpaper

Figure 1. *Keys, buttons, and ports on the BlackBerry Curve*

Inside Your Curve

You have to get inside your Curve to access your battery, SIM card slot, and media card slot. The following instructions and Figure 2 show you how.

To Remove the Back Cover:
Insert your fingernail into the opening at the bottom of the Battery cover and gently lift up. Take it out of the two notches at the top.

To Remove or Replace the Battery:
Gently put your fingernail at the top edge of the battery and pry the top edge out first. Then, remove the battery. To replace it, insert the bottom edge of the battery with the metal contacts and push down the top edge.

To Insert a Memory Card (MicroSD format):
Gently place the media card with the metal contacts facing down and slide it completely into the memory card slot (see below) from the top.

To Insert a SIM Card (required to connect to a GSM phone network):
Remove the battery and slide the SIM card completely into the SIM card slot from left to right (see Figure 2).

To Replace the Back Cover:
Insert the two notches at the top (near the top of the battery) and press the cover down from the bottom of the BlackBerry until it clicks into place.

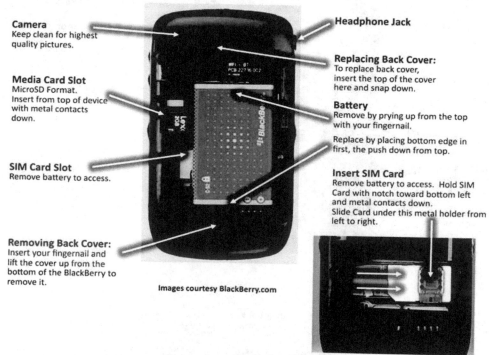

Camera
Keep clean for highest quality pictures.

Media Card Slot
MicroSD Format. Insert from top of device with metal contacts down.

SIM Card Slot
Remove battery to access.

Removing Back Cover:
Insert your fingernail and lift the cover up from the bottom of the BlackBerry to remove it.

Headphone Jack

Replacing Back Cover:
To replace back cover, insert the top of the cover here and snap down.

Battery
Remove by prying up from the top with your fingernail.

Replace by placing bottom edge in first, the push down from top.

Insert SIM Card
Remove battery to access. Hold SIM Card with notch toward bottom left and metal contacts down. Slide Card under this metal holder from left to right.

Images courtesy BlackBerry.com

Figure 2. *Inside your Curve: the Battery, Media Card, and SIM Card slots*

Starting and Exiting Icons

You use the **Trackpad**, **Menu** key, and **Escape** key to navigate around your BlackBerry, open folders, and select icons (see Figure 3). The **Escape** key will get you back out one step at a time, the **Red Phone** key will jump you all the way back to your **Home** screen. You can change the background image (wallpaper) also called the **Home** screen image, from your media player or camera. You can change the look and feel or theme of your Curve by going into the **Options** icon and selecting **Theme** (see page 178). You will learn how to move icons on page 169 or hide icons on page 1711.

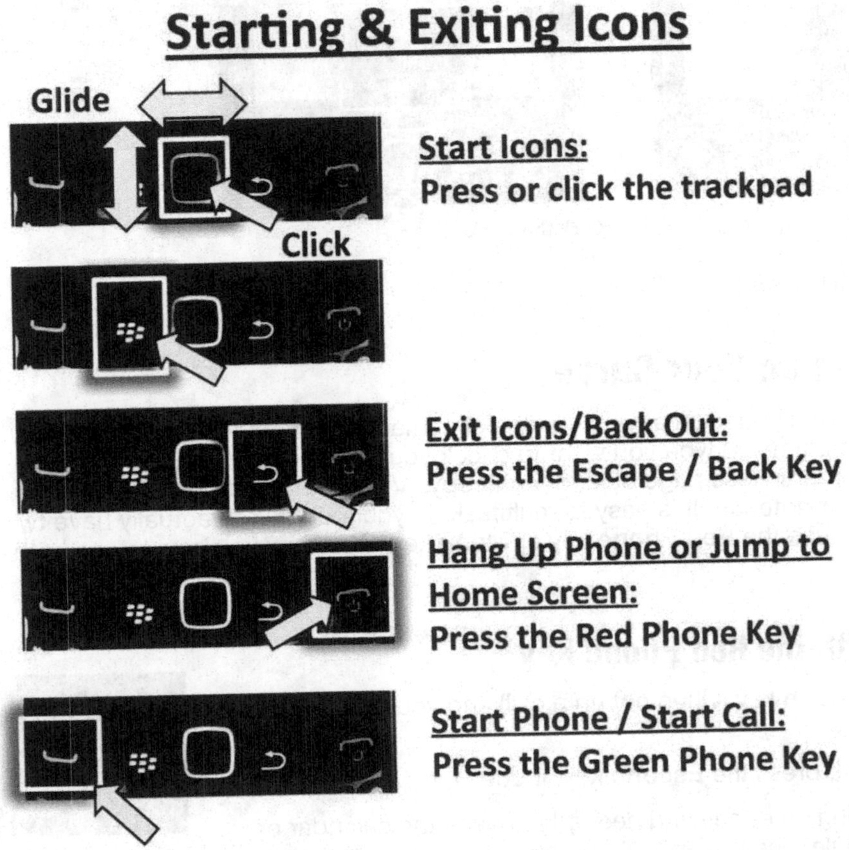

Starting & Exiting Icons

Glide

Start Icons:
Press or click the trackpad

Click

Exit Icons/Back Out:
Press the Escape / Back Key

Hang Up Phone or Jump to Home Screen:
Press the Red Phone Key

Start Phone / Start Call:
Press the Green Phone Key

Figure 3. *How to start and exit icons (Apps)*

Two Types of Menus (Full and Short)

One useful thing on your BlackBerry is the two types of menus: Full and Short (Figure 4). You see the Full Menu by pressing the **Menu** key and the Short Menu by pressing the **Trackpad**. You will notice that the Short Menu will often times have exactly the thing you want to do highlighted, like **Send** or **Forward**, saving you time with common tasks.

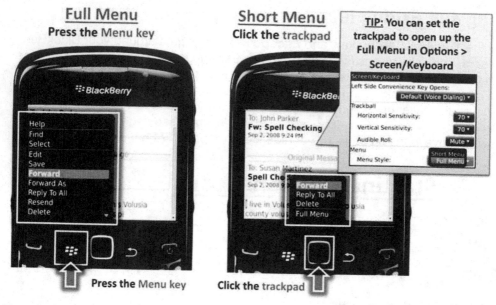

Figure 4. *Full and short menus*

Multitasking on Your Curve

Once you start using your Curve, you will almost immediately want to start doing a few things at the same time. Maybe you want to check your **Calendar** while listening to **Pandora** internet radio (see page 384), or cut, copy, and paste text from an e-mail message into your notepad. It is easy to multitask on your curve. You actually have two choices: you can use the **Red Phone** key or **Menu** key. We show you how to use both below.

Multitask with the Red Phone Key

Press the **Red Phone** key (when not on a call) and you jump right to the home screen.

Or when on a call, press the **Escape** key, it does the same thing.

Say you are writing an e-mail and needed to check the calendar or wanted to schedule a new event.

1. Press the **Red Phone** key to jump to the **Home Screen**.

2. Start the **Calendar** to check your schedule.

3. Press the **Red Phone** key again to return to the **Home Screen**.

4. Click on the **Messages** icon to return exactly to where you left off composing your e-mail message.

Remember, though, that if you always use the **Red Phone** key to jump out of icons and leave them running in the background, over time your blackberry will slow down.

Multitask with the Menu Key

You can also multitask using the **Menu** key. Just press and hold it to bring up the multitasking pop-up window.

1. Press and hold the **Menu** key to see the pop-up window of running apps.

2. Glide the **Trackpad** to the app you want to start.

3. Click on the **Home** app, if you don't see the icon you want to start. Then click on the icon you want to start from the **Home screen**.

4. Repeat the procedure to return to the app you started in.

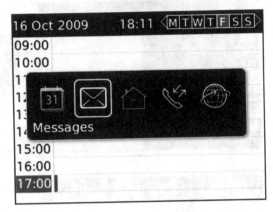

Jump to First Letter Trick for Menus and Drop-Downs

Getting around on your Curve, you will probably access at least 20 menus every day, sometimes many more. Since you use menus so often, saving a little time on every menu will result in a lot of overall time savings. You can do this by pressing the first letter of the menu item, list, or drop-down item on your keyboard to instantly jump down to it. See Figure 5.

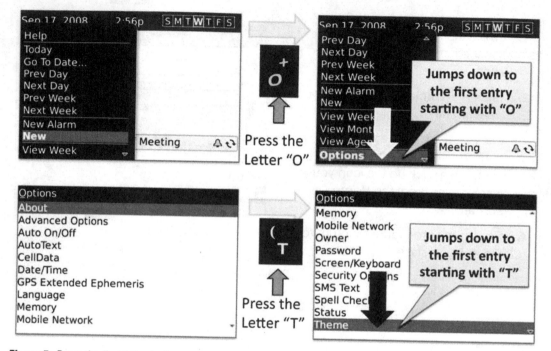

Figure 5. *Press the first letter to Jump to a particular menu item or list item.*

Save Time with the Space Key

Pressing the **Space** key will save you time when you type e-mail or web addresses (Figure 6). Hitting the **Space** key in an e-mail address instead of an "@" sign or a dot inserts those characters into an e-mail address or web address. Also, pressing it twice at the end of a sentence will automatically insert a period and capitalize the first letter of the next sentence.

Save Time with the Space Key

- Use the **Space** key when typing:
  Email Addresses
  - Type:
    - susan **Space** company **Space** com

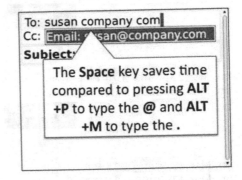

The **Space** key saves time compared to pressing **ALT** +P to type the @ and **ALT** +M to type the .

  Web Addresses
  - Get the dot "." in the address:
  - Type:
    - www **Space** google **Space** com

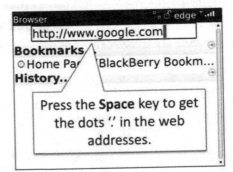

Press the **Space** key to get the dots "." in the web addresses.

TIP: Save time typing by pressing the **Space** key twice at the end of each sentence. You will get an automatic period and the next letter will be uppercase.

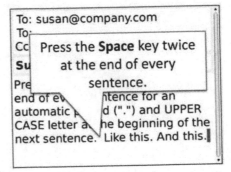

Press the **Space** key twice at the end of every sentence.

Figure 6. *Use the **Space** key to quickly type e-mail and web addresses*

Setting Dates and Times with the Space Key

When you are setting dates or times, try using the **Space** key to jump to the next month, day, hour, or 15 minutes (Figure 7). It can be a great time saver if you want to schedule something just a month, day, hour, or 15 minutes ahead.

- The **Space** key will jump to the next item in a date, time or drop-down list field. Will jump to next 15 minutes in minute field.

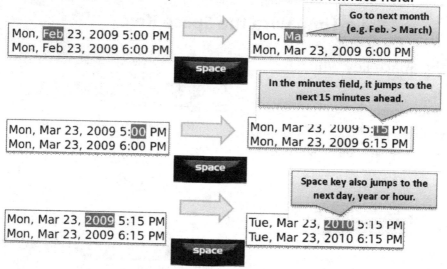

Figure 7. *Use Space key to advance a month, day, year, or 15 minutes*

Setting Dates and Times with Number Keys

When you are setting dates or times, you can save time rolling and clicking by using the **number** keys to enter an exact date or time. For example, if you want to go to the 19th, type **1** and **9** and you're done. See Figure 8.

- The **number** keys will allow you to type exact numbers in date/ time fields. Like "2" "5" for the 25th of the month.

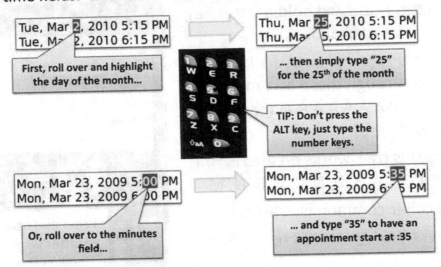

Figure 8. *Use number keys to set dates and times*

Space Key as Page Down

Save your thumb from the pain caused by constantly moving or gliding down to read more in an e-mail, web page, or other item. Tap the **Space** key instead which works as your **Page Down** key.

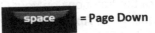 = Page Down

- The **Space** key also doubles as a **Page Down** key.

- This can be very useful when reading:

  - E-mail
  - Web pages
  - E-mail attachments

Quickly Typing Accented or Special Characters

The fastest way to type accented or special characters on your BlackBerry is to press and hold the underlying letter key, such as **a**, and then roll the **trackpad** until you see the character you need. Using this trick you can even quickly type special characters such as a trademark or copyright symbol. Remember, you can also use the **Sym** key for basic symbols (see Figure 9).

- To type an accented letter or special character, press and hold a letter key and roll the **trackpad**.

- Example: Press and hold the letter A to scroll through these accented characters: À Á Â Ã Ä Å Æ (both upper and lower case).

- Letters this trick works on are: E, R, T, Y, U, I, O, P, A, S, D, K, C, V, B, N, M

- Some other common characters:
    - V key for ¿, T key for ™, C key for ©, R key for ®

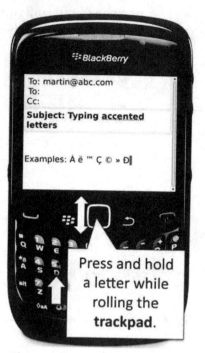

Press and hold a letter while rolling the trackpad.

Figure 9. *How to quickly type accented letters or special characters*

Working with the Wireless Network

Since most of the functions on your Curve work only when you are connected to the Internet (e-mail, Web, **App World**, **Facebook**, and so forth), you need to know when you're connected. Understanding how to read the status bar can save you time and frustration. You will also want to know how to quickly turn off your wireless radio or other radios (e.g. Bluetooth, Wi-Fi) when you get on an airplane.

Reading Your Wireless Network Status

Table 1 shows you how to read the status icons on the top of your Curve screen so you can save time and keep yourself connected.

Table 1. *Reading Your Wireless Network Status*

In the upper right corner, If you see letters & symbols...	E-mail & Web	Phone Calls	SMS Text	Speed of Data Connection
3G (3G with logo)	✓	✓	✓	High
1XEV or EDGE	✓	✓	✓	Medium
1X or GPRS	✓	✓	✓	Slow
Wi-Fi With any letters shown	✓	✓	✓	High
Wi-Fi Without letters	✓	✗	✗	High
1x, edge, gprs, GSM or 3G	✗	✓	✓	None
OFF Wi-Fi logo grayed out	✗	✗	✗	None

The following shows the various wireless signal strength icons that will appear (signal strength varies between one and five bars):

Strong signal:

Weak signal:

No signal:

Radio off:

Traveling with Your Curve: Airplane Mode

When you travel, on most airlines you can simply turn off all your wireless connections (Mobile Network radio and Bluetooth) and continue using your BlackBerry.

Here's how to turn off all your wireless connections:

1. Click the Manage Connections icon.

2. Then click Turn All Connections Off until you see the word Off next to your wireless signal strength indicator.

3. When you land and want to turn your connections on again, go back into **Manage Connections** and click the top option: **Restore Connections**.

TIP: To check/uncheck any option, just highlight and hit the **Space** KEY.

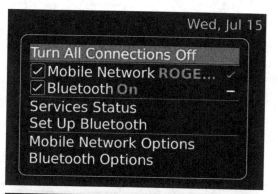

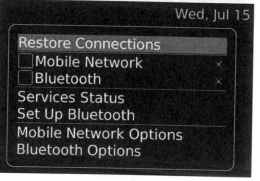

4. **Bluetooth On, Network Off:** Some airlines will allow you to keep your Stereo Bluetooth connection turned on while in flight. This allows you to listen to your music or watch a video using a Stereo Bluetooth headset. In order to keep Bluetooth on, but turn off your radio, uncheck **Mobile Network** but leave **Bluetooth** checked as shown.

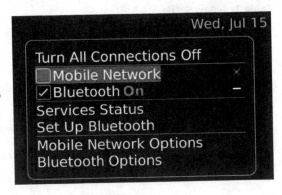

App Reference Tables

This section includes a number of tables that group the apps on your Curve, and other apps you can download. Each table gives you a brief description of the app and tells where to find more information in this book.

NOTE: The hotkeys listed in the following tables only work after you turn them on (see page 548 for instruction on this).

Getting Set Up

Table 2 lists some icons and quick links to help you get your e-mail, Bluetooth, contacts, calendar, and more loaded on to your device. You can even boost the memory by adding a memory card, which is important to install if you like to have more pictures, videos, and music on your Curve.

Table 2. *Getting Set Up*

To Do This...	Use This... *(Hotkey)*	Where to Learn More
Find Your Setup icons	**Setup folder**	Click on this icon to see your other Setup icons.
E-mail Setup, Date/Time, Fonts, and more	**Setup Wizard**	Page 37.
Setup Your Internet E-mail	**Personal E-mail Setup**	Page 37.
Setup your Bluetooth headset	**Setup Bluetooth**	Page 451.
Share Addresses, Calendar, Tasks and Notes with your Computer	**BlackBerry Desktop Manager (for Windows)** **BlackBerry Desktop Manager (for Apple Mac)**	Page 67. See Videos at www.MadeSimpleLearning.com. Page 125.
Add memory to store your Music, Videos, and Pictures	**Media Card** © SanDisk Corp.	Inserting it - Page 367.
Load up your Music, Pictures and Videos	Windows or Mac **Mass Storage Mode**	Page 144.
Fine-tune your Internet E-mail Setup& More	**Your Wireless Carrier Website**	See list of web sites on page 56.
Turn Off	**Power Off**	Click this icon to turn off your BlackBerry.
Lock Your Keyboard (Avoid speed dial in pocket or purse)	**Keyboard Lock** **(K)**	Click this icon, or tap the lock key on the top of your BlackBerry to lock it.

Staying In Touch

Getting familiar with the icons and buttons in Table 3 will help you stay in touch with your friends and colleagues. Whether you prefer calling, e-mailing, texting,or using instant messaging, your BlackBerry has many options. Use the browser to stay up-to-date with the latest happenings on the web.

Table 3. *Staying In Touch*

To Do This...	Use This... *(Hotkey)*	Where to Learn More
Read & Reply to E-mail	**Messages (M)**	Email - page 239. PIN Messaging - page 349. Attachements -page 250.
Send & Read SMS Text and MMS Messages	**SMS & MMS**	SMS Text - page 335. MMS Message - page 343.
View all your Saved Messages	**Saved Messages (V)**	Click to see all messages you have saved in your Messages inbox.
Get on the Internet / Browse the Web	**Browser (B / W)**	Page 471.
Call Voicemail	**Press & Hold 1**	Page 215.
Start a Call Dial by Name View Call Logs	**Phone & Call Logs**	Phone – page 211. Call Logs - page 221. Conference Call – page 235.
Dial by Voice	**Voice Dialing**	Page 227.
Send an Instant Message to another BlackBerry user	**BlackBerry Messenger (N)**	BBM - page 352.

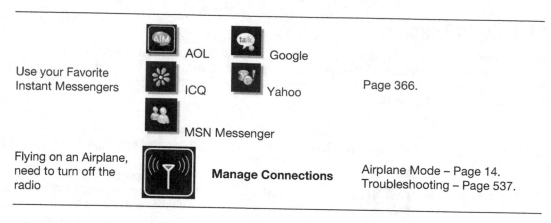

Use your Favorite Instant Messengers	AOL ICQ MSN Messenger Google Yahoo	Page 366.
Flying on an Airplane, need to turn off the radio	**Manage Connections**	Airplane Mode – Page 14. Troubleshooting – Page 537.

Staying Organized

From organizing and finding your contacts to managing your calendar, taking written or voice notes, and calculating a tip using your built-in calculator, your BlackBerry can help you do it all. Table 4 provides information for helping you to stay organized.

Table 4. *Staying Organized*

To Do This...	Use This... (Hotkey)	Where to Learn More
Manage Your Contact Names & Numbers	**Contacts (C)** **Address Book (A)**	Basics – Page 275. Add New – Page 278.
Manage Your Calendar	**Calendar (L)**	Calendar - Page 295. Sync to PC – Page 67. Sync to Mac – Page 125.
Set a wakeup alarm, use a countdown timer or stopwatch	**Clock**	Page 516.
Store all your important passwords	**Password Keeper**	Page 519.
Find lost names, e-mail, calendar entries, and more	**Search (S)**	Page 521.

Being Productive

Sometimes you need to get work done on your Curve. Use the icons in Table 5 to complete tasks on your BlackBerry.

Table 5. *Being Productive*

To Do This...	Use This... (Hotkey)	Where to Learn More
Manage your To-Do List	**Tasks** *(T)*	Tasks - Page 317. Sync to PC – Page 67. Sync to Mac – Page 125.
Find Things, Get Directions, See Traffic	**Google Maps**	Page 504.
Take notes, store your grocery list, and more!	**MemoPad** *(D)*	MemoPad - Page 323. Sync to PC – Page 67. Sync to Mac – Page 125.
Cannot type a note? Leave yourself a quick Voice Note!	**Voice Note Recorder**	Page 518.
View & Edit Microsoft Office Word, Excel and PowerPoint	**Word to Go, Sheet to Go, Slideshow to Go**	Page 251.
Calculate your MPG, a meal tip, and convert units!	**Calculator** *(U)*	Page 515.

Being Entertained

Use the icons and hotkeys listed in Table 6 for entertainment on your BlackBerry.

Table 6. *Being Entertained*

To Do This...	Use This... *(Hotkey)*	Where to Learn More
Quickly get to all your Music	**Music**	Page 371.
Listen to Free Music – with customized music stations	**Pandora**	Page 384.
Listen to Free Music – with customized music stations	**Slacker**	Page 386.
Play Music, Videos, and watch Pictures	**Media**	Music – Page 371. Videos – Page 407. Ring Tones – Page 401. Pictures – Page 402. Voice Notes –Page 518.
Snap Pictures of Anything, Anytime	**Camera**	Page 391.
Capture Video of anything, anytime	**Video Camera**	Page 408.
Take a Break and Play a Game	**Games folder**	Page 488.
Use the built in Text-Based help (*What, you can't find it in this book!*)	**Help** *(H)*	Page 159.

Networking Socially

Connect and stay up to date with friends, colleagues, and professional networks using the social networking tools on your Curve (Table 7).

Table 7. *Networking Socially*

To Do This...	Use This...*(Hotkey)*	Where to Learn More
Connect with Facebook Friends	Facebook	Page 416.
Follow people and Tweet using Twitter	Twitter	Page 420.
Connect with Colleagues	Linked In	Page 426.

Personalize Your Curve

Use the icons and hotkeys in Table 8 to personalize the look and feel of your Curve.

Table 8. *Personalize Your Curve*

To Do This...	Use This...*(Hotkey)*	Where to Learn More
Change your Phone Ringer, if e-mails vibrate or buzz and more...	**Sounds**	Page 193.
Change your Background Home Screen Picture	Media / Pictures	Pictures - Page 184. Home Screen – Page 178.
Change your Theme	Options *(O)*	Theme – Page 179.
Change your Font Size	Options *(O)*	Screen/Keyboard – Page 176.
Change your programmable Convenience Keys	Options *(O)*	Screen/Keyboard – Page 187.

Add and Remove Software

Use the icons and hotkeys in Table 9 to add and remove software and other capabilities on your BlackBerry.

Table 9. *Add and Remove Software*

To Do This...	Use This... *(HotKey)*	Where to Learn More
Add new software (also remove it)	App World	Page 441.
You can also add software using the Web Browser	Browser *(B)*	Page 485.
Find the icons you download	Downloads Folder	Glide to and click on this folder to see your downloaded icons.
Remove icons and programs	Options *(O)*	Page 491.

Part II

Introduction

Welcome to your new Curve. In this section, we will introduce you to how the book is organized and where to find useful information. Inside the front and back cover, check out the **Day in the Life** section where we give you scenarios describing how you can use your Curve for work and play. We even show you how to find great tips and tricks sent right to your Curve.

Congratulations on Your BlackBerry Curve!

In your hands is one of the most capable and powerful smartphones available—the BlackBerry Curve 8500 Series. While you may have an 8520 or 8530 model, they are all Curve 8500 Series BlackBerry Smartphones.

Key Features on the BlackBerry Curve

Your BlackBerry Curve has many shared features with the BlackBerry family including a few unique features as well.

Multimedia and Network Features

- Camera (2.0 megapixel)
- Media player (pictures, video, and audio)
- Video recording
- Built-in Wi-Fi
- Messaging and social media capability

Media Card—Expansion Memory Card

Enhance the usable memory on your BlackBerry by a significant amount with an eight or 16 gigabyte (GB) or higher capacity MicroSD memory card.

Getting the Most Out of
BlackBerry Curve Made Simple

This book can be read cover to cover, but you can also peruse it in a modular fashion by chapter or topic. You may want to check out the app world, try the Web browser, get set up with your e-mail or contacts, or upload your music. You can do all of this and more with our book.

You will soon realize that your Curve is a very powerful device. There are, however, many secrets "locked" inside that we help you "unlock" throughout this book.

Take your time—this book can help you on your way to learning how to best use, operate, and have fun with your new Curve. Think back to when you tried to use your first Windows or Apple computer. It may have taken a while to get familiar with how to do things. It's the same with the Curve. Use this book to help you get up to speed and quickly learn the best tips and tricks.

Remember that devices as powerful as the Curve are not always easy to grasp—at first.

You will get the most out of your Curve if you can read a section and try out what you read. Reading and then doing an activity can give you a much higher retention rate than simply reading alone.

In order to learn and remember what you learn, we recommend reading a little, trying a little on your Curve and repeat

How This Book Is Organized

Knowing how this book is organized can help you quickly locate things important to you. Here, we show you the main organization of this book. Remember to take advantage of our abridged table of contents, detailed table of contents, and comprehensive index to help you quickly pinpoint items of interest.

Day in the Life of a Curve User

Located inside the front and back cover is an excellent piece of information full of easy-to-access cross-reference page numbers. If you see something you want to learn, thumb to that page and learn it—all in just a few minutes.

Part 1: Quick-Start Guide

Learning Your Way Around: Learn about the keys, buttons, and ports on your Curve and how to change the battery, SIM card, or memory card. Learn many timesaving tips about navigating quickly and how to multitask.

Working with the Wireless Network: Learn how to read letters, numbers, and symbols at the top of your Curve screen so you know when you can make phone calls, send SMS text messages, send and receive e-mail, or browse the Web. Also learn how to handle your Curve on an airplane.

App Reference Tables: Quickly peruse the icons or apps grouped by category. Get a thumbnail of what all the apps do on your Curve including quick page numbers to jump right to the details of how to get the most out of each app in this book.

Part 2: Introduction

You are here now . . .

Part 3: You and Your BlackBerry Curve

This is the meat of the book organized in 36 easy-to-understand chapters packed with loads of pictures guiding you every step of the way.

Part 4: Hotkey Shortcuts

Check out this section for a complete listing of all the hotkey shortcuts to get things done quickly on your Curve. Save yourself countless hours of rolling, searching, and clicking by using **Home** screen hotkeys, **E-mail** hotkeys, **Calendar** hotkeys, **Web Browser** hotkeys and **Media Player** hotkeys. These hotkeys will allow you to do things much more quickly with your Curve.

Quickly Locating Tips, Cautions, and Notes

As you flip through this book, you can instantly see these items based on their formatting. For example, if you wanted to quickly find all the **Calendar** tips, you would flip to the **Calendar** chapter.

TIPS, **CAUTIONS**, and **NOTES** are all formatted like this, with a gray background, to help you see them more quickly.

Free BlackBerry E-mail Tips and Free Videos

Check out the author's web site at www.madesimplelearning.com for a series of very useful, "bite-size" chunks of BlackBerry tips and tricks. We have taken a selection of great tips from this book and added a few new ones. Click the **Free Tips** section and register for tips in order to receive a tip right in your Curve inbox about once a week. Learning in small doses can be a great way to master your Curve.

The authors also offer free videos showing you how to use **Desktop Manager** for Windows at madesimplelearning.com. In addition, there are over 100 video tutorials showing you how to use your Curve that you can watch on your computer and your BlackBerry.

BlackBerry OS 4.6 and OS 5.0

If you purchased your BlackBerry Curve in mid- to-late 2009, it is likely you were running BlackBerry Operating System (OS) version 4.6. As of today, you have been given the opportunity to upgrade to OS 5.0. Also, from about February 2010, all new BlackBerry Curve smartphones are shipping with OS 5.0 pre-installed. Most of the screens shown in this updated Curve book are from OS 5.0.

The differences between the two operating systems are largely cosmetic, with the option menus having more drop downs to use for configuration. The 5.0 **Options** menus also have more white space around each of the drop down box items. See the following example:

BlackBerry OS 4.6

Date/Time	
Time Zone:	Eastern Time (-5)
(GMT-05:00) Eastern Time (US & Canada)	
Time:	22:26
Time Format:	24 hour
Date:	Wed, Jul 15, 2009
Date/Time Source:	Network
Network Time:	22:14
Network Date:	Wed, Jul 15, 2009

BlackBerry OS 5.0

Date/Time	
Time Zone:	Eastern Time (-5) ▼
(GMT-05:00) Eastern Time (US & Canada)	
Time:	12:50 PM
Time Format:	12 hour ▼
Date:	Wed 23 Sep 2009
Date/Time Source:	Network ▼
Network Time:	7:50 PM
Network Date:	Wed 23 Sep 2009

Notice the space around **Eastern Time**, and **12 hour** compared to the 4.6 version. This is to help with current and future touch screen models like the BlackBerry Storm.

Significant differences are in how you customize your **Sound** profiles. We have a special section in the **Sounds** chapter dealing specifically with 5.0 profiles.

Determining the Operating System Version on your Curve

It is easy to tell what version of Operating System (OS) your Curve is running.

1. Method 1: **Options** App

   a. Click your **Options** icon.

   b. Select **About**.

2. Method 2: Help Me! Screen

   c. Press and hold three keys simultaneously.

   d. Press and hold **Alt**, **cap**, and **H** to see the **Help Me!** screen shown to the right.

```
Help Me!
BlackBerry
By Research In Motion Limited.

If you are having problems, please
call technical support.
Vendor ID:                      107
Platform:                  4.3.0.16
App Version:         5.0.0.90 (91)
PIN:                      207b28ba
IMEI·          2FF2FF 02 0FF021 2
```

The first two digits next to the **App Version** are your OS version—the image above shows this BlackBerry is running 5.0.

TIP: You can view things like **Free memory** and **Battery strength** if you scroll to the bottom of the **Help Me!** screen.

How Can I Update My BlackBerry Operating System?

You can update your BlackBerry operating system software in two ways—using **Desktop Manager** on your computer or updating it wirelessly over the network. It is probably safer to use **Desktop Manager** in case something goes wrong during the update process, because with **Desktop Manager** you will have a back up of your BlackBerry data before completing the update process.

Using Desktop Manager

You can use **Desktop Manager** software and we describe the process in detail later in this book. If you use **Desktop Manager** for Windows (see page 94) or **Desktop Manager** for Mac (see page 125), you will be notified of OS (also called Firmware) updates and be able to update using either software.

Using Wireless Update

Most BlackBerry smartphones now offer the ability to update your OS directly from the device itself using the **Options** icon.

1. To begin, click the **Options** icon. The faster way is pressing the letter **O** if you have already turned on **Home Screen** hotkeys (see page 548).

2. Click **Advanced Options** and press the letter **W** to jump down and click **Wireless Update**.

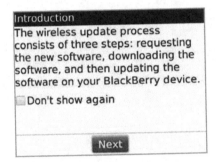

3. Click **Next** at the bottom of the screen to get to the **Available Updates** screen.

4. Click the **Check for Updates** button at the bottom.

5. If updates are found, you will see the status on the screen. Follow the on-screen instructions to install the update.

NOTE: A full update can take an hour or more, so you may want to complete the update only at night.

6. Once the update is complete, you will see a status message as shown to the right.

7. If there are no updates, you will see a message similar to the one below.

You and Your Blackberry Curve

This is the heart of *BlackBerry Curve Made Simple*. In this section, you'll find clearly labeled chapters each explaining the key features of your Curve. You'll see that most chapters focus on an individual application (app) or a specific type of app. Many of the chapters discuss apps that come with your Curve, but we also include some fun and useful apps you can download from BlackBerry **App World**. Sure, the Curve is for fun, but it's also for much more, so you'll learn how to be productive with **Word To Go, Sheet To Go,** and **Slideshow To Go** in this section. We finish with handy troubleshooting tips that can help if your Curve isn't working quite right.

Chapter 1

E-mail Set Up

This chapter focuses on getting your e-mail setup as well as wireless syncing of your contacts if you use Google Mail (Gmail) or have a BlackBerry Enterprise Server (BES). Sometimes e-mail setup can cause problems, and we show you how to fix common errors and make sure you receive all your e-mail on both your computer and BlackBerry. While you can adjust e-mail setup from your BlackBerry, you may also want to adjust your e-mail settings from your computer (we also cover that in this chapter).

If your BlackBerry is tied to a BES, we show you how to get connected (or activated) on the server. More recently, Research In Motion (BlackBerry's maker) announced free BES Express software. This can be a fantasic value if your organization uses Microsoft Exchange and would like to take advantage of the BES features without additional software licensing and, in most cases, without additional hardware costs.

Learn Your BlackBerry and Getting Around

Much of the basics about the keys, buttons, and using your Curve including great tips and tricks are located in our **Quick Start Guide** at the beginning of this book. In the **Quick Start Guide** we also show you how to use the **trackpad**, **Escape,** and other keys including how to save time with many shortcuts and multitasking.

Your Home Screen

Depending on the particular phone company that supplied your BlackBerry, you may see more or fewer icons on your **Home** screen similar to your computer's desktop. You may also see a different background picture than shown in the figure to the right. Your BlackBerry is fully customizable, so you can change the look and feel (called the **Theme**) and even the picture you see as the background.

TIP: To change your background wallpaper, from your **Home** screen press the **Menu** key twice until you see a menu appear. Select **Options** from the menu. Scroll down to **Set Wallpaper** and click **Change Wallpaper**. Select from a number of pre-loaded background images or snap a picture and set it as your wallpaper.

Getting Around Your Home Screen, Folders, and Icons

Depending on the particular phone company that supplied your BlackBerry, you may see more or fewer icons on your **Home** screen–similar to your computer's desktop. You will see a different background picture than the one shown in Figure 1-1. The background wallpaper in that figure was taken with the BlackBerry Curve Camera.

TIP: Check out Home Screen Hotkeys in Part 4 of this book on page 548 to learn how to enable single key startup of all your most-used icons, such as Messages (in Figure 1-1), Contacts, Calendar, and more.

1. Press the **Menu** key to go from your limited set of icons to see all your icons.

2. Scroll the **trackpad** down to see any icons that might be off the bottom of the screen.

3. Click on any folders, such as **Media**, to see more icons inside the folders

4. Press the **Escape** key to back out of a folder or return to your **Home** screen with just a few icons and your picture.

5. Your BlackBerry is fully customizable, so you can change the look and feel (called the **Theme**) and even the picture you see as the background.

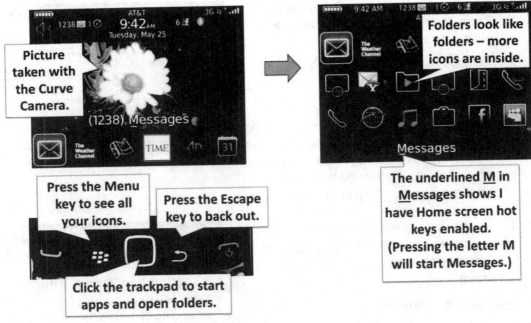

Figure 1-1. *Use Your* **Menu** *key,* **trackpad,** *and* **Escape** *keys to navigate around your Curve*

The Setup Wizard

When you first turn on your BlackBerry, you will likely be presented with the **Setup Wizard**. If you ignored or closed it, you can return by locating and clicking the **Setup Wizard** icon. You may need to click the **Setup** folder in order to find the **Setup Wizard** icon.

You will be presented with a number of screens that are not shown in this book because they are self-explanatory. Follow the suggested steps. They will give you a good jump-start on getting your BlackBerry set up and teach you some of the basics.

1. Click any field, including **Date, Time,** or **Time Zone** to make an adjustment and glide down and click **Next**.

2. Remove the unused languages to save space.

3. Next, you will see a few screens giving you some tips about how to use the basic keys on your Curve. (The screens you see in the Setup Wizard vary depending on which wireless carrier you have, so we have not included them in the book.

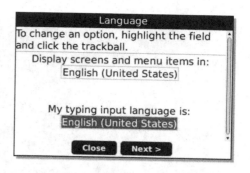

4. Finally, you will see a screen similar to the one to the right with the following items (you may also see a few different items listed):

Language – see page 261.

Date and Time—see page 37.

Navigation and Typing Tutorials – see our Quick Start guide and Chapter 6 "Typing, Spelling and Help."

E-mail setup—continue reading this chapter.

Set up Bluetooth— see page 451.

Import SIM Card Contacts—see page 22

Font—see page 176.

Help—see page 159.

Setting Up E-mail the First Time

Your BlackBerry is designed to retrieve your e-mail from up to 10 different e-mail accounts and, if you are connected to a (BES), one corporate e-mail account. When your BlackBerry receives your e-mail, all your messages will be displayed in your **Messages** inbox.

You can set up your basic e-mail right from your BlackBerry, but for things like your automated e-mail signature **Sent from my (carrier name) BlackBerry**, you will need to log in to your carrier's web site (see page 60).

NOTE: If you want to set up your BlackBerry to work with e-mail coming from a BES, skip to the Setting Up Your Corporate E-mail section on page 62.

Personal or Internet E-mail Setup

You can set up your personal or internet e-mail from two places:

the **Setup Wizard** icon and the **Personal E-mail Set Up** icon (both of which

may be inside the **Setup** folder).

1. If you're already using the **Setup Wizard**, click **Next** to get to the **Personal E-mail Setup** screen.

2. If you see a list of items, click **Personal E-mail Setup**.

3. Select **I want to create or add an e-mail address** and click **Next** to get to the login screen shown to the right.

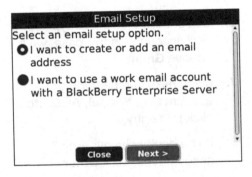

NOTE: You may need to create a new account if this is the first time you are logging into **E-mail Setup** on your BlackBerry. IF SO, BE SURE TO Click the check box next to **Remember me on this device** and you won't have to keep entering your username/password every time.

4. Click the **Log In** button. Any accounts you have already set up will be listed at the top as shown in the screen on the right.

5. To add an account, click the **Add** button.

6. Select from the various types of e-mail accounts. In this case, we'll choose **Gmail.**

7. If you have another type of account (e.g. **Yahoo!**, **AOL**, etc.), click that entry.

8. If you don't see your e-mail account type, click **Other**.

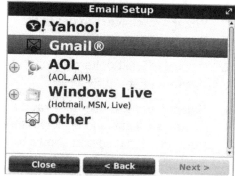

9. Type your full e-mail address, (name@gmail.com) and password, then click **Next** to attempt the login.

> **TIP:** Click the **Show Password** check box to see the letters in your password. This can be helpful to prevent mistyping it.

If everything is correct, you will see a screen (see Figure 1-2).

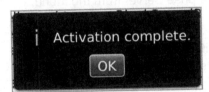

Figure 1-2. *The final setup screen on* **E-mail** *setup and the* **Activation Complete** *pop-up window*

Once each e-mail account is set up correctly, you will see an **Activation** e-mail message in your **Messages** inbox and within 15 minutes, e-mail should start flowing into your BlackBerry. Now, with full wireless e-mail, you will begin to see why so many are addicted to their BlackBerry smartphones.

From: Activation Server
Email account information
Dec 10, 2009 12:24 PM

Congratulations, you have successfully set up martintrautschold@yahoo.com with your BlackBerry(R) device. You should begin receiving new messages in approximately 20 minutes.

Setting Up Your Corporate E-mail

Your help desk or information technology department can typically set up your corporate e-mail (i.e. Enterprise Activation). If not, you need your activation password and you can set this up on your own right from the BlackBerry using the **Setup Wizard** or from an **Enterprise Activation** icon

NOTE: If you have not received your activation password, you need to ask your help desk or information technology department for that password before you may complete this process.

Set up Corporate E-mail Using the Setup Wizard

1. Click your Setup Wizard icon and select E-mail Setup, and choose I want to use a work e-mail account with a BlackBerry Enterprise Server from the menu.

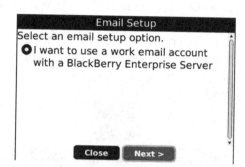

2. Verify your Enterprise Activation password.

3. Type the e-mail address along with the activation password you received from your help desk or information technology department.

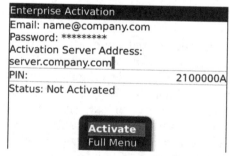

4. Press the **Trackpad** and select **Activate**.

5. You will see many messages on the screen, such as Establishing Secure Connection, Downloading Contacts, Downloading Calendar. The entire process may take 15 minutes or more depending on how much data is being sent as well as the strength of your wireless connection.

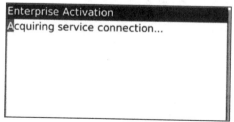

6. If you see an error message, verify your password, that your wireless radio is turned on, and that you are in a strong coverage area. If you still have problems, please contact your help desk.

7. Once you have seen all the Enterprise Activation messages go by and you see a completion message, click **E-mail** and check your address book and calendar to see if everything was loaded correctly. If not, contact your help desk for support.

How Can I Tell if I Am Activated on the BlackBerry Server?

A simple rule of thumb for knowing whether you're connected to the BlackBerry server is that if you can send and receive e-mail and you have names in your BlackBerry address book (**Contacts** icon), then it has been successfully set up (the Enterprise Activation is complete).

To verify if your BlackBerry successfully configured with your Server:

1. Click your BlackBerry **Contact List** / **Address Book**.

2. Click the **Menu** key to the left of the **Trackpad**.

3. Glide the **Trackpad** up or down to find a menu item called **Lookup.**

4. If you see **Lookup**, then you are connected. (This **Lookup** command allows you to do a **Global Address List** (**GAL**) lookup from your BES to find anyone in your organization. You can then add them to your personal address book on your BlackBerry.)

Maintaining Your E-mail Accounts

You may need to add, edit, or delete e-mail accounts. You may want to fine-tune your e-mail signature (**Sent from my BlackBerry**) attached to the bottom of each e-mail you send from your Curve.

Adding More E-mail Personal Addresses

You can add up to 10 e-mail addresses to your Curve. Only one can be an Enterprise or corporate e-mail address, but the rest can be personal addresses including POP3 or IMAP addresses.

1. Click you're the **Personal E-mail Setup** icon (possibly in the **Setup** folder).

2. Enter your username and password (if requested) and click **Log In**.

3. Scroll to the bottom of the list of e-mail addresses and click the **Add** button.

4. Follow the steps to add the new account as described earlier.

Hiding Extra E-mail Account Icons

As you setup each e-mail account, you will notice a new icon appearing on your **Home** screen tied to that particular account. If you like having individual icons, you can leave them alone. However, since all of your e-mail goes into your main **Messages** icon, you can hide these icons to clean up your **Home** screen. Follow these steps to hide these extra icons.

1. Highlight the icon you want to hide.

2. Press the **Menu** key.

3. Select **Hide**.

If you want the icon back, follow the steps as shown in the **Hiding and Un-hiding Icons** shown in Chapter 8.

Edit or Delete an E-mail Account (Signature and Advanced Settings)

To change your e-mail account name, password, signature, advanced settings, or synchronization options, you need to edit your e-mail account settings. If you don't use a certain e-mail account anymore, you may want to delete that particular address:

1. Click the **Personal E-mail Setup** icon.

2. Log in if requested.

3. Click the **Trackpad** on a particular e-mail account you want to edit or delete.

4. To delete the account, select **Delete** from the short menu and confirm your selection. When done, press the **Escape** key to exit to your **Home** screen.

5. To edit the account, select **Edit** from the short menu.

6. You can adjust the following items:

    a. General Options

    b. E-mail account name (the name for the e-mail account icon)

    c. Your Name (the name that appears instead of the e-mail address when you send messages, also known as the Friendly Name)

    d. Signature (the signature attached to each e-mail you send from your BlackBerry . . . usually, you will want to change this from the Sent from my (wireless carrier) BlackBerry Device to something more personal like your name and phone number or your company name)

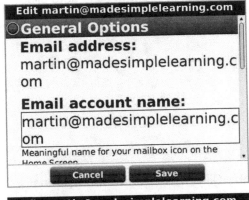

7. Scroll down and click **Login Information** to change your password for this account.

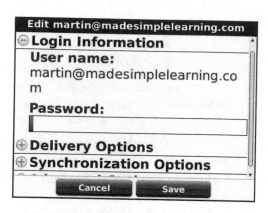

8. Click **Delivery Options** to add an e-mail account to send auto blind carbon copies of every e-mail you send from your BlackBerry.

9. Click **Synchronization Options** to adjust whether or not e-mail messages you delete on your BlackBerry are synced wirelessly to also be deleted in your main e-mail inbox. To check or uncheck the box, highlight it and press the **Space** key.

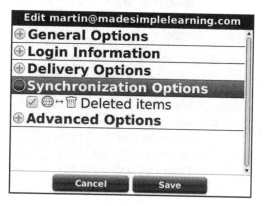

10. Scroll down to Advanced Options to adjust the **E-mail Server** name. Contact your E-mail Administrator for help if you are not sure about the **E-mail Server** name.

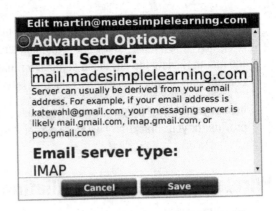

11. Scroll down to select whether or not you use **Secure Socket Layer (SSL)**. This is a security protocol that scrambles your e-mail messages for added safety. Contact your e-mail administrator for help if you are not sure about SSL.

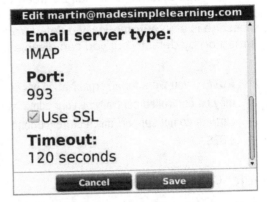

TIP: Press the **Space** key to get the at (@) and dot (.) symbols whenever typing an e-mail. For example, for sara@company.com, type **sara SPACE company SPACE com.**

Change Your "Sent from (carrier) Wireless" Signature

Every e-mail message you send from your BlackBerry will have an auto signature attached at the end. Typically, it will have your carrier name on it. For example, if your carrier is AT&T, your default auto-signature may say **Sent from my AT&T BlackBerry.** To change this signature, follow the steps shown earlier in the **Edit or Delete E-mail Account** section on page 42.

NOTE: If you are not sure of your advanced e-mail settings, open your mail client on your computer. If using MS Outlook or something similar, click Accounts or E-mail Accounts from the menu. Review the advanced settings for that account. If you use web mail exclusively, contact your service provider and ask for assistance with getting your BlackBerry set up.

If you are still having trouble with e-mail setup, then please contact your e-mail service provider or your BlackBerry wireless carrier (Phone Company) technical support.

Wireless E-mail Reconciliation

The BlackBerry allows you to turn on or off the **Wireless Reconciliation,** the feature that synchronizes deletion of e-mail between your regular mailbox and your BlackBerry. If you deleted an e-mail on your BlackBerry, you could set it up so the same e-mail message is also automatically deleted from your regular e-mail account. Usually, this is turned on by default, but you can disable it.

NOTE: If you work for an organization or company that supplied your BlackBerry, this feature may be controlled centrally by your administrator and may not be adjustable. Some wireless carriers do not support this feature (or don't support it fully) unless your BlackBerry is tied to a BES.

1. Click your **Messages** icon.

2. Click the **Menu** key and click **Options.** You may also press the letter **O** to jump down to **Options.**

3. Select E-mail Reconciliation.

4. Set Delete On to Handheld.

5. Set **Wireless Reconcile** to **Off**.

TIP: To turn **E-mail Reconciliation** back on, set **Delete On** to **Mailbox & Handheld**, and set **Wireless Reconcile** to **On.**

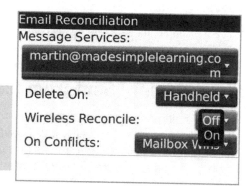

If you have turned on the **Wireless Reconcile** and
want to get rid of old e-mail that you have deleted
from either your main e-mail inbox or from your
BlackBerry, press the **Menu** key, select **Purge
Deleted Items,** and select the e-mail address.

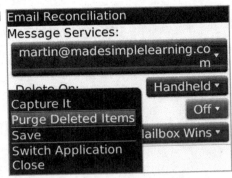

Clean Up Your Main E-mail Inbox On the Road

If you like to keep your main e-mail inbox (which you view on your computer) cleaned up, make
sure to keep **Wireless Reconcile** turned **On**. Just use downtime during the day to clean up your
BlackBerry e-mail inbox. This way, any e-mail messages you delete on your BlackBerry (such as
spam or other unnecessary e-mails), will not appear in your computer's e-mail inbox. It is quite
refreshing to come back to a very clean inbox after a day away from your desk.

Sync Google Contacts Using E-mail Setup

If you use Google for e-mail and managing your contacts, you can set up a wireless
sync for your **Google Contacts**. This is a useful feature because you no longer need to
connect your Curve with a sync cable to your computer to update contact changes
between your Curve and Google. The contact updates, like e-mail, all happen
automatically and wirelessly.

Setting Up Google Wireless Contacts Syncing

A new feature with BlackBerry 5.0 system software and BlackBerry Internet Service
software (assuming your carrier has upgraded) is that you now can select wireless
contact syncing for Google. To do so, follow these steps:

CAUTION: You can also sync your **Google Contacts** using the **Google Sync** app (see page
311). Do not sync **Google Contacts** with both methods—you are asking for trouble. Instead,
if you choose to use this method below for **Contacts** syncing, use **Google Sync** for only your
Google Calendar.

TIP: If you forgot to check this sync box in the first-set up, you can get to it in the **Edit E-mail Account** area shown on page 42.

1. Highlight your e-mail account from the main list of accounts, click the **Trackpad,** and select **Edit**.

2. Scroll down and click **Synchronization Options** and check / uncheck your boxes.

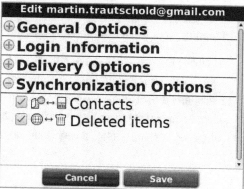

The first time you enable this **Contact Sync** feature, you will see a screen showing the progress of the initial sync. If you have a significant number of contacts (e.g. 1,000 or more), it could require over 10 minutes to finish the first-time sync.

You may also have to try it a few times if it fails the first time.

As of publishing time, this only worked with Google/Gmail accounts, but we believe more account types could be added in the future.

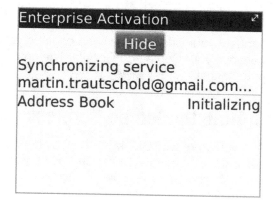

Turning On or Off Wireless Contact Syncing

If you have enabled wireless **Contact Syncing** with Google or another service, you can adjust the sync from your **Contacts Options** screen as follows:

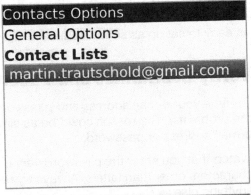

1. Click the **Contacts** icon, press the **Menu** key, and click **Options** to see this screen.

2. Roll down and click the e-mail account under the **Contact List** to make adjustments using the screen shown.

3. To disable **Wireless Synchronization**, change the **Yes** to a **No** by pressing the **Space** key.

4. This screen also shows you how many contact entries are being synced. Save your changes.

Handling Issues with Google Contacts Wireless Sync

Unfortunately, sometimes your **Google Contacts** do not sync correctly with your BlackBerry. Below are tips to help you get up and running:

1. Make sure you are trying to sync a **Google Mail** account.

2. As of publishing time, you could not sync **Google Mail** contact groups.

3. Make sure you have enabled **Wireless Synchronization** on your BlackBerry smartphone. To verify this, click the **Contacts** app, press the **Menu** key, and click **Options**. Scroll down to and click your Gmail address under **Contact Lists**. The setting next to **Wireless Synchronization** should be set to **Yes** (see earlier steps and images).

Troubleshooting Your E-mail Accounts

Sometimes your e-mail accounts just don't operate correctly. This section provides a few tips for handling some of the more common errors. Unfortunately, e-mail will not be as easy to set up as shown earlier.

Verify Usernames and Passwords

Re-type your e-mail address and password (this typically handles about 80 percent of the problems). The reason could be as simple as an incorrect character typed in your e-mail address or password.

Watch that you enter the password very carefully, especially if you have numbers or characters other than letters. Always try retyping them a few times before doing anything else.

Verify Your E-mail Server is POP3 or IMAP

Some E-mail servers cannot be accessed by the BlackBerry Internet Service, so you cannot use these types of e-mail accounts on your Curve. Contact your e-mail service provider and tell them you are trying to access your e-mail from a BlackBerry smartphone and verify the server is of a type called POP3 or IMAP.

Verify Your E-mail Server Settings (Advanced Settings)

Another setup issue might be that your server uses SSL security or might have a non-standard e-mail server name. Contact your service provider to learn about these settings. To change these settings on your Curve, follow the steps shown earlier in the **Edit or Delete E-mail Account** section on page 42.

Solving a Gmail Enable IMAP Error Message

If you receive an error message in your e-mail inbox telling you to turn on IMAP settings in Gmail, log in to your Gmail account from your computer and follow these steps:

1. Click the **Settings** link (usually in the top right corner).

2. Click the **Forwarding and POP/IMAP** tab.

3. Set **IMAP Access** to **Enable IMAP** (see Figure 1-3).

4. Click the **Save Changes** button.

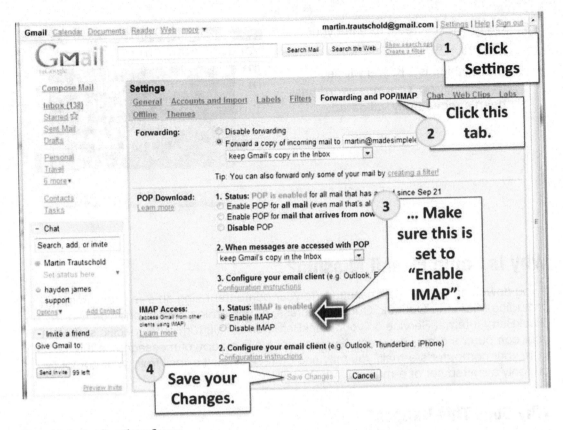

Figure 1-3. *Gmail settingssScreen.*

5. After you make this change, click your BlackBerry **Personal E-mail Setup** icon.

6. Highlight the **Invalid Account** (in this case Gmail) and click the **Trackpad** or **Menu** key to select **Validate**.

7. On the next screen, re-enter your password and click **Next**.

8. If everything is OK, you will see a pop-up saying **Your password has been successfully validated**.

Why Is Some E-mail Missing?

If you download your e-mail messages to your computer using an e-mail program (including Microsoft Outlook, Outlook Express, or something similar) and you use BlackBerry Internet Service on your BlackBerry for e-mail, turn on a specific setting in your computer's e-mail program. If you do not leave a copy of messages on the server from your computer's e-mail, you may end up receiving all e-mail from your computer, but only a limited set of e-mail on your BlackBerry.

Why Does This Happen?

By default, most e-mail programs pull down or retrieve e-mail from the server every one to five minutes and erase the retrieved messages from the server. By default, the BlackBerry Internet Service usually pulls down e-mail about every 15 minutes. If your computer has pulled down the e-mail every five minutes and erased it from the server, your BlackBerry will only receive a limited set of messages (those that haven't yet been pulled down by your computer).

How Do I Fix This?

To fix this, set your computer's e-mail program to keep your messages on the server. This way, the BlackBerry will always receive every e-mail message. Here's how:

1. In your computer e-mail program (e.g. Microsoft Outlook), find the location where you can configure or change your e-mail accounts including **Tools, Configure Accounts, Account Settings,** or something similar (see Figure 1-4).

2. Select or change the appropriate e-mail account. (sometimes you double-click the account to edit it).

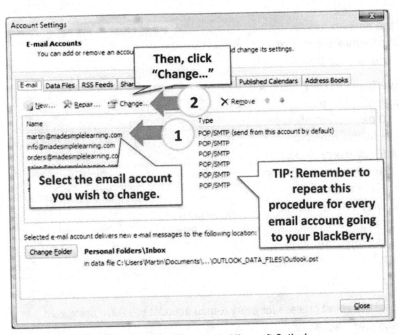

Figure 1-4. *E-mail account settings screen in Microsoft Outlook.*

3. Typically you will go to an **Advanced** settings area to make changes to **Leave a copy of the message on the server**. In Microsoft Outlook, click the **More Settings** tab and the **Advanced** tab (see Figure 1-5).

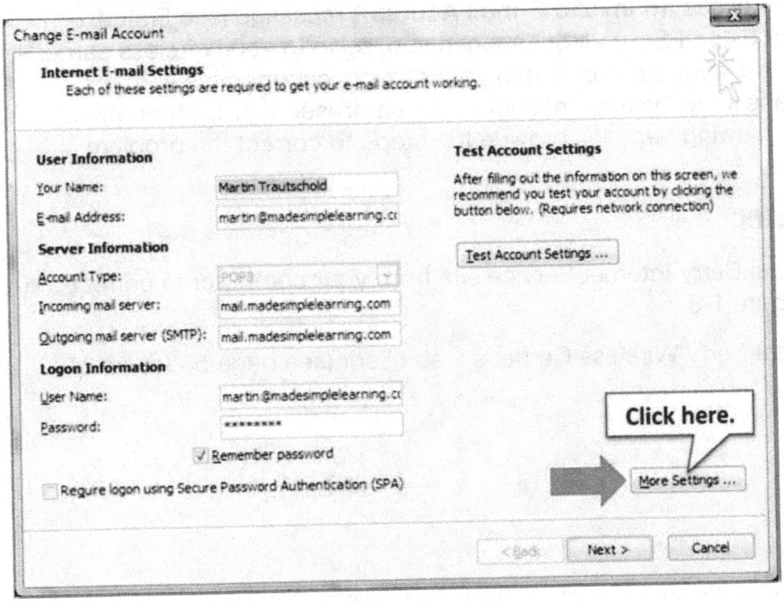

Figure 1-5. *Internet e-mail settings in Microsoft Outlook.*

4. At the bottom of the screen, under **Delivery**, check the **Leave a copy of the message on the server** box.

5. Check the **Remove from server after X days** box. We suggest changing the number to about **10** days. This allows you time to make sure the message reaches both your BlackBerry and your PC but doesn't clutter the server for too many days. If you make the number of days too high, you may end up with a **Mail Box Full** error and have your incoming e-mail messages bounced back to the senders.

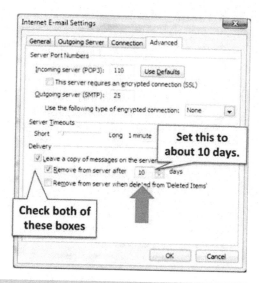

NOTE: Remember to repeat the above process for every e-mail account you have being sent to both your computer and your BlackBerry.

Correcting the "Invalid Account. Please Validate" Message

From time to time, you may see **an Invalid E-mail Account** message (see Figure 1-6), either in your BlackBerry **E-mail Setup** icon or when you log in to your wireless carrier's web site. This may happen if you have changed your e-mail account password, or sometimes it just happens if the system encounters an unforeseen error (through no fault of your own). The following sections provide the steps to correct the problem.

Using Your Computer

You can log in to the BlackBerry Internet Service site from your computer to correct the invalid account. See Figure 1-6.

1. Log in to your BlackBerry Wireless Carrier's web client (see page 56 for list of sites).

Email Accounts

Manage the accounts you are using with your BlackBerry device.

Valid	Email Account	Edit	Filters	Delete
✉	info@blackberrymadesimple.com	✎	▼	🗑
✉	martin@blackberrymadesimple.com	✎	▼	🗑

Note: Email accounts marked with ✉ are invalid. Please click on the ✉ beside the email account to try to validate it.

Figure 1-6. *BlackBerry Internet Service showing invalid e-mail Accounts.*

2. Click the **Edit** icon ✎, enter your information including your password, and save your changes. You will see the message **Your e-mail account has been successfully validated.** The invalid account icon will change to a check mark in the **Valid** column as shown (see Figure 1-7).

Email Accounts

Manage the accounts you are using with your BlackBerry device.

Valid	Email Account	Edit	Filters	Delete
✔	info@blackberrymadesimple.com	✎	▼	🗑

Figure 1-7. *E-mail account successfully validated in BlackBerry Internet Service*

Using Your BlackBerry

1. Log in to your **E-mail Setup** icon (usually in the **Setup** folder).

2. After logging in, you will see a screen similar to the image shown to the right..

3. To correct the **Invalid Account** errors, highlight the account and click the **Trackpad** to select **Validate**.

4. Re-type your password and click **Next** to validate the account.

5. You will see a message similar to the one shown to the right for each validated account.

6. Repeat the process for any other accounts shown as invalid.

Set up or Adjust E-mail Accounts from Your Computer

Your personal e-mail accounts can also be set up from your computer using your carrier's web site. Notice that when you send an e-mail from the BlackBerry, the signature is something very basic like "Sent from BlackBerry Device via T-Mobile," or "Sent from AT&T Wireless," depending on your carrier. You can easily change your **E-mail Signature** and perform other tasks from your carrier's web site, but you'll first need to create an account. If your account was already set up when you activated your phone, log in with your username and password and skip ahead to the **Changing Your E-mail Auto Signature** section.

Setting Up BlackBerry E-mail from Your Computer

From your computer, find your way to your carrier's web site (see partial list below) using your Web browser and, once there, log in to your personal account page.

> **NOTE:** These web sites change frequently. Some carriers imbed or include the BlackBerry E-mail Setup pages within the main carrier web site. Please check with your wireless carrier if the link below is incorrect, or you don't see your carrier listed. You may also want to check for updated sites at the bottom of this web page:
>
> na.blackberry.com/eng/support/blackberry101/setup.jsp#tab_tab_e-mail

Alltel (USA): http://www.alltel.blackberry.com

AT&T/Cingular (USA): http://www.att.blackberry.com/

Bell / Solo Mobile (Canada): https://bis.na.blackberry.com/html?brand=bell

Cellular South (USA): https://bis.na.blackberry.com/html?brand=csouth1

Rogers Wireless (Canada): https://bis.na.blackberry.com/html?brand=rogers

Sprint/Nextel (USA): https://bis.na.blackberry.com/html?brand=sprint

T-Mobile (USA) – (Login to main site): http://www.t-mobile.com/bis/

T-Mobile (Germany): http://www.instantemail.t-mobile.de/

Telus Mobility (Canada): https://bis.na.blackberry.com/html?brand=telus

Verizon Wireless (USA): https://bis.na.blackberry.com/html?brand=vzw

Virgin Mobile (Canada): https://bis.na.blackberry.com/html?brand=virginmobile

Vodafone (UK): https://bis.eu.blackberry.com/html?brand=vodauk

If you do not see a link directly to your phone company's BlackBerry Internet Service site from the list above or from na.blackberry.com/eng/support/blackberry101/ setup.jsp#tab_tab_email, log in to your own phone company's web site and look for a button or tab that says something like **Phone and Accessories**, **Device**, **Handheld** or **Support** from your home page and **Setup BlackBerry E-mail** or **Setup Handset E-mail**. If you still cannot get to your BlackBerry Internet e-mail setup, contact your phone company.

On many of the sites above, however, you will first need to create your BlackBerry Internet Service account on a screen similar to the one shown to the right.

Create a New Account

To create a new account, follow these steps:

1. Click the **Create New Account** button at your provider's site.

2. You see a **Legal Agreement**. In order to continue, check the **I have read this agreement** box and click the **I Agree** button. After accepting the legal agreement, you should see a screen (see Figure 1-8).

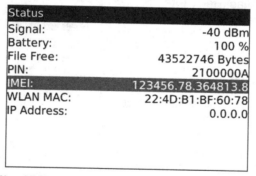

Account Setup

To begin creating your BlackBerry Service account, type your device details below.

Device PIN:

Device IMEI:

Cancel   Continue

To find your PIN perform one of the following actions:
- In the BlackBerry device options or settings, click **Status**.
- Look for the PIN and IMEI information on the outside of the box that your BlackBerry device or BlackBerry-enabled device came in.
- Turn the BlackBerry device off and remove the battery. Look for the sticker on the BlackBerry device with the PIN information where the battery is usually located.

Figure 1-8. *Set up BlackBerry Internet Service Account—requesting PIN and IMEI*

3. Both of the numbers you need are under your **Options** icon on your BlackBerry. Click the **Options** icon, and press the letter **S** on your keyboard a few times until you get to the **Status** item and click it.

4. Once in Status, look at the lines marked PIN and IMEI shown in Figure 1-9.

Options
Language
Memory
Mobile Network
Owner
Password
Screen/Keyboard
Security Options
SMS Text
Spell Check
Status

Status	
Signal:	-40 dBm
Battery:	100 %
File Free:	43522746 Bytes
PIN:	2100000A
IMEI:	123456.78.364813.8
WLAN MAC:	22:4D:B1:BF:60:78
IP Address:	0.0.0.0

Figure 1-9. *Locating your PIN and IMEI on your BlackBerry in the Options app.*

5. Type in the **PIN** and **IMEI** into the web site screen, but remove any spaces or dots. You should come to a series of screens on the **Main BlackBerry Internet Service** web page (see Figures 1-10 through 1-12).

6. Log in or click the link from your carrier's web site to access a screen similar to the one in Figure 1-10.

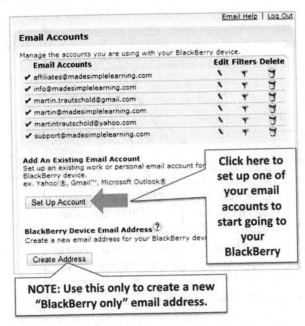

Figure 1-10. *E-mail accountaSettings on the BlackBerry Internet Service web site.*

7. Click the **Setup Account** button to input your e-mail address and password (see Figure 1-11). Click **Next** and your account will be set up.

Figure 1-11. *Adding an existing e-mail account to the BlackBerry Internet Service.*

After the e-mail account is successfully set up, you will receive a confirmation e-mail on your BlackBerry usually titled **Activation.**

    ✉ 10:30a **Activation... Congratulatio...**
    ✉ 10:29a **Activation... Congratulatio...**
    ✉ 10:29a **Activation... Congratulatio...**
    ✉ 10:29a **Activation... Congratulatio...**

Shortly thereafter, your first e-mail will come in on the BlackBerry.

Repeat step 7 for each of your e-mail accounts.

Once you have all of your e-mail accounts configured, you will see them listed (see Figure 1-12). You can customize (**Edit**), filter e-mail (**Filter**), or remove them (**Delete**) by selecting the icons on the right side.

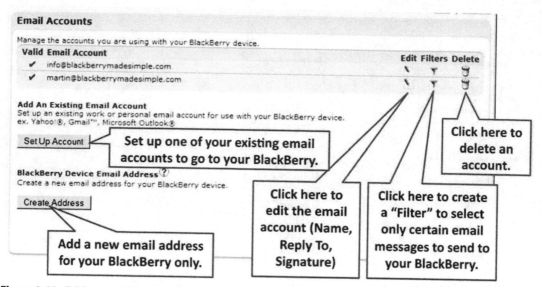

Figure 1-12. *Editing or adding e-mail accounts in the BlackBerry Internet Service.*

Changing Your E-mail Auto-Signature

On your **E-mail Accounts** page, you should see an icon for editing each of your set-up accounts. You can add a unique signature for each account.

> **TIP:** You can also change this signature directly from your BlackBerry (see page 42).

1. Select the **Edit** icon next to the e-mail account you would like to work with (see Figure 1-12).

2. Make changes in the provided fields (see Figure 1-13).

3. In the signature box, type in the new signature at the bottom of that particular e-mail account.

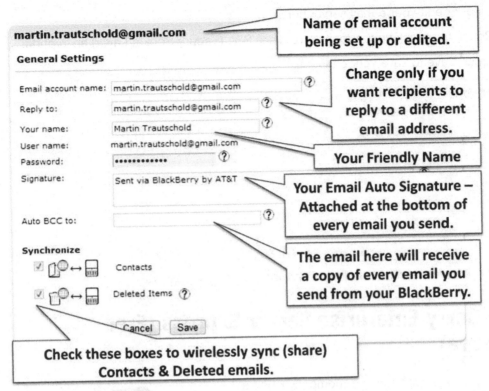

Figure 1-13. *Adjusting settings including **Auto-Signature** and **Sync Settings** from BlackBerry Internet Service.*

4.   Click the **Save** button.

> **NOTE:** As of publishing time, only Gmail has the ability to wirelessly sync or share **Contacts.** We expect more services to be added in the future (e.g. Yahoo!, etc.).

We recommend you test your new settings by sending an e-mail from your Blackberry to yourself or another e-mail account and verify that the new signature is included.

You can also add signatures that can be selected "on the fly" from your BlackBerry while writing e-mails, using the **AutoText** feature (see page 22).

Adjusting Advanced E-mail Account Settings

From the e-mail settings screen, you can also adjust advanced e-mail settings which you will need if your e-mail is not working correctly on your BlackBerry.

1.   Click on the **Advanced Settings** link (sometimes it does not look clickable) at the top of the e-mail **Edit** screen to see the screen shown in Figure 1-14.

2.   Enter or edit your e-mail server name.

3. Enter or edit your e-mail server port.

4. Check the box if your e-mail server uses SSL (Secure Socket Layer) encryption.

5. Press Save to save your changes.

---

martin@madesimplelearning.com

General Settings | **Advanced Settings**

Email server: mail.madesimplelearning.com
Email server type: IMAP
Port: 993
Timeout: 120 seconds
SSL: ☑

[Cancel] [Save]

10 Research In Motion Limited. All rights reserved. End User Agreement. Legal Information.

Figure 1-14. *Advanced Settings screen on the BlackBerry Internet Service web site.*

BlackBerry Enterprise Server Express (Free Software)

If you work at an organization or company using a Microsoft Exchange or Microsoft Windows Small Business Server, you can now acquire the BES Express software for free (see the advantages of having a BES below).

A BES is a server that typically sits behind your organization's firewall and securely connects your BlackBerry to corporate e-mail, corporate data, and also wirelessly synchronizes (shares) contacts, calendar, tasks, and memo items between your corporate computer and your BlackBerry.

BES allows your organization to gain all the benefits of a BlackBerry Server with no additional software costs. This saves thousands of dollars over the old pricing model by Research In Motion. Talk to your information technology department about this new deal if you use BlackBerry devices at your workplace and are not already using it.

Image courtesy of `blackberry.com`

You should be able to support up to 75 BlackBerry users on the same box as your e-mail server. You can support up to 2,000 users by putting the BES Express software on a separate server.

How Do I get the BES Express software?

To acquire BES Express, visit blackberry.com and follow these steps:

1. Click the **Software** link at the top.

2. Click **BlackBerry Enterprise Server Express** under **Business Software** on the left column to see a screen (see Figure 1-15). (You might be able to go straight to the page by visiting na.blackberry.com/eng/services/business/server/express/.

3. Follow the on-screen steps to begin the free download.

Figure 1-15. *BlackBerry Enterprise Server Express software web site.*

4. Once downloaded, the administrator uses a web-based console to set up and administer all users. The full set up instructions for BES Express are beyond the scope of this book, but please follow the on-screen help and tutorials found at blackberry.com see Figure 1-16.

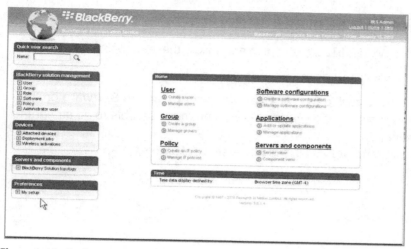

Figure 1-16. *Setting up the BES Express Software.*

Benefits of Being Connected to a BlackBerry Server

Individuals and small office BlackBerry users can gain easy access to a BES. Perform a web search for **Hosted BES** or **Hosted BlackBerry Enterprise Server** to locate a number of providers.

> **TIP:** See the BES Express section above for free BES software.

Connecting your BlackBerry to a BES (v4.0 and higher) will give you all of the following benefits:.

Strong Encryption of E-mail Within Your Organization

All e-mail sent from your BlackBerry to other users in your organization will be fully encrypted with military-grade Triple-DES encryption provided by the server.

Full Two-Way Wireless Synchronization

Full two-way wireless updates between your BlackBerry and corporate desktop account for:

- Address Book
- Calendar
- Task List
- MemoPad (Notes)

This means you will be able to add new information or make changes to anything in your **Address Book, Calendar, Task List,** or **MemoPad** on your BlackBerry and in minutes it will appear on your desktop computer.

Securely Connect to Your Corporate Data

The BES server provides a highly secure connection to corporate data behind your firewall. This can provide productivity benefits to your organization or company by providing access to view and update important information in the field.

Push Applications Wirelessly to All Your BlackBerry Users

The BES administrator can create software configurations for groups of users and push them out wirelessly to any or all BlackBerry users. This saves on IT support costs.

Global Address List Lookup

Using Global Address List (GAL) Lookup (**Lookup** for short), you can immediately **Lookup** anyone in your organization or company from your BlackBerry, even if there are thousands.

Out-of-Office Auto Reply and E-mail Signature

Your **Out-of-Office Reply** and **E-mail Signatures** are adjustable right from your BlackBerry if you are connected to a BlackBerry Server:

1. Go to **Messages** (e-mail).

2. Press the **Menu** key.

3. Select **E-mail Settings** to adjust these items.

Meeting Invitations

Just like on your desktop computer, you may check people's availability and invite attendees to meetings you schedule right on your BlackBerry. And, just like on your desktop, you may accept, decline, or tentatively accept meeting invitations you receive on your BlackBerry. Learn more on page 309.

> **NOTE:** Sending and responding to meeting invitations is an available feature without having your BlackBerry tied to a BES.

Chapter 2

Windows PC Setup

This chapter shows you how to install Desktop Manager Software on your Windows computer. We show you how to synchronize your contacts, calendar, tasks and memos, backup and restore, and more.

If you want to transfer files and media, check out our chapter on transferring files for Windows users (page 105). (You may need some of the instructions in this chapter on how to install Desktop Manager if you want to use it as your method to transfer files.)

Do you have an Apple Mac computer? Please see the **Apple Mac Setup** chapter on page 125.

Unless you work for an organization or company providing you access to a BES, if you are a Windows computer user you will need to use BlackBerry Desktop Manager Software to do a number of things:

1. Transfer or synchronize your personal information (addresses, calendar, tasks, and notes) between your computer and your BlackBerry (see page 73).

2. Backup and restore your BlackBerry data (see page 96).

3. Install or remove application icons (see page 90).

4. Transfer or sync your media (songs, videos, and pictures) to your BlackBerry (see page 105).

> **CAUTION:** Do not sync your BlackBerry with several computers, especially if you are syncing separately to an online service like Google. You could corrupt your BlackBerry and/or other databases ultimately ending up with duplicates or deleted items (even worse).

Download Desktop Manager for Windows

Each new version of Research In Motion's (maker of BlackBerry smartphones, also known as RIM) Desktop Manager Program has come with more functionality and more versatility than the previous versions. It is always a good idea to keep up-to-date with the latest version of the Desktop Manager software.

The Disk from the BlackBerry Box

It is likely that the disk that arrived with your brand new BlackBerry has a version of Desktop Manager that is already out-of-date. Oftentimes, the company produced the CDs months ago, and in the mean time a new version has been released. We recommend downloading the latest version from the Internet directly from blackberry.com as shown below.

Check Your Current Version

If you have already installed Desktop Manager, check which version you currently have. Start up your Desktop Manager program, click **Help** and **About Desktop Manager**. You will see the version number of your particular version shown here. If you don't have version 5.0.1 or higher, it is time to upgrade.

To get the latest version of Desktop Manager, follow these steps:

1. From your computer, open a web browser and go to na.blackberry.com/eng/services/desktop/ or perform a Web search for **BlackBerry Desktop Software download** and choose the appropriate search results for going to the blackberry.com site.

2. This should bring you to the BlackBerry web site. Follow the links to get to the download screen (see Figure 2-1).

3. Click the **Download** button at the bottom to get started.

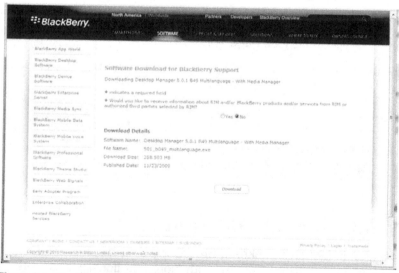

Figure 2-1. *BlackBerry Desktop Manager download web site.*

4. Save the file to a place where you will remember it. This is a large file so it may take some time to download.

Install Desktop Manager

1. Locate and double-click the installation file you've downloaded. It will typically be in your **Downloads** folder unless you changed the default (see Figure 2-2).

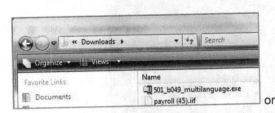 or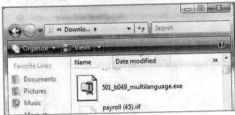

Figure 2-2. *Locating the Downloaded Installation File on your computer.*

2. What the file looks like will depend on your **View** in Windows Explorer (e.g. small icons, large icons, list, or details). The first few numbers in the file name correspond to the version of Desktop Manager (in Figure 2-2 it is 501 for version 5.0.1).

3. After you double-click the install file, follow the directions to complete the installation. Choose **Integrate with a personal e-mail account** unless your BlackBerry is tied to a BES.

Overview of BlackBerry Desktop Manager

One of the benefits of your BlackBerry is the amount of information, entertainment, and fun that you can carry in your pocket at all times. What would happen if you lost your BlackBerry or lost some of your information? How would you get it back? What if you wanted to put music from your computer on your BlackBerry? Your BlackBerry comes with BlackBerry Desktop Manager that can back up, synchronize, add media, and load new applications on your BlackBerry.

To get started, click the **Desktop Manager** icon on your computer, or go to **Programs, BlackBerry**, and **Desktop Manager.** When it starts, you should see a screen similar to Figure 2-3. Make sure your BlackBerry is plugged into the USB cable provided and attached to the computer.

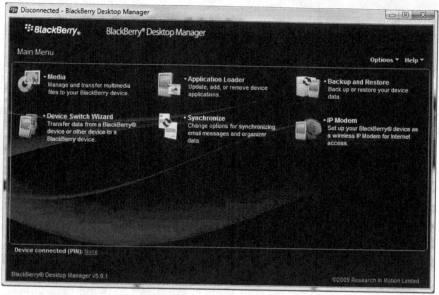

Figure 2-3. *BlackBerry Desktop Manager main screen.*

NOTE: Version 5.0.1 is shown in Figure 2-2; your version may be higher.

You will see the following five or six icons (the **IP Modem** icon may not show up for you, we tell you why below) in **Desktop Manager**:

The **Media** icon is for transferring media (songs, videos, pictures, and ringtones) between your computer and your BlackBerry. We discuss the **Media** icon (**Media Manager** and **Media Sync** on page 105).

The **Application Loader** is for installing or removing BlackBerry icons and upgrading your BlackBerry System Software version.

The **Backup and Restore** icon is for making a full backup of all your data on your BlackBerry and restoring (or selected databases) at a later time.

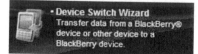

Along the second row is the **Device Switch Wizard**. This **Wizard** can be very helpful for moving your data from an old device (BlackBerry or non-BlackBerry) to a new BlackBerry.

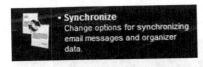

Next is the **Synchronize** icon that controls the settings for synchronizing your data including your address book, calendar, tasks, memos and more to keep your computer and your BlackBerry up-to-date with one another.

The **IP Modem** icon allows you to connect your Laptop computer to the Internet using your BlackBerry. You may not see the **IP Modem** icon. Some wireless carriers disable this feature within Desktop Manager causing the icon to disappear once you connect your BlackBerry to your computer. Learn more about this **IP Modem** feature on page 464

TIP: You can install new software icons wirelessly right on your BlackBerry (see page 22).

NOTE: Most wireless carriers require you purchase a separate **BlackBerry as a Modem** or **Tethering** data plan in order to use this feature.

Entering Your Device Password

If you have enabled **Password Security** on your BlackBerry, you will need to enter your password on your computer right after connecting your BlackBerry to your computer (see Figure 2-4).

Figure 2-4. *BlackBerry Desktop Manager* **Device Password** *screen.*

Device Switch Wizard

1. If you are upgrading from another BlackBerry, a Palm device, or Windows Mobile device, use the **Device Switch Wizard** in Desktop Manager.

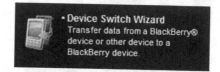

2. After clicking the **Device Switch Wizard**, you have two options depending on the type of device you were using before your BlackBerry Curve (see Figure 2-5).

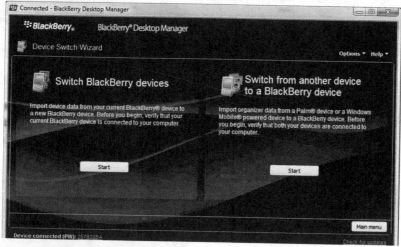

Figure 2-5. *Device Switch Wizard main screen in Desktop Manager.*

Moving from Another BlackBerry

1. Connect the old (called "current") BlackBerry to your computer.

2. Click the **Start** button and follow the on-screen instructions. Your current BlackBerry data will be backed up to your computer.

3. Connect your new Curve to the computer so all data (including e-mail setup and other settings) can be restored.

NOTE: Not all third-party icons (applications) you added to your old BlackBerry will be able to be copied to your new BlackBerry. The Curve will have a newer operating system and may have a different screen size, so some third-party apps that worked on your old BlackBerry will not work on the Curve.

Moving from a Palm or Windows Mobile Device

1. Connect both your Palm/Windows Mobile handheld and your new BlackBerry to your computer at the same time..

2. Click the **Start** button to see Figure 2-6.

3. Follow the on-screen directions.

NOTE: Because the devices use different operating systems, not all the information from the Palm or Windows Mobile device will be copied to your BlackBerry.

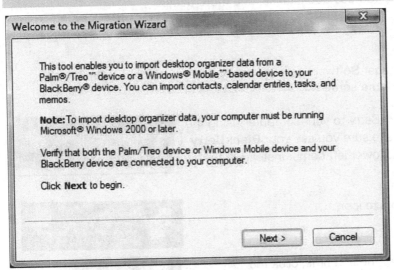

Figure 2-6. *BlackBerry Desktop Manager Migration Wizard.*

NOTE: You will not be able to copy any icons or software from your Palm/Windows Mobile device to your BlackBerry. If you have a favorite application from Palm/Windows Mobile, check out the **BlackBerry App World** (see page 441) or the software vendor's web site to see if there is a compatible version for your BlackBerry Curve.

Synchronize Your BlackBerry

You may have come to rely on your BlackBerry more and more as you get comfortable using it. Think about how much information you have stored in your BlackBerry.

> **TIP:** If you use Google for your **Contacts,** you may already have set up synchronization when you set up your Gmail account (see the **Sync Google Contacts** section of **Chapter 1: E-mail Set Up** on page 47).

At this point, you may want to ask yourself a couple questions: "Is all my information safely stored in my computer?" and "Is all my BlackBerry information synchronized or shared with the information in my computer software?"

Synchronizing your BlackBerry with Desktop Manager is very important. Your data will be safe and backed up or shared with the correct program on your computer—making things like your calendar, address book, tasks, and more useful.

Set up the Sync

Open your Desktop Manager Software as you usually do by clicking the **Desktop Manager** icon on your **Home** screen:

1. Connect your BlackBerry to your computer using the USB cable and make sure you see your **BlackBerry PIN number** in the lower left corner instead of the word **None**.

2. Click the **Synchronize** icon.

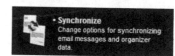

3. Before you Sync for the first time, click the **Synchronization** link right below where it says **Configure** on the left-hand side of the screen.

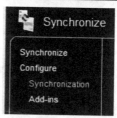

4. Click the Synchronization button on the right side next to Configure synchronization settings for my desktop program.

NOTE: If the **Synchronization** button is grayed out and not clickable, please make sure your BlackBerry is connected to your computer. If you see **None** instead of your **PIN number** in the lower left corner, your BlackBerry is not connected to your computer.

Device connected (PIN): None

BlackBerry® Desktop Manager v5.0

5.   You will see the main **IntelliSync Program** window (see Figure 2-7).

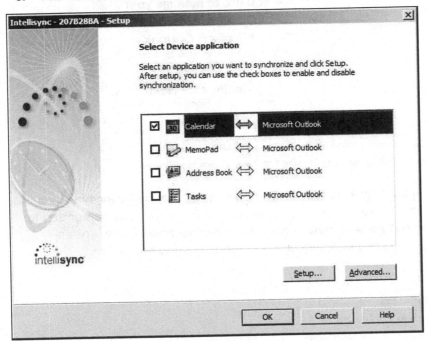

Figure 2-7. *Intellisync **Main Setup Screen** in Desktop Manager.*

6.   To get started, check the box next to the icon you want to sync or on the name of the icon. You can also click the check box and click the **Setup** button at the bottom. For example, clicking **Calendar** and **Setup** will bring you to a few screens with details for how to sync your computer's calendar to your BlackBerry.

7.   Select your **Desktop** app from the list (see Figure 2-8) and click **Next**.

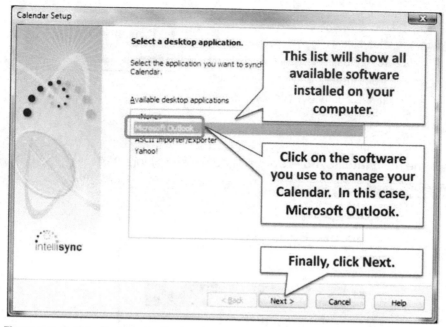

Figure 2-8. *Select a Desktop Application to sync using Intellisync in Desktop Manager.*

8. You will see options for **Two way** or **One-way sync**. The **Two way sync** means any changes you make on your computer or BlackBerry will be synchronized to the other device (**Two way sync** is typically more desirable). Under special circumstances, you might require or want **One-way sync** see Figure 2-9.

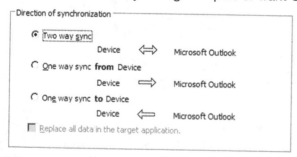

Figure 2-9. *Select One way sync or Two way sync for your Information.*

9. Click **Next** to see an advanced screen with more options. This shows options for the **Calendar. Address Book, Tasks,** and **MemoPad** may have different options. We recommend settings as shown below to ensure you never miss out on any data you enter on your BlackBerry (if you forget to sync every day). These settings will sync calendar events up to 30 days old from your BlackBerry and 180 days into the future (see Figure 2-10).

Microsoft Outlook options for Calendar

These settings are used during data exchange operations involving Microsoft Outlook.

Outlook user profile

| Outlook |

Calendar date range

○ Transfer all scheduled items
○ Transfer only future items
◉ Transfer items within a range of days

| 30 | Days prior to today |
| 180 | Days after today |

Alarm settings

☑ Remove alarm for past items

Figure 2-10. *Select **Additional Options** for your **Calendar** sync.*

10. Repeat the procedure for all the apps you want synced. Click **Next** and click **Finish** on the next screen. You will see similar screens for all four apps with some minor variations (see Figure 2-11).

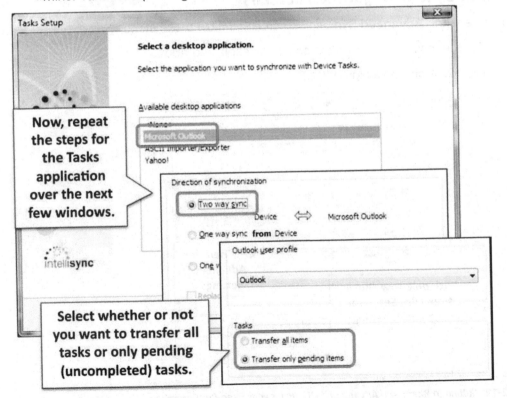

Figure 2-11. ***Task Sync Options*** *in Desktop Manager.*

11. Once the setup is complete for **Two way sync** for all four applications, your screen should look similar to the one on the left below. If you are using **Google Contacts** wireless sync (see page 311), do not check the box next to **Address Book** as shown below on the right.

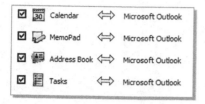

12. After the **Configuration** is set, go back to the main **Synchronization** screen and put a check mark in the **Synchronize Automatically** box if you want the Desktop Manager to automatically synchronize as soon as you connect your BlackBerry to your computer.

13. Close out all **Sync** setup windows to save your changes.

Advanced Sync Configuration Screens

In order to see the **Advanced Sync** setup screens, follow these steps:

1. Go to the main synchronization screen as explained above.

2. Click **Advanced** (see Figure 2-12).

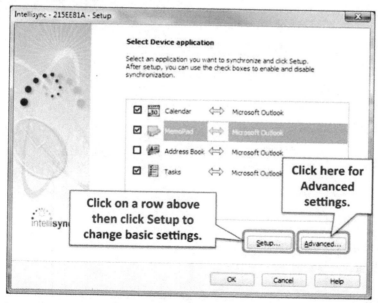

Figure 2-12. *Getting to Basic and Advanced Settings for your Sync Configuration.*

3. After clicking **Advanced**, you will see a screen similar to the one in Figure 2-13.

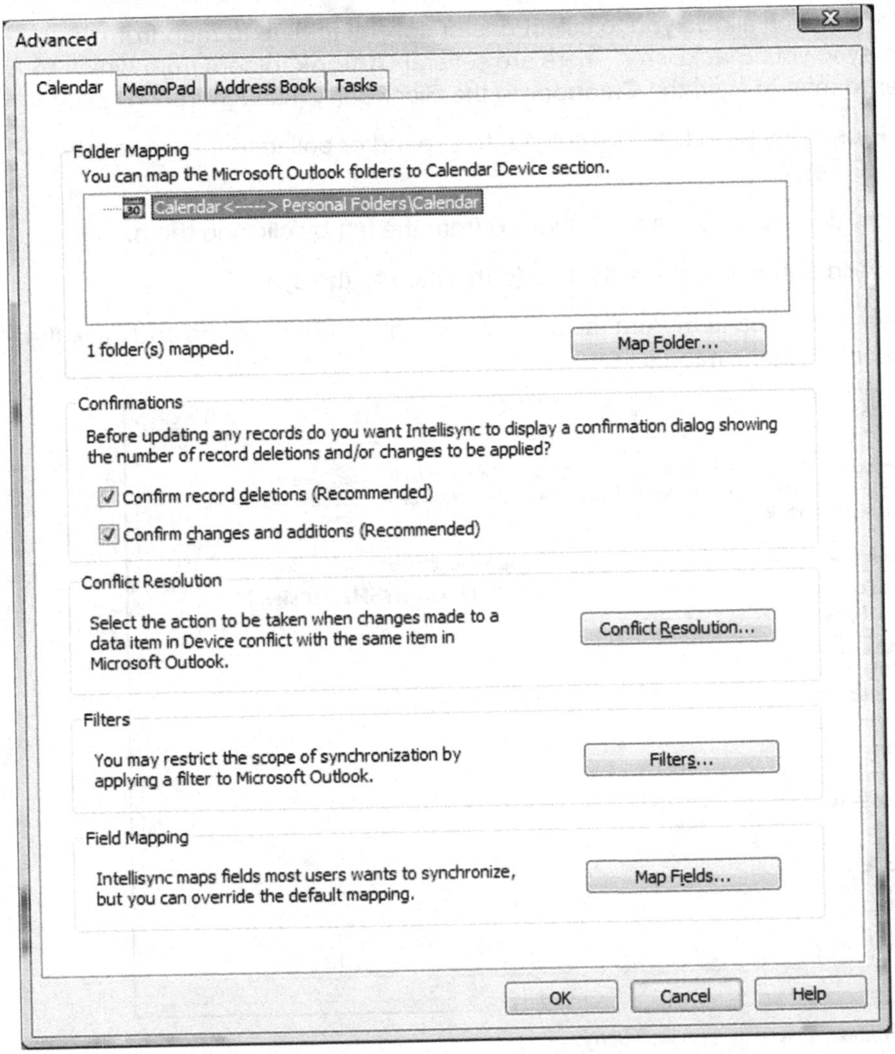

Figure 2-13. *Advanced Settings tabbed screen for your **Sync Configuration**.*

From this **Advanced** settings screen, you can perform any of the following actions:

- Map Folder
- Conflict Resolution
- Filters
- Field Mapping

Map Folder

The **Map Folder** function allows you to select one or several folders to map from your desktop app to sync your BlackBerry. There are several **Outlook** folders from which to choose in order to map to sync the **Calendar** to the BlackBerry (see Figure 2-14).

1. Use the **Plus** signs (+) in the right column to expand or collapse the views (see Figure 2-13 below).

2. Select individual items (such as **Calendar**) from the left by clicking them.

3. Click the **Add** button in the middle to add this item to the sync.

4. To remove a selected item from the sync, click it in the right column and click the **Remove** button in the middle.

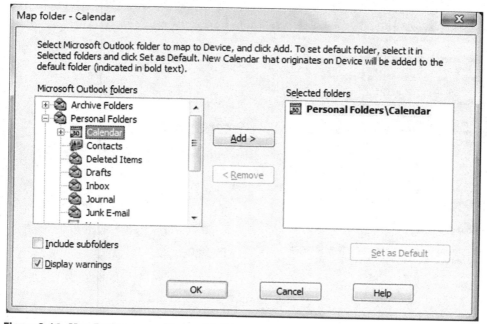

Figure 2-14. *Map Folders to sync to your BlackBerry.*

Conflict Resolution

The **Conflict Resolution** function allows you to review each sync change and determine whether in **Conflicts** the handheld or your computer will "win" (or you should be asked each time). Being asked each time is the default and recommended setting (see Figure 2-15).

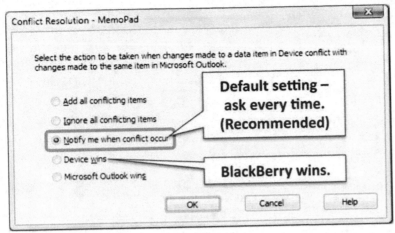

Figure 2-15. *Conflict Resolution choices window from **Advanced Sync Settings** (for **MemoPad** app).*

Filters

The **Filters** function allows you to filter synchronized data. This can be extremely useful if you have specific data that you do or do not want to be synchronized to your BlackBerry from your computer. With filters and creative use of information typed in your desktop app, you can really fine-tune the data that is transferred to your BlackBerry. To set up a new filter, click the **Filters** button (see Figure 2-12) and follow the steps shown below (also see Figure 2-15):

1. Click **New**.

2. Enter a name for your **Filter.**

3. Click **OK**.

4. Click the drop down for **Field.**

5. Select an **Operator** such as **Starts with, Contains**, or **Equals**.

6. Type a **Value** to use to compare for the selected field and operator.

7. Click the **Add to List** button. Repeat steps 4-7 for additional fields.

8. Click the **Rules** tab at the top.

9. Select one of the two conditions: **All Conditions** or **One or more.**

10. Click **OK** to return to the screen shown in the upper right corner (see Figure 2-16).

11. Check or uncheck the box stating **Delete from device any data that does not match the filter** as desired. Click **OK** and **Save**.

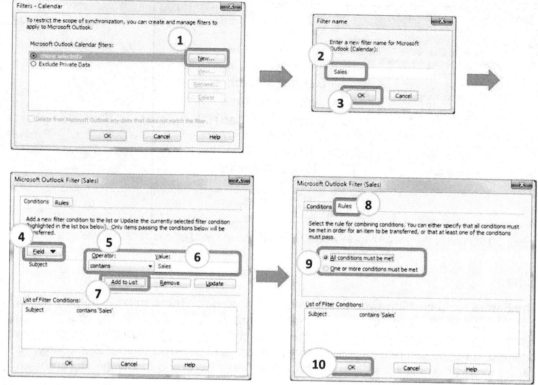

Figure 2-16. *Creating a new sync filter in Desktop Manager.*

Field Mapping

The **Field Mapping** function allows you to map individual fields from your computer app into your BlackBerry. This can be useful if you need to fine-tune the information added to your BlackBerry (see Figure 2-17). You can complete the following actions:

- To **map** a field, click between the left and right columns until you see the double-arrow.

- To **unmap** a field, click between the left and right columns until it is blank (the double-arrow goes away).

- To **change which field is mapped** on the right column, drag it up or down and drop it.

- You may need to scroll down the list to see all the possible fields to be mapped.

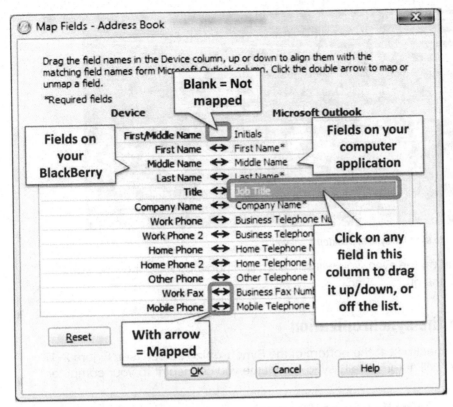

Figure 2-17. *Adjusting field mapping for the sync.*

To return to the main **Synchronize** screen, click **OK** or **Save.**

Running the Sync

To start the sync for the first time, follow these steps: (You can automate the sync so you don't have to do these steps every time. We show you how to automate the sync in the next section.)

1. Click the **Synchronize** link in the very left-hand column (Figure 2-18).

2. Make sure the box next to **Synchronize organizer data** is checked.

3. Click the **Synchronize** button in the middle of the window to start your sync.

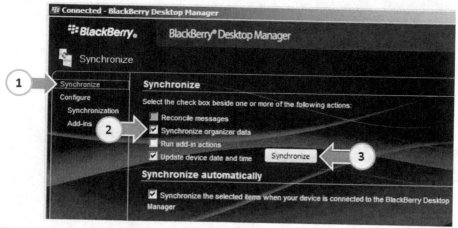

Figure 2-18. *Steps to start the sync in Desktop Manager.*

4. After starting the sync, you will see a small window pop-up showing you the status of the current sync.

Automating the synchronization

If you click the checkbox at the bottom of the **Synchronize** screen (see Figure 2-17), your BlackBerry will automatically sync every time you connect it to your computer.

Accepting or Rejecting Sync Changes

During the sync, if there are additions or deletions found in either the BlackBerry or the computer app, a dialogue box will appear giving you the option to **Accept** or **Reject** changes. Click **Details** if you want to see more about the specific changes found (see Figure 2-19).

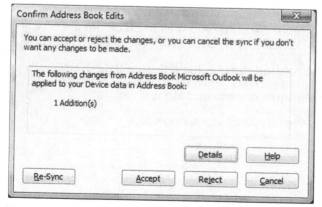

Figure 2-19. *Accepting or Rejecting Changes found during the sync.*

We recommend **Accepting** the changes unless something looks strange. Finally, the **Synchronization** process will end and your data will be transferred to both your BlackBerry and your computer. For more details on what has changed on your BlackBerry and computer, click the **Details** button.

Troubleshooting Your Sync

Sometimes you will encounter errors or warning messages when you try to sync. In this section, we try help you through some of the more common issues.

"Default Calendar Service Has Changed" Message

Sometimes you may see a warning message (see Figure 2-20). When you add a new e-mail address, it typically takes precedence as the default e-mail address or service for all new calendar entries you add on your BlackBerry. Click **Cancel** and follow the steps below to verify everything is how you would like it before syncing again:

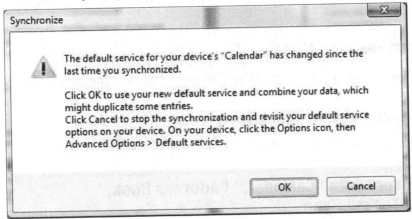

Figure 2-20. Default Calendar Service Message Has Changed message.

After clicking the **Cancel** button, follow these steps:

1. Click the **Options** icon on your Curve.

2. Click **Advanced Options.**

3. Click **Default Services**.

4. You will see a screen similar to the one shown. Verify that the e-mail address under the **Calendar** item at the top is set correctly. If not, click and adjust it.

5. Click the **Menu** key and select **Save**.

6. Re-sync using Desktop manager. If you see the same error, ignore it by clicking **OK**.

Close and Re-Start Desktop Manager

Try closing down Desktop Manager and re-starting it as this can sometimes help.

Remove and Re-Connect your BlackBerry

Sometimes a simple disconnect and re-connect can also help.

Fixing Specific Errors with "Calendar," "Address Book," "MemoPad," or "Tasks" Sync

Try the sync again after it fails and watch it closely—you should note where it fails whether on the **Calendar, Address Book, MemoPad,** or **Tasks**—by watching the status screen. Once you determine where the sync fails, clear out or delete the problem database from your BlackBerry and start the sync again:

CAUTION: Doing this will force you to lose any changes you have made on your BlackBerry since your last successful sync.

1. From the main **Desktop Manager** screen, click **Backup and Restore.**

2. Click **Backup** (see Figure 2-21). Make a note of the file name and location. You may need to use it later to restore data if this troubleshooting does not work. In the image above, the backup file name is **Backup-(2008-12-12)-1.ipd.**

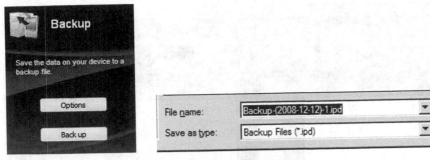

Figure 2-21. *Perform a **Full Backup** and note the file name.*

3. Once your full backup is complete, click the **Advanced...** button from the **Backup and Restore** screen (see Figure 2-22).

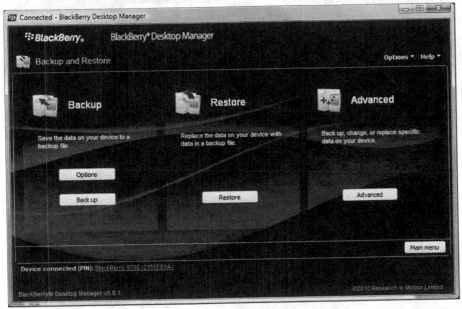

Figure 2-22. *Main Backup and Restore screen in Desktop Manager.*

4. Now, you will be on a new screen (see Figure 2-23). Locate the problem database in the right-hand window (BlackBerry) and click the **Clear** button at the bottom. In the image below, get ready to clear out the **Address Book** and **Address Book-All** from the BlackBerry. (Press the **Ctrl** key to click and select more than one.)

5. Both are selected in the right-hand window **Device Databases**. Press and click the **Clear** button.

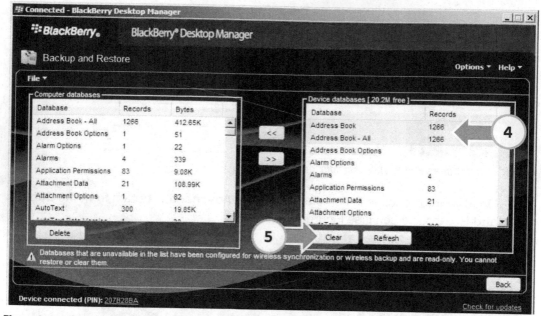

Figure 2-23. *Clear or erase a specific database from the BlackBerry.*

6. Once they have been cleared out, click the **Back** button.

7. Try to **Sync** again. This will hopefully correct the sync problem.

If the problem has not been corrected, you can restore the **Address Book** by following these steps:

8. Return to the **Advanced Backup and Restore** window shown above.

9. In the upper-right corner, click **File** and click **Open to open** the full backup file you just created (see Figure 2-24).

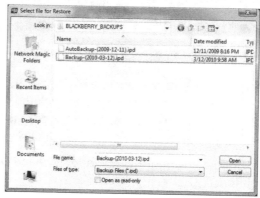

Figure 2-24. *Opening a previous backup file to restore.*

Now you can highlight the correct databases from the **Full Backup** in the left-hand window (**Computer databases**). In this example we have clicked the **Address Book-All** database (see Figure 2-25).

To restore the selected database to your BlackBerry, click the **>>** button in the middle of the screen.

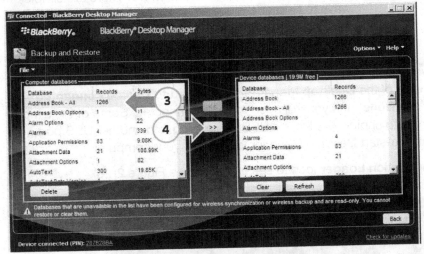

Figure 2-25. *Restoring a particular database to your BlackBerry.*

Getting More Help for Desktop Manager Issues

Some of the Desktop Manager sync issues can be particularly tricky. Before you pull out too much hair, try the **BlackBerry Technical Knowledgebase**. You should also try some of the more popular BlackBerry online discussion forums to see if others have experienced and solved similar issues.

BlackBerry Knowledgebase:

10. From your computer web browser, go to na.blackberry.com/eng/support/.

11. Click the **BlackBerry Technical Solution Center** link (or similar) in the left column.

Web Search:

Pull up your web browser and do a web search for the particular issue you are facing.

BlackBerry Forums:

- crackberry.com
- blackberryforums.com
- pinstack.com
- blackberrycool.com

Application Loader

Use this icon to add or remove software from your BlackBerry. This is also used to update your BlackBerry operating system or system software. There are simpler ways to load or remove software from your device (see the **App World** chapter on page 441 and the **Add / Remove Software** chapter on page 485).

1. Make sure your BlackBerry is connected to your computer and it is shown in the lower-left corner of the **Desktop Manager** screen next to **Device connected (PIN).** If you see **None** then you will need to get it connected. Some of the simpler things to do are to unplug/re-plug the USB cable, plug into another USB port, shut down and re-start Desktop Manager, or re-start your computer.

2. Click the **Application Loader** icon to see a screen (see Figure 2-26).

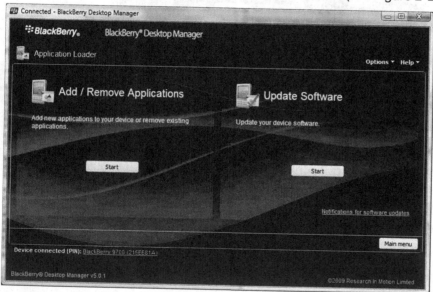

Figure 2-26. *Application Loader main window in Desktop Manager.*

Add / Remove Apps

To add or remove apps, which could be third-party or portions of the main system software and core apps (such as language files), follow these steps:

1. Click the **Start** button under **Add / Remove Applications** (see Figure 2-26).

NOTE: You will first see a **Task in Progress** window showing you that the software is reading your current BlackBerry configuration and installed software.

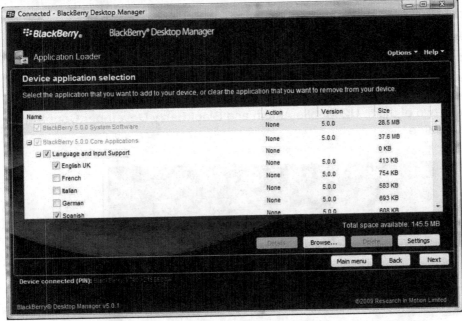

Figure 2-27. *Add / Remove Software screen in **Application Loader** of Desktop Manager.*

2. Listed at the top of the screen (see Figure 2-27) is your current BlackBerry System Software. This device is running 5.0.0, and your device may show a different version.

3. You can add or remove languages using this tool.

   a. To add an item, place a **check** in the checkbox next to it.

   b. To remove an item, **uncheck** a checkbox next to it.

4. Scroll down using the scroll bar on the right edge to see more language options. Part of the way down you will notice **Supplemental SureType Wordlists** (see Figure 2-27).

5. If you work in the finance, legal, or medical professions, you may want to add some of these customized dictionaries. These can help when you use **SureType** or when the spell checker guesses what you are trying to type. Add **English Financial** and **Medical** terms by checking both boxes (see Figure 2-28).

6. Notice the **Action** column shows **Install** as a status.

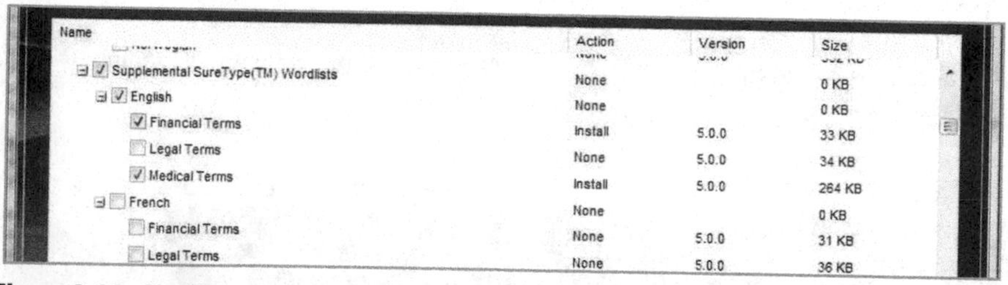

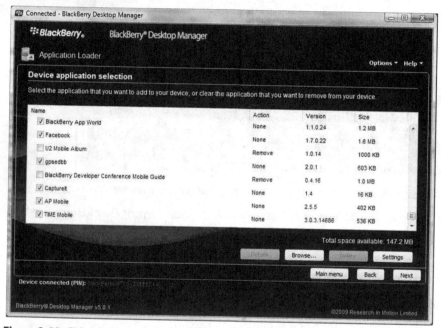

Figure 2-28. *Supplemental wordlLists for financial, legal, and medical terms.*

7. To see all installed **Third Party** applications, scroll to the bottom of the list (see Figure 2-29). You have a number of apps installed and decided to remove or uncheck two of them: **U2 Mobile Album** and **BlackBerry Developer Conference Mobile Guide**.

Figure 2-29. *Third Party Applications are shown at the bottom of the list.*

8. To complete the adding or removing of apps, click the **Next** button in the lower-right corner to see the **Summary** screen (see Figure 2-30).

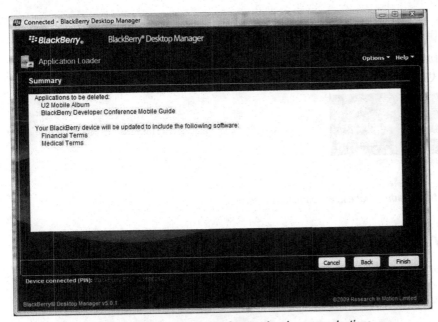

Figure 2-30. *Application Loader Summary Screen showing your selections.*

9. If you have made a mistake, click **Back** to return to the previous screen. Otherwise click the **Finish** button to execute the listed actions. While the software is working, you will see a status window (see Figure 2-31).

In some cases, this process can be very fast taking just a minute or so. However in other cases, especially if you are updating the system software or any part of it (like adding or removing core dictionaries), you will see a message that **This task might take up to 30 minutes to complete.**

In our testing, the process took about six minutes, but it felt like 30 minutes!

Figure 2-31. *Application Loader Status screen.*

Have patience while this is happening. If you disconnect your BlackBerry from your computer while this reboot is happening, your BlackBerry might become unusable.

10. When the process is finished, you should see a small status message in the upper left corner (see Figure 2-32).

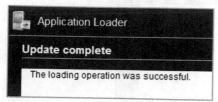

Figure 2-32. *Application Loader Successful* completion message.

Update Your BlackBerry Device Software

Also in **Application Loader,** you can update the device software, or the System Software running on your BlackBerry smartphone. You can upgrade and downgrade using this feature:

1. Click the **Start** button under the **Update Software** section of the **Application Loader** main screen (see Figure 2-26).

2. The software will check your BlackBerry and the Internet for available updates.

3. You will see a screen (see Figure 2-33).

4. Depending on what version you have installed on your BlackBerry and what is available, you may see one or more rows with **(Current), (Upgrade),** or **(Downgrade)** next to them.

    a. To upgrade your software, check the box next to the **(Upgrade)** item and click the **Next** button.

    b. To downgrade your software, check the box next to the **(Downgrade)** item and click the **Next** button.

    c. To make no changes, click the **Main Menu** button.

Figure 2-33. *Update System Software screen in Application Loader.*

5. If you are upgrading or downgrading software, you will see screens telling you it is backing up your BlackBerry, erasing it and re-installing software, and restoring your data. This process could take more than 10 minutes.

6. You will see a **Summary** screen (see Figure 2-34).

7. Click the **Main Menu** button to finish the process and return to the main **Desktop Manager** window.

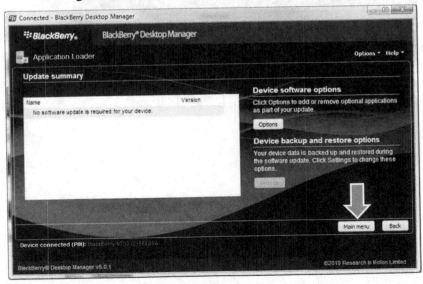

Figure 2-34. *Update System Software screen in Application Loader.*

Backup and Restore

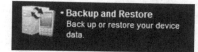

• Backup and Restore
Back up or restore your device data.

Use this feature to protect important data on your BlackBerry. You can use some of the advanced features to help with troubleshooting your **Desktop Manager** sync (see page 85).

Click the **Backup and Restore** icon to see a screen (see Figure 2-35).

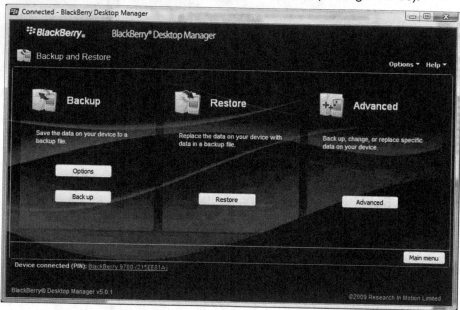

Figure 2-35. *Backup and Restore main qindow.*

On the **Backup and Restore Options** screen, click the **Options** button under the **Backup** heading on the left side of the page to see the options screen (see Figure 2-35).

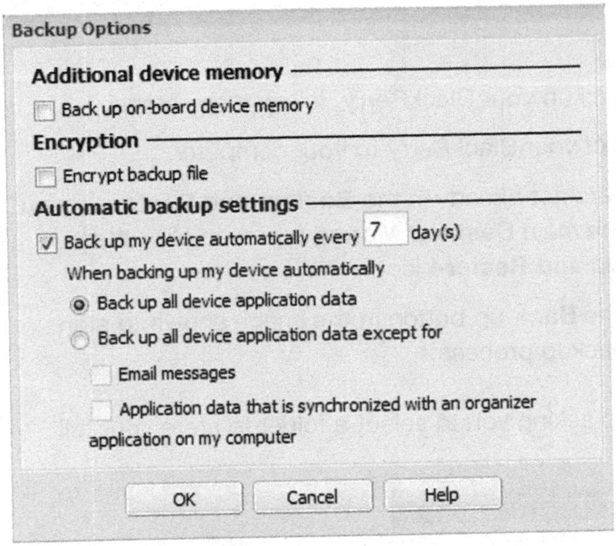

Figure 2-36. *Backup Option screen.*

If you want to backup data stored in your main BlackBerry memory (including pictures, video recordings, voice notes, or other information), check the box **Back up on-board device memory.**

If you had confidential information and wanted to encrypt your backup file for added security, check the box next to **Encrypt backup file.**

The default for **Automatic Backup Settings** is every seven days for backing up all device data. You can adjust this to be any number of days. Try fewer days if you are concerned about your data being lost.

The backup can take several minutes or more depending on how much information you have stored on your device. The easiest way to speed up the backup is to back up less information. Since your e-mail is already on your computer or e-mail server, you may check **E-mail Messages.** This would skip backing up e-mail. If you sync regularly with your computer, you could check the box next to **Application data that is synchronized with an organizer application on my computer.** Click **OK** to save your **Options** settings.

Backup Your BlackBerry

In order to backup your BlackBerry, follow these steps:

1. Connect your BlackBerry to your computer.

2. If you are not already in the **Backup and Restore** menu, from the main **Desktop Manager** screen click the **Backup and Restore** icon.

3. Click the **Back up** button in the image shown to start your backup process.

4. You will see a dialog box pop up asking you to select a folder to store your full backup file (see Figure 2-37).

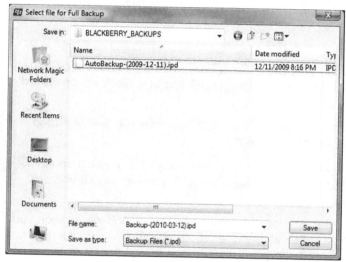

Figure 2-37. *Choose a folder in which to store the backup file.*

5. Use the drop-down list at the top or one of the icons to the left to select your backup file location.

6. Notice the format of the file name **Backup-(2010-03-12).ipd** is in year-month-date format so you can easily see the date of your backup.

> **NOTE:** We have both experienced computer hard disk failures. We highly recommend storing the backup on at least one external location. This could be a USB thumb drive, an external USB drive, another computer on your network, or any location not on your hard disk.

7. Once you have selected the location of your backup file, click the **Save** button to start the backup.

8. You will see a status window (see Figure 2-38).

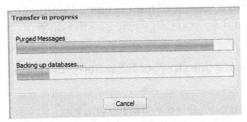

Figure 2-38. *Backup Status window.*

9. You will see a **Backup Successfully Created** message at the end. If you see an error message, look at any help available on the screen. Sometimes just re-doing the backup will solve the issue. If that does not help, try the BlackBerry discussion forums (see page 544) or **BlackBerry Technical Knowledge** base for help.

Restore Your BlackBerry

To restore from a previously saved backup file, follow these steps:

1. Connect your BlackBerry to your computer.

2. If you are not already in the **Backup and Restore** menu, from the main Desktop Manager screen click the **Backup and Restore** icon.

3. Click the **Restore** button as shown in the image.

4. You will see a dialog box pop up asking you to select a folder in which to store your full backup file (see Figure 2-39).

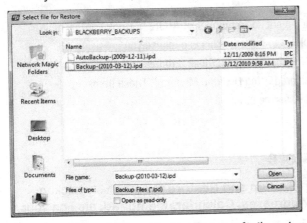

Figure 2-39. *Select folder and backup file to use for the restore.*

5. Use the drop-down list at the top or one of the icons to the left to locate your backup file to from which to restore. Notice the format of the file name **Backup-(2010-03-12).ipd** is in year-month-date format so you can easily see the date of your backup.

6. Once you have located the file to use to restore data to your BlackBerry, click the **Open** button.

7. You will see a list of details of the information contained in the file you just opened. This allows you to confirm that you want to use this restore file. Scroll down to see total number of contacts (**Address Book**) and **Calendar** entries. Make sure they seem reasonable.

8. Click **Yes** to start the restore process (see Figure 2-40).

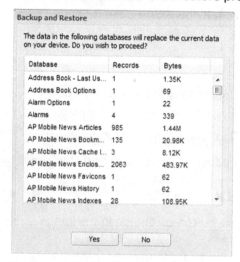

Figure 2-40. *Confirm Restore* screen.

NOTE: In the screen (see Figure 2-39), you do not see a number of **Address Book** entries, only **Address Book Options** and **Address Book—Last Used**—this is because you are using a wireless sync with Google contacts. With any wireless sync, those databases (**Addresses, Calendar,** etc.) cannot be backed up or restored using Desktop Manager. These items are essentially backed up all day with the wireless sync process.

Advanced Backup and Restore

You would use the **Advanced** feature in **Backup and Restore** to selectively backup, restore, or erase individual databases (**Addresses, Calendar, MemoPad,** etc.) on your BlackBerry. Use the following steps:

NOTE: We showed how to erase only your **Address Book** and restore it to help with troubleshooting the Desktop Manager sync in the **Fixing Specific Errors** section on page 86.

1. Connect your BlackBerry to your computer.

2. If you are not already in the **Backup and Restore** menu, from the main **Desktop Manager** screen click the **Backup and Restore** icon.

3. Click the **Advanced** button in the right portion of the screen (see Figure 2-41).

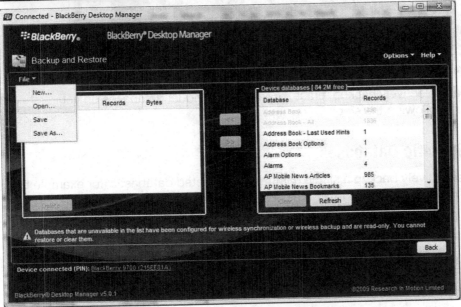

Figure 2-41. *Opening a Backup File in the Advanced Backup and Restore screen.*

4. The left side of the screen shows a backup file from your computer. If the left side is blank, open a backup file to use. Select **File** and **Open** (see Figure 2-41).

5. Navigate to a specific folder and backup file to open and click **Open**.

6. When the file is open, you will see the left-hand window fill up with the contents of that backup file (see Figure 2-42).

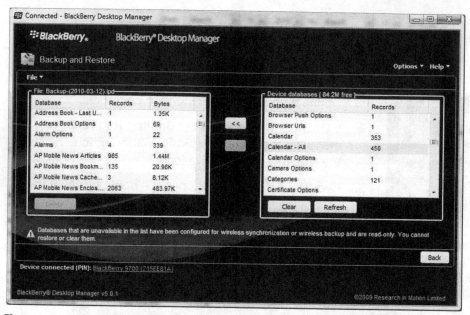

Figure 2-42. *Advanced Backup and Restore screen with backup file open in left window.*

Now, you can selectively backup, erase, or restore individual databases on your BlackBerry by following the steps in the next section.

Backup Specific Databases

In order to selectively backup a single database or selected databases (for example the **Calendar**, **Address Book,** or **NotePad**) use the following steps (and see Figure 2-41):

1. Click the right-hand window (**Device Databases**) to highlight and select a database or hold the **Control** key to select several databases.

2. Click the << button in the middle to copy the information to the backup file on the left.

Erase or Clear Specific Databases

In order to selectively erase or clear a single database or several databases from your BlackBerry, use the following steps (and see Figure 2-42):

1. Click the right-hand window (**Device Databases**) to highlight and select a database or hold the **Control** key to select several databases.

2. Click the **Clear** button under the right-hand window.

3. Click **Yes** to confirm and delete the listed databases (see Figure 2-43).

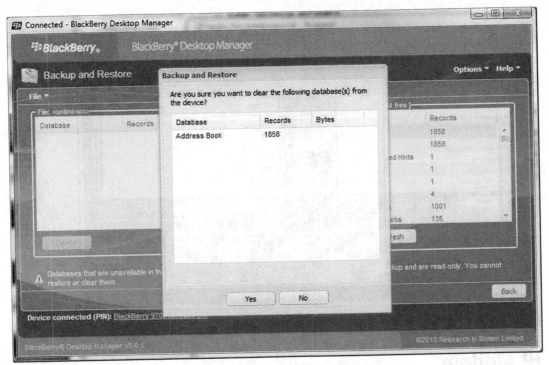

Figure 2-43. *Confirm you want to clear or erase databases from your BlackBerry.*

How to Restore Specific Databases

In order to restore a file to your BlackBerry, use the following steps (and see Figure 2-43):

1. Open a backup file in the left window. If the left window is blank, click **File** and **Open** in the upper-right corner.

2. Click to select one or more database files in the left-hand window under **File: Backup-(year-month-day).ipd**.

3. Click the **>>** button in the middle to copy the information to your BlackBerry on the right side. Select the **Calendar** database with 450 entries from the **Backup** and copy it to the BlackBerry (see Figure 2-44).

4. Begin the restore process by clicking **Yes** on the next screen (see Figure 2-43).

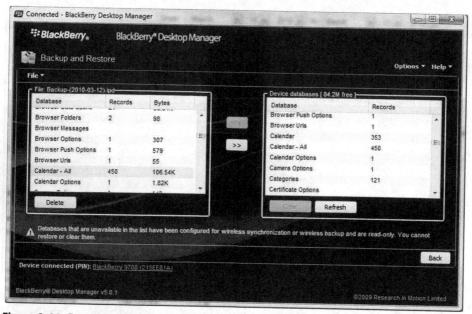

Figure 2-44. *Restoring specific databases from a backup file to your BlackBerry.*

IP Modem

You may not see this icon in Desktop Manager because your wireless carrier may have disabled it or may provide separate software. See the **Modem** chapter starting on page 461 to set up your BlackBerry as an IP modem or dial-up Internet connection for your laptop computer.

Chapter 3

Windows PC Media and File Transfer

In this chapter we will help you get your important files and media from your Windows computer to your Curve. Your Curve is quite a capable media player on which you can enjoy music, pictures, and videos. Like your computer, your BlackBerry can even edit Microsoft Office documents.

You have a variety of choices about how to transfer documents and media and we explore all the most popular ones in this chapter. You will quickly see that some methods such as Mass Storage Mode transfer work well for large numbers of files, whereas you will want to use the Media Sync program to transfer your music playlists. There are a few ways to load up media (music, videos, pictures) and Microsoft Office documents (for use with Documents to Go) onto your BlackBerry:

- Desktop Manager Media Manager (page 114)

- Desktop Manager BlackBerry Media Sync (page 105)

- Mass Storage Mode Transfer (page 144)

- E-mail the files to yourself as attachments (*if they are small enough*)

Having all that functionality is great, but first, you have to get your media onto the BlackBerry. That's where the Media Manager and the Media Sync features in are useful in Desktop Manager.

Before we begin, we strongly recommend that you install a Micro SD memory card into your BlackBerry handheld. With the price of memory coming way down, you can get a 2 GB, 4 GB, or even an 8GB Micro SD card for little money. Obviously, the bigger the card, the more media files you can store on your device. (See our chapter on Media Cards on page 367 to learn how to insert a media card)

Using the Media Manager (in Desktop Manager)

> **NOTE:** Remember, you should use BlackBerry Media Sync instead of Media Manager if you want to sync iTunes or Windows Media playlists (see page 105).

To use the **Media Manager**, follow these steps.

1. Start **BlackBerry Desktop Manager**.

2. Plug in your BlackBerry Device with the USB Cable.

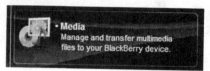

3. Click the **Media** icon.

4. Click the **Launch** button under the Media Manager icon.

5. You may see a license agreement that you need to accept before you can continue.

Scanning Your Computer for Media Files

When you start the Media Manager for the first time, it may ask if you want it to scan your computer for all music, video, and picture files that you could use on your BlackBerry device. This takes a while to do, but it is worthwhile if you have lots of pictures, music, and videos scattered over your computer. So click **Yes**

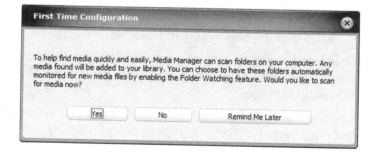

> **CAUTION:** If you have a lot of media on your computer, this scanning process could take **more than 10 minutes to complete.**

After you do this, you can see that the **Media Manager** tells you exactly how many of each kind of file it contains. Under the icon for each type of media, you can click on **Manage Media** to rename, regroup, or organize your media.

Watched Folder Settings

You may see another window for Watched Folder Settings. These are folders that are scanned by the Media Manager to see if any changes have occurred (new songs, videos, pictures, and so forth) that should be synchronized with your BlackBerry.

Once you click **OK**, you will see the software scanning the selected Watched Folders and see a status window. You can **Pause** or **Cancel** the process if it takes too long.

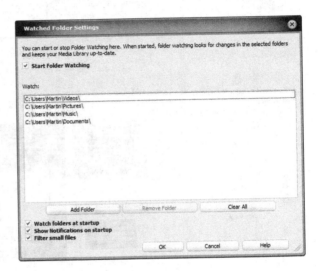

Enter Password

If you have a device password set on your BlackBerry, you will need to enter it before Media Manager can see the files stored on your BlackBerry.

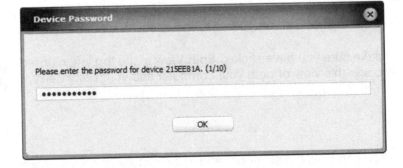

The Main Media Manager Window

Once the program loads, you will see a window similar to Figure 3-1.

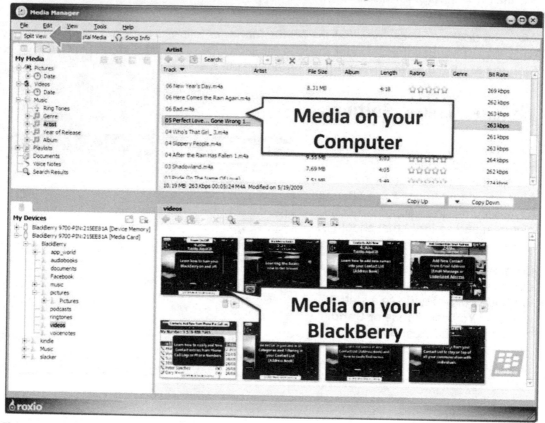

Figure 3-1. *Media Manager Main Window*

The **Media Manager** window show you the media files that are stored on your computer in the top half and on your BlackBerry and on your media card in the bottom half.

Make sure you have clicked **Split View** in the top left in order to see this view of both your computer and your BlackBerry.

You can drag the slider bar above the pictures/media to increase or decrease their size.

Locating Media on Your Comptuer

Use the top left portion of the Media Manager window to look for media you want to copy to your computer.

Click on the plus sign (+) next to any item to expand the view. You can use any of the following items to help you find media.

- Click on **Music** and then under that **Genre**, **Artist**, **Year of Release**, **Album**, or **Playlists** to further refine your view.

- Click on **Pictures** to view pictures and click on the **Date** item to narrow views by dates.

- Click on **Videos** to view your videos.

- Click on **Documents** to view documents compatible with your BlackBerry.

- Click on **VoiceNotes** to view voice notes.

- Type in a **Search** string in the top row to search for particular media.

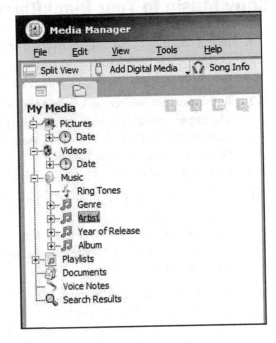

Copy Music to Your BlackBerry

1. In the top half of the **Media Manager** screen, click on a folder to view your music or playlist.

2. In the bottom left corner of the **Media Manager** screen, click the plus sign (+) next to the BlackBerry with the **[Media Card]** at the end of it to see all the folders stored on your media card.

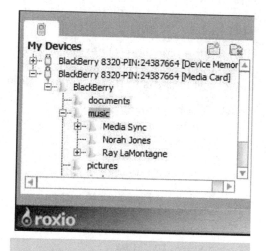

3. Click on the folder to which you want to copy your media–music, videos, ringtones, and so forth. In this case, because we want to transfer music, we click on the **music** folder.

4. Now, you should see the music you want to copy from your computer in the top half of the screen and the music folder from your BlackBerry media card in the bottom half of the screen.

NOTE: On your **Media Manager**, your will see *your* BlackBerry model number instead of the one shown.

5. Now, click to highlight songs, playlists, videos, or any other media in the top window.

6. Click the **Copy Down** button in the middle of the screen.

7. Repeat the procedure for more songs or any other type of media.

8. You may see a window asking you if you want the Media Manager program to copy the song and convert it for optimal playback on the BlackBerry–you can select either copy with conversion, without conversion, or look at advanced conversion options.
   We generally recommend letting the Media Manager convert your media for optimal playback on your BlackBerry. *(However, this conversion may not work with videos, which are much more challenging to convert than music and are beyond the scope of this book.)*

9. Select **OK** and the song (or songs) will now be copied onto your BlackBerry media card. Verify the copy by looking on the lower window and seeing the song on your *media card.*

Copying Pictures

The only difference between copying pictures and copying music is that on the **Media Manager** screen, in the top window, under **My Media**, just select **Pictures** and your pictures will be displayed in the top window. Make sure that down below, you collapse the **Music** menu and open up your **pictures** folder on your media card to ensure that your files will be copied to that folder.

Select your pictures (if you want more than one, just hold down the **Ctrl** key on your keyboard and then press and click each picture you want; they will all highlight.) Then, click the **Copy Down** button and let them be **converted** and they will go right on your media card (see Figure 3-2).

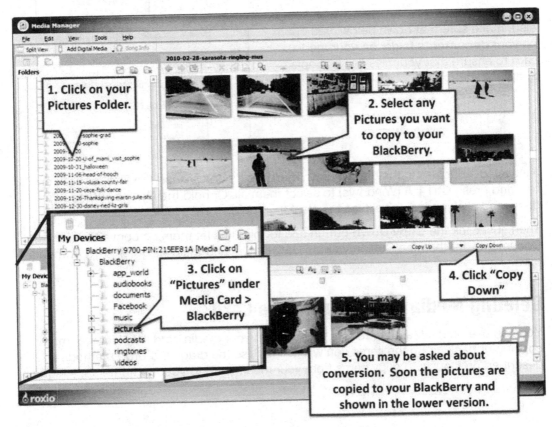

Figure 3-2. *Copying pictures and other items to your BlackBerry using Media Manager*

Copying (Microsoft Office) Documents

Repeat the steps for copying pictures and music, but in
the top window under **My Media,** just select **Documents**
and your documents folders on your computer will be
displayed in the top window. Navigate to the correct
folder for your particular documents.

Also, make sure that down below, you open
up your **documents** folder on your media
card to ensure that your files will be copied
to that directory.

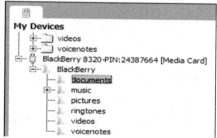

Just select your files in the top window. Then draw a box around the files, or click on
one and press **Ctrl + A** (Windows) to select them all. Or hold the **Ctrl** key (Windows)
down and click on individual files to select them.

Then, just click the **Copy Down** button and for pictures let them be converted (for
Documents, let them be Copied with no Conversion) and they will go on to your media
card.

Deleting Media from Your Media Card

You can use Media Manager to free up space on your media card. We first recommend
copying or backing up the items you will delete. Use the drag–and–drop methods
described previously to copy items from your media card to your computer (see Figure
3-3).

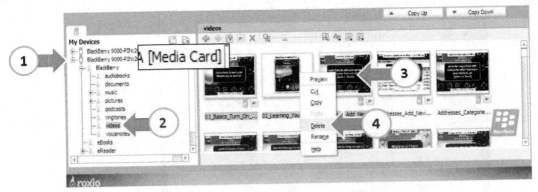

Figure 3-3. *Selecting and deleting media from your BlackBerry with Media Manager*

1. Click the + sign next to the **BlackBerry nnnn-PIN:xxxxxxx [Media Card]** in the lower left window to see all the folders on the media card.

2. Then click on a folder from which you wish to delete media on the media card.

3. Select the items, using **Ctrl + click** or **Shift + click** to select a list of items.

4. Once the items to delete are selected, press the **Delete** key on your keyboard, or right-click and select **Delete**.

> **TIP:** Videos and songs will usually be the largest items on your BlackBerry–deleting these items will free up more space than deleting individual pictures.

Troubleshooting Media Manager

Sometimes when you are previewing a file or performing some other function, Media Manager might crash and stop responding. If this is the case, you can stop the program by following these steps:

1. On your Windows computer, press three keys simultaneously: **Ctrl + Alt + Del**.

2. If you are given a choice, then select **Start Task Manager**.

3. From the **Window Task Manager** (Figure 3-4), click on the **Processes** tab.

4. Scroll down and highlight the Image Name of **MediaManager**, as shown.

5. Click the **End Process** button at the bottom.

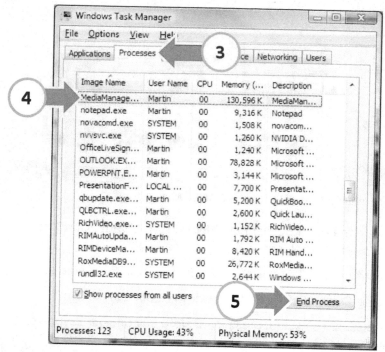

Figure 3-4. *Windows Task Manager*

6. On the next screen that says **Do you want to end this process?**, click **End process** to stop the program.

7. Now, you can restart the program and try again.

BlackBerry Media Sync

NOTE: You should use the BlackBerry Media Manager instead of the Media Sync if you want to sync non-iTunes media and you need to convert music and video to be viewable on your BlackBerry (see page 105).

Perhaps the easiest way to get music into playlists (and now your album art) is using the BlackBerry Media Sync program. If you are an iTunes user and you have playlists already in your iTunes program, the Media Sync program allows you to transfer those playlists directly to your BlackBerry.

RUNNING MEDIA SYNC SEPARATELY FROM DESKTOP MANAGER

Normally, you just launch Media Sync from inside Desktop Manager; however, you can download and run Media Sync separately from BlackBerry Desktop Manager. To do this:

Open up a web browser on your computer and go to: www.blackberry.com/mediasync

Click the **Download for PC** link.

Once you have the file downloaded, just run the installation program. A window will appear letting you know the application has been installed properly.

To launch the application, just go to Start→All Programs→BlackBerry Media Sync and click on the icon. Make sure that your BlackBerry is connected via the USB cable to your computer—but **don't** have Desktop Manager running when you do this.

Start Media Sync from Desktop Manager

To use the **Media Sync** from within Desktop Manager, follow these steps.

1. Start BlackBerry Desktop Manager.

2. Plug in your BlackBerry Device with the USB Cable.

3. Click the **Media** icon.

4. Click the **Launch** button under the BlackBerry Media Sync icon. You may need to accept a license agreement to continue.

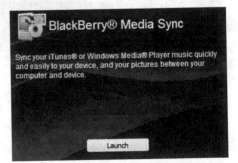

5. After clicking **Launch**, you may see a window telling you an update is available. Click the **Download** button and follow the steps to install the updated software.

NOTE: If a song is in iTunes and is DRM-protected (see page 122), then it is NOT possible to sync it to your BlackBerry.

Enter BlackBerry Password for Media Sync

If you have set a password to protect your BlackBerry, then you will need to enter your password to continue.

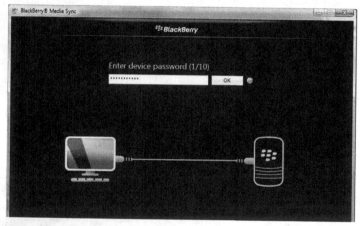

Figure 3-5. *Media Sync Password screen.*

Media Sync Setup

When you first start Media Sync, it may show you a setup screen similar to Figure 3-6.

1. Change the name of your device, if you like.

2. Select where your media should be stored; leave this on your media card (see page 22 to learn about media cards).

3. Use the slider bar to keep more or less space free after the sync. The default is 10% and should be fine.

4.   Click on **iTunes** or **Windows Media Player** for where you store your music.

5.   Click **OK** to continue.

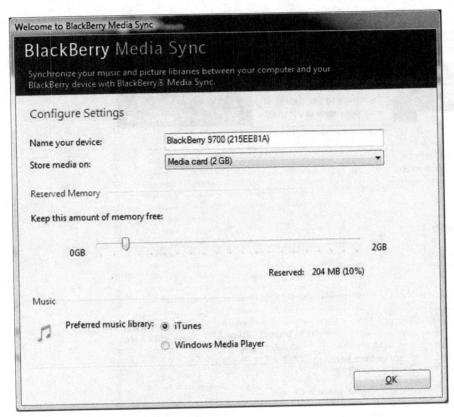

Figure 3-6. *Media Sync options (device).*

After your initial **Configure Settings** screen is complete, you should then see a screen similar to the one shown in Figure 3-7.

Media Sync—Syncing Music

You are now ready to set up your Music Sync.

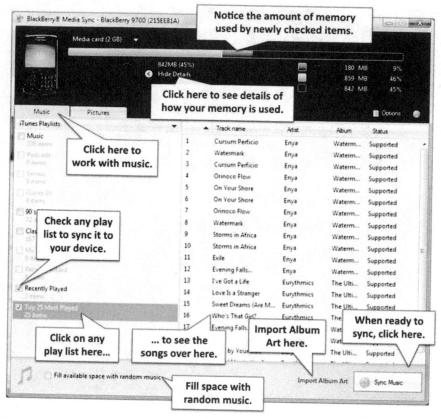

Figure 3-7. *Media Sync screen (Music tab).*

Make sure to click on the **Music** tab in the upper left corner as shown in Figure 3-7 to configure your music sync.

To import your Album Art, just click the **Import Album Art** link next to the Sync Music button in the lower right corner of Figure 3-3. If you are importing from iTunes, iTunes will automatically start automatically (Figure 3-8).

> **NOTE:** If iTunes has a dialog box open when it automatically starts, you will have to close out the dialog box and re-try the **Import Album Art** button.

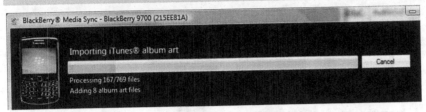

Figure 3-8. *Status screen for importing Album Art in BlackBerry Media Sync*

Once the import is done, you will see a little pop-up window saying it is **Finished importing Album Art**.

To select a playlist to sync to your device, just check the box next to the playlist. When you check it, watch the **Memory Bar** at the top to make sure that you have not **Exceeded Available Memory** with your selections. If you have, just uncheck the playlists until you get back under 100% of memory usage.

If you want to fill the available space with random music, then place a check next to the box in the lower left corner that says **Fill available space with random music**.

In order to see the details of what is occupying the space on your memory card, click the **Show Details** button underneath the Available memory after sync number in the middle upper part of the window.

Once you are done with your selection of playlists, click the **Sync Music** button in the lower right corner. You will see the sync status in the upper portion of the window (Figure 3-9).

Figure 3-9. *Status screen for syncing files to the BlackBerry*

Media Sync—Syncing Pictures

If you would like to transfer or sync pictures between your BlackBerry and your computer, click the **Pictures** tab in the upper left corner, as shown in Figure 3-10.

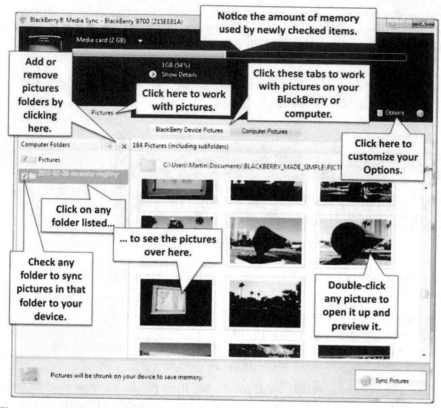

Figure 3-10. *Media Sync screen (Pictures tab)*

To switch between viewing pictures on your computer and on your BlackBerry, click the buttons in the middle upper section of the screen (Figure 3-4).

To add or remove picture folders on your computer, click the folder + and – icons at the top of the folder column.

Once you have folders listed, then click on a folder to display all pictures in that folder.

Check the box next to the folder to sync all the pictures in that folder to your device. If you have previously synced a folder, you can uncheck it to remove those pictures from your device to save space.

When you check each pictures folder, watch the **Memory Bar** at the top to make sure that you have not **Exceeded Available Memory** with your selections. If you have, just uncheck the folders until you get back under 100% of memory usage.

In the lower left corner of Figure 3-4, you see the text **Pictures will be shrunk on your device to save memory**. That is a setting you can change by clicking on the **Options** link in the upper right corner. See Figure 3-5 and related descriptions for help.

In order to see the details of what is occupying the space on your memory card, click the **Show Details** button underneath the Available Memory after sync number in the middle upper part of the window.

Once you are done with your selection of pictures, click the Sync Pictures button in the lower right corner. Your sync status will be shown in the top portion of the window.

Some Songs Could Not Be Synchronized

Look carefully at the **Synchronization complete** message (Figure 3-11). If some songs are protected, then they will not be synced to your BlackBerry. In this example, 35 songs were protected.

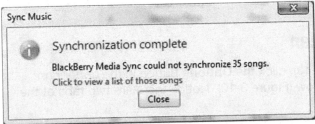

Figure 3-11. *Synchronization complete message*

To see the list, click the **Click to view a list of those songs** link. Then you should see a window similar to Figure 3-12. Click the plus sign **(+)** next to **Protected** to see all the protected songs.

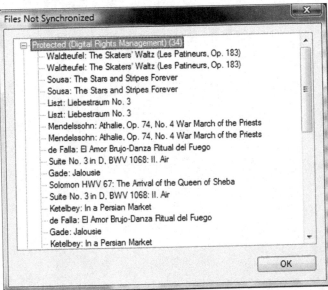

Figure 3-12. *Viewing songs that could not be synced due to Digital Rights Management protection*

Defining DRM (Digital Rights Management) Protected Media

Some music and other media purchased on iTunes contains **DRM (Digital Rights Management)** restrictions–that means that most iTunes music can only be played on iPods and through iTunes. Most likely, these are older songs purchased before the middle of 2009.

Any other music you might have put in your iTunes library–such as CDs you loaded into your computer or music that does not have DRM restrictions—will transfer into the appropriate playlist. Make sure that you don't disconnect your BlackBerry while the music is transferring.

Once the Sync is done, close out the **Media Sync** window. Now jump to page 371 to learn how to use music on your BlackBerry.

Media Sync Options Screen

To see the **Options** screen (Figure 3-13), click the **Options** button in the upper right corner of the main **Media Sync** window (Figure 3-10). Notice there are two tabs at the top: **General** and **Device**.

General Tab

Click the **General** tab at the top of the **Options** screen to see the screen shown in Figure 3-13.

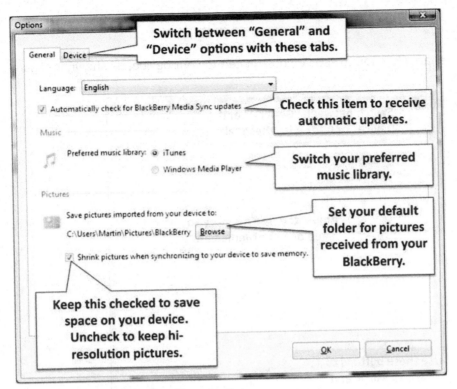

Figure 3-13. *Media Sync Options (General tab)*

On the **General** tab, you can do the following:

- Select your **language** from the drop-down list.

- Select **Automatically check for Media Sync Software updates** by checking the box (it is checked by default).

- Select your **Preferred music library**. If you have changed from **iTunes** to **Windows Media Player** or vice-versa, you can select either here.

- Select the folder to store pictures that are transferred from your BlackBerry to your computer by clicking the **Browse** button.

- You can also decide how high the resolution should be for pictures you sync to your BlackBerry. The default is to **Shrink pictures when synchronizing to your device to save memory**. Uncheck it if you want higher-resolution pictures and aren't worried about the extra storage space required.

Device Tab

Click the **Device** tab at the top to see settings related to your device, as shown in Figure 3-14 below.

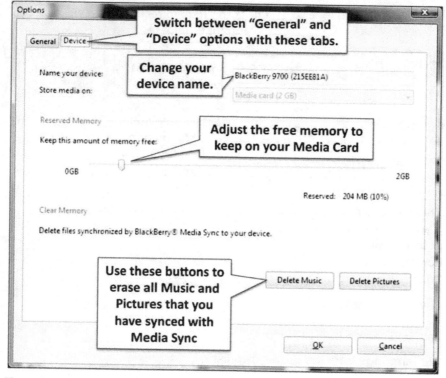

Figure 3-14. *Media Sync Options (Device tab)*

On the Device tab, you can do the following.

- Change your **Device Name** for your BlackBerry.

- Change the amount of **Reserved Memory** on your device after the sync. Use the **slider bar**.

- Erase all the music and pictures synced to your BlackBerry by clicking the **Delete Music** or **Delete Pictures** buttons.

Chapter 4

Apple Mac Setup

This chapter shows you how to install the new BlackBerry Desktop Manager Software on your Apple Mac computer and complete the basics of synchronizing your contacts, calendar, tasks, memos, and backup and restore. If you want to transfer files and media with your Mac, see the chapter on transferring files for Mac users (see page 141).You may need some of the instructions in this chapter on how to install Desktop Manager if you want to use it as your method to transfer files.

> **CAUTION:** Do you use more than one computer (e.g. work, home, etc.)? If so, check the **Sync with other computers** option if you plan on syncing your BlackBerry with multiple computers using Desktop Manager. Otherwise, you could end up corrupting your BlackBerry and/or computer databases.

Do you want a wireless, two-way automated sync? Try using **Google Contacts, Google Calendar,** and **Google Sync** for your BlackBerry. All of these are free apps and give you a full two-way wireless sync.

BlackBerry Desktop Manager for Mac

For years, Windows users have enjoyed the seamless Synchronization of their contacts, calendar, notes, and tasks with their PC via the BlackBerry Desktop Manager Software. Now, for the first time, this peace of mind that comes with knowing your data is fully backed up and available to the Mac user.

If you are a Windows user, this will seem familiar yet very much streamlined for the Mac. If you have never used BlackBerry Desktop Manager, you will be able to not only synchronize your data, but backup, restore, sync your **iTunes** playlists, and more.

Download and Install Desktop Manager for Mac

Desktop Manager for Mac software was is available for free at BlackBerry.com. To download it, use the following steps:

1. Open your Web browser and go to the download page at `na.blackberry.com/eng/services/desktop/mac.jsp` (see Figure 4-1).

2. Fill out the required information on the download page and click to download the software.

Figure 4-1. *Locating the download file on BlackBerry.com web site.*

3. Once the file is downloaded, you will see a screen (see Figure 4-2).

Figure 4-2. *Starting the installation.*

4. Double-click the **BlackBerry Desktop Manager.mpkg** file to begin the installation process.

5. Your Mac will display a warning message (see Figure 4-3).

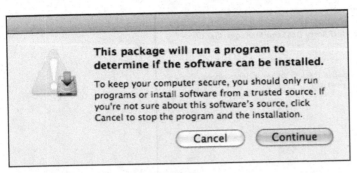

Figure 4-3. *Mac Installation Warning* screen.

6. Select **Continue** to move forward with the installation process.

NOTE: If you have been using either Pocket Mac or The Missing Sync to synchronize your BlackBerry with your Mac, you will receive another warning note telling you that in order to proceed, the connection between your BlackBerry and the third-party synchronization software will need to be discontinued.

7. If you already have other software installed, you will see another warning message (see Figure 4-4). Click **Install Anyway** to move forward with the installation process.

Figure 4-4. *Additional Warning* screen about additional BlackBerry software.

8. The installation process will begin (Figure 4-5). Follow the on-screen prompts as your Mac installs the new Desktop Manager Software.

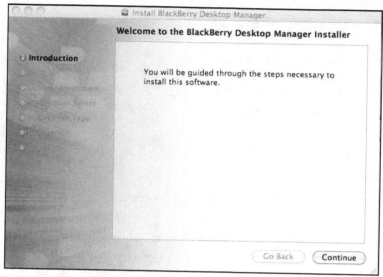

Figure 4-5. *First Installation* screen.

9. Click **Read License** to read the software license or click **Agree** to proceed (Figure 4-6).

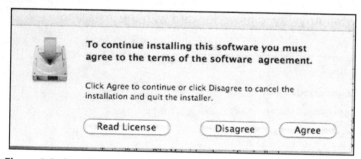

Figure 4-6. *Installation License Agreement* pop-up window.

10. For most Mac users, one drive will be shown. It is possible that you may have more than one possible location for the install. Choose the correct drive and click **Continue** (Figure 4-7).

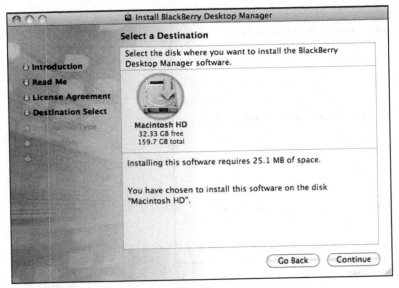

Figure 4-7. *Choose location of installation.*

11. If you have a **Password** set on your Mac, you will be prompted to enter it at this time in order to proceed with the installation (see Figure 4-8).

Figure 4-8. *Password required to complete installation.*

12. You will be asked to restart your computer when the installation is complete—agree to this by clicking **Continue Installation** (see Figure 4-9).

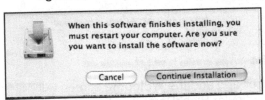

Figure 4-9. *Request to restart after installation.*

13. When the installation is complete (and before the restart), you should see a screen (see Figure 4-10) indicating the software was installed successfully.

Figure 4-10. *Successful Software Installation screen.*

Starting Desktop Manager for the First Time

To locate the **Desktop Manager** app, click the **Finder** icon and click your **Applications** icon. The **BlackBerry Desktop Manager** icon will be in your **Applications** directory (Figure 4-11).

Figure 4-11. *Locating BlackBerry Desktop Manager for Mac.*

Double-click the **BlackBerry Desktop Manager** app and the **Welcome** screen will appear showing you information about your particular BlackBerry (see Figure 4-12). On this **Welcome** screen you can adjust your device options.

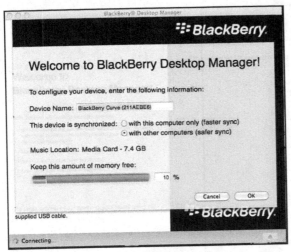

Figure 4-12. *BlackBerry Desktop Manager for Mac Welcome* screen.

Select how to synchronize your BlackBerry in the **This Device Is Synchronized** field.

If you synchronize your BlackBerry with other computers, a network server, or **Google Sync** for **Calendar** or **Contacts**, select **With other computers (safer sync).**

CAUTION: If you want to sync with more than one computer, check the option **Sync with other Computers (Safer Sync)**. Otherwise you could corrupt your BlackBerry and/or computer databases.

If you are planning on syncing your BlackBerry with this one Mac, you can choose **With this computer only (faster sync)**.

Main View in Desktop Manager

Desktop Manager will display a picture of your BlackBerry device and a clean interface displaying information along the left-hand bar and **Commands** along the top bar (see Figure 4-13).

NOTE: You will see your own BlackBerry device (Figure 4-13 displays a Curve 8900).

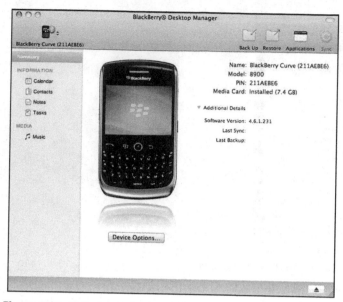

Figure 4-13. *Main view in Desktop Manager.*

Using Desktop Manager for Mac

One of the first things you will notice is the **Device Options** button below the picture of your BlackBerry (see Figure 4-13). Clicking this brings you to the **Options** screen (the same screen displayed when you first started Desktop Manager (see Figure 4-14).

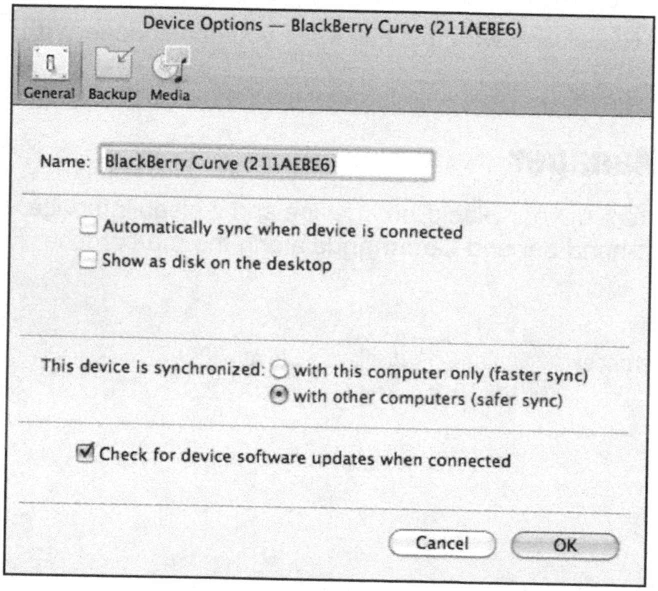

Figure 4-14. *Device options in Desktop Manager for Mac.*

Device Options

You can rename your device (the default is your model and PIN number). If you want to **Automatically Sync** your device each time you connect, check the first check box. If you want to see a desktop icon showing your BlackBerry as an external disk, check the **Show as disk on the desktop** box. You can then easily transfer files between your Mac and your BlackBerry using the drag and drop method you have used on your Mac to copy between folders and disks.

Device Is Synchronized with One or Several Computers

You have the option of choosing whether your BlackBerry syncs only with this Mac or with other computers. If your BlackBerry syncs with your PC and with your Google account, select the **With other computers** option to avoid duplicating entries in your contacts and calendars.

Backup Options

1. Click the **Backup** 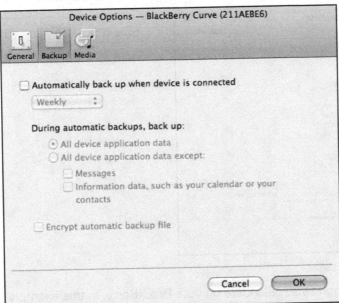 tab on the top of the **Device Options** screen.

Figure 4-15. *Backup options in Desktop Manager for Mac.*

2. 2. To create a backup each time you connect your device, check the **Automatically back up...** box (Figure 4-15). You can specify exactly what you would like backed up. We cover the **Backup** options a bit later.

Set Up Your Sync Options

Click **OK** or **Cancel** to return to the main screen of Desktop Manager (see Figure 4-13) and notice the left column below **Information** (see Figure 4-16).

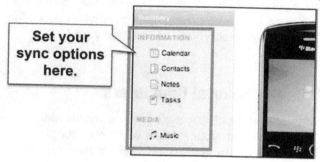

Figure 4-16. *Sync options in Desktop Manager for Mac.*

This is where you set the **Sync** options for the **Calendar, Contacts, Notes,** and **Tasks.**

1. Click any of the items below **Information.** In this case, we will begin with the **Calendar** on the **Sync setup** screen (Figure 4-17).

2. This screen has a similar look and feel to the **Calendar Sync** screen within **iTunes** for those who are familiar with syncing an iPhone or iPod Touch and a Mac.

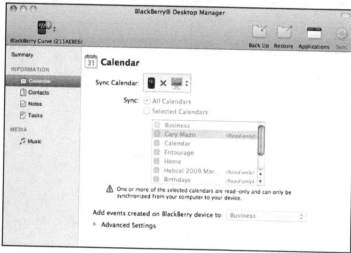

Figure 4-17. *Calendar Sync Options screen.*

3. Desktop Manager will recognize all calendars on your BlackBerry. In this example, we use **Google Calendar** and have different calendars, all set to a unique color. You can see this in the list of calendars.

4. Click the box with the **Sync Calendar** option. The **Red X** on this icon shows that the BlackBerry calendar will not be synced with the Mac calendars.

5. Click the box and select the next item in the dropdown and the picture will change to show that now you want a two-way sync between the Mac **Calendar** and the BlackBerry **Calendar.**

6. Select which calendar you would like events to be stored to that you create on your BlackBerry. The default is **Business Calendar**, but that can be changed to any calendar you have set up on the device.

Add events created on BlackBerry device to: Business

Advanced Settings

Click the **Advanced Settings** tab `▶ Advanced Settings` at the bottom and the options shown in Figure 4-18 are revealed:

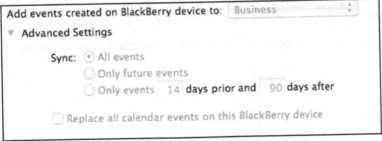

Figure 4-18. *Advanced sync settings in Desktop Manager for Mac.*

Like Desktop Manager for the PC, you can specify whether you want to sync **All events, Only Future Events,** or you can set individual parameters for synchronization.

> **TIP:** We recommend not selecting **"Only Future Events"** unless you have a strong reason to do so. Let's say you made some notes to an event that was held the previous day in the BlackBerry **Calendar** notes field. If you select **"Only Future Events,"** these notes would not be transferred to your Mac.

To replace all calendar events on the BlackBerry with events from your Mac's calendar, click the check box at the bottom of the screen.

Syncing Contacts, Calendar, Notes, and Tasks

The procedure for setting the **Sync Options** for the **Contacts, Tasks,** and **Notes** is identical to what we explained above. Groups or events to choose within each category are the only items that change.

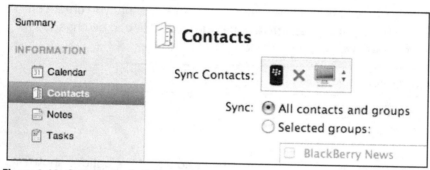

Figure 4-19. *Sync Contacts Setup screen.*

In the screen shown in Figure 4-19, you can click next to **Sync Contacts** as done above and you can choose either to not sync with the Mac or to perform a two-way sync.

Select to sync either **All Contacts or groups** or only **Selected groups** from **Address book.**

Automating the Synchronization

In order to have your BlackBerry sync every time you connect it to your Mac, you will need change a setting on the **Device Options** screen.

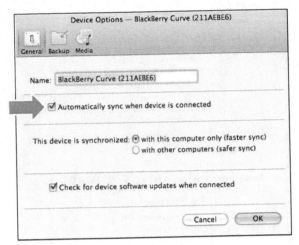

1. Click the **Device Options** button below the picture of your BlackBerry on the main screen.

2. Then check the check box next to **Automatically sync when device is connected.**

Backup and Restore

One of the features now available to Mac users is the ability to **Backup** and **Restore** either you entire BlackBerry contents or selected information on your Mac. **Backup** and **Restore** begins with the two icons at the top of the main screen in Desktop Manager.

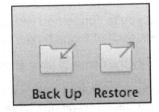

Using Backup

1. Click the **Backup** icon and you will be taken to the next screen (Figure 4-20) where you specify exactly which information you would like to back up on your Mac.

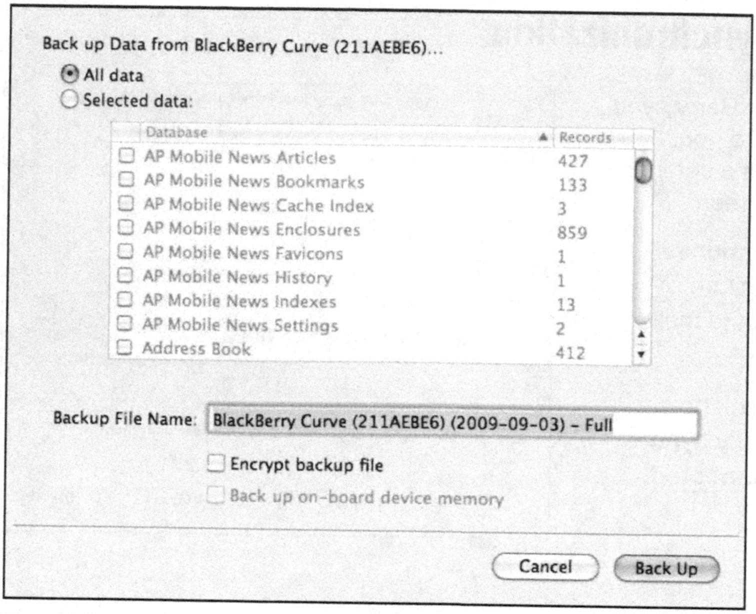

Figure 4-20. *Backup screen in Desktop Manager for Mac.*

2. Select either **All data** or **Selected data** and choose exactly which items you wish to back up.

3. Let's say that you're concerned with backing up your **Contacts, Calendar,** and **Notes**—check each of those boxes and your backup will complete much faster.

4. You can specify the name of your **Backup** for easy retrieval in the future.

5. Once you have made your backup selections, click the **Back Up** button and the progress of the back-up will be displayed in a dialog box.

Restoring from Backup

Sometimes unexplained things happen and you can lose information on your BlackBerry. Maybe you try to update the operating system and make a mistake or maybe sync with other computers and information gets corrupted. Now, Mac users have a reliable and safe way to restore data on their devices. Use the following steps:

1. Click the **Restore** icon  along the top row of the main screen in Desktop Manager. You will be taken to the **Restore options** screen (see Figure 4-21).

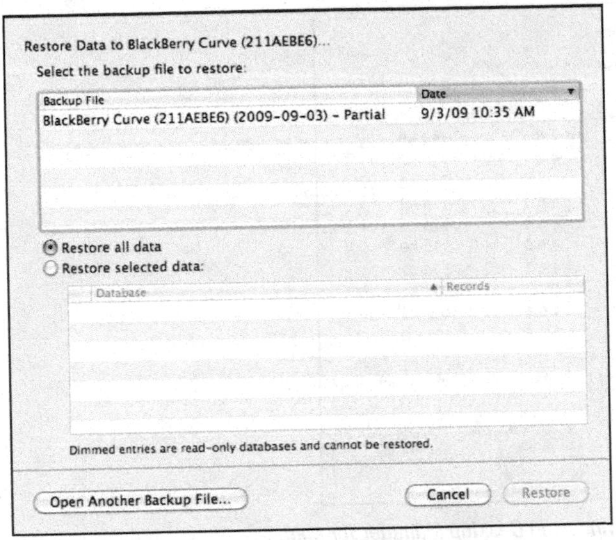

Figure 4-21. *Restore* screen in Desktop Manager for Mac.

2. If you have made a backup file on your Mac (required so you have a file you can restore), it will be shown in the top box under **Backup File.** If you have multiple backup files, they will all be listed here.

3. Select the file from which you would like to restore information (if you did a selective backup, selected data will be displayed in the second screen below).

4. Click the **Restore** button and your BlackBerry will be restored as it was when you made the backup file.

Add or Remove Applications

For the first time, Mac users are able to add or remove apps on their BlackBerry from the Desktop Manager environment.

1. Click the **Applications** icon  in the upper-right corner of the main screen and you will be taken to the **Applications** screen in Desktop Manager (Figure 4-22).

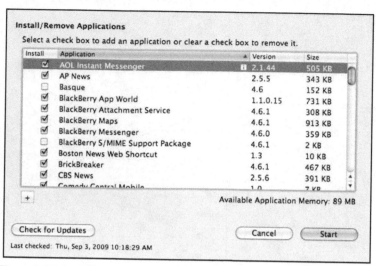

Figure 4-22. *Install or Remove Applications* window in Desktop Manager for Mac.

2. To check for updates, click the **Check for Updates** button in the lower-left hand corner.

3. Place a check mark in any app that isn't already checked and it will be installed on your device. Conversely, uncheck any box and that app will be removed from your BlackBerry.

4. Click the **Start** button and the selected or unselected apps will be either installed or uninstalled depending on your selection.

> **TIP:** For peace of mind, it can be a good idea to perform a backup both before and after you add or delete apps from your Blackberry.

Update Your BlackBerry Device Software

When BlackBerry has issued a new version of device software for your BlackBerry smartphone, you will see an alert window in Desktop Manager when you connect your device to your Mac.   This window will tell you that a new version of device system software is available and ask you if you would like to update your BlackBerry. To update your device, click OK or Update depending on the screen shown.

Setting up the BlackBerry as a Modem for Your Mac

See our **Tethered Modem** chapter starting on page 461 for help with setting up your BlackBerry to connect your Mac to the Internet as a dial-up modem.

Chapter 5

Apple Mac Media and File Transfer

Your BlackBerry can be a great media player. In order to get all your songs, videos, and other media on your BlackBerry, you'll need to learn some of the information in this chapter.

There are two ways to load media and Microsoft Office documents (for use with **Documents to Go**) on your BlackBerry

1. Use BlackBerry Desktop Manager for Mac Software.

2. Use Mass Storage Mode transfer

Syncing Media with Desktop Manager for Mac

Start Desktop Manager for Mac (shown on page 130) and make sure your BlackBerry is connected to your Mac with your USB cable. Click the third tab along the top called

Media (shown in Figure 5-1).

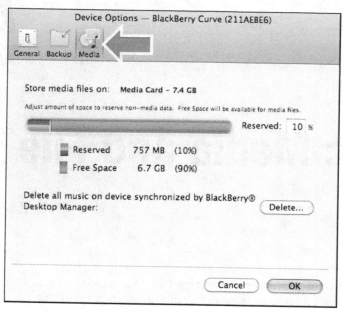

Figure 5-1. *Media Sync* in Desktop Manager for Mac.

By default, Desktop Manager will reserve 10 percent of the space on your media card for non-media data. You can adjust this amount in the box. The smaller the number you input the more space you will have for media files on the media card.

Delete All Music

Click the **Delete** button below the **Delete all music on device...** statement and you can remove any or all music stored on your device.

When asked **Why would you want to do that?** say you have been dragging and dropping music on your BlackBerry (one of the only options for Mac users unless you were using Pocket Mac or the Missing Sync). Let's say you were using a program like the **Missing Sync** (syncing **iTunes** playlists but not bringing in the album art) .You now have the option of syncing **iTunes** playlists complete with album art. You might want start fresh and get rid of other music on your BlackBerry.

Syncing Music

BlackBerry Desktop Manager allows you to sync your **iTunes** playlists to media card of your BlackBerry. Click the **Music** icon under the media line along the left-hand column of the main screen.

You will be taken to the **Music Sync** screen (Figure 5-2). There are efficient options in this screen.

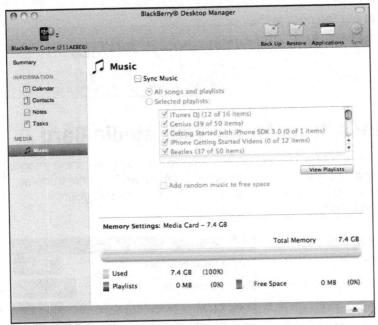

Figure 5-2. *Sync Music screen in Desktop Manager for Mac.*

Like **iTunes,** you can choose to sync **All Songs and Playlists** or **Selected Playlists.**
Use the following instructions:

1. Place a checkmark in the **Sync Music** box at the top of the screen and select
    which playlists you would like to sync between your Mac and your BlackBerry.

2. Place a checkmark in the **Add random music to free space** box and additional
    songs will be randomly placed on the media card.

3. In Figure 5-3, you can see four playlists were selected for the BlackBerry. Check
    marks were placed in the appropriate boxes.

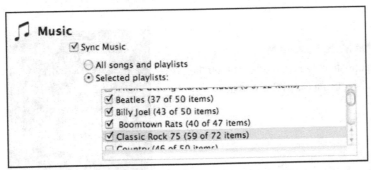

Figure 5-3. *Sync-specific playlists in Desktop Manager for Mac.*

4. Click the **Sync** icon at the top right of the screen to perform the **Music Sync** to your BlackBerry.

Mass Storage Mode Transfer for Your Media Card -

Whether you have a Windows or a Mac computer, this feature works. It will show images for the Mac computer process and will be fairly similar for a Windows PC. This transfer method assumes you have stored your media on a MicroSD media card in your BlackBerry. Use the following steps:

1. Go to your **Options** icon and scroll down to click **Memory.**

2. Make sure your media card **Mass Storage** mode support is **On** and other settings are as shown.

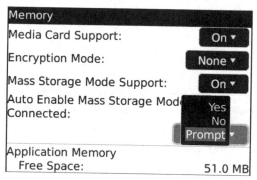

3. Connect your BlackBerry to your computer with the USB cable. If you selected **Prompt** for **Auto Enable Mass Storage Mode** on the previous screen, you will see a question reading **Turn on Mass Storage Mode?**

4. Answer **Yes** (check the box that says "**Don't Ask Me Again**"). When you answer **Yes,** your media card looks like another hard disk to your computer (similar to a USB flash drive).

TIP: If you set the **Auto Enable Mass Storage Mode** setting to **Yes**, you won't be asked this question and the media card on the BlackBerry will automatically look like a **Mass Storage** device (disk drive letter).

5. After your BlackBerry is connected and is in **Mass Storage** mode, open your computer's file management software.

6. Start your Finder. Look for another hard disk or BlackBerry (model number) that has been added.

> **NOTE:** You will see your BlackBerry model number (Curve_8500).

7. When you plug your BlackBerry into your Mac, it will identify the **Main Memory** and the contents of the Micro SD card as two separate drives and place them on your desktop for easy navigation.

8. To copy pictures from your BlackBerry, select the files from the **BlackBerry / pictures** folder.

9. Draw a box around the pictures or click and press **Command + A** (Mac) to select them all (you can also press the **Command** key (Mac or for Windows **CTRL + Click**) and click the individual pictures. Once selected, click **Control + click** (Mac) or Windows (**right click** on one of the selected pictures) and select **Cut** (to move) or **Copy** (see Figure 5-4).

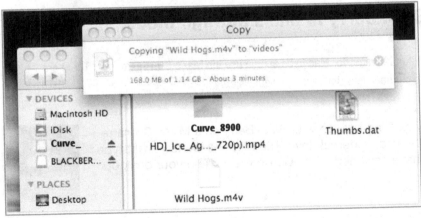

Figure 5-4. *Status of copying files to your BlackBerry.*

10. Click any other disk/folder (like **My Documents)** and navigate to where you want to move / copy the files. Right-click again in the right window where all files are listed and select **Paste.**

11. On your Mac, click the **Finder** icon in the lower left-hand corner of the **Dock.** On Windows, click the disk drive letter (your BlackBerry media card).

12. You will see your **Devices** (including both BlackBerry drives) on the top and your **Places** (where you can copy and paste media) on the bottom.

13. You can also delete the pictures/media/songs from your BlackBerry in a similar manner. Navigate to the BlackBerry/(media type) folder like **BlackBerry/videos.** Press the key combination shown above to select all files. Press the **Delete** key to delete all files.

You can also copy files from your computer to your BlackBerry using a similar method. Go to the files you want to copy, highlight, and right- click to copy and paste them into the correct BlackBerry / (media type) folder.

> **IMPORTANT:** Not all media (videos), pictures (images), or songs will be playable or viewable on your BlackBerry. Use Desktop Manager for Mac to transfer the files. Most files will be automatically converted for you.

Using your BlackBerry in Mass Storage Mode

> **NOTE:** Install Desktop Manager for Mac to be able to use the **Mass Storage** option. There are drivers required to connect your BlackBerry to your Mac.

Once connected, your Mac will see your BlackBerry as a **Mass Storage Device** and mount it as an external drive. The Mac will identify what type of BlackBerry you have assigned the device in the icon on your desktop.

The BlackBerry will also be visible if you click your **Finder** icon in the dock, listed under **Devices.**

Explore the drive

Right click the icon for the BlackBerry and choose **Open** (or double-click on the **Desktop** icon and open the drive (see Figure 5-5).

You can explore your BlackBerry as you would any drive. Copy **Pictures, Music,** or **Video** files by dragging and dropping to the correct folder. You can also delete files from your BlackBerry by clicking the appropriate folder, selecting a file or files, and dragging them to the trash.

NOTE: Your music, video, ringtone, and picture files are in the folder named **BlackBerry**.

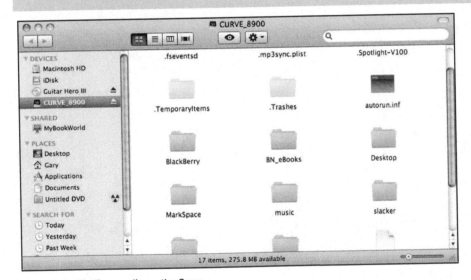

Figure 5-5. *Finding media on the Curve.*

Chapter 6

Typing, Spelling, and Help

In this chapter we help you get typing as fast and accurately as you can on your small BlackBerry keyboard and show you where to get help on your Curve.

TIP: If you have not already done so, please check out our "Quick Start Guide" in the front section of this book (page 1) for a picture of what every key does on your BlackBerry and some good navigation tips and tricks.

The Trackpad

One great navigation feature on your BlackBerry is the front trackpad, which can glide any direction as well as be clicked. While this may take some getting used to for seasoned BlackBerry users (if you were used to the familiar trackball or side trackwheel), you will quickly see that the trackpad gives you lots of freedom to scroll up and down and left to right using your thumb. It is incredibly intuitive to use.

The other thing that is great is that clicking in the trackpad will give you an innovative "short menu" that is context sensitive. Sometimes, it is so sensitive that it almost seems as if it reading your thoughts. Type an e-mail message, and then click the **trackpad**. Notice that **Send** is highlighted, so you can simply click the trackpad again to send your e-mail message.

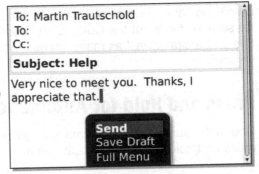

There are also some great features that are user-adjusted with regards to the trackpad.

Trackpad Sound and Sensitivity

Each user has a different preference for how quickly he or she likes to navigate the Home screen and the sensitivity of the trackpad. To adjust the trackpad sensitivity, follow these steps.

1. Click the **Options** icon.

2. Scroll down and click **Screen/Keyboard**.

3. Scroll down and you will see trackpad, and under it three user-adjustable fields.

4. Click the **Horizontal Sensitivity** or **Vertical Sensitivity** field (70 is the default) and change it. Higher is more sensitive, lower is less.

5. Click in the **Audible Roll** field to set **Click** or **Mute**. **Click** will produce an audible click when you move the trackpad, and **Mute** makes trackpad movement silent.

6. Press the **Menu** key and select **Save**.

Screen/Keyboard	
	Messages ▾
Trackpad	
Horizontal Sensitivity:	40 ▾
Vertical Sensitivity:	70 ▾
Audible Roll:	Mute ▾
Menu	
Menu Style:	Short Menu ▾

TIP: You may find that your trackpad moves too quickly up or down lines. If so, then reduce the **Vertical Sensitivity** to 50 or lower.

Typing Tips for Your Curve

Below we have a number of typing tips to help you get more proficient with your Curve. Be sure to check out the Quick Start Guide at the beginning of this book for even more tips and tricks as well as many images to help understand some of the topics covered in this chapter.

Press and Hold for Automatic Capitalization

One of the easiest tips is to capitalize letters as you're typing them. To do this, simply press and hold the letter to capitalize it.

Caps Lock and Num/Alt Lock

If you want to lock the **Caps** key to type ALL UPPERCASE, press the **Alt** key, and then press the right **Shift** key. Tap the either **Shift** key to turn off **Caps** lock.

If you want to type only numbers or the symbols shown on the top of the keys, then you need to turn on **Num/Alt** lock by pressing the **Alt** key, then pressing the left **Shift** key. Tap either **Shift** key to turn off the **Num/Alt** lock.

Automatic Period and Cap at the End of the Sentence

At the end of a sentence, just press the **Space** key twice to see an automatic "." (period) and the next letter you type will be automatically capitalized.

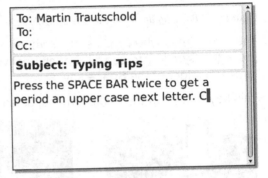

Typing Symbols: Two Types—Alt and Sym Keys

There are two types of symbols you can type on your BlackBerry—those shown on the top of the keys, which you can access by pressing and holding the **Alt** key while pressing the key, and the other set of symbols not shown on the keyboard, which are accessed by pressing the **Sym** (Symbol) key on the keyboard. Both ways allow you to quickly add symbols to your text.

To type any symbol shown on the top of the keys on the keyboard, like the pound sign (#) or the parentheses, you would press and hold the **Alt** key while pressing the other key, e.g., **Alt+Q** gives you a **#**, and so on. See Figure 6-1.

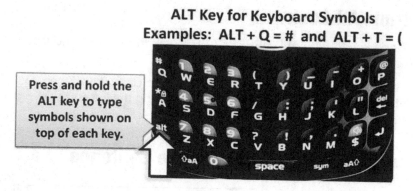

Figure 6-1. *Pressing the Alt key to type symbols shown on the top of each key*

There are times when you need a symbol not shown on the keyboard. Then you need to press the **Sym** key to see a list of alternative symbols available to you. Press the **Sym** key to the right of the **Space** key.

This key brings up the Symbol menu, as shown in Figure 6-2.

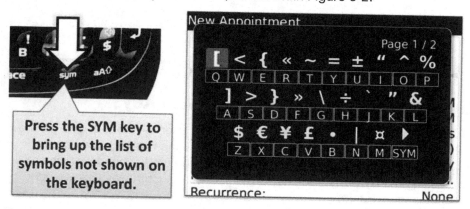

Figure 6-2. *Locating symbols not shown on the keyboard*

Select the symbol by pressing the associated letter or gliding and clicking the trackpad. In the image above, if you press the letter **C** on your keyboard, you would get the symbol for the Japanese Yen currency.

Quickly Typing Accented Letters and Other Symbols

You can easily type standard accented characters such as Á by pressing and holding a letter on the keyboard and gliding the trackpad. (See page 12 of the **Quick Start Guide**.)

Example: Press and hold the letter **A** to scroll through these accented characters related to A: À Á Â Ã Ä Å Æ (both upper and lower case).

- Letters this trick works on are E, R, T, Y, U, I, O, P, A, S, D, K, C, V, B, N, M.

- Some other common characters are **V** key for ¿, **T** key for trademark symbol, **C** key for copyright symbol, **R** key for registered trademark symbol.

Editing Text

Making changes to your text is easy with the BlackBerry. See Figure 6-3.

1. Glide the trackpad left or right to position the cursor.

2. Edit text by pressing the **Del** or **Alt+Del** keys.

   a. Use the **Del** key to erase characters to the left of the cursor.

   b. Hold the **Alt** key and press **Del** to delete characters under the cursor.

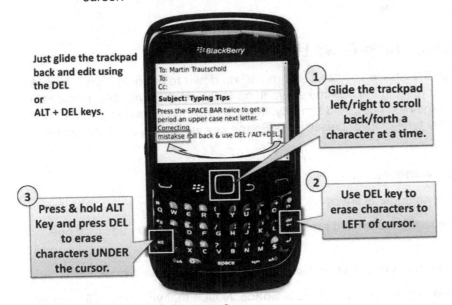

Just glide the trackpad back and edit using the DEL or ALT + DEL keys.

1 Glide the trackpad left/right to scroll back/forth a character at a time.

3 Press & hold ALT Key and press DEL to erase characters UNDER the cursor.

2 Use DEL key to erase characters to LEFT of cursor.

Figure 6-3. *Editing text on your BlackBerry Curve*

The Mighty Space Key

Like many of the keys on the BlackBerry, the **Space** key can do some very handy things for you while you are typing.

Using the Space Key While Typing an E-mail Address

On most handhelds, when you want to put in the "@" or the "." in your e-mail message, you need a complicated series of commands—usually a **Shift** or **Alt**.

On the BlackBerry, you don't need to take those extra steps. While you are typing the e-mail address, after the user name (e.g., martin) just press the **Space** key once and the BlackBerry will automatically insert the "@" "martin@".

Type the domain name, press the **Space** key again, and—presto—the BlackBerry automatically puts in the "." in "martin@madesimplelearning." No additional keystrokes are necessary. Just finish the e-mail address with the "com" in "martin@madesimplelearning.com".

Quickly Changing Drop-Down Lists

Another thing that the **Space** key does is to move you down to the next item in a list. In the **Minutes** field, pressing the **Space** key will jump to the next 15 minutes. In the **Hour** field, you jump to the next hour. And similarly, in the **Month** field, you jump to the next month. In any other type of field, pressing the **Space** key will jump you to the next entry.

Give it a try.

1. Click your **Calendar** icon.

2. Open a new calendar event by clicking the trackpad anywhere in the Day view.

3. Glide down to the month and press the **Space** key—notice you advance one month.

4. Glide over to the hour and press **Space**—notice you advance 1 hour.

5. Finally, glide to the minutes and press **Space**. Notice that you move 15 minutes forward.

6. These are all great tricks to quickly re-schedule calendar events.

Using Letter Keys to Select Items in Lists and Menus

You can even use the letter keys on your keyboard to instantly jump down to the first item matching either letter on the key (if there are two letters), or jump down to a matching menu item, or jump down to a matching item in a list (like the long list in the **Options** icon).

Using Number Keys to Type Dates and Times

You can even use the number keys on your keyboard to instantly type a new date or time, or select an entry in a drop-down list with that number.

Examples include the following:

- Typing **40** in the **Minutes** field to set the minutes to 40

- Typing **9** in the **Hour** field to get to 9 AM or PM

This also works in the fields where drop-down list items start with numbers, like in the **Reminder** field in the calendar or tasks. Typing a number **9** would immediately jump you to the 9 Hours setting.

Using Your Spelling Checker

Your BlackBerry comes with a built-in spelling checker. Normally, your spelling checker is turned on to check everything you type. The little dotted underlining while you type things on your BlackBerry goes away when the spelling checker matches your words with those in the dictionary. Normally, you will need to turn it on to have it check your outgoing e-mail messages.

When your spelling mistakes are not auto-corrected with the AutoText feature (see page 22), the other way to quickly correct many typing errors is to use the built-in spelling checker on your BlackBerry. When your BlackBerry finds what it thinks is a misspelled word, it will underline it, as shown in Figure 6-4.

Figure 6-4. *Words that the spelling checker thinks are misspelled are underlined.*

To correct one of these words, just glide the cursor back into the word with the trackpad and click. You will see a list of suggested changes, just glide to and click the correct word. If the word is spelled correctly and you want to add the word to your custom word list (custom dictionary), press the **Menu** key and select **Add to Dictionary**. We show you more on the custom dictionary in Figure 6-5.

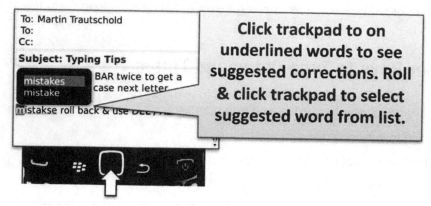

Figure 6-5. *Working with your spelling checker*

Custom Spelling Dictionary

You will quickly find out that you need to add or delete words in your custom dictionary (e.g., a name or other unique word that is spelled correctly but not in the default standard dictionary).

Adding Words to the Spelling Custom Dictionary

Sometimes, you might use unique words (e.g., local place names) in your e-mail messages that are not found in the standard dictionary. One of the options offered to you is to add the word to your own unique custom dictionary. The advantages of this are (1) that you will never again be asked to replace that word with something suggested and (2) if you misspell this custom word, you will be given the correct spelling.

To add a new word, follow these steps, as shown in Figure 6-6.

1. During the spell checking process, the spell check program will notice a word that it believes is misspelled.

2. In this example, we are using Flagler, a county in Florida, which is not in the standard dictionary.

3. You will see that the spelling checker suggests options for replacing the word, none of which are correct.

4. Press the **Menu** key.

5. Click **Add to Dictionary** to add the word to your own custom dictionary.

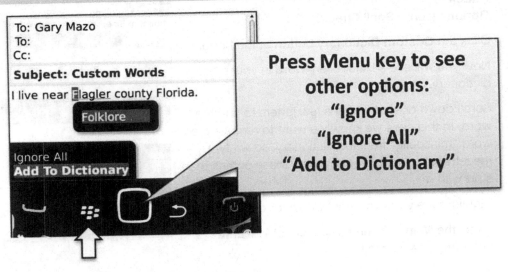

Figure 6-6. *Adding new words to your custom dictionary*

Next time we spell Flagler, it will not be shown as misspelled. What's even better is that next time we misspell Flagler (e.g., Flaglr), the spelling checker will find it and give us the correct spelling.

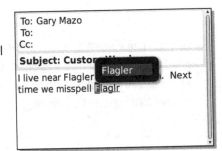

Edit or Delete Words from the Spelling Custom Dictionary

Mistakes will happen, and it's fairly easy to click the wrong menu item and inadvertently add wrong words to the custom dictionary. The authors have done this plenty of times!

1. Get into the Spell Check options screen in either of these two ways:
   Messages icon **->** **Menu** key **->** **Options** **->** **Spell Check** or
   Options icon **->Spell Check**.

2. Click the **Custom Dictionary** button at the bottom.

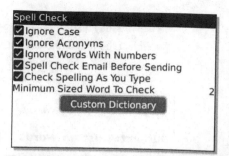

3. Now you will see a list of every word in your custom dictionary.

4. Scroll down or start typing a few letters to find the word. In this case we know we want to remove the word "misspellg" from the dictionary, so we type the letter **m** to instantly show only those entries that start with m.

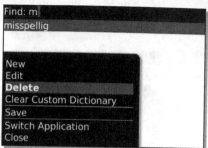

5. Highlight the word you want to edit or delete.

6. Press the **Menu** key and select **Delete** or **Edit**. Enter any changes to the word.

7. Press the **Menu** key or **Escape** key and save your changes.

> **TIP:** You Can Force A Spell Check Before Sending E-mail Messages. By default, most BlackBerry smartphones will not do a spell check before sending e-mail messages. You can actually ignore all misspelled (underlined) words and send. Below we show you how to force the spelling checker to be enabled for outgoing e-mail messages.

Enable Spell Check for Outbound E-mail Messages

One of the great features of your new BlackBerry is that you can automatically check the spelling of your e-mail messages before you send them out. Many times, this feature must be enabled; it is not turned on when you take your BlackBerry out of the box. Like your spelling checker on your computer, you can even create additions to the dictionary for frequently used words. Spell check will save you embarrassing misspellings in your communication, which is especially important with such a small keyboard.

1. Click your **Messages** (E-mail) icon.

2. Press the **Menu** key and select
   Options.

   TIP: You can also start with the **Options** icon
   and select **Spell Check**.

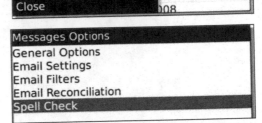

3. Click **Spell Check**.

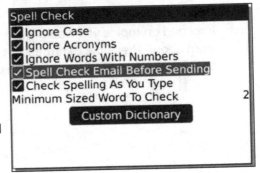

4. Make sure to select the **Spell Check E-
   mail Before Sending** check box to
   enable spell checking on outbound e-
   mail messages. Click it with the
   trackpad or press the **Space** key to
   check it.

5. Press the **Menu** key or **Escape** key and
   save your changes.

Using BlackBerry Text-Based Help

There might be times when you don't have this book or our video tutorials handy, and
you need to find out how to do something right away on your BlackBerry.

You can get into the Help menu from the **Help** icon, and almost every
application on the BlackBerry has a built-in contextual help menu that can
answer some of your basic questions.

Using the Help Menus Inside Icons

The Help menu can be accessed from virtually any application. For our purposes, we will
take a look at the Help menu built into the **Calendar** icon.

1. Click your **Calendar** icon, or press the Home screen hot key **L** (see page 548 for
   help with Home screen hotkeys).

2. In most applications on your BlackBerry, Help is the top or almost-top menu item. Press the **Menu** key, scroll up to and click **Help**.

3. To select any of these options, just glide the trackpad to highlight the item (such as **Calendar basics,** as shown) and click the trackpad.

Calendar

- Calendar basics
- Meetings
- Conference call meetings
- Calendar options
- Multiple calendars
- Calendar shortcuts
- Calendar troubleshooting

Related information
Personal organizer

Contents

4. Continue to glide and click the trackpad on topics you would like to learn about. Press the **Escape** key to back up one level in the Help menus.

Calendar basics

- About calendar views
- Switch calendar views
- Move around a calendar
- Schedule an appointment
- Schedule an appointment quickly in Day view
- Schedule a meeting
- Recurrence fields
- Schedule an alarm
- Check spelling
- Open an appointment, meeting, or alarm
- Delete an appointment, meeting, or alarm
- Switch days in Day view

5. Finally, you will see a screen like this one showing you the actual steps to follow to complete the task.

Move around a calendar

1. On the Home screen, click the **Calendar** icon.
2. Press the **Menu** key.
3. Perform one of the following actions:
   - To move to a specific date, click **Go To Date**.
   - To move to the current date, click **Today**.
   - To move forward or back by a time period, click **Prev** or **Next**.

Related information
Calendar basics

Contents

6. At the bottom in the gray bar, usually you will see related Help topics. To jump to these topics, simply scroll down with the trackpad and click them.

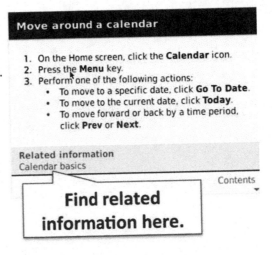

Find related information here.

Overall Help Contents and Finding Text

To jump back to a list of all the main Help topics, click **Contents** in the lower right corner.

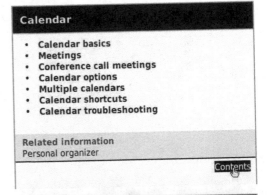

If you want to find text on the currently displayed Help page, then press the **Menu** key and select **Find**. You can also get to this **Find** menu item if you glide the cursor to the top of the screen and click the trackpad. Not sure how useful this is, because ideally the Find feature should search the entire Help database, not just the current screen.

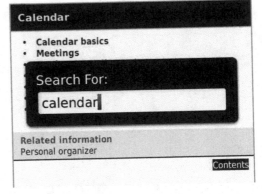

Chapter 7

Save Time with AutoText

In this chapter we show you some great tips and tricks to save time and increase accuracy for things that you may have to type many times. You can also come up with new AutoText for things like directions, or unique things like creating a date and time stamp with a two-letter shortcut. This is great if you are taking notes and don't want to bother typing out the current date and time—two letters of AutoText does the trick!

Saving Time with Auto-Correcting AutoText

Sometimes, typing on the little BlackBerry keyboard produces less than desirable results. Fortunately, for the more common misspellings, you can create an AutoText entry to solve this problem. The pre-loaded AutoText is used to correct common typing mistakes, like leaving out an apostrophe in the word "aren't" or misspelling "the" (Figure 7-1).

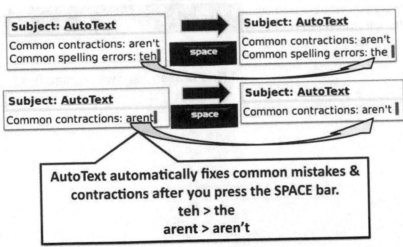

Figure 7-1. *AutoText fixes common spelling mistakes and contractions to save you time.*

> **TIP:** Knowing AutoText is there helping you get things right will allow you to type with greater abandon on your BlackBerry. Take a few minutes to browse the AutoText pre-loaded entries, especially the the contractions, so you can learn to type them without ever using the apostrophe.

You can also use AutoText for more advanced things like automatically typing an e-mail signature (Page 22), driving directions, a "canned" e-mail message, routine text describing your products or services, legal disclaimer text, or anything!

Creating a New Custom AutoText Entry

You can get into the AutoText list from the **Edit AutoText** menu item when you are typing an e-mail message (by pressing the **Menu** key) or from the main **Options** icon. To create a new entry, follow these steps.

1. Click your **Options** icon.

2. Click **AutoText** to see the list of entries.

> **TIP:** Learn the contractions to save you time as you type future e-mail messages. (Skip typing the apostrophe.)

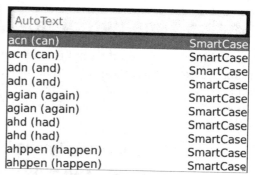

3. Type the new entry you want to add (in this case **dirh** for **Directions to home**) and make sure you see no entries that exactly match.

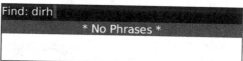

* No Phrases * shows no matches.

4. Just hit the **Enter** key to start adding your new entry.

5. Glide down under the **With** field and type the text you want to appear when you type your new AutoText word "dirh."

```
AutoText: New
Replace:
dirh
With:
1. Take I-95 to exit 268
2. Exit onSR-40 West
3. Follow 3 miles, turn right on Creek Rd.
4. Follow 2.3 Miles, turn left onForest
5. We are the 3rd house on right, #235
Using:                    SmartCase ▼
Language:                 All Locales ▼
```

6. Press the **Menu** key and select **Save**.

TIP: Type these directions on your computer and e-mail them to yourself, then copy/paste them into AutoText from the e-mail message.

Using New AutoText Entries

Now when someone wants directions, all you have to do is type your new AutoText entry, dirh.

```
To: susan@company.com
To:
Cc:
Subject: Directions to house
Here's how to get to my house:
Dirh
```

After pressing the **Space** key, the full directions appear from your new AutoText entry.

```
To: susan@company.com
To:
Cc:
Subject: Directions to house
Here's how to get to my house:
1. Take I-95 to exit 268
2. Exit on SR-40 West
3. Follow 3 miles, turn right on Creek Rd.
4. Follow 2.3 miles, turn left on Forest.
5. We are the 3rd house on right, #235
```

Advanced AutoText Features: Macros—Time Stamp

With AutoText, you can actually insert macros or shortcuts for other functions, such as displaying the current time and date, your PIN number, or owner information, or even simulating pressing the **Backspace** or **Delete** keys.

Creating a New Entry with Macros

Let's create the new entry called "ts" ("Time Stamp") that will instantly show the current time and date.

1. Start creating a new entry as you did previously, and use the letters **ts** for **time stamp**.

2. Press the **Menu** key and select **Insert Macro**.

   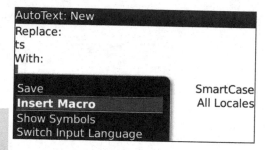

   TIP: All macros start with the percent sign (%), and you could simply type them instead of selecting them from the menu.

3. Scroll up or down and select the macro you want.

4. In this case, we want **Short Date (%d)**, which is mm/dd/yy format.

   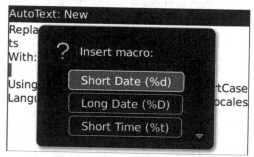

5. Type a space, "-", and then a space again.

6. Now press the **Menu** key and select **Short Time (%t)**.

More with AutoText Macros

Now whenever you want to put the current date and time, just type your new entry, **ts**, and press **Space**.

> **Title: Meeting ts**

Press the **Space** key to see the date/time.

> **Title: Meeting 1/31/2009 - 9:25a**

Here is a list of the standard AutoText macros. Here's what they look like:

%d	Short date
%D	Long date
%t	Short time
%T	Long time
%o	Owner name
%O	Owner information
%p	Your phone number
%P	Your PIN number
%b	Backspace
%B	Delete
%%	Percent

> **Title: Macros List**
>
> Short Date: 9/22/2008
> Long Date: Mon, Sep 22, 2008
> Short Time: 8:12p
> Long Time: 8:12:29 PM
> Owner Name: Martin Trautschold
> Owner Info: If found, please contact
> Martin Trautschold office: 1-386-506-8224.
> 123 Main Street
> Anytown, STATE 38928

TIP: Instead of pressing the **Menu** key and selecting the macro, just type the letters, like "**%t**" for short time.

Edit or Delete an AutoText Entry

Sometimes you may need to edit or remove an AutoText entry. The steps to get this done are very similar to creating a new one.

Return to the AutoText list by selecting **Edit AutoText** while typing an e-mail message or from the **Options** icon. Type a few letters to find the AutoText entry. Press the **Menu** key and select **Edit** or **Delete**.

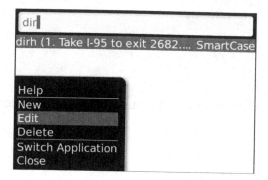

Chapter 8

Personalize Your BlackBerry

In this chapter you will learn some great ways to personalize your BlackBerry like moving and hiding icons, organizing with folders, setting your Convenience keys, changing your theme or "look and feel," and adjusting font sizes and types.

TIP: Change Your Home Screen Image (Wallpaper). If you go into the **Media** icon, you can select from a number of pre-loaded background images, or you can even snap a picture and immediately set it as your background image. (See exactly how to get this done on page 184.)

Moving Icons, Hiding, and Deleting Icons

You may not need to see every single icon on your Home screen, or you may have your most popular icons and want to move them up to easy access on the top row. We show you how to work with icons when you are in one of the standard themes on your BlackBerry (see page 178); however, the steps may vary a little depending on which theme is active on your BlackBerry.

Moving Your Icons Within a Folder

Press the **Menu** key to see an array of all your icons. If the icon you want to move is inside a particular folder, like **Downloads** or **Applications**, glide to and click that folder.

Glide over it to highlight the icon you want to move using the trackpad. In this case, we are going to move the **Maps** icon, because it is highlighted.

Press the **Menu** key (to the left of the trackpad) to bring up the **Move** menu item as shown.

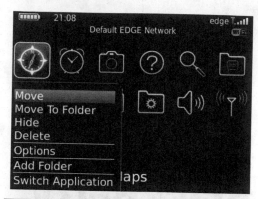

Once you select **Move,** then you see arrows pointing around the icon (as shown). Start moving it wherever you want by rolling the trackpad.

Finally, click the trackpad to set the moved icon at the new location.

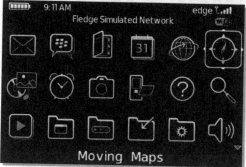

How Do You Know When You're in a Folder?

When you are in a folder you see a little icon at the top of your screen with a folder tab image and the name of the folder. In the image here, you see that you are in the **Applications** folder.

Moving Your Icons Between Folders

Sometimes you want to move icons to your **Home** folder to make them more easily accessible. Or, you might want to move some of the icons you seldom use from your **Home** folder into another folder to clean up your Home screen.

Let's say we wanted to move our **Docs to Go** icon 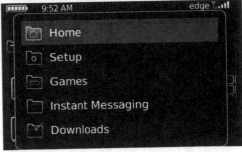 from the **Applications** folder to our **Home** folder, so it's more easily accessible.

Highlight the **Docs to Go** icon as shown. Then, press the **Menu** key to bring up the left of the trackpad to select **Move to Folder**.

Now, we want to move this out of our **Applications** folder into the **Home** folder, so we click **Home** at the top of the list.

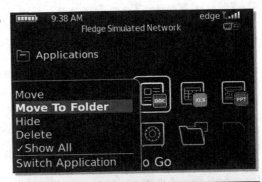

Now we press the **Escape** key to exit the **Applications** folder back to the **Home** folder to locate our newly moved **Docs to Go** icon. In this case, it is near the bottom of the list of icons.

Hidingand Un-hiding Icons

Sometimes you may want to hide an unused icon to make your BlackBerry easier to use. Hiding and un-hiding icons is easy—you follow the similar steps that you did to move icons.

First, if you see only six icons, you have to press the **Menu** key to the left of the trackpad to see all your icons on the Home screen. If the icon you want to hide is inside a folder, then go ahead and click the folder so you can see the icon. Now, highlight the icon you want to hide and press the **Menu** key. Select **Hide** as shown.

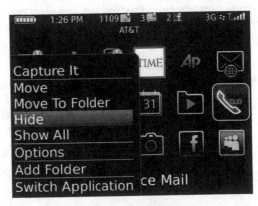

To unhide an icon, press the **Menu** key, select **Show All**, highlight the grayed-out (hidden) icon, press the **Menu** key, and click **Hide** to turn off the check mark.

Setting Your Top Icons

Depending on what theme you have selected on your BlackBerry, you may have noticed that only a few icons show up on your main Home screen. These happen to be the top icons in the list of icons after you press the **Menu** key. So, it's simple to get icons on the limited list—just move them up to the top. Let's say we want to move our **Word to Go** icon into one of the top spots.

Highlight the icon we want to move, press the **Menu** key, select **Move**, and glide it up into one of the top six spots. Click the trackpad to set it into place.

Now we see **Word to Go** on our limited set of icons on the Home screen.

Using Folders to Organize Your Icons

On your BlackBerry you can create or delete folders to better organize your icons. There may already be a few folders created by default. Typically, you will see **Applications**, **Settings**, **Downloads**, and **Games** folders. You can add your own folders and then move icons into your new folders to better organize them.

Creating a New Folder

NOTE: At the time of publication, you could create folders only one level deep. In other words, you can create new folders only when you are in the **Home** folder, not when you are already inside another folder. This may change with new software versions.

To create a new folder, first press the **Menu** key to see all your icons. Then press the **Menu** key again and select **Add Folder**.

> **NOTE:** If you don't see the **Add Folder** menu item, then press the **Escape** key to get back to your **Home** folder.

After you select the **Add Folder** menu item, then you will see this screen.

Type your folder name. You can click the on the **Folder** icon and glide left/right to check out all the different folder colors/styles possible.

Once you're done selecting the **Folder** icon style, then click it and glide down to click the **Add** button to finish creating your folder. Then you will see your new folder.

Moving Icons Between Folders

Once you create your new folder, you will want to move icons into it to organize them, so that your Home screen is not too crowded. Please see our instructions on page 170 on how to do this.

Editing a Folder

You can edit a folder by highlighting it, pressing the **Menu** key, and selecting **Edit Folder**. Then you can change the name and folder icon and save your changes.

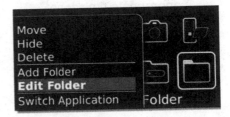

Then you can change the name and the folder icon color, and save your changes.

Deleting a Folder

Whenever you want to get rid of a folder, just highlight it, press the **Menu** key, and select **Delete** as shown.

Setting the Date, Time, and Time Zone

There might be times when you want to adjust your date, time, and time zone. While you can set the time and time zone in the setup wizard, you can also adjust it directly from your **Options** icon. To do so, follow these steps.

1. Click to open your **Options** icon or press the letter **O** from your Home screen to start **Options**. (See "Home Screen Hotkeys" in Part 4.)

2. Press the letter **D** to jump down to **Date/Time**, or scroll down and click it.

3. Click the trackpad to see all the time zones, and glide up / down to select the appropriate time zone.

4. Scroll down to set the **Auto Update Time Zone** field. You can select the default **Prompt** (which asks you if you want to change the time zone whenever it detects you are in a new time zone), **Off** (which never adjusts), or **On** (which will adjust the time zone without asking you). We recommend leaving it as **Prompt**.

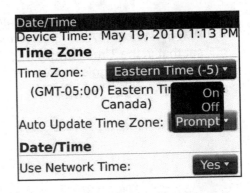

5. Roll down to the **Use Network Time** field and select **Yes** or **No**. The default is **Yes**, which uses the Network Time shown at the bottom of the screen. We recommend leaving this set to **Yes** unless you want to manually override the time. To manually set the time, select **No**.

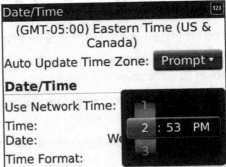

6. If you selected **No** in the **Use Network Time** field, then you can manually adjust the **Time** and **Date** fields by clicking and rolling up or down.

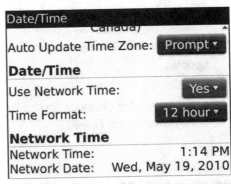

> **TIP:** You can also use the number keys to change the years, date, hours, or minutes. For example, simply type **26** in the **Minutes** field to jump right to 26. Another trick is the **Space** key—tap it to advance one number.

7. If you prefer the 12 hour (7:30 AM/ 4:30 PM) or 24 hour (07:30/16:30) format, you set that in the **Time Format** field. Tap the **Space** key to toggle between the two options.

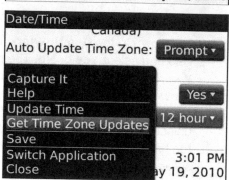

TIP: You can force the time zones and the network time to update if you press the **Menu** key and select **Update Time** or **Get Time Zone Updates**.

8. To save your changes, press the **Menu** key and select **Save**.

Changing Your Font Size and Type

You can fine-tune the font size and type on your BlackBerry to fit your individual needs.

Do you need to see more on the screen and don't mind small fonts? Then go all the way down to a micro-size 7-point font.

Do you need to see bigger fonts for easy readability? Adjust the fonts to a large 14-point font and make it BlackBerry type.

Here's how to adjust your font size and type:

Click the **Options** icon. You may need to press the **Menu** key and glide up or down to find it.

Inside the **Options** icon, click **Screen/Keyboard** to get to the screen where you can change your fonts among other things (Figure 8-1).

Figure 8-1. *Changing your font size*

Click the trackpad to select a different font family, size, style, or type as shown. You can even see a preview of your currently selected style and size to make sure it will fit your needs.

Changing Your Currency Key (Dollar, Pound, Euro, or Yen sign)

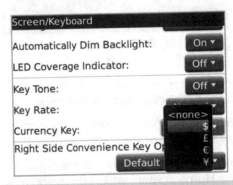

You will notice that the key next to your **Enter** key in the lower right corner of your keyboard has a currency symbol on it. It may be a dollar, pound, Euro, or Yen sign. You can change the currency character that this key types in the **Options -> Screen and Keyboard** section.

TIP: This key also doubles as your **Speakerphone** hotkey to turn on or off your speakerphone.

Home Screen Preferences and Options (Download Folder, Layout, Wallpaper, Theme, Reset Icons)

On your BlackBerry, you can customize many things about your Home screen by pressing the **Menu** key from the Home screen and selecting **Options** (Figure 8-2).

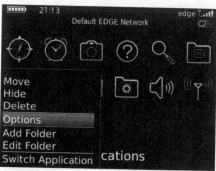

Then you will see the Home screen Preferences screen. Glide the trackpad down to see all the settings options.

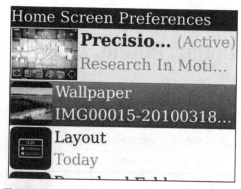

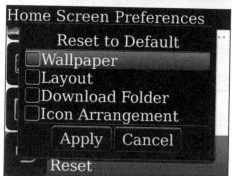

Figure 8-2. *Setting Home screen preferences*

Wallpaper: You can select any picture on your BlackBerry to set as your desktop background, or even click a picture with the camera.

Layout: The Zen layout is the default where there are just a few icons on the bottom of the Home screen, which gives you a nice view of the background wallpaper. The Today layout gives you a preview of recent messages (E-mail), phone calls, and upcoming calendar events. See Figure 8-3 for both of these.

Download Folder: Use **Downloads** as the default or change to any folder or even the **Home** folder. This can be convenient if you download a lot of apps and you want easy access to the icons from your Home screen.

Figure 8-3. *Zen layout and Today layout of the homescreen*

Theme Defaults: This will allow you to change the entire look and feel of your BlackBerry by changing the theme. Read the section on themes to learn more.

Reset to Default: Highlight **Theme Defaults** and press the trackpad and then place a checkmark in those items you with to Reset to Default.

Selecting New Themes: The Look and Feel of Your BlackBerry

You can customize your BlackBerry and make it look truly unique. One way to do this is to change the theme or look and feel of your BlackBerry. Changing themes usually changes the layout and appearance of your icons, and the font type and size you see inside each icon. There are several different themes already included on your BlackBerry, and literally dozens more available for download at various web sites or App World (learn how on page 181.)

Carrier-Specific Themes: Depending on your BlackBerry wireless carrier (phone company) you may see various customized themes that are not shown in this book.

More Standard/Generic BlackBerry Themes: Most of the standard themes shown here are pre-installed on every BlackBerry.

Glide and click the **Option** icon on your BlackBerry. You may have to press the **Menu** key to see all your icons, and then locate the **Options** icon. Or if you have Home screen hotkeys enabled, just tap the letter **O** (see page 548).

9. Once in **Options**, scroll down to **Theme** and click.

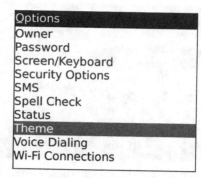

TIP: Press the letter **T** to jump right down to the first entry starting with T. which should be Theme.

10. Inside the Theme screen, just glide and click the theme you want to make active. Your currently selected theme is shown with the word Active next to it.

11. Press the **Escape** key to get back to the Home screen to check out your new theme.

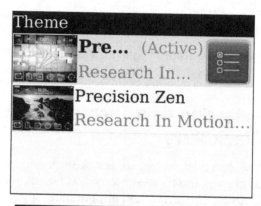

Precision Silver Theme

This theme is like the Zen theme, with a limited set of five icons on the main Home screen; however, all icons are gray/monotone. Unless your BlackBerry provider has specifically removed these themes, they should be available on your BlackBerry.

Precision Zen Theme: Icons

This them has full-color icons with a limited set of five shown on the main Home screen. They look very similar—it is fairly hard to tell the difference between these two themes. The Zen theme has some slight color to the icons.

Your screen should look similar to one of the screens shown here, with possible slight deviations.

Downloading New Themes from BlackBerry App World

Figure 8-4 shows some examples of dozens of new themes that you can download from App World on your BlackBerry.

Figure 8-4. *Customizing the Home screen with new themes*

The one on the left is Sky2 PrimeTheme, from DreamTheme, and the one on the right is Animated Winter Wonderland, from Motek Americas Inc., which is animated so the snowflakes actually fall on the Home screen. Some of the themes are animated so that there is some movement (e.g., the wind blows the leaves of a palm tree and there are waves moving in the ocean). Themes range from free to about US $9.99, with many in the $4.99 to $6.99 range.

> **NOTE:** If you need help getting started with BlackBerry App World, check out our chapter starting on page 441.

1. Start the **App World** icon by clicking it.

2. Click the **Categories** icon in the lower left corner (looks like a bunch of folders).

3. Notice that when this shot was taken, the Sky2 theme was one of the featured items.

4. 4. Roll down and click **Themes**.

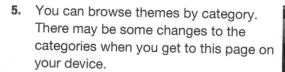

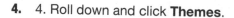

5. You can browse themes by category. There may be some changes to the categories when you get to this page on your device.

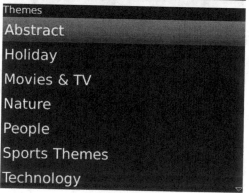

6. 6. Within each category, you can find a theme by typing a few letters of its name.

7. Click the theme you want to check out.

8. Each theme will have a description, rating (1–5 stars), reviews, and screen shots.

9. For themes, we recommend checking out the screen shots before you purchase.

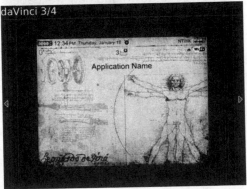

10. Just roll the trackpad back and forth to see the various screen shots. Press the **Escape** key to return to the main page for the theme to buy or download it.

For most themes, after you download and install them using App World, they will ask if you want to activate the theme. If you want to start using the theme right away, then you should select **Yes**. If you want to change themes, see page 179.

CAUTION: The authors have downloaded many themes on their BlackBerry smartphones. Some themes can cause problems with your BlackBerry.

TIP: Besides App World, you can also download themes from some of these vendors and BlackBerry community sites such as the following:

bPlay: `http://www.bplay.com`

CrackBerry.com: `www.crackberry.com`

BlackBerry Forums: `www.blackberryforums.com`

BerryReview: `www.berryreview.com`

BlackBerry Cool: `www.blackberrycool.com`

Also, try a web search for "BlackBerry themes, wallpaper, or ring tones." There are probably new sites all the time!

Changing the Home Screen Background Image or Wallpaper

Now that you have the font size, type, and theme that you like, you may also want to change the background image or picture on your Home screen, also called the Home screen image or wallpaper. You already saw how to download new themes—use the same steps to download new wallpapers.

In addition, since you have a built-in camera, you can simply snap a picture and immediately use it as wallpaper. Finally, you may use any image that is stored on your BlackBerry—either in the BlackBerry's main memory or on the memory card as wallpaper. Grab a picture of your favorite person, a beautiful sunset, or any landscape for your own personalized BlackBerry background wallpaper.

Changing Your Wallpaper or Home Screen Image Using a Stored Picture

1. Click the **Media** folder.

2. Highlight the **Pictures** icon and click it.

> **TIP:** You can also change the wallpaper by pressing the **Menu** key from the Home screen and selecting **Options**, as shown on page 178.

3. Once in **Pictures**, use the trackpad to navigate to the location of the picture you wish to use—either in **All Pictures**, **Picture Folders**, or **Sample Pictures**. You may also see an option to select the **Camera** at the top, to take a new picture.

4. Highlight the thumbnail of the picture you wish to set as your wallpaper, and then press the **Menu** key to select **Set As Wallpaper**.

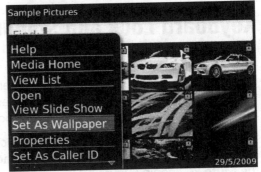

5. Then press the **Escape** key a few times to check out your new wallpaper on your Home screen.

Using a Picture or Image Directly from Your Camera

Take the picture. (Learn all the details about the camera on page 22.)

Click the **Crop** icon as shown and select **Set as Home Screen Image**.

Keyboard Lock and Standby Mode (Avoid Butt Dialing!)

Have you ever needed to put your BlackBerry into your pocket, purse, or bag and don't want keys to be accidentally pressed? If yes, then you can use either the **Keyboard Lock** key or the **Mute** key to lock the keyboard.

Standby Mode (On/Off): Just press and hold the **Mute/Play** key on the top of your BlackBerry until you see the **Entering Standby** message. To exit standby mode, just tap the **Mute** key again (Figure 8-5).

Mute/Play key

Lock or Unlock the Keyboard: Just tap once the **Keyboard Lock** key on the BlackBerry. Tap the same key again to unlock the keyboard.

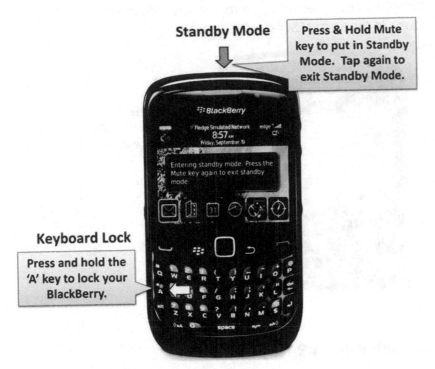

Standby Mode

Press & Hold Mute key to put in Standby Mode. Tap again to exit Standby Mode.

Keyboard Lock

Press and hold the 'A' key to lock your BlackBerry.

Figure 8-5. *Putting BlackBerry into standby mode*

What If You Receive a Phone Call When in Standby Mode?

Don't worry, your BlackBerry will still ring or vibrate to notify you of an incoming phone call when it is in standby mode.

What's the difference between the two options? You will notice a difference if you have your password security enabled (page 528). Pressing the **Lock** key will force you to enter your password to unlock it. Pressing the **Mute** key (standby mode) will not force you to enter your password (unless the security timeout has elapsed). The other difference, according to some blogs, is that standby mode is supposed to save your battery more than the keyboard lock mode.

Changing Your Convenience Keys

The two keys on the middle of the sides of your BlackBerry are actually programmable keys called Convenience keys (Figure 8-6). This is because each of the two keys can be set to conveniently open any icon on your BlackBerry, even new third-party icons that you add to your BlackBerry.

Convenience Keys: Start Icons

(Can be changed to open any icon, even newly installed icons in Options > Screen/Keyboard)

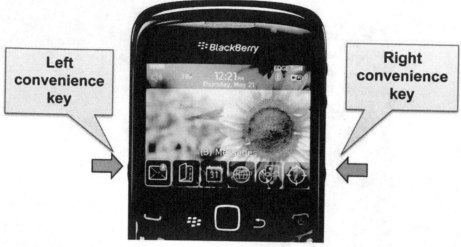

Figure 8-6. *Convenience keys*

Changing Your Convenience Keys

1. Click the **Options** icon (press the **Menu** key if you don't see it listed).

2. Press the letter **S** a few times to jump down to the **Screen/Keyboard** item and click it.

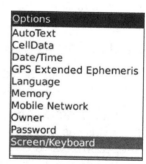

3. Scroll down the screen until you see the fields for **Right Side Convenience Key Opens** and **Left Side Convenience Key Opens**.

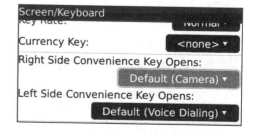

4. To change the icon or application these keys open, just click the item to see the entire list. Then glide and click the icon you want.

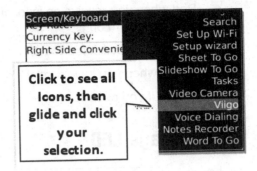

Click to see all Icons, then glide and click your selection.

5. Then press the **Menu** key and select **Save**.

6. Now, give your newly set Convenience keys a try.

> **TIP:** The Convenience keys **work from anywhere**, not just the Home screen. Also, you can set your Convenience keys to open any app, even newly installed ones!
>
> After you install new apps, you will notice that they show up in the list of available icons to select in the Screen/Keyboard options screen. So if your newly installed stock quote, news reader, or game is important, just set it as a Convenience key.

Understanding that Blinking LED (Repeat Notification)

One of the features that BlackBerry users love is the little LED that blinks in the upper right-hand corner.

You can customize this notification light in several way, which we will show you in this chapter.

The light not only tells you when you have a message, it can also tell you when you are connected via Bluetooth, in signal coverage or when you need to charge your battery. It is possible to have this light blink different colors:

- Red when you receive an incoming message (MMS, SMS or e-mail) or calendar alarm rings
- Blue when connected to a Bluetooth device
- Green when you have wireless coverage
- Amber if you need to charge your BlackBerry or it is charging

Red Message LED

1. Start your **Sounds** icon.(See page 22 for detailed help on profiles.)

2. Select **Set Ringtones/Alerts** at the bottom of the list of profiles.

3. Click **Messages** and then **E-mail** to see the screen shown. Notice that one of the fields is **LED**, and that when clicked, you can choose to disable the LED by selecting **No**.

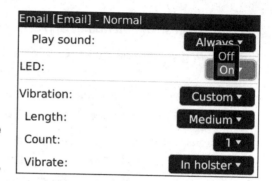

Blue Bluetooth LED

1. From your Home screen, click the **Options** icon, scroll to **Bluetooth**, and click.

2. Press the **Menu** key and select **Options**.

3. Go down to **LED Connection Indicator** and set it to **On** or **Off**.

4. Press the **Menu** key and save your settings.

Green Coverage LED

Go into your **Options** icon and scroll to **Screen/Keyboard** (or press the letter **S** to jump there) and click. Scroll down to the **LED Coverage Indicator** field and select either **On** or **Off**.

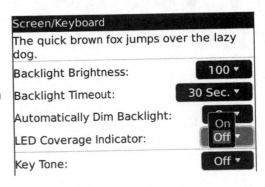

Hearing a Different Tone When Someone Special Calls

You may decide that you want to customize a particular profile to meet your specific needs. You can make adjustments in any number of custom fields for a particular type of notification, or you can create a totally new custom profile on your BlackBerry. See page 200 if your Curve is running OS 4.6 or page 207 if your Curve is on OS 5.0 or higher.

Chapter 9

Sounds: Ring and Vibrate

Your BlackBerry can be customized in many ways. One area that lends itself to customization on the BlackBerry is the area of sound and ring tones. In this chapter we will explain the various profiles that can be adjusted.

You will learn how to make your BlackBerry ring, vibrate, ring and vibrate, or make no sound at all.

You will find that you can customize your BlackBerry for individual situations and even individual contacts by setting unique ring tones and vibrations, so you can immediately tell who is calling, texting, or even e-mailing you.

Set Phone Ring Tones from the Music App

The BlackBerry gives you a couple options for using media files as ring tones. You can choose to use songs or pre-loaded files when your phone rings.

Setting a Song as Your Ring Tone

You can set a song as a ring tone with only a couple of steps:

1. Navigate to and play the song you want to use as a ring tone, as described previously.

2. Press the **Menu** key and select **Set as Ring Tone**.

Now, the next time you receive a call, the specified song will be played.

Using a Pre-Loaded Ring Tone

If you want to use a pre-loaded ring tone instead of a song, then follow these steps:

1. Select Ring Tones.

2. Select All Ring Tones, My Ring Tones, or Preloaded Ring Tones.

3.

4. Next, scroll down the list and click the Trackpad to listen to a selected ring tone.

5. You can also type a few letters to the Find: field to find a ring tone that matches the letters you type.

> **TIP:** Type in Ringer to find all your phone's ring tones.

6. Once you find the ring tone you want, press the **Menu** key and select **Set As Ring Tone**.

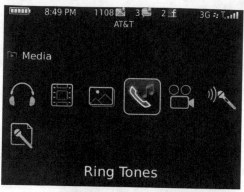

Finding a Louder Ring Tone or Downloading a New Ring Tone

Sometimes, you may find that your stock ring tones are not loud enough for you to hear, even when you turn the volume up to loud. We have found that you can download a new ring tone from mobile.blackberry.com to help with this problem.

Open your BlackBerry web browser. If you can type a web address, type **mobile.blackberry.com** and click the trackpad. If you cannot type a web address, press the **Menu** key, select **Go To...**, and then type **mobile.blackberry.com**.

1. Scroll down the home page until you see the **Personalize** topic. Then click the **Ringtones** link.

2. Then, you will have to accept the terms and conditions to continue.

3. From there you will see a list—click any ring tone listed and give it a try.

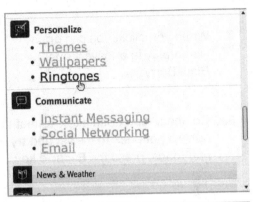

4. At the top of the page you may see the top five ring tones, as shown here.

5. Click any Download link to download and try out the ring tone.

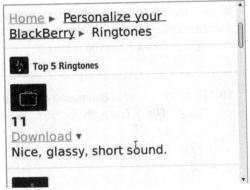

6. If you scroll further down the page, you should get to a section with ring tone categories.

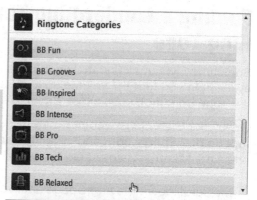

> **TIP:** The BB Intense and BB Pro categories seem to have some of the louder ring tones.

7. When you click, you can open (listen/play it) or save it on your BlackBerry.

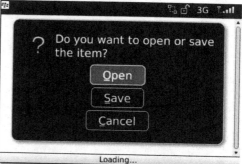

8. Go ahead and open a few to test them out. To get back to the list and try more ring tones, press the **Escape** key.

9. If you like the ring tone, then press **Menu** key after you listened to it, and select **Save** from the menu.

10. This time, select **Save** and select the **Set as Ring Tone** check box.

You are done. Next time you receive a phone call, the new louder ring tone should play.

> **TIP:** New ring tones are available on many BlackBerry user web sites, like www.crackberry.com, where many are free or you can choose to purchase ring tones at web stores like www.CrackberryAppStore.com.

Also check out the other web stores and discussion sites listed on page 556.

Understanding Sound Profiles

Your BlackBerry is highly customizable—everything from ring tones to vibrations to LED notifications can be adjusted. Traveling on an airplane but still want to use your calendar or play a game without disturbing others? (See page 14 to turn off your radio.) No problem. In a meeting or at the movies and don't want the phone to ring, but you do want some sort of notification when an e-mail message comes in? No problem.

Virtually any scenario you can imagine can be dealt with preemptively by adjusting the Profile settings.

BlackBerry OS 4.6 and OS 5.0 Differences

Setting and customizing your sound profiles are something that will change slightly depending on which version of BlackBerry Operating System (OS) you have installed on your BlackBerry.

How can I tell what version of OS is installed on my BlackBerry? See page 28.

- For OS 4.6 users, please continue reading.

- For OS 5.0 (and higher) users, please skip to page 203.

Sound Profiles for Curves running OS 4.6

If your BlackBerry Curve is running OS 4.6, then this section applies to you.

By default, the BlackBerry is set to a Normal profile, meaning that when a call comes in, the phone rings, and when a message comes in, the phone plays a tune.

Select a New Sound Profile (for OS 4.6)

> **NOTE:** This section and the next few that follow are for BlackBerry smartphones running OS 4.6. If you are running OS 5.0, then see page203. If you need help determining which version you are running, see page 28.

To set or change the Profile settings, do the following:

Depending on your selected theme and BlackBerry carrier (phone company), how you get to your **Profiles** icon will be slightly different.

If you don't see this speaker icon on your screen, press the **Menu** key to see the entire list of icons, then scroll to the **Profiles** icon and click it.

Six basic preset settings are available from which you can choose: Loud, Vibrate, Quiet, Normal, Phone Only, and Off. Next to one of those options the word "Active" will be displayed.

For most users, **Normal** will be the active profile that rings during phone calls and either vibrates or plays a tone when a message arrives.

Loud increases the volume for all notifications.

Vibrate enables a short vibration for meetings, movies, or other places where cell phone rings are discouraged.

Quiet will display notifications on the display and via the LED.

Phone Only will turn off all e-mail and SMS notifications.

Off will turn off all notifications.

Fine-Tuning Your Sound Profiles (for OS 4.6)

There may be some situations where you want a combination of options that one profile alone cannot satisfy. The BlackBerry is highly customizable so that you can adjust your profile options for virtually any potential situation. The easiest way to accomplish this is to choose a profile that is closest to what you need and edit it, as shown here.

To enter the Advanced Profile menu, do the following:

1. Click the **Profiles** icon as you did previously. (Or press the hotkey letter **F** from your Home screen.)

2. Scroll down to **Advanced** and click.

3. Each of the profiles can be adjusted by scrolling to the profile you desire to edit, pressing the **Menu** key, and selecting **Edit**.

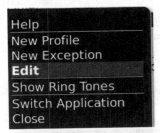

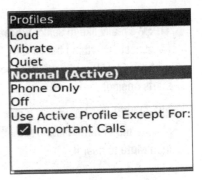

4. There are profile settings for almost every alert you could have on your BlackBerry:

BlackBerry Messenger (Alert and New Messenger), Browser, Calendar, Level 1 Messages (High Priority), E-mail, Messenger (Alert and New Message,) Phone, SMS, and Tasks.

> **TIP:** Even a new application icon that you install, like some news readers, can have profile categories in this screen.

5. For example, choose **E-mail** and notice that you can make adjustments for your BlackBerry when it is both out of the holster and in the holster.

> **NOTE:** A **holster** may be supplied with your device or sold separately. This is a leather or plastic carrying case that clips to your belt and uses a magnet to notify your BlackBerry it is in the holster and should turn off the screen immediately, among other things.

Vibrate + Tone = Vibrate first then ring.

Number of Beeps = number of times it repeats the Ring Tone.

LED Flashing = Red LED light flashes.

TIP: We really like to select **Vibrate + Tone** for almost everything because it allows us to grab the BlackBerry most times before it starts ringing!

REMEMBER THAT If you set a tone, then change the **Volume** field to something other than **Mute** to hear it.

```
Messages [Email] in Normal
Out of Holster:              Vibrate+Tone
Ring Tone:                BBPro_Sanguine
Volume:                            Medium
Number of Beeps:                        1
Repeat Notification:         LED Flashing
Number of Vibrations:                   2
In Holster:                       Vibrate
Ring Tone:                BBPro_Sanguine
Volume:                              Mute
Number of Beeps:                        1
Repeat Notification:         LED Flashing
```

Remember to adjust the **In Holster** field at the bottom, press the **Menu** key, and select **Save**.

After saving, press the **Escape** key a few times in order to get out of the Profiles screen.

```
Messages [Email] in Normal
Out of Holster:              Vibrate+Tone
Ring Tone:                BBPro_Sanguine
Volume:                            Medium
Number of Beeps:                        1
Repeat Notification:         LED Flashing
Number of Vibrations:                   2
Change Option               Vibrate+Tone
Save                      BBPro_Sanguine
Switch Application                 Medium
Close                                   1
                             LED Flashing
```

Now every time you receive a new e-mail message, you will experience this new profile setting.

TIP: If you have several e-mail accounts integrated to your BlackBerry, you can customize every single e-mail account to have a separate profile (ring, vibrate, or mute).

```
Normal
Calendar
Level 1
Messages [info@blackberrymadesimple.c...
Messages [martin.trautschold@gmail.com]
Messages [martin@blackberrymadesimpl...
Messages [martinbb2008@att.blackberry...
Messages [orders@blackberrymadesimpl...
Messages [videocontact@blackberrymad...
Messages [Web Client]
MMS
Phone
```

Hearing a Different Tone When Special People Call (Exceptions for OS 4.6)

You may decide that you want to hear a different ring tone when someone special calls. You can do this in the **Profiles** icon and in your **Contacts** icon (address book) by assigning a custom phone tune to a particular contact. Below we show you the **Profiles** app method, which has the added benefit of allowing you to assign as many names as you want to a single ring tone.

1. Start your **Profiles** icon.

2. Scroll and click the **Advanced** menu in the **Profiles** menu, as shown previously.

3. Press the **Menu** key, scroll to **New Exception**, and click.

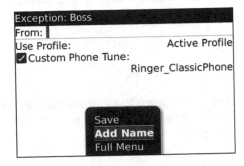

4. Type any name for this new profile in the field marked **Exception**, like **Boss**.

5. Then, glide down to the **From** field and click the trackpad to select **Add Name**.

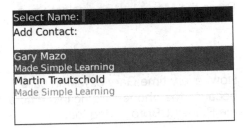

6. Now, you can select a contact from your address book for whom this new profile will apply.

7. Press the **Escape** key and save the new profile. In the example here, I want the phone to ring loud specifically when my friend Martin calls, so I don't miss the important call.

You now see the name listed next to the **From** field.

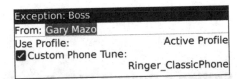

Need to add another name?

Just press the **Menu** key and repeat the Add Name process.

Need to change or remove a name?

Highlight the name and click the **Menu** key to select **Delete Name** or **Change Name**.

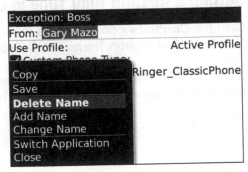

Glide down to **Use Profile** and select either **Active Profile** to make this exception active all the time, or select only one specific profile for this exception to be active.

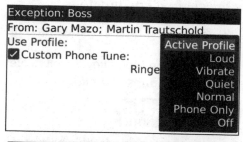

Then glide down to **Custom Phone Tune** and select a specific ring tone to use for this exception.

Press the **Menu** key and select **Save**.

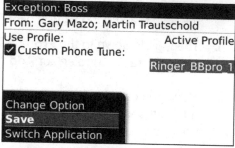

Now, every time Gary or Martin calls, I will know because the phone will ring in a different way—the Ringer_BBpro_1 ring tone.

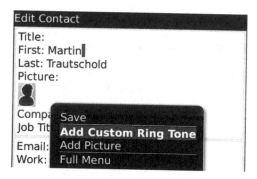

Setting a Custom Ring Tone in Contacts (for OS 4.6)

Start the **Contacts** icon and type a few letters to find the contact you wish to edit, e.g., "Ma Tr" to find "Martin Trautschold." Click the **Menu** key and select **Edit**.

Now, in the Edit Contact screen, click the trackpad and select **Add Custom Ring Tone**.

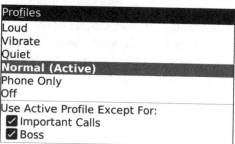

Now click the **Browse...** button to select the custom ring tone for this person. You will be able to pick from any pre-loaded ring tones and any ring tone you have placed in the **Ring Tones** folder.

Once you select your ring tone, you will see it listed at the very bottom of the contact entry. Press the **Menu** key and select **Save** when you are done.

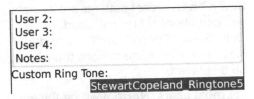

Want to know how to remove a custom ring tone?

Edit the contact entry as shown previously, glide to the very bottom to highlight the ring tone, and then press the **Menu** key and select **Delete Field**.

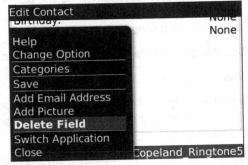

Sound Profiles for Curves running OS 5.0+

The following sections will help you work with sound profiles if your Curve is running OS 5.0 or higher.

Selecting a New Sound Profile (for OS 5.0+)

NOTE: This section and the next few that follow are for BlackBerry smartphones running OS 5.0 or higher. If you are running OS 4.6, then see page 197. To determine which version you are running, see page 28.

To set or change the profile settings, do the following:

Depending on your selected theme and BlackBerry carrier (phone company), how you get to your **Sounds** icon will be slightly different.

Profiles (Normal)

If you don't see this **Speaker** icon on your screen, press the **Menu** key to see the entire list of icons, then scroll to the **Sounds** icon and click it.

Seven basic preset settings are available from which you can choose: Normal, Loud, Medium, Vibrate Only, Silent, Phone Calls Only, and All Alerts Off. Next to one of those options the word "Active" will be displayed.

For most users, **Normal** will be the active profile that rings during phone calls and either vibrates or plays a tone when a message arrives.

Loud increases the volume for all notifications.

Medium is between Loud and Quiet.

Vibrate Only enables a short vibration for meetings, movies, or other places where cell phone rings are discouraged.

Silent will display notifications on the display and via the LED.

Phone Calls Only will turn off all e-mail and SMS notifications.

All Alerts Off will turn off all notifications.

Fine-Tuning Your Sound Profiles (for OS 5.0+)

There may be some situations where you want a combination of options that one profile alone cannot satisfy. The BlackBerry is highly customizable so that you can adjust your profile options for virtually any potential situation. The easiest way to accomplish this is to choose a profile that is closest to what you need and edit it, as shown here.

To enter the Advanced Profile menu:

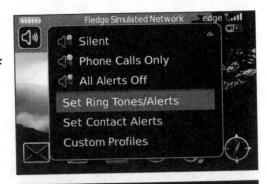

1. Click the **Sounds** icon as you did previously. (Or press the hotkey letter **F** from your Home screen.)

2. Scroll down to **Set Ringtone Alerts** and click.

3. Once you choose **Set Ring Tones/Alerts**, you can adjust the tones and alerts for the phone, messages, instant messages, reminders, or browser by choosing the field to edit.

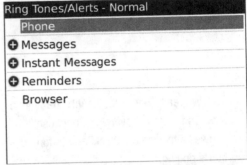

4. There are profile settings for almost every alert you could have on your BlackBerry:

5. BlackBerry Messenger (Alert and New Messenger), Browser, Calendar, Level 1 Messages (High Priority), E-mail, Messenger (Alert and New Message,) Phone, SMS, and Tasks.

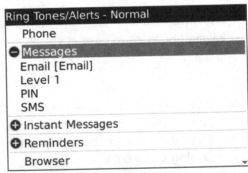

TIP: Even a new application icon that you install, like some news readers, can have profile categories in this screen.

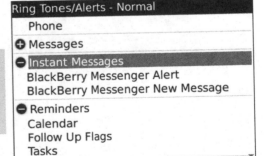

6. For example, choose **E-mail** and notice that you can make adjustments for your BlackBerry when it is both out of the holster and in the holster.

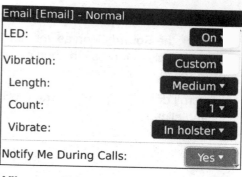

NOTE: A **holster** may be supplied with your device or sold separately. This is a leather or plastic carrying case that clips to your belt and uses a magnet to notify your BlackBerry it is in the holster and should turn off the screen immediately, among other things.

Vibrate + Tone = Vibrate first then ring.

Count = number of times it rings.

LED = Red LED light flashes.

TIP: We really like to set the **Vibrate** field to **Always** for almost everything because it allows us to grab the BlackBerry before it starts ringing.

CAUTION: If you set a tone, then change the **Volume** field to something other than **Mute** to hear it.

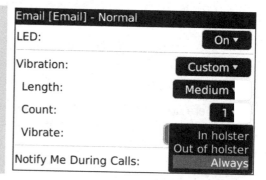

7. If you want to be notified during phone calls of an incoming message or alerts, just select **Yes** for the **Notify Me During Calls** field.

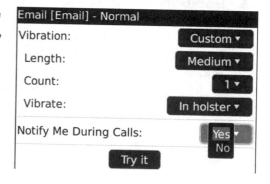

Now every time you receive a new e-mail message, you will experience this new profile setting.

> **TIP:** If you have several e-mail accounts integrated to your BlackBerry, you can customize every single e-mail account to have a separate profile (ring, vibrate, or mute).

```
Normal
Calendar
Level 1
Messages [info@blackberrymadesimple.c...
Messages [martin.trautschold@gmail.com]
Messages [martin@blackberrymadesimpl...
Messages [martinbb2008@att.blackberry...
Messages [orders@blackberrymadesimpl...
Messages [videocontact@blackberrymad...
Messages [Web Client]
MMS
Phone
```

Hearing a Different Ring for People (For OS 5.0+)

You may decide that you want to hear a different ring tone when someone special calls. You can do this in the **Sounds** icon and in your **Contacts** icon (address book) by assigning a custom phone tune to a particular contact. Here we show you the **Sounds** icon method, which has the added benefit of allowing you to assign as many names as you want to a single ring tone.

Set Custom Rings in Sounds App (for OS 5.0+)

To set a custom notification profile, do the following:

1. Start your **Sounds** icon.

2. Scroll and click **Custom Profiles**.

3. Press the **Menu** key, scroll to **New**, and click.

4. Type any name for this new profile in the field marked **Name**, like **Boss**.

5. You can set each individual tone or alert as you did previously.

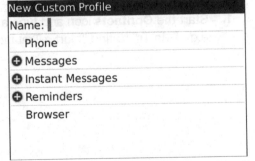

6. You can also set contact alerts from the Sounds menu. Just click the Profile icon, scroll down to Contact Alerts, and click the trackpad. Then click Add Contact Alert, press the trackpad, and select Add **Name**.

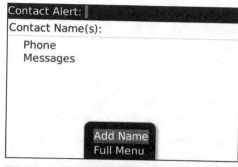

7. In the example here, I want the phone to ring loud specifically when my friend Martin calls, so I don't miss the important call.

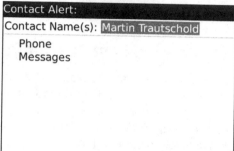

8. You now see the Martin's name listed next to the **Messages** field.

9. All the various options for customizing his ring tone, volume, etc., are now available for to customize.

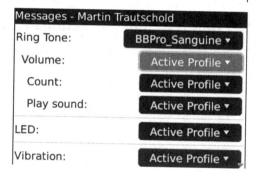

Set Custom Ring Tone in the Contacts App (for OS 5.0+)

In addition to using the Sounds app, you can use the Contacts app to set custom ring tones or alerts for people.

1. Start the **Contacts** icon and type a few letters to find the contact you wish to edit, e.g., "Ma Tr" to find "Martin Trautschold." Click the **Menu** key and select **Edit**.

2. Now, in the Edit Contact screen, scroll down to **Custom Ring Tones/Alerts**.

3. Click the **Phone** field and all the available ring tones on the BlackBerry will be displayed.

4. Just scroll up to the very top, and you can even browse your music and turn a song into a ring tone.

5. Now click the **Browse...** button to select the custom ring tone for this person. You will be able to pick from any pre-loaded ring tones and any ring tone you have placed in the **Ring Tones** folder.

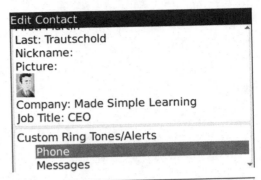

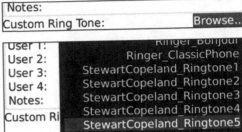

6. Once you select your ring tone, you will see it listed at the very bottom of the contact entry.

7. Press the **Menu** key and select **Save** when you are done and save the changes.

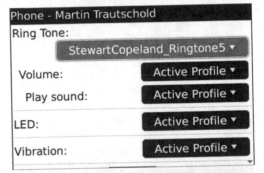

Want to know how to edit a custom ring tone?

Edit the contact entry as shown previously, glide to the **Custom Ring Tone** field, and click the trackpad. Just select any other tone for the contact.

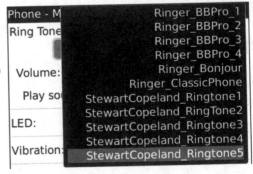

Chapter 10

Phone and Voice Dialing

Sometimes, it is easy to forget that your BlackBerry is first and foremost a phone, and a very capable phone at that. You have many extra phone features on your phone as well as the ability to use voice dialing to place your calls (see Figure 10-1).

In this chapter, we will show you how to place calls, answer calls, mute calls, use voice dialing, and use your call log. We will also show you how to set up and use speed dial on your BlackBerry.

Figure 10-1. *Important keys for phone and voice dialing*

Basic Phone Features

In our next chapter, we will take a look at some of the more advanced features of your phone. Now, let's look at how to get up and running quickly with all the basic phone features of the BlackBerry.

Call Any Underlined Phone Number

You may have noticed that most phone numbers you see are underlined on your BlackBerry. This allows you to place a call to any underlined number you see (Figure 10-2). This works anywhere, in an e-mail signature, calendar event, MemoPad item, or even a web browser screen.

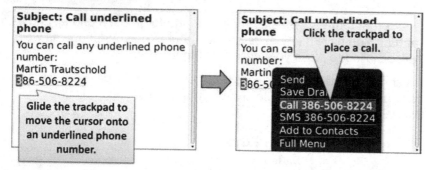

Figure 10-2. *Calling any underlined phone number*

Adjusting the Volume on Calls

There may be times when you are having trouble hearing a caller. The connection may be bad (*because of their old fashioned phone, e.g., a non-BlackBerry*) or you may be using a headset. Adjusting the volume is easy. While on the phone call, simply use the two volume keys on the right-hand side of the BlackBerry to adjust the volume up or down.

⬅ **Volume Up**

⬅ **Volume Down**

Muting Yourself on the Call

There are times you want to be able to mute yourself on the call. It might be so you can discuss something in private or you just want to be quiet as you listen to a conference call. To mute or un-mute the call, just tap the **Mute** key on the top of the BlackBerry.

What's Your Phone Number?

You have your phone, and you want to give your number to all your friends. You just need to know where you can get your hands on that important information. There are a couple of ways of doing this:

Press the **Green Phone** key to see "My Number" at the top of the screen.

Above your call log it should say your number next to My Number. In the image, the phone number of this BlackBerry is 1 519 888 7465.

11:44 AM		3G
GSM Test Network 2		WiFi
My Number: 1 519 888 7465		
David Parker	(M)	9:05a
+16065551923		9:04a
3865555712		9:04a
Gary Mazo	(W)	9:00a
Martin Trautschold	(W)	12/13

Adding Pauses and Waits in Phone Numbers

There are times when you are entering phone numbers in your address book that require either a pause or a wait (see Figure 10-3). These might be when you are dialing a conference call number, entering your password/PIN number for a voice mail access system, or auto-dialing an extension at the end of a number, but need the extra pause. If you need more than a 3-second pause, just add a few more pauses—you can put as many pauses together as you need.

Pause = 3-second pause, then continues dialing automatically

Wait = Waits for you to click the trackpad, then continues dialing

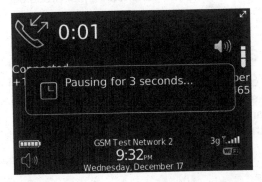

Figure 10-3. *Adding a pause when dialing*

Add pauses and waits by pressing the **Menu** key (or sometimes the trackpad works) and select **Add Pause** or **Add Wait** from the menu.

> **TIP:** Typing a phone number, then an **X**, and the extension, is the same as adding a pause. For example, typing **1 800 555 1212 x 1234** is the same as adding a pause after the phone number and before the extension. If you frequently have to dial a number that has several pieces (like calling in for your work/home voice mail messages), you can add an entry into your contact list (address book) with pauses or waits (see page 280) and assign this new entry to a speed dial (see page 224).

Changing Your Phone Ring Tone

To select any of your songs or pre-loaded ring tones on your BlackBerry as a new phone ring tone, please check out the steps in our "Media" section on page 193.

Making a Call—Just Dialing a Phone Number

Press the **Green Phone** key at any time to get into the **Phone** application.

Just start dialing numbers.

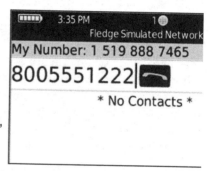

First, the BlackBerry will try to match the letters you are typing to address book entries. If it cannot find any, then it will just show you the digits you have typed, as shown.

You will notice that a small image of the **Green Phone** key is immediately after the cursor. Once all the numbers are punched in, just press the **Green Phone** key and the call will be placed.

Answering a Call

Answering a call couldn't be easier. When your call comes in, the number will be displayed on the screen. If you have that particular number already in your address book, the name and/or picture will also be on the screen (if you have entered that information into that particular contact.)

When a call comes in, do the following:

Press either the **Green Phone** key or click the trackpad to answer the call.

If you are using a Bluetooth headset, you can usually click a button on the headset to answer the call—see page 22.

Calling Voice Mail

The easiest way to call voice mail is to press and hold the number **1** key. This is the default key for voice mail. If it is not working correctly, then please call your phone company technical support for help in correcting it.

To set up voice mail, just call it and follow the prompts to enter your name, greeting, password, and other information.

When Voice Mail Does Not Work

Sometimes, pressing and holding the **1** key will not dial voice mail. This happens if the voice mail access number is incorrect in your BlackBerry. You will need to call your phone company (wireless carrier) and ask them for your local voice mail access number.

This sometimes happens if you move to a different area or change cell phones, then restore all your data onto your BlackBerry.

Once you have the new phone number from the carrier, you need to enter it into your BlackBerry.

1. Start your phone by pressing the **Green Phone** key. Press the **Menu** key, press the letter **O** to jump down to the **Options** item, and select it.

2. Now click **Voice Mail**.

    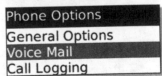

3. Enter the phone number you received into the voice mail **Access Number** field.

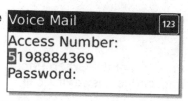

TIP: You can even enter your voice mail password if you like.

Why Do You See Names and Numbers in Your Call Logs?

You will see both phone numbers and names in your phone call logs. When you see a name instead of a phone number, you know that the person is already entered in your BlackBerry address book.

It is easy to add entries to your contacts right from this phone call log screen. Here we show you how.

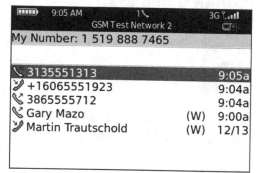

How Can You See Missed Calls on Your Home Screen?

Many of the themes will show you your missed calls with an icon with a phone and an X next to it, and a pop-up window, as shown here. Here is an image with one missed call showing on the Home screen.

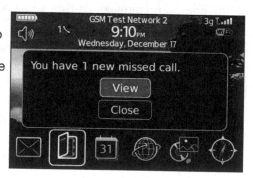

Quickly Dial from the Contact List

You can quickly dial from your contact list by pressing and holding the **Green Phone** key from just about anywhere, except when you are already in the phone or if you have a phone number underlined. (Pressing it in those cases will start a phone call from the highlighted number or person.)

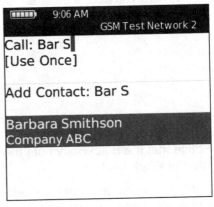

When you let go of the **Green Phone** key you should see your contact list. Finally, quickly find an entry by typing a few letters of the first name, last name, nickname, or company name.

Add a New Contact Entry from Phone Call Logs and Copy/Paste

If you see a phone number in your call log screen, then there is a good chance you might want to add that phone number as a new contact entry.

Call log entries are generated whenever you receive, miss, ignore, or place a call from your BlackBerry.

1. Get into the call log screen by tapping the **Green Phone** key once.

2. Highlight the phone number you want to add to your address book from the Call Log screen.

3. Now press the **Menu** key and select **Add to Contacts**.

4. Type as much information as possible. The more you add, the better your BlackBerry will help you communicate!

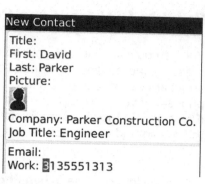

Notice that the BlackBerry puts the phone number into the **Work** field.

Is this phone number not the work number? Just cut and paste it into another field.

Cut and Paste

1. With the cursor at the beginning of the phone number, press the **Shift** key to start highlighting the phone number.

2. Glide the trackpad down one click to highlight the entire number.

3. With the phone number highlighted as shown, press the trackpad and select **Cut**.

4. Now move to the correct phone field, e.g., the **Mobile** field shown here, and click the trackpad to paste the number.

5. Enter the rest of the address book entry information for this person. Finally, press the **Menu** key and select **Save**.

Put the cursor at the beginning of the phone number you want to cut.

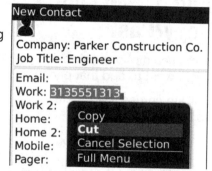

6. Now you see that David Parker's name replaced his phone number in the call logs, since he is now in your contact list.

> **TIP:** Learn more tips on entering new addresses on page 278.

Ignoring and Muting Phone Calls

Sometimes, you can't take a call, and you need to make a decision to ignore or perhaps mute the ringing of an incoming call. Both of these options can be achieved quite easily with your BlackBerry.

Ignoring a Call and Immediately Stopping the Ringing

When the phone call comes in, simply press the **Red Phone** key to ignore the call, send to voice mail, and stop the ringer.

> **TIP:** Need to silence the ringer but still want to answer the call? Just gliding the trackpad up or down will give you a few more seconds in which to answer the call before the caller is sent to voice mail. Also, if the ringing or vibrating had started while your BlackBerry was still in the holster (carrying case), then simply pulling the BlackBerry out of the holster should stop the vibrating and ringing, but still give you time to answer.

Ignoring a call will immediately send the caller to your voice mail.

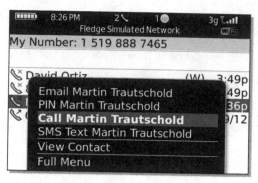

The missed call will be displayed on your Home screen. Click the missed call with the trackpad, and a small menu pops up, allowing you to do various things depending on whether this phone number is already in your address book.

Benefits of Adding People to Your Contact List / Address Book

- Call them and any number for this person (that is entered into your address book).

- Send them an e-mail message (if this person has an e-mail address entered).

- Send them an SMS text message.

- Send them an MMS message (multimedia message with pictures or other media like songs).

- Send them a PIN message.

- View the contact information.

Muting a Ringing Call

If you would prefer not to send the call immediately to voice mail and simply let it ring a few times on the caller's end, but you don't want to hear the ring (perhaps you are in a movie theater or a meeting), when the call comes in, press the **Mute** key on the top of your BlackBerry. The **Mute** key has the small **Speaker** icon with the line through it. All this will do is silence the ring.

You may still pick up the call or let the caller go to voice mail.

Using the Call Log

The call log is an especially useful tool if you make and receive many calls during the day. Often, it is hard to remember if you added that individual to your address book—but you definitely remember that they called yesterday. Here is a perfect situation to use your call log to access the call, add the number into your address book, and place a return call.

Checking Your Call Log

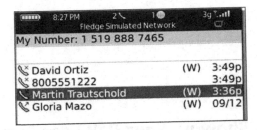

Just tap the **Green Phone** key from anywhere to see your call logs, a sequential list of calls placed, missed, or received.

TIP: Change the way call logs are displayed by pressing the **Menu** key from the phone and selecting **Options**. Then select **General Options** and finally change the **Phone List View** field to the option you desire: **Most Recent**, **Most Used**, or **Name**.

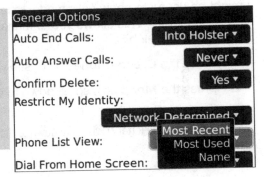

Placing a Call from the Call Log

Go to the call logs as you did previously, and scroll through the list.

TIP: If you want to call the number listed—in this case, Susan's mobile number (M)—then skip pressing the trackpad, but press the **Green Phone** key to immediately start the call.

If you want to call one of the other numbers for this person, either press the **Menu** key or click the trackpad.

You will be given a choice as to which number to call, such as **Work**, **Mobile**, or other numbers you have in your contact list for this person.

Showing Your Call Logs in the Messages Icon (Inbox)

It might be useful to show calls made, received, and missed in your message list for easy accessibility. This allows you to manage both voice and message communication in a single unified inbox.

1.   Press the **Green Phone** key to see your call logs.

2.   Press the **Menu** key, scroll down to **Options**, and click.

> **TIP:** Pressing the letter **O** will jump down to the first menu item starting with O. This should be **Options**.

3.   Scroll to **Call Logging** and click.

4.   In the **Show These Call Log Types in Message List** field, select one of the following:

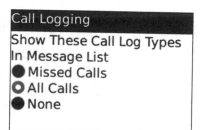

Missed Calls (see only missed calls)

All Calls (see all placed, missed, received)

None (this is the default, see no calls)

5.   Press **Menu** and select **Save**.

Adding a Note to a Call Log

1. Press the **Green Phone** key to get into the phone logs if you are not already there. Press the **Menu** key and select **View History**.

2. Select the call history item to which you want to add your notes by gliding the trackpad up or down.

3. Once selected, press the **Menu** key again and click **Add Notes**.

4. When you are done typing your notes, click the trackpad and select **Save**.

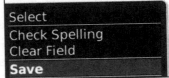

TIP: You can even add notes when you are still talking on the phone.

You may want to use the speakerphone or your headset so you can hear while typing.

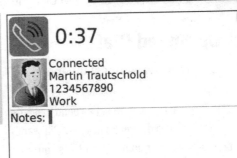

Forwarding a Call Log

1. Go to your call log and highlight the log entry you wish to forward.

2. Press the **Menu** key and click **View History** just as you did previously.

3. While viewing the call history entry, press the **Menu** key again and select **Forward**.

4. Type your e-mail message or make changes to the notes, then click the trackpad and select **Send**.

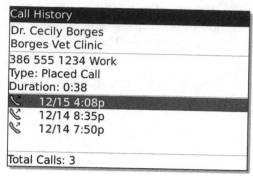

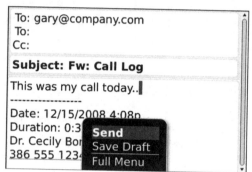

Speed Dial

Speed dialing is a great way to call your frequent contacts quickly. Just assign them a one-digit number key (or character key) that you hold, and their number is automatically dialed. You have up to 26 speed dial entries.

Set Up Speed Dial

There are a few ways to set up speed dialing on your BlackBerry.

TIP: The easiest way to set a speed dial letter on your keyboard is to press and hold it from your Home screen. You will be asked if you want to set it as a speed dial. Select **Yes** and select the person from your contacts list to assign.

Option #1: Use Call Logs

1. Press the **Green Phone** key to see your call logs.

2. Highlight the call log entry (either phone number or name) that you want to add to speed dial and press the **Menu** key.

3. Select **Add Speed Dial.**

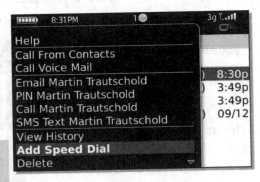

> **NOTE:** If this person is already on speed dial, then you will see a **Remove Speed Dial** menu option instead.

4. You may be asked to confirm you want to add this speed dial number with a pop-up window looking something like this.

5. In the Speed Dial list use the **Trackpad** and move the phone number into a vacant slot.

6. Once the correct speed dial key is chosen, just click the **Trackpad**. The number or symbol you selected is now set as the speed dial key for that phone number.

> **TIP:** You may want to reserve the **H** key to be your home number.

Option #2: Press and Hold a Key

Follow these steps to easily assign a key for speed dial.

1. Press and hold any letter key from your Home Screen that is not reserved (1, A, and Q are reserved) or already assigned.

2. You will be asked if you want to assign this key to a speed dial number. (Figure 10-4)

Set up Speed Dial

Press & Hold any of
your letter keys to set
up Speed Dial.

The only exceptions are: W/1
key – Voice Mail
Q key – Turn on/off Quiet
profile (Vibrate mode)

Figure 10-4. *Setting up speed dial*

3. Select **Yes** to assign it.

4. Then you will be shown your Contacts
List. You can either select an existing
entry or click on **[Use Once]** at the top
of the list to type in a new phone
number that is not in your Address
Book.

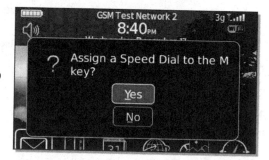

5. If you are using an existing contact
entry, click on the selected name.

6. If the entry has more than one phone
number, you will need to select the
phone number such as Home, Mobile
or Work.

7. After selecting or entering a new number, you will see the **Speed Dial Numbers** screen.

8. If you want to move this entry to a different letter in the Speed Dial list, press the **Menu** key and select **Move**.

9. Press the **Escape** key to back out and save your settings.

10. Give your new speed dial a try by pressing and holding the letter from your **Home Screen** or **Messages** app.

Option #3: Use a Contact Phone Number

1. Tap the **Green Phone** key and start entering a contact name or number.

2. When you see the contact listed, scroll to it and highlight it.

3. Press the **Menu** key, select **Add Speed Dial**, and follow steps to select the speed dial letter as shown previously.

Using Speed Dial

Once you set up your speed dial numbers, all you need to do is press and hold the letter key you assigned to start dialing the phone.

You can use speed dial letters from three places:

- Home screen,
- Messages app and,
- Phone app.

Remember these three keys are reserved:

1 key = Voice Mail

A key = **Lock** your BlackBerry

Q key = Toggle your **Sound** profile to **Vibrate** or back to the previous profile.

Using Voice Dialing

One of the powerful features of the BlackBerry is the voice command program for voice dialing and simple voice commands. Voice dialing provides a safe way to place calls without having to look at the BlackBerry and navigate through menus. Voice command does not need to be trained like on other smartphones—just speak naturally.

Using Voice Dialing to Call a Contact

The **Left Convenience** key is (usually) set for voice command—simply press this key. What is a Convenience key and how do you set it? See page 187.

The first time you use this feature, the BlackBerry will take a few seconds to scan your address book.

When you hear "**Say a Command**" just speak the name of the contact you wish to call using the syntax "**Call Martin Trautschold.**"

You will then be prompted with "**Which number.**" Again, speak clearly and say "**Home,**" "**Work,**" or "**Mobile.**" Say "**Yes**" to confirm and the BlackBerry will dial.

Using Voice Dialing to Call a Number

1. Press the **Left Convenience** key as you did previously (assuming your Convenience key is set to voice dialing—if it's not, you can change it, as shown on page 187).

2. When you hear "**Say a command,**" say "**Call**" and the phone number. Example: "**Call 386-555-8888.**"

3. Depending on your settings, you may be asked to confirm the number you just spoke, or it will just start dialing.

Chapter 11

Advanced Phone

Now that you have the basics down for using your BlackBerry as a phone, it is time for some more advanced phone topics.

In this chapter we will show you how to set unique caller IDs for contacts, how to use advance voice dialing options, and how to use call forwarding and call waiting.

We will also show you how to set up and manage conference calling on your BlackBerry.

Advanced Phone Topics

For many of us, the basic phone topics covered in the previous chapter will cover most of our phone needs with the BlackBerry. For others of us, however, we need to eke out every possible phone feature. Let's get started!

Using Your Music As Ring Tones (Phone Tune)

The BlackBerry supports using any type audio file listed previously as a ring tone. You can set one general ring tone (phone tune) for everyone or set up individual tones for your important callers.

> **CAUTION:** In some BlackBerry handhelds, when you are attempting to set a ring tone for a specific person in the address book or in Profiles, you can browse only to the **Ring Tones** folder, not the **Music** folder. If this is the case, then you must copy your ring tones to the **Ring Tones** folder using the methods to transfer media found in this book.

To set one Song (MP3) as your general **Ring Tone**, do the following:

1. Navigate to your list of music as you did above.

2. Find the MP3 file you wish to use as the general phone tune.

3. Press the **Menu** key, scroll to **Set As Ring Tone**, and click.

Help
Music Library
Replay
Repeat
Shuffle
Show Playlist
Activate Handset
Activate XPLOD
Set As Ring Tone
Switch Application
Close

TIP: Set up unique ring tones for each of your important callers. This way you will know when each of these people is calling without looking at your BlackBerry screen.

Set a Custom Ring Tone for a Single Caller (Set One Song (MP3) as an Individual Person's Ring Tone)

See how to do this on page 208.

More with Voice Dialing

The last chapter concluded with an overview of voice command. Voice Dialing is a powerful tool for enabling not only basic phone calls, but other functions of the BlackBerry without having to push buttons or input text.

Other Voice Commands

You can use the voice command software to perform other functions on the BlackBerry. These are especially useful if you are in a position where you can't look at the screen (while driving) or in an area where coverage seems to fade in and out.

The most common are the following:

Call Extension will call a specific extension.

Call Martin Home will call the contact at the home number.

Check Battery will check the battery status.

Check Signal will let you know the strength of your wireless signal and whether you have no signal, a low signal, a high signal, or a very high signal.

Turn Off Voice Prompts will turn off the "Say a command" voice and replace it with a simple beep.

Turn On Voice Prompts turns the friendly voice back on.

Changing Your Voice Dialing Options

You can control various features of voice dialing by going into your **Options** icon and selecting **Voice Dialing** (Figure 11-1).

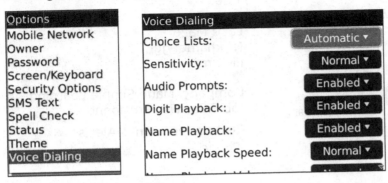

Figure 11-1. *Voice Dialing option screen*

Change the **Choice Lists**: If you do not want to be confronted with lots of choices after you say a command, your options here are **Automatic** (default), **Always On**, or **Always Off**.

Sensitivity: You can adjust the acceptance/rejection ratio of voice commands by adjusting the field that initially reads **Normal**. You can go up to **3 (Reject More)** or down to **-3 (Reject Less)**.

Audio Prompts: These can be enabled or disabled from this screen or by saying "**Turn Prompts On/Off**."

Digit Playback: This repeats the numbers you say and **Name playback**, which repeats the name you say, can also be enabled or disabled.

Finally, you can adjust the playback speed and playback volume of the voice dialing program.

Voice Dialing / Voice Command Tips and Tricks

There are a few ways to speed up the voice command process. You can also customize the way that voice dialing works on the BlackBerry.

Making Voice Dialing Calls More Quickly

When using voice command, give more information when you place the call. For example, if you say "**Call Martin Trautschold, Home**," the voice dialing program will ask you to confirm only that you are calling him at home.

The call will then be placed.

Giving Your Contacts Nicknames

Make a shortcut entry for a contact—especially one with a long name.

In addition to my **Gary Mazo** contact, I might also make a contact with the same information, but put "**gg**" as the name.

I would then simply say, "**Call gg.**"

> **TIP:** This nickname also works when you are addressing e-mail messages, SMS text messages, and more.

Edit Contact
Title:
First: Gary
Last: Mazo
Nickname: gg
Picture:

Company: Made Simple Learning
Job Title: Vice President
Custom Ring Tones/Alerts
Phone

Call Waiting—Calling a Second Person

Like most phones these days, the BlackBerry supports call waiting, call forwarding, and conference calling, all useful options in the business world and in your busy life.

Enabling Call Waiting (Chances Are That This Is Already On)

1. Press the **Green Phone** key to get into the Phone screen.

2. Press the **Menu** key, scroll to **Options**, and click the trackpad.

3. Scroll to **Call Waiting** and make sure the **Call Waiting Enabled** field is set to **Yes**.

4. Press the **Menu** key and select **Save**. To turn off or disable call waiting, just repeat the previous steps and set the field to **No**.

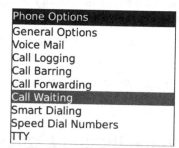

Phone Options
General Options
Voice Mail
Call Logging
Call Barring
Call Forwarding
Call Waiting
Smart Dialing
Speed Dial Numbers
TTY

Call Waiting
Call Waiting Enabled: Yes ▾

Using Call Waiting

Start a phone call with someone. Or receive a phone call from someone.

Now you can receive a call from a second person.

Press the **Green Phone** key while on a call to dial a second phone number or call someone else from your BlackBerry address book. This will put the previous caller on hold.

> **TIP:** If a second person calls you while you are speaking to a first caller, just press the **Green Phone** key to answer the second caller—the first caller will still be waiting for you on hold.

Press the **Green Phone** key to toggle between calls (Figure 11-2).

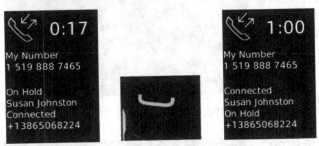

Figure 11-2. *Using the **Green Phone** key to toggle between calls*

Working with a Second Caller

When you are speaking to a person on the phone and your phone rings again with a second caller, you can do a number of things. It just takes a little practice to get smooth doing it.

Option #1: Answer and put the first caller on hold.

This is probably the easiest option.

1. Just press the **Green Phone** key
   (**Answer – Hold Current**).

2. Then to swap between the callers, just
   press the **Green Phone** key again.

3. With two callers on the phone, pressing
   the **Menu** key allows you to do a
   number of other things including
   conference calling.

Option #2: Hang up with the first caller and answer the second caller.

Click the trackpad and select **Answer-Drop
Current** to hang up with the first caller and
answer the second caller.

Option #3: Press the **Red Phone** key to send the second caller to voice mail (ignore
them).

Conference Calling

Conference calling is very helpful to get people together and share ideas, or when you need to get two people on the phone so they can transfer information directly to each other.

Take a recent scenario from one of the authors (Martin), where conferencing together two parties was a faster (and safer) way to transfer needed information. Martin was trying to lease a car. The car dealer left a voice mail for Martin to call the insurance company to approve the proof of insurance being faxed to the dealer. Martin called the insurance company, surprised that they did not have the dealer's fax number.

Instead of hanging up and calling the dealer to get the fax number and then calling the insurance company back, Martin did a quick conference call between the dealer and insurance company. The conference call allowed the dealer's fax number to be immediately relayed to the insurance company along with any special instructions and approvals.

Setting Up a Conference Call

1. Place a call as you normally would.

2. While on the call, press the **Green Phone** key (Figure 11-3).

(or if this does not show you a New Call screen, then press the **Menu** key and select **New Call**) and either choose a contact from your contact list or type a phone number and place the call.

3. While on the second call, press the **Menu** key, scroll to **Join Conference**, and click.

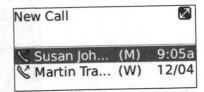

Figure 11-3. Press **Green Phone** key to initiate a second call.

If you add more than two callers to the conference call, just repeat the process starting with another **New Call** (press the **Green Phone** key).

1. Join the calls as you did previously. Repeat as needed.

2. To speak with only one of the callers on a conference call, press the **Menu** key while on the conference call, and select **Split Call**. You will then be able to speak privately with that one caller (Figure 11-4).

Figure 11-4. *Splitting calls when on a conference call*

Ending or Leaving a Conference Call

To hang up on everyone and end the conference call for all, press the **Red Phone** key or press the **Menu** key and select **Drop Call**.

Dialing Letters in Phone Numbers or on the Phone

You can dial letters like **1-800-CALLABC** when you are on a phone call or even put phone numbers with letters in your address book. To do this dialing while on the phone, just press the **Alt** key (lower left-most key) and type the letters on your keyboard.

Hold **Alt**, then type **TRAUTS**.

So when you hear "In order to use this phone directory, please dial the first three letters of the person's last name to look them up," just press the **Alt** key and type the letters!

When typing phone numbers with letters in your address book or in the phone, use the same technique. If you had to enter 1-800-CALLABC into your address book, you would type **1 800**, then press the **Alt** key, and type **CALLABC**.

> **TIP:** When you are not on a phone call (e.g., when editing a contact), pressing and holding a letter key (without holding the **Alt** key) will also produce a letter.

Edit Contact

Picture:

Company: Red Sox
Job Title: DH

Email:
Work: 617-114-6788
Work 2:
Home: 1800CALLABC
Home 2:
Mobile: 1386556133
Pager:

TTY or Teletype Support

TTY or Teletype is a common name for the telecommunications device for the deaf (TDD). Your BlackBerry is designed in such a way that it can convert received calls into text that can be read on a TTY device. You need to connect your BlackBerry to the TTY device and then enable that option.

Make sure that your wireless carrier supports TTY (most do). You will have to start the phone call logs with the **Green Phone** key if you are not already in the phone. Then press the **Menu** key and select **Options**. Then select **TTY** to see this screen and make sure that the TTY mode is set to **Yes**. Save your changes.

Make sure that the TTY device operates at the universal standard of 45.45 BPS. Connect the TTY device to the headset jack on the BlackBerry. (There are other adapters, but this is the easiest way to connect the BlackBerry to a TTY device.)

Chapter 12

E-mail Like a Pro

BlackBerry smartphones are known for their e-mail capabilities. You will truly be amazed with how easy it is to get started with e-mail on your BlackBerry.

There is so much you can do, however, with the e-mail application on the device. In this chapter, we will show you how to compose, send and reply to e-mail messages as well as how to work with e-mail attachments.

Finally, we will show you how to use the search commands and features to find and organize your messages.

Getting Started with E-mail

The BlackBerry, even though small and stylish, is a BlackBerry to the core—a powerful e-mail tool. This chapter will get you up and running with your e-mail. In minutes, you will be an e-mailing pro!

E-mail Inbox (Messages) Shortcut Hotkeys

You can find a complete set of e-mail hotkeys (one-key shortcuts) to help you really speed up your e-mailing at the beginning of this book on page 169, with all the other hotkey lists.

Composing E-mail Messages

The BlackBerry, like all BlackBerry smartphones, gives you the freedom to e-mail on the go. With the cellular network, e-mail is available to you at all times almost anywhere in the world.

Option #1: E-mailing from the Messages Icon (Hotkey: M)

This first option is perhaps easiest for learning how to initially send an e-mail message.

Select your **Messages** icon on the Home screen and click. (Or press the **M** Home screen hotkey.)

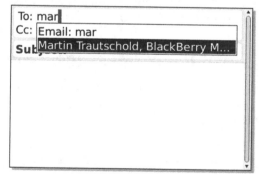

A fast way to start writing a new e-mail message is to click a date row separator and click the trackpad to select **Compose E-mail**. (Shortcut: from the same **Date Row separator line**, just press the **Enter** key.)

You may also press the **Menu** key and scroll down to **Compose E-mail** and click.

Type the recipient's e-mail address in the **To** field. If your BlackBerry finds a match between what you are typing and any Address Book entries, those are shown in a selectable drop-down list. Then you may select the correct name by clicking it.

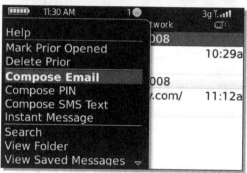

Repeat this to add additional **To** and **Cc** addressees.

If you need to add a blind carbon copy (**Bcc**), then press the **Menu** key and select **Add Bcc** (Figure 12-1).

 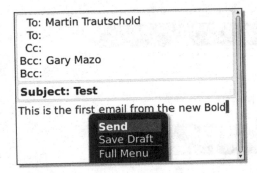

Figure 12-1. *Adding a Bcc in an e-mail message*

Then type the subject and body of your e-mail message. When you are done, press the trackpad and click **Send**. That's all there is to it.

TWO-LETTER NICKNAMES FOR POPULAR CONTACTS

Martin has set up the nickname "pp" as part of his own contact entry (**Nickname** field). This allows him to almost instantly call up his name whenever he wants to find his contact entry (e.g., to look up the company's DUNS number or tax ID in his contact notes) or add himself as a quick carbon copy on an e-mail message, or even when he wants to quickly send a note or reminder to himself as an e-mail message. How do you get this done?

Step 1: Simply edit any contact and add a 2-letter nickname to the **Nickname** field.

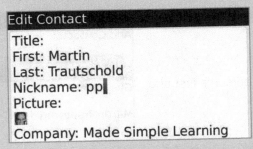

Step 2: Whenever you type the two letters (e.g., 'pp') in the **ToE-mail** field, this person instantly appears.

This also works in the phone and when addressing SMS/MMS messages.

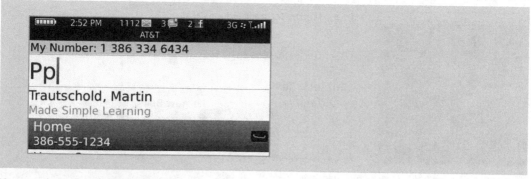

If you have several e-mail addresses integrated with your BlackBerry, you can select which one to send your e-mail message from using the **Sent From** or **Send Using** field.

1. Just glide and click the field next to **Send Using** at the top of the E-mail Composition screen.

2. Click the trackpad and select which e-mail account to use.

Sending E-mail Messages from Your Contacts App

After you have entered or synced your names and addresses to your BlackBerry, you may send e-mail messages directly from your contacts. (See page 67 for help on sync setup for Windows PC users, or page 125 for Apple Mac users.)

1. Navigate to your **Contacts** icon (address book) and click the trackpad.

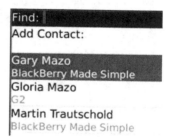

2. Begin to type a few letters from your person's first and last name to find them.

3. Once you see the name you want, press the **Menu** key and select **E-mail (name)**. The only time you will not see the option to **E-mail** someone is if you do not have an e-mail address stored for that contact.

4. Alternatively, if you are already looking at the person's detailed address screen, then you can glide to the **E-mail** field, click the trackpad to see the short menu, and select **E-mail**.

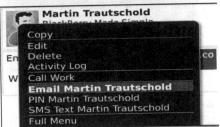

5. Click that option with the trackpad and the name now appears in the **To** field. Complete and send the e-mail message as outlined previously.

Using "Q" to Quickly See a Person's E-mail Address

When you receive e-mail messages on your BlackBerry, many times you will see the person's real name, e.g., "Margaret Johnson," and not his or her e-mail address in the **From** field.

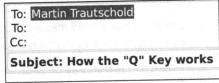

Sometimes you want to quickly see the e-mail address, since it may tell you exactly where they work. The trick to do this is to glide up, highlight the e-mail address, and press the **Q** key. Press **Q** again, and it switches back.

Press **Q** to see the e-mail address:

Or, you can simply highlight the person's name and see the e-mail address in a little pop-up window, as shown here.

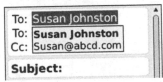

Replying to Messages

Once you get the hang of e-mailing on your BlackBerry, you will quickly find yourself checking your e-mail and wanting to respond quickly to your e-mail messages. Replying to messages is very easy on the BlackBerry.

> **TIP:** R = Reply, L = Reply All, C = Compose E-mail, F = Forward
>
> The shortcut hotkeys to reply, reply all, and forward are very easy. You can press any of these keys when either reading a message or just viewing a received message in the message list (inbox). See page 169 for all E-mail hotkeys.

1. Open your e-mail inbox by clicking the **Messages** icon.

> **NOTE:** The **Messages** icon will usually have a red asterisk, or it might be flashing to indicate you have received new mail.

2. Scroll to the e-mail message you wish to open, and click the trackpad to open it and read it.

3. Press the **Menu** key or click the trackpad, scroll to **Reply**, and click, or simply press the **R** shortcut key. (See page 169 for all e-mail shortcut keys.)

4. The recipient is now shown in the **To** field.

5. Type your message, and click the trackpad when done. Choose **Send** and your e-mail message is sent.

Flag for Follow Up

After receiving an e-mail message, have you ever found yourself thinking one of the following:

"This is important, but I can't deal with it now."

"I need to spend more time on this e-mail message and get back to them later."

"I need to give them a call about this message on Wednesday."

If so, then the follow-up flag is a great feature.

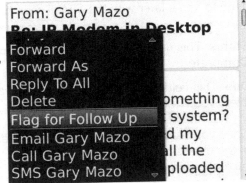

You can set flags of many types and colors, with or without due dates, from the main e-mail inbox or while you are reading a particular message.

To set a flag, press the **Menu** key and select **Flag for Follow Up** as shown previously.

You can set various flag properties on this screen.

Keep in mind that you can use the messages search command to find flags or specific colors of flags.

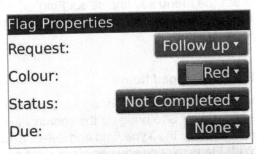

Request type: There are quite a few types of follow-ups that you can select. Click the **Request** field to see them all. In some cases, you might even want to select **No response necessary**.

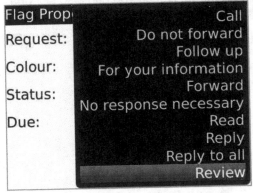

Color / Colour: You can change the color of the flag, which can help you locate the flagged items later with the e-mail search feature.

Status: This field is either **Not Completed** or **Completed**.

Due: This field is either **None** or **By Date** and it lets you specify a due date.

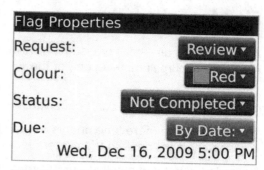

Once you set the flag, you will see it in the top of the message under the addresses and subject information.

Changing Flag Properties

Click the flag itself in an e-mail message or press the **Menu** key and select **Flag Properties**. This will allow you to change all the properties.

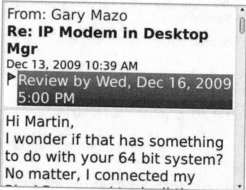

Finding Flagged Items

In your e-mail inbox (Messages), press the hotkey letter **S** to bring up the search window. Roll down to the **Type** field and select **E-mail With Flags**. Notice you can also select a specific color or all colors.

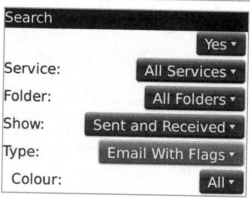

Setting a Hotkey for your Search

Before you execute your search, press the **Menu** key and select **Save**. This allows you to name your search and set a hotkey combination, such as **Alt** + some letter.

Try **Alt + Q** (**Alt + F** did not seem to work).

Now, in your e-mail inbox, you can quickly find all flagged items by pressing **Alt + Q**.

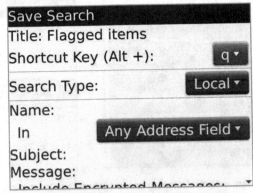

When a flagged item alarm rings, you will see a pop-up screen similar to the one shown here.

You will also notice a flag on your top status bar with a number next to it showing how many flag due dates have passed.

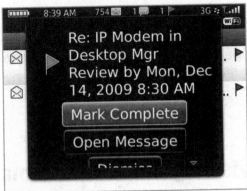

Attaching a Contact Entry (Address Book Entry) to an E-mail Message

At times, you might need to send someone an address that is contained in your BlackBerry contacts.

Start composing an e-mail message by pressing the **L** key or selecting **Compose E-mail** from the menu in the **Messages** icon.

Press the **Menu** key and scroll to **Attach Contact** (Figure 12-2).

Figure 12-2. *Attaching contact information to an e-mail message*

Either type the name of the contact or use the trackpad to scroll and click a contact name. You will now see the attached contact shown as a little address book icon at the bottom the main body field of the e-mail message.

Viewing Pictures in E-mail Messages You Receive

In some e-mail messages, you may see blank spaces where images should be. If you see this, then press the **Menu** key and select **Get Image** to retrieve just one image, or **Get Images** to retrieve them all. You may see a warning message about exposing your e-mail address; you need to click **OK** or **Yes** in order to get the image.

Attaching a File to an E-mail Message

The BlackBerry is a powerful business tool. As such, there are times that you might need to attach a file (much like you would do on your computer) to the e-mail message you send from the BlackBerry.

> **NOTE:** Depending on the version of your BlackBerry software, this **Attach File** menu option may not be available for you.

1. Start composing an e-mail message and press the **Menu** key.

2. Select **Attach File** from the menu.

3. Next, you need to locate the directory in which the file is stored. Your two initial options are **Device Memory** or **Media Card**.

Figure 12-3. *Attaching a picture to an e-mail message*

4. Use the trackpad to navigate to the folder where the file is stored. Once you find the file, simply click it and it will appear in the body of the e-mail message (Figure 12-3).

TIP: You can add several files to your e-mail message—simply repeat the procedure.

Setting the Importance of the E-mail Message

Sometimes, you want your e-mail message to be noticed and responded to immediately. The BlackBerry lets you set that importance so that your recipient can better respond.

High = Exclamation point,

Normal = Nothing,

Low = Arrow pointing down.

It's easy to set the importance of a new e-mail message as you are writing it.

1. Press the **Menu** key and select **Options**. (Shortcut: pressing the letter key that matches the first letter of the menu item (e.g., the **O** key) a couple of times will jump you down to that item.)

2. In the Options screen, you will see the **Importance** field.

3. Select from **Normal** and you will see the options **High** or **Low**.

4. Press the **Menu** key and save.

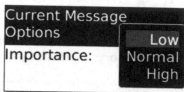

Verifying Delivery of E-mail Messages

On some, but not all e-mail messages you send, you will see a little D inside the checkmark. These are messages that have been confirmed delivered to the recipient. It does not mean they have opened the message—just that it was successfully delivered to their inbox. Notice the D next to the two check marks in Figure 12-4.

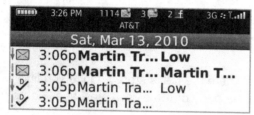

Figure 12-4. *Verifying delivery of your e-mail messages*

Spell Checking Your E-mail Messages

Please see page 22 to learn how to enable spell checking on e-mail messages you type and send. The spelling checker may not be turned on when you take your BlackBerry out of the box the first time.

Working with E-mail Attachments

One of the things that makes your BlackBerry more than just "another pretty smartphone" is its serious business capabilities. Often, e-mail messages arrive with attachments of important documents, such as Microsoft Word files, Excel spreadsheets, or PowerPoint presentations. Fortunately, the BlackBerry lets you open and view these attachments and other common formats, wherever you might be.

Supported E-mail Attachment Formats

- Microsoft Word (DOC)
- Microsoft Excel (XLS)
- Microsoft PowerPoint (PPT)
- Corel WordPerfect (WPD)
- Adobe Acrobat PDF (PDF)
- ASCII text (TXT)
- Rich Text Format files (RTF)

- HTML
- Zip archive (ZIP)
- (Password protected ZIP files are not supported)
- MP3 – Voice Mail Playback (up to 500Kb file size)
- Image files of the following types: JPG, BMP, GIF, PNG, TIFF

NOTE: Multi-page TIFF files are not supported.

NOTE: Additional file types may be supported in newer versions of the system software running on your BlackBerry.

Here are features available in attachment viewing:

- Images: Pan, zoom, or rotate.
- Save images to view later on your BlackBerry.
- Show or hide tracked changes (e.g., in Microsoft Word).
- Jump to another part of the file instead of paging through it.
- Show images as thumbnails at the bottom of the e-mail message.

Using Documents to Go to View and Edit E-mail Attachments

Your BlackBerry also comes with the **Documents to Go** program icons from DataViz. This is an incredibly comprehensive program that allows you to not only view, but also edit Word, PowerPoint, and Excel documents, while preserving the native formatting. That means that the documents can open on your BlackBerry and look just like they do on your computer.

How Do You Know If You Have an E-mail Attachment?

You will see an envelope with a paperclip, as shown here.

= The message has an attachment.

= The message has no attachment (or it has an attachment that cannot be opened by the BlackBerry).

Opening an Attached File

1. Navigate to your message with the

   Attachment icon showing

   (paperclip on envelope) and click it.

2. At the very top of the e-mail message, you will see **1 Attachment** or **2 Attachments**, depending on the number of attachments.

3. 3. Click the trackpad and select **Open Attachment**.

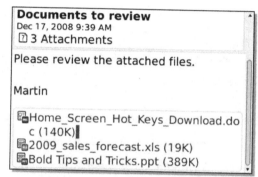

4. If the document is a Microsoft Office document format, you will then be presented with the option to **View** or **Edit with Documents to Go**.

5. For a quick view, without the option to edit or change the document, select **View**.

The View mode document is shown here.

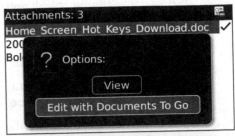

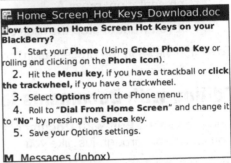

6. To really see the document the way it was meant to be seen, and get the option to edit the document, we suggest you select **Edit with Documents to Go**.

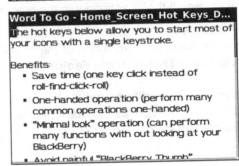

If you get an error message such as "**Document Conversion Failed**" it is very likely that the attachment is not a format that is viewable by the BlackBerry Attachment Viewer. Check out the list of supported attachment types on page 250.

E-mail Attachment Viewer Tips and Tricks

Like all features of your BlackBerry, there are some shortcuts and tricks that might prove helpful when working with attachments using the generic BlackBerry attachment viewer:

- To search for specific text inside an attachment, press **F**.
- To switch between showing tracked changes and showing the final version, press **H**.
- To jump to the top of the attachment, press **T**.
- To jump to the bottom of the attachment, press **B**.

- (Spreadsheet/table only) If you want to change the width of a column in a spreadsheet, press **W**.

- (Spreadsheet/table only) If you want go to a specific cell inside a spreadsheet, press **G** and then type the cell name, e.g., **C3**.

- (Spreadsheet/table only) If you wish to view the content of a cell in a spreadsheet, press the **Space** key or simply click the trackpad.

- (Pictures/PowerPoint presentation only) To view a slide show presentation, press **A**.

- If you want to stop the slide show presentation, hold the **Escape** key.

To switch views in the presentation, press **Z**.

Editing with Documents to Go

Once you select **Edit with Documents to Go** the document will open on your screen. You can scroll through just like you were reading a Word document on your computer.

What are all those asterisks in the menus?   ***Check Spelling**

These are items that are only available in the Premium edition of Documents to Go. You can upgrade right from one of the menu items in the application. Press the **Menu** key and select **Try Premium Features**.

If you want to edit and make changes to the document, just press the **Menu** key and select **Edit Mode** from the menu.

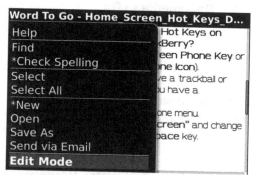

If you want to adjust the formatting of the document, just press the **Menu** key and select **Format**. You will then see the formatting options available to you (Figure 12-5).

> **NOTE:** Sometimes Documents to Go gets updated in BlackBerry App World. Every so often, check App World to see if a new version is available.

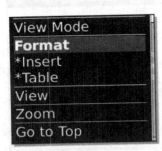

Figure 12-5. *Formatting text in Documents to Go*

Using the Standard Document Viewer

You may decide you don't want to use Documents to Go. In that case, just select the **View** option when you go to open the attachment.

The document won't have the same look, but you will be able to navigate through it quickly.

> **Home_Screen_Hot_Keys_Download.doc**
>
> **How to turn on Home Screen Hot Keys on your BlackBerry?**
>
> 1. Start your **Phone** (Using **Green Phone Key** or rolling and clicking on the **Phone Icon**).
> 2. Hit the **Menu key**, if you have a trackball or **click the trackwheel,** if you have a trackwheel.
> 3. Select **Options** from the Phone menu.
> 4. Roll to "**Dial From Home Screen**" and change it to "**No**" by pressing the **Space** key.
> 5. Save your Options settings.
>
> **M** Messages (Inbox)

Using Sheet to Go or Slideshow to Go (MS Excel or PowerPoint)

Follow the same steps you did earlier when you opened the word processing document.

Sheet to Go View Mode:

	A	B	C	D
	Sheet1			
1	2009 Sales Forecast			
2		West	East	Combi...
3	Q1	100	300	**400**
4	Q2	150	400	**550**
5	Q3	200	500	**700**
6	Q4	250	600	**850**
7	Total	**700**	**1800**	**2500**

Sheet to Go Edit Mode:

Opened with Sheet to Go (you can view formulas and edit).

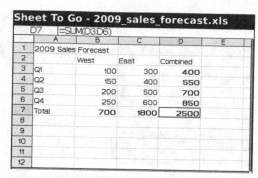

Here is a Microsoft PowerPoint document opened with Slideshow to Go.

Just click the trackpad and select **Edit Slide Text** to change any slide text items.

Now, just click and type your changes.

Then you can save a copy on your BlackBerry, or send it via e-mail.

If you send via E-mail, then you will see a new e-mail message screen come up with the edited file as an attachment. **You can truly get work done on the road with your BlackBerry!**

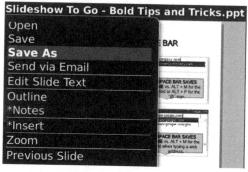

Send the edited file and you're done.

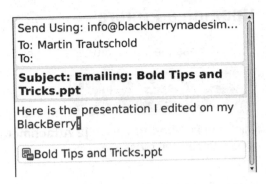

Finding Text in an Attachment

1. Open up the attachment as described previously.

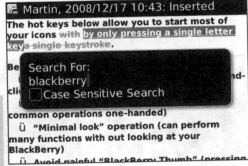

2. Then, to find text in an E-mail attachment, press the trackpad and select **Find**, or use the shortcut key **F**.

3. Type text to search for and select whether you want the search to match the case (upper/lower) of your search term. Finally, click the trackpad to start the search.

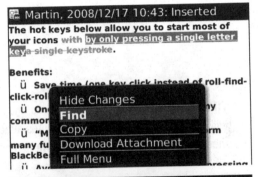

TIP: To quickly find the same text again later in the document, press the **F** key again. To search for different text, click the trackpad and select **Find**.

To change the way the attachment looks on the BlackBerry:

1. Open up the attachment as described previously.

2. Press the **Menu** key and select **Options**.

3. Choose a new font from the **Font Family** to change the display font of the document.

Opening a Picture

Open a message with pictures attached.

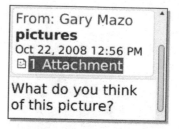

From: Gary Mazo
pictures
Oct 22, 2008 12:56 PM
📧1 Attachment

What do you think
of this picture?

Click the **[1 Attachment]** or **[2 Attachments]**, etc. at the
top of the e-mail message.

Select **Open Attachment** or **Download Attachment** (to
save it on your BlackBerry). Then click the image file names
to open them.

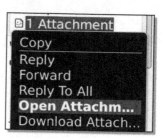

TIP: Once you have opened the pictures, then the next time you view that e-mail message, you
will see the thumbnails of all the pictures attached to that e-mail message at the bottom of the
message. You can then just glide down to them and click them to open them.

To save the picture, press the **Menu** key or click the trackpad and click **Save Image**
(Figure 12-6). The picture will be saved where you specify, either on your media card or
the main device memory.

Figure 12-6. *Saving an image you received in an e-mail message*

Other menu options include **Zoom** (to expand the image), or **Rotate** (to rotate the
image), **Send as E-mail** (E-mail as an attachment), or **Send as MMS** (multimedia
message = imbed image as part of e-mail message).

To save it as a caller ID picture in contacts, select **Set as Caller ID** from the menu and then begin to type the contact name. Navigate to the correct contact and save as prompted.

Searching for Messages (E-mail, SMS, MMS)

Some common scenarios when you might want to search your messages inbox are the following:

- You are trying to find that funny e-mail message from "Susan" you received a few days ago to forward to a friend. Type **Susan** next to the **Name** field.

- You want to find all invoice related e-mails. Type **invoice** next to the **Message** field.

- You need to quickly find that e-mail about your trip to San Francisco. Type **San Francisco** in the **Message** field.

You might find that you use your messaging so often, since it is so easy and fun, that your messages start to really collect on your BlackBerry.

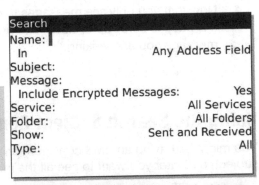

> **TIP:** Need to search other places like your **Contacts**, **Calendar**, **Task**, or other icons? Use the **Search** icon shown on page 521.

Sometimes, you need to find a message quickly, rather than scroll through all the messages in your inbox. There are three primary ways to search through your messages: searching the entire message through any field, searching the sender, and searching the subject.

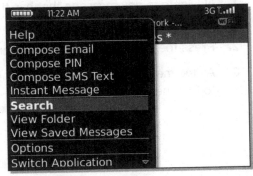

Using the Search Sender or Search Recipient Command

> **TIP:** The Search, Search Sender, Search Recipient, and Search Subject commands work on SMS messages, E-mail, MMS—anything in your messages inbox!

Sometimes, you have many messages from one particular sender, and you want to see only the list of your communication with that particular individual.

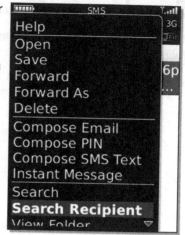

1. From the messages list, scroll to any message from or to the person you wish to search and press the **Menu** key.

2. Select **Search Recipient** or **Search Sender**.

3. Only the list of messages sent by or sent to that particular person (in this case, Martin) is now displayed.

4. Now that you only see messages to or from Martin, it is easy to scroll up or down and quickly find the message you are seeking.

Using the Search Subject Command

You might be having an SMS conversation with several people about a particular subject, and later you want to see all the messages about that subject on your device.

1. Navigate to any message that has the subject displayed that you are searching for.

2. Press the **Menu** key and select **Search Subject**.

3. All the messages with the same subject are now displayed. It is easy to navigate to the one you wish to read.

Chapter 13

Advanced E-mail Topics

Given the E-mail power of the BlackBerry, there might be some things that you would want to do right from your handheld that before were done only from your computer. You can write e-mail messages in other languages, select any one of your integrated e-mail accounts to send from, and easily create and select various e-mail signatures and auto-signatures.

Switching Input Language for E-mail and More

Let's say you have a client in Latin America and you wish to compose your e-mail messages in Spanish. Because of the spell checking feature and special characters and accents, you will want to change your typing or input language selection to the one in which you are composing the e-mail message.

NOTE: Don't see the **Switch Input Language** option or it does not do anything when you select it?

During the setup wizard process, the BlackBerry will remove unused input languages based on your selections.

If you removed all languages except your display language, then the **Switch Input Language** menu item won't be visible or it will not do anything when you select it.

If you are a Windows PC user, you can use the application loader inside Desktop Manager to add back languages you have previously removed (see page 90). If you are a Mac user, please contact your service provider and ask them how to put languages back on your BlackBerry.

1. Start composing a new e-mail message.

2. Press the **Menu** key and select **Switch Input Language**.

3. Scroll down to the input language you want, e.g., **Español**, and click.

4. When you begin typing, you will now have the Spanish language dictionary loaded and you can type your e-mail message in the new language.

Messages Inbox Housecleaning (Delete Prior)

It is possible for your messages mailbox to get a little unwieldy. Just follow these suggestions to manage and clean your mailbox.

Cleaning Out Old Messages

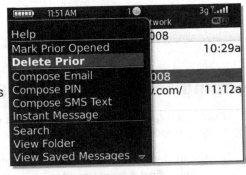

1. Start your **Messages** icon and press the **Menu** key.

2. Highlight the date row separator (e.g., "**Mon, Aug. 11, 2008**") under the most recent message you desire to keep, press the **Menu** key, and select **Delete Prior**.

3. All older messages will then be deleted

4. To delete an individual message, just click the message, press the **Menu** key, and choose **Delete**.

NOTE: If you have turned on call logs in your messages inbox, then Delete Prior will also delete all your call logs.

Sending from a Different E-mail Account (Send Using)

Like many of us, you might have a separate e-mail account for business and for personal matters, or several just for work. You can easily change which e-mail account you use to send e-mail messages on your BlackBerry.

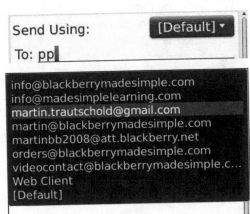

Start composing an e-mail. Scroll to the **Send Using** field.

The default is chosen, but you can highlight the word Default and click, and all your available e-mail accounts will show up in the window.

Just click the e-mail account you wish to use to send this particular e-mail message.

Send Using:	martin.trautschold@gmail...
To:	
Cc:	
Subject:	

Setting Your Default "Sent From" E-mail Address

You can change your default **Sent From** e-mail address on your BlackBerry. To get this done, you need to do the following:

1. Go into your **Options** icon. Options may be located within the **Setup** folder if you cannot find it from your Home screen of icons.

2. Click **Advanced Options**.

3. Click **Default Services** (or if you don't see this item, then click **Message Services**).

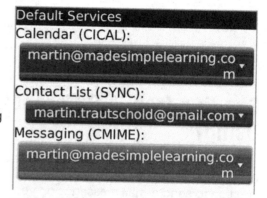

4. Then you will see a screen that shows you **Messaging (CMIME)** or something similar.

5. Click the item to see a list of all your integrated e-mail accounts.

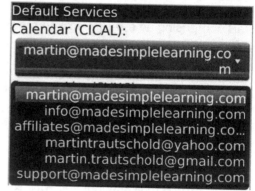

6. Select your new default e-mail account for sending new messages you compose on your BlackBerry.

7. Finally, press the **Menu** key and select **Save**.

Now compose a new e-mail message—notice that your new default e-mail account is used at the top in the **Send Using** field.

Changing the Way Your E-mail Looks and Functions

You can change many of the more advanced options for e-mail by doing the following:

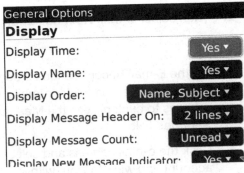

1. Navigate to your **Messages** icon and click.

2. Press the **Menu** key, scroll down to **Options**, and click.

3. Click **General Options**.

Probably the best way to see more messages on your list is to set the **Display Message Header On** field to **1 line**.

1 line

For **Display Message Header On** field

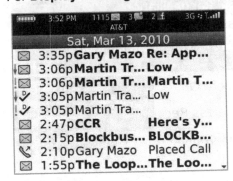

2 lines

For **Display Message Header On** field

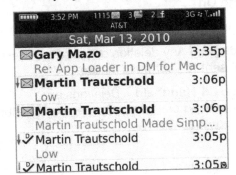

You can choose whether to display the time, name, message header, and new message indicator, confirm the deletion of messages, hide files and sent messages, and change the level of PIN messages. (Learn more about PIN messages on page 349.)

Click the desired change. When done, press the **Menu** key to save your changes, and they will now be reflected in your e-mail screen.

E-mail Reconciliation (Deletes and Sometimes Your E-mail Opens)

Depending on the type of e-mail accounts you have set up and your messaging services, you may be able to wirelessly share your actions (Deletion and maybe even Open actions) between your main e-mail inbox and your BlackBerry.

1. Open your **Messages** icon, press the **Menu** key, and select **Options**.

2. Then select **E-mail Reconciliation**.

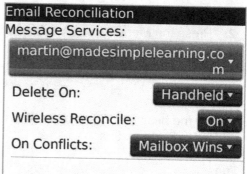

3. On the E-mail Reconciliation screen, you can select a particular e-mail address to customize in the **Message Services** field.

4. Click the e-mail address and select the account you want to work with.

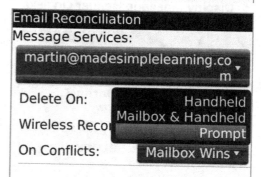

Delete On

Prompt = This option asks you each time.

Handheld = Any deletion on your BlackBerry is not sent to your main mailbox.

Mailbox & Handheld = Deletions are synchronized or shared between your mailbox and your BlackBerry.

Wireless Reconcile

On = Yes, share deletions and other information between your BlackBerry and main mailbox.

Off = No, don't share information.

On Conflicts

Lastly, you can choose whether your server or your handheld wins if there is a reconciliation conflict. default The setting is **Mailbox Wins**, which means that your main e-mail box changes win over changes from your BlackBerry.

TIP: If you want to be able to delete e-mail messages from your BlackBerry and not have it also delete from your main e-mail inbox, then set the **Wireless Reconcile** field to **Off**.

IMPORTANT: If you choose **Mailbox and Handheld** and set **Wireless Reconcile** to **On**, then whenever you delete e-mail messages from your BlackBerry, they will also be deleted from your regular e-mail inbox and vice-versa.

Easily Adding Signatures to Your E-mails

There are various ways to setup e-mail signatures for messages you compose and send from your BlackBerry. Probably the easiest one is to use is the one right in your e-mail setup program on your BlackBerry. You can also set up signatures from your carrier's BlackBerry Internet Service web site. You can also create customized AutoText signatures that you can adjust on-the-go to select a specific signature whenever you need it.

Setup Custom AutoText Signatures You Can Choose While Composing the Message

TIP: This AutoText option works for both Personal/Internet E-Mail users and Corporate (BlackBerry Enterprise Server) users.

If you want to be able to select different signatures as you are writing your messages, then you will need to use the **AutoText** feature.

1. Locate and click on the **Options** icon. It may be inside the **Applications** or **Setup** folder on your BlackBerry. It usually looks like a wrench

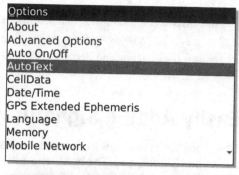

2. Select **AutoText** near the top of the list and click.

3. Press the **Menu** key and select **New**.

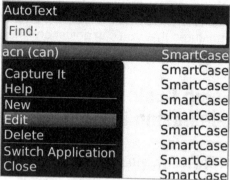

4. In the **Replace** field type any combination of letters – we would recommend putting your initials. If you plan to have several different signatures, possibly one for work and one for personal use, then you might want to use a number or extra letter after your initials like "(initials)w" (for work) and "(initials)p" for personal.

5. In the **With** field, type in your full e-mail signature exactly as you would like it to appear in your e-mails.

6. Choose **SmartCase** if you want the BlackBerry to capitalize the letters according to the correct context in the sentence when they are replaced. Select Specify Case to replace these letters with the capitalization exactly as you have entered them in the AutoText entry. For example, if you entered "DeSoto" with Specified Case then it would always replace the words as "DeSoto" never "Desoto".

7. In this example we can put in Gary's full name, title and E-mail just by setting up an AutoText for "gam."

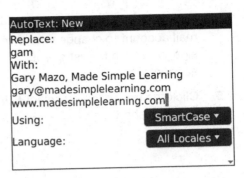

AutoText: New
Replace:
gam
With:
Gary Mazo, Made Simple Learning
gary@madesimplelearning.com
www.madesimplelearning.com
Using: SmartCase ▾
Language: All Locales ▾

8. Then, in language, select **All Locales** for this AutoText entry (signature) to work in every language or specify only one language for this to work. This setting would be useful if you had different signatures for different languages.

9. Press the Menu when you are done and select **Save**.

10. Now, each time you type in your initials and press the **Space** key, your complete signature will appear instantly.

Personal or Internet Service E-mail Users

If you have integrated personal or internet e-mail (POP3 and IMAP 4 Accounts) to your BlackBerry, you have a few options for e-mail signatures.

Setting up Signatures from your BlackBerry Carrier's Web site

This option is described in detail on page 60. Using this feature, you have the ability to add a unique **Auto Signature** to each of your integrated e-mail accounts.

Setting up E-mail Signatures Using E-mail Setup on Your BlackBerry

If you use BlackBerry Internet E-mail (POP3 and IMAP 4 Accounts) there are a couple of ways to set up your e-mail signature right from your BlackBerry.

Option #1: Setting up from the BlackBerry E-mail settings

1. Go to your **Setup** folder.

2. Click on the **Personal E-mail Setup** icon. (It may be called E-mail settings).

3. Login, if requested.

4. Roll up or down to highlight the e-mail account to change your e-mail signature from the list of your accounts.

5. Click the trackpad and select **Edit** from the short menu.

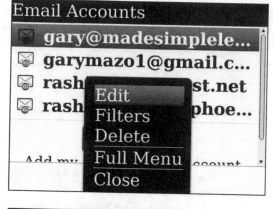

6. Scroll down to **Signature** and type your new e-mail signature.

7. When you are done, select **Save**.

8. Press the **Escape** key to exit e-mail settings.

Corporate or BlackBerry Enterprise Server E-Mail Users

If you are a corporate or BlackBerry Enterprise Server user, then you can setup your Signature right in your Messages app.

1. From your **Messages** list, press the **Menu** key.

2. Select **Options.**

3. Then click on **E-mail Settings**

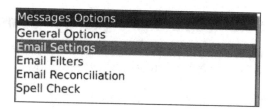

4. Scroll down to **Use Auto Signature** field and change **No** to **Yes**.

5. Scroll down and type your e-mail signature in the field.

6. Press the **Menu** key and save your new Auto Signature.

Email Settings	
Send Email To Handheld:	Yes
Save Copy In Sent Folder:	Yes
Use Auto Signature:	Yes
▶ Martin Trautschold	
Made Simple Learning	
www.madesimplelearning.com	
386-506-8224	
Use Out Of Office Reply:	No

NOTE: Please see page 22 to learn how to turn on and use the **Spell Checking Your E-mail Messages** feature.

Filtering Your Messages for SMS, Calls, and More

Sometimes, your messages can really start to add up on your BlackBerry, and it can get quite overwhelming. Fortunately, it is easy to set up filters to show you only the messages you want to see at a particular moment.

TIP: The shortcuts to filter your messages inbox are the following:

Alt + S = Show only SMS text messages

Alt + L = Show only MMS multimedia messages

Alt + I = Show only incoming messages and phone calls

Alt + O = Show only outgoing messages and phone calls

Alt + P = Show only phone calls

Alt + V = Show only voice mail messages

Press the **Escape** key to "un-filter" and see your entire inbox again.

Just like on your computer, using e-mail folders can help you be more organized and productive. Also, if you have saved many messages and are not sure which are e-mail inbox messages and which are SMS inbox messages, using the folder commands can help.

1. Start your **Messages** app.

2. Press the **Menu** key.

3. Scroll down to **View** Folder and click. You will now see a listing of all the message folders on your device.

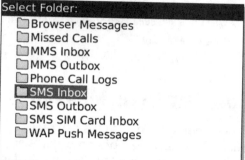

4. Choose **SMS inbox** and you will now see only the SMS messages in your inbox and none of the other messages.

5. You can also use these folders to see your missed calls, MMS messages, WAP Push messages and your Browser Messages.

Filing a Message in a Folder

Make sure that (in the previous E-mail Reconciliation section) wireless synchronization is turned on. This is necessary in order to file messages.

1. Click the **Messages** icon from your Home screen.

2. Highlight the message you wish to file.

3. Press the **Menu** key and select **File**.

4. Then choose the folder in which you wish to store the message.

Changing Folder Names or Adding Folders

In order to do this, you must be using your BlackBerry together with a BlackBerry Enterprise Server with wireless synchronization. If you are unsure whether you are using wireless sync, most likely you are not using it.

On your desktop (or notebook) computer that you use to sync your BlackBerry, simply change or add a folder to the e-mail client you use to sync the BlackBerry.

Changes you make on the desktop or notebook will be reflected in the folders available on the BlackBerry.

E-mail Message Filters (Only for BlackBerry Enterprise Server users)

While receiving your e-mail messages on your BlackBerry is a wonderful thing, there might be some e-mail messages that, for whatever reason, you don't want sent to your BlackBerry. Fortunately, you can use an e-mail filter to see just which messages you want sent to your BlackBerry and which ones stay on the server.

Create E-mail Filter

1. Click your **Messages** icon. (Or press **M** if you have enabled Home screen hotkeys.)

2. Press the **Menu** key.

3. Scroll down to **Options** and click.

4. Click **E-mail Filters**, press the **Menu** key, and click **New**.

5. Press the **Menu** key and choose **Save**.

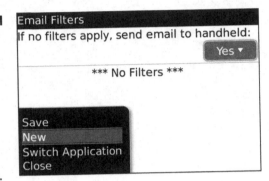

Use E-mail Filters

1. Click your **Messages** icon.

2. Press the **Menu** key and select **E-mail Filters**.

3. Just use the trackpad and click the radio button next to the filter you wish you use.

Chapter 14

Your Contact List

Your BlackBerry excels as a contact manager. You will turn to your **Contacts** app, perhaps more than any other app on the device. From a contact, you can e-mail, sent a text message, call, fax or even "poke" someone if you have the **Facebook** app installed.

One rule of thumb you will hear us say often is to add anything and everything to your contacts. Whenever someone calls, add them to your contacts. Add contacts from e-mails and messages—you will always go back to them.

The Heart of Your BlackBerry

Your **Address Book** program is really the heart of your BlackBerry. Once you have your names and addresses in it, you can instantly call; e-mail; and send text (SMS) messages, PIN-to-PIN BlackBerry messages, and even pictures or Multi-Media Messages (MMS). Since your BlackBerry came with a camera, you may even add pictures of anyone in your **Address Book**; if you do so, a contact's picture shows up as a **Picture Caller ID** when the contact calls.

Picture Caller ID
"Gary with the warm blue glow"

Transferring Contacts off the SIM Card

If you are using your SIM (Subscriber Identity Module) card from another phone in your BlackBerry, and you have stored names and phone numbers on that SIM card, it's easy to transfer your contacts into your **Contact** list.

Follow these steps to transfer contacts on a SIM card into your **Contact** list:

1. Click on your **Contacts** icon.

2. Press the **Menu** key, scroll to **SIM Phone book**, and click.

3. Next, press the **Menu** key and scroll to **Copy All To Contacts**.

4. Now you will see a screen that says **Contacts Imported** or **No Contacts are saved on your SIM Card**.

After this process is complete you should see the entire name and phone number list from your SIM card in your **Contacts** list.

> **TIP:** Your SIM Card only contains the bare minimum **Name** and **Phone** information. Sometimes a SIM card stores names in all caps, so be aware you might need to do some additional cleanup after the import. You should also review your imported contacts and add in e-mail addresses, mobile/work phone numbers, and home/work addresses to make your BlackBerry more useful.

Getting Contacts onto the BlackBerry

You can manually add contact addresses one-at-a-time (see page 278). You can also mass load or sync up your computer's contacts with your BlackBerry.

If your BlackBerry is tied to a BlackBerry Enterprise Server, the synchronization is wireless and automatic. Otherwise, you will use either a USB cable or Bluetooth wireless to connect your BlackBerry to your computer to keep it up-to-date. If you use a Windows PC, see page 67; if you use an Apple Mac, see page 125.

 If you use Gmail (Google Mail), you can use the BlackBerry Internet Service e-mail set up for Google to wirelessly sync contacts (see page 47) or use the **Google Sync** program to wirelessly update your contacts on your BlackBerry with your address book from Gmail, see page 311.

Making Your Contact List Useful

Your **Contacts** program is most useful when two things are true:

- You have many names and addresses in it.
- You can easily find what you need.

Trying Our Recommendations

We recommend keeping two rules in mind to help make your Contacts most useful.

Rule 1: Add anything and everything to your Contacts.

You never know when you might need that obscure restaurant name/number, or that plumber's number, etc.

Rule 2: As you add entries, make sure you think about ways to easily find them in the future.

We have many tips and tricks in this chapter to help you enter names so that they can be instantly located when you need them.

TIP: Whenever you enter a restaurant into your **Contact** list, make sure to put the word *restaurant* into the **Company Name** or **Nickname** field, even if it's not part of the name. If you type the letters *rest*, then you should instantly find all your restaurants!

What Fields are searched to find Contacts

At the top of the Contacts list, you will see a **Find:** field. As long as you know which fields in your contact entries are searched, you can easily find all your contacts. Just keep these fields in mind when you enter new information into your address book.

The following fields are used when you type in letters to search for contacts.

- First name
- Last name
- Nickname
- Company name

Add New Addresses Easily

On your BlackBerry, your **Address Book** program is closely tied to all the other applications (e.g., **Messages/E-mail**, **Phone**, and **Web Browser**), so you have many methods to easily add new addresses:

- **Choice 1:** Add a new address inside the **Contacts** app.

- **Choice 2:** Add an address from an e-mail message in **Messages** app.

- **Choice 3:** Add an address from a phone call log in the **Phone** app.

- **Choice 4:** Add a new address from an underlined e-mail address or a phone number from any source (e.g. the **Web Browser**, **E-mail**, **Tasks**, or **MemoPad** apps).

In the next few sections, we will walk you through how to take advantage of all these choices.

Choice 1: Adding an Address into Contacts

1. Use the trackpad and navigate and click on the **Contacts** icon.

2. Press the **Menu** key and select **New Contact** or just glide to the top and click on **Add Contact** at the top of the Contact List.

OR

3. Add as much information as you know because the more you add, the more useful your BlackBerry will be.

4. Below we show you more details about how to add information to your contact entries.

TIP: Press the **Space** key instead of typing the @ and "." in the e-mail address.

If you add a contact's work or home address, you can easily map it to get directions right on your BlackBerry.

Edit Contact
First: David
Last: Parker
Picture:

Company: Parker Construction Co.
Job Title: Engineer

Email: david@parkerconstruction.com
Work: 6175551234
Work 2: 1800REDSOX1

Entering More than One E-mail Address for a Contact

Sometimes you will want to enter more than one e-mail address for a contact. If so, just press the **Menu** key and select **Add E-mail Address** as you are adding or editing that contact.

New Contact

Help
Categories
Save
Add Email Addr...

Be sure to save your changes by pressing the **Menu** key and selecting **Save**.

Company: Parker Construction Co.
Job Title: Engineer

Email: david@parkerconstruction.com
Email: davidparker@gmail.com
Work: 6175551234
Work 2: 1800REDSOX1

Entering a Phone Number with Letters

Some phone numbers have letters, such as *1 800-REDSOX1*. These characters are easier than you might think to add to your BlackBerry **Address Book** (or type while on the phone). The trick is to

hold down your **Alt** key (the lower left key with up/down arrows on it), and then type the letters on your keyboard. You can also just press and hold a key to see a letter appear.

> **Edit Contact**
>
> Company: Parker Construction Co.
> Job Title: Engineer
>
> Email: david@parkerconstruction.com
> Email: davidparker@gmail.com
> Work: 617 555 1234
> Work 2: 1 800 RED SOX 1|
> Home:
> Home 2:

> **TIP:** Putting spaces in the phone number can make it easier to read; do so by hitting the **Space** key.

> Work: 617 555 1234
> Work 2: 1 800 RED SOX 1|

Entering a Phone Number with Pauses or Waits

Sometimes you need to dial a phone number that has several components, such as a dial-in number and a separate password. For example, a voice mail system for your home or office phone number might require such delays. Or, assume you have to dial an 800 number, wait four seconds, enter your own number, wait two seconds, and then enter your own password. You can do it all with pauses or waits. A *pause* is a two second pause, after which your BlackBerry continues dialing; a *wait* causes your BlackBerry to wait for you to manually click a button before it continues dialing.

> **New Contact**
>
> Title:
> First: Work
> Last: Voicemail
> Picture:
>
> Company:
> Job Title:
>
> Email:
> Work: 18005551234|

For example, you might need to enter the number **1-800-555-1234**, pause four seconds, enter the number **386-506-8224**, pause another two seconds, and then enter password **12345**. You'd do so by following these steps:

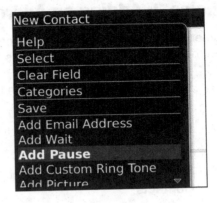

1. Type 1-800-555-1234.

2. Tap the **Menu** key, select **Add Pause**, and set a value of two seconds.

3. Tap the **Menu** key, select **Add Pause**, and set a value of two more seconds.

4. Input 386-506-8224.

5. Tap the **Menu** key, select **Add Pause**, and finally input your password, 12345.

When you're done, the screen should look similar to what you see on the right.

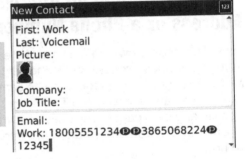

> **TIP:** Try adding several pauses in a row or using the **Add Wait** option if a single pause does not work.

Choice 2: Add an Address from an E-mail Message

Another easy way to update your **Address Book** is to simply add the contact information from e-mails that are sent to you. This process requires several steps:

1. Navigate to your message list and scroll to an e-mail message in your **Inbox**.

2. Click the e-mail message and press the **Menu** key.

3. Scroll to **Add to Contacts** and click it.

4. Add the information to the appropriate fields, then push the **Menu** key and click **Save**.

Choice 3: Adding an Address from a Phone Call Log

Sometimes you will remember that someone called you a while back, and you want to add their information to your **Address Book**. Follow these steps to accomplish that:

1. Press the **Green Phone** button to bring up your call logs.

2. Scroll to the number you want to add to your **Address Book**.

3. Press the **Menu** key and select **Add to Contacts**.

4. Add the address information, press the **Menu** key, and select **Save**.

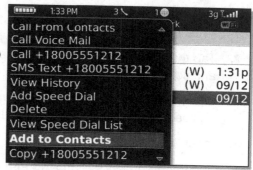

Choice 4: Adding an Address from an Underlined E-mail Address or a Phone Number from Anywhere

One of the most powerful features of the BlackBerry is that you can add your contacts from just about anywhere. While the next steps show you how to do this on the **MemoPad**, but you can follow these same steps to add contacts from **Tasks**, e-mails (e.g., e-mail addresses in the **To:**, **From:**, and **CC:** fields, as well as from the body of the e-mail), and web pages. Let's say you wrote down a contact's name and phone number in a memo, but you never added this information to your **Address Book**, but want to do so now:

1. Locate and click your **MemoPad** icon.

TIP: Press the hotkey **D** to instantly start it (see page 548).

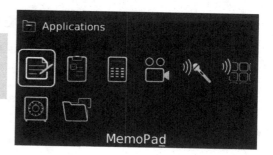

2. Locate the memo you wrote earlier with the phone number and open it.

3. Glide to the underlined phone number to highlight it, press the **Menu** key or click the Trackpad, and select **Add to Contacts**.

4. Input all the contact information for this person.

5. Finally, click the Trackpad and select **Save**.

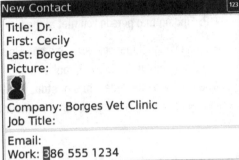

At this point, you are back in the **Memo** item. Now try highlighting the number and clicking the Trackpad. Notice that you now see a **Call (name)** option because you have added this person to your **Address Book**.

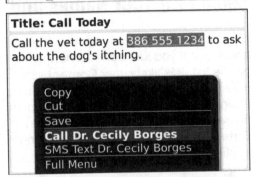

TIP: You can also call any underlined number. See Figure 14-1 showing an underlined phone number in an e-mail message. You will typically see phone numbers in e-mail signatures.

Figure 14-1. *Placing a call from a phone number in an e-mail*

TIP: Finding that person you met at the bus stop

Assume you just met someone at a bus stop and want to find that person. Enter the person's first and last name (if you know it), but also enter the words **bus stop** in the **Company** name field. When you type the letters **bus** or **stop**, you should now find everyone you've ever met at the bus stop instantly, even if you cannot remember the person's name!

Seeing All Your Names and Addresses

If you are not seeing any names, seeing only a few names, or if you just added a new name but do not see it on the list, it is likely your **Contact** list is **filtered**. This means it is showing you only those names that are assigned to a particular **Category**. The tip-off that it's filtered is the black bar (or other color) at the top with the **Category** name. In the image to the right, the **Category** applied for the filter is **Business**.

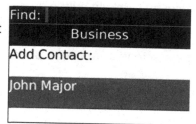

You can learn how to see your entire **Contact** list again on page 292 or learn more about **Categories** on page 290.

Finding Names and Addresses Easily

Once you get the hand of adding contact information into the **Contacts** app, you will begin to see how useful it is to have all that information at your fingertips. The tricky part can be actually locating all the information you have input into the BlackBerry. Fortunately, your BlackBerry gives you three basic ways of finding this information, which we'll cover next.

Option 1: Using the Find Feature in Contacts

The **Contacts** app has a great **Find:** feature at the top of the app that will search for entries that match the letters you type in one of these fields:

- **First**
- **Last**
- **Nickname**
- **Company**

Follow these steps to find information in your **Contacts** app:

1. Inside the **Contacts** app, type a few letters of a person's first name, last name, and/or company name (separated by spaces) to instantly find that person. In this example, assume you want to find someone whose first, last name, or company has an *M* in it.

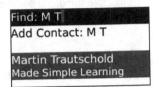

2. Press the letter **M** to see only entries where the **first name**, **last name**, or **company name** start with the pressed letter; doing so might bring up the following names:

   - **Martin Trautschold**: This match is on the contact's first name.

   - **Gary Mazo**: This match is on the contact's last name.

   - **Cathy Carollo**: This match is on the contact's company name, "Made Simple Learning."

3. Now press the **Space** key and type another, such as **T** to narrow the list to people with an *M* and a *T* as the starting letters in the first, last, or company names. In this case, **Martin Trautschold** is the only match.

Option 2: Using the Find feature in the Phone

You can also locate people in your **Contact** list when you are dialing the phone:

1. Tap the **Green Phone** key to start the **Phone** app.

2. Now type a few letters of someone's first name, last name, or company name.

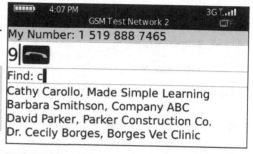

> **TIP:** If no matching entries can be found, you just see the digits being dialed.

3. Press the **Space** key and type a few more letters to narrow the list.

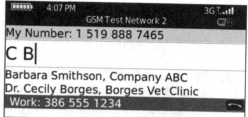

4. Now scroll down to the correct entry and phone number (e.g., work, home, or mobile number).

5. Press the **Green Phone** key to start the call.

6. Or, if you decide you want to e-mail or SMS this person instead, highlight their name and press the **Menu** key to select **E-mail** or **SMS**. You will only see these Menu options if there is an e-mail address and phone number for this contact.

Managing Your Contacts

Sometimes, your contact information can get a little unwieldy. Multiple entries for the same individual, business contacts mixed in with personal ones, and so on. There are some very powerful tools within the **Contacts** application that can easily help you get organized.

> **TIP:** Finding Your Neighbors
>
> If you just moved into a new neighborhood, it can be quite daunting to remember the names of everyone you've just met. One tip is to add the word **neighbor** into the **Nickname** name field for every neighbor you meet. Now you can instantly call up all neighbors you've ever met by inputting the letters **neigh**.

Adding More Information to Your Contact Entries

One of the first things to do is to make sure that all the information included in your contacts is correct. Follow these steps to do so:

1. Select the **Contacts** app and click it or press the **C** hotkey (see page 548 for hotkeys).

2. Type in a few letters of the first, last, or company name for a contact into the **Find:** field. Or, you can just scroll through the list until you find the desired contact.

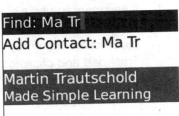

3. Highlight the contact you want to manage with the Trackpad.

4. Press the **Menu** key and choose **Edit** to access the detailed contact screen, and then add any information missing in the fields.

Adding a Picture to the Contact for Caller ID

Sometimes it is nice to attach a face with a name. If you have loaded pictures onto your media card or have them stored in memory, you can add them to the appropriate contact in your **Contact** list. Since you have a BlackBerry with a camera, you can simply take the picture and add it with the **Picture Caller ID** option right from your camera. Follow these steps to do so:

1. Select the contact to edit with the Trackpad as you did previously.

2. Scroll down to the **Picture** option or click the **Picture** icon and click the Trackpad.

3. Choose either the **Add Picture** or **Replace Picture** option.

You have the choice of finding a picture already stored on your BlackBerry or taking a new one with the camera. Follow these steps to add a picture to a contact:

1. If you want to use a stored picture, then navigate to the folder in which your pictures are stored by rolling the Trackpad and clicking the correct folder.

2. Once you have located the correct picture, click the Trackpad on the picture, and you will be prompted to **Crop and Save** the picture.

Alternatively, you can follow these steps to use the BlackBerry's camera to take a picture right now:

1. Click the camera and take the picture.

2. Move the box to center the face, click the Trackpad, and select **Crop and Save**.

The picture will now appear in several places:

- On the screen when you speak with that person on the phone

- In their contact entry.

- It will also appear next to their e-mail address.

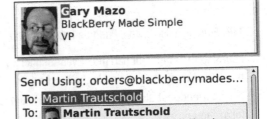

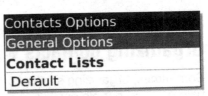

TIP: On any menu, you can jump down to an entry by pressing the key with the first letter. For example, you can press the **O** key to jump down to **Options**.

Changing the Way Contacts Are Sorted

You can sort your contacts by first name, last name, or company name by following these steps:

1. Click your **Contacts** icon – but don't click any particular contact.

2. Press the **Menu** key and select **Options**.

3. Click **General Options**.

4. In the **Sort By:** field, click the Trackpad and choose the way you want your contacts to be sorted. You may also select whether to allow duplicate names and whether to confirm the deletion of contacts from this menu.

TIP: First Letter Trick for Menus/Lists

On any drop down **Sort By:** list, such as *First Name, Last Name, Company*, pressing the first letter of the entry will jump you there. For example, you can press the letter **L** will jump to the **Last Name** entry in the aforementioned list.

TIP: Finding Your Child's Friend's Parents Names

Learning the names of parents of your school age children can be fairly challenging. However, this trick can make it easier. In the **First name** field, you should add in not just the name of your child's friend, but also that child's parents' names, as well. For example, you might make the following entry:

First Name: Samantha (Mom: Susan Dad: Ron)

Add the text *school friend* to the **Nickname** field, as well:

Nickname: Cece school friend

Now, just typing your child's name in your **Contact** list's **Find:** field will instantly find every person you've ever met at your child's school, enabling you to say, "Hello Susan, great to see you again!" without missing a beat. Try to conceal your BlackBerry when you are doing your name search.

Organizing Contacts with Categories

Sometimes, organizing similar contacts into **Categories** can be a very useful way to help you find people quickly. Even better, the **Categories** you add, change, or edit on your BlackBerry are kept fully in sync with those on your computer. Follow these steps to associate a contact with a **Category**:

1. Find the contact you want to assign to a **Category**.

2. Click the Trackpad to view the contact, then click it again and select **Edit** from the short Menu.

3. Click the **Menu** key and select **Categories**. Now you will see a list of available categories. (The default **Categories** are **Business** and **Personal**.)

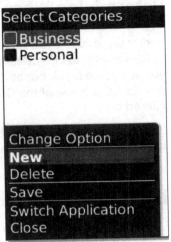

4. If you need an additional **Category**, press the **Menu** key, choose **New**, and type in the name of the new **Category**. This **Category** will now be available for all your contacts.

5. Scroll to the **Category** you wish to add this contact to and click it.

TIP: You can create and assign contacts as many **Categories** as you want!

Filtering Your Contacts by Category

Now that you have your contacts assigned to **Categories**, you can filter the names on the screen by their respective **Categories**. So, let's say that you want to quickly find everyone you have assigned to the **Business** category. You can do so by following these steps:

1. Click your **Contacts** app.

2. Press the **Menu** key, scroll up, and select **Filter**.

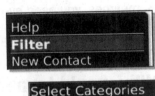

3. You now see the available **Categories** listed. At this point, you can click the Trackpad (or press the **Space** key) on the **Category** you wish to use as your filter. Once you do this, only the contacts in the **Category** you selected are available to scroll through.

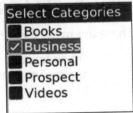

Determining When Your Contact List Is Filtered

Earlier we showed you how to filter. Now you'll see how to filter contacts into certain categories. If a list is filtered, you will see a black bar at the top of your **Contact** list that lists the name of the **Category** the contact is being filtered by.

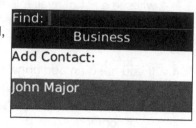

In this image to the right, the contact list is being filtered to show only contacts in the **Business** category.

Unfiltering Your Contacts by Category

Unlike when toggling off the **Find:** feature, you cannot just press the **Escape** key to toggle off filtering your **Categories**; instead, you need to reverse the **Filter** procedure. Do so by following this pair of steps:

1. Inside your **Contacts** app, press the **Menu** key.

2. Select the **Filter** option, glide down to the checked **Category**, and uncheck it by clicking it or pressing the **Space** key when it is highlighted.

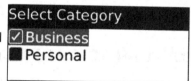

Use Groups as Mailing Lists

Sometimes, you need even more organizing power from your BlackBerry. Depending on your needs, grouping contacts into mailing lists might be useful, so you can send mass mailings from your BlackBerry.

Why would I want to use a mailing list?

There are many reasons to create mailing lists including:

- If you have your team members on mailing list, you can instantly notify them of project updates.

- Let's say you're about to have a baby. Put everyone in the notify list into a **New Baby** group. Then you can snap a picture with your BlackBerry and instantly send it from the hospital!

Creating and Using a Group Mailing List

You can create and use a group mailing list by following these steps:

1. Scroll to the **Address Book** and click the Trackpad.

2. Press the **Menu** key, scroll to **New Group**, and click it.

3. Type in a name for your new group.

4. Press the **Menu** key again, scroll to **Add Member**, and click it.

TIP: Make sure each member you add to a group has a valid e-mail address; otherwise, you will not be able to send that person e-mail from your group.

5. Scroll to the contact you want to add to that group and click it. That contact's name is now listed under the name of the group you just added.

6. Continue to add contacts to that group or make new groups and fill them using the steps just described.

TIP: You can add either a mobile phone number (for SMS groups) or an e-mail address for **E-mail** groups – we recommend keeping the two types of groups separate. In other words, you should have an SMS-only group and an e-mail-only group. Otherwise, if you mix and match, you will always receive a warning message that some group members cannot receive the message.

Sending an E-mail to the Group

Sending an e-mail to your group is straightforward. Just use the group name as you would any other name in your **Address Book**. If your group name is **My Team**, then you can compose an e-mail and address it to **My Team**. Notice that you see a separate **To:** for each person you have added to the group after you send the message.

Editing or Deleting SIM Card Contacts

It's also easy to edit or delete contacts from your SIM card. Simply follow these steps:

1. Click the **Address Book**, scroll to your SIM card's **Phone Book** app, and click it.

2. Scroll to the contact you wish to edit or delete, and press the **Menu** key.

3. Choose the desired action from the menu.

Storing SMS Messages on the SIM Card

Sometimes you want to make sure you save a message. SMS messages are sometimes purged after a certain period of time or deleted accidentally; you can preserve them by storing them on your SIM card. Follow these steps to preserve them on the SIM card:

1. From your **Home** screen, locate and click the **Options** icon.

2. Press the **S** key a few times or glide the Trackpad down to the **SMS Text** line and click it.

3. The second option is to leave your SMS messages on the SIM card. The default setting is **No**, but if you click this option, you can change the setting to **Yes**.

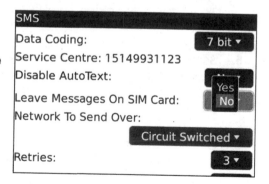

Securing Your SIM Card

See page 531 to learn how to secure or protect your SIM card in case it gets stolen.

Chapter 15

Managing Your Calendar

The BlackBerry **Calendar** app is both intuitive and powerful. In this chapter, we will show you how to add events, schedule individual and recurring appointments, accept meeting invitations, search, as well as utilize all the other features of your **Calendar** app.

Organizing Your Life with Your Calendar

For many of us, our calendar is our lifeline. Where do I need to be? With whom am I meeting? When do the kids need to be picked up? When is Martin's birthday? The calendar can tell us all these things and more.

The **Calendar** app on the BlackBerry is simple to use, but it also contains some very sophisticated options for the power user.

Sync Your Computer Calendar with Your BlackBerry

You can also mass load or sync your computer's calendar with your BlackBerry **Calendar** app.

If your BlackBerry is tied to a BlackBerry Enterprise Server, the synchronization is wireless and automatic. Otherwise, you will use either a USB cable or Bluetooth wireless to connect your BlackBerry to your computer to keep it up to date. If you use a Windows PC, see page 67; if you use an Apple Mac computer, see page 125.

If you use **Google Calendar**, you can receive wireless and automatic updates to your BlackBerry **Calendar** app using Google Sync. Learn how on page 311.

Adding Calendar Shortcut Keys and Hotkeys

We have put many of the hotkeys and shortcuts in the beginning of the book both for easy access and to keep them all together. Please go to page 169 to see the complete list of the **Calendar** app's hotkeys.

Switching Views and Days in the Calendar

The calendar is where you look to see how your life will unfold over the next few hours, days, or weeks (see Figures 15-1 and 15-2). It is quite easy to change the view if you need to see more or less time in the Calendar screen.

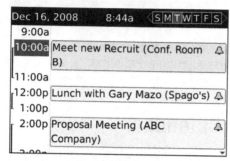

Day View   **Week View**

Figure 15-1. *Day and week view in the Calendar app*

Month View   **Agenda View**

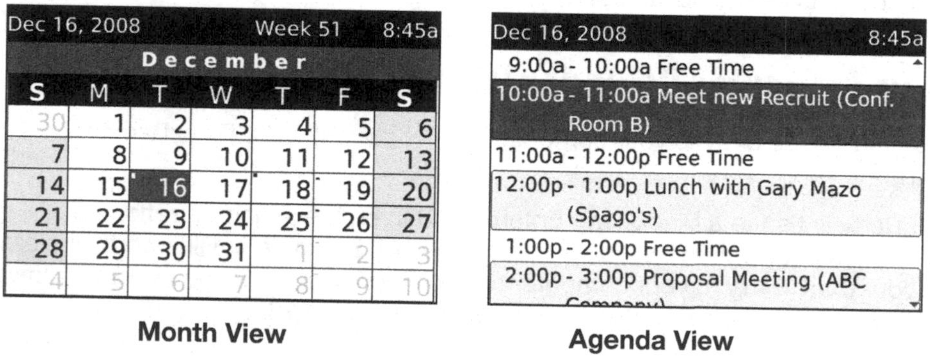

Figure 15-2. *Month and agenda view in the Calendar app*

Option #1: Using the Trackpad (Fastest way)

Follow these steps to change day you're viewing in the **Calendar** app with the Trackpad:

1. Navigate to your **Calendar** icon and click it. The default view is the **Day** view, which lists all appointments for the current calendar day.

2. Move the Trackpad left or right to a previous day or an upcoming day. Notice that the date changes in the upper left-hand corner.

Option #2: Using the Menu key

Follow these steps to change the day you're viewing in the **Calendar** app with the **Menu** key:

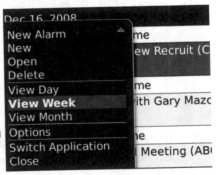

1. Click the **Calendar** icon, as you did above.

2. Press the **Menu** key and select **Go to Date...** from the list of options shown.

3. After you click **Go to Date...** you can input the date you wish to view.

Changing to Week, Month, or Agenda View

Follow these steps to change the type of view you see in the **Calendar** app:

1. Inside the **Calendar** app, press the **Menu** key and select **View Week**, **View Month**, or **View Agenda**.

2. Use the Trackpad to navigate left and right to view past or future weeks or months.

3. Glide the Trackpad up and down to move an hour at a time in **Week** view, a week at a time in **Month** view, or up/down to move through your scheduled appointments or free time in **Agenda** view. The current view you have selected will not appear in the menu. As the image to the right shows – **Agenda View** is missing because you are already in Agenda View.

Scheduling Appointments

Putting your busy life into your BlackBerry is quite easy. Once you start to schedule your appointments or meetings, you will begin to expect reminder alarms to tell you where to go and when to go there. Soon you will wonder how you lived without your BlackBerry for so long!

Using Quick Scheduling

1. It is amazingly simple to add basic appointments (or reminders) to your calendar.

2. In **Day View**, glide the trackpad to the correct day and time, press the **Enter** key, and start typing your appointment right in **Day View**.

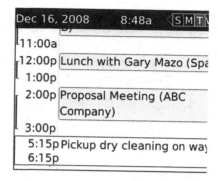

3. If you need to change the **start time**, press the **ALT** key (up/down arrow in lower left corner) while rolling the trackpad up/down.

4. To change the **ending time**, just glide the trackpad by itself. When you're done, click the trackpad or press the **Enter** key.

It is amazingly simple to add basic appointments (or reminders) to your calendar.

1. In **Day View**, glide the trackpad to the correct day and time, press the Enter key, and start typing your appointment right in **Day View**.

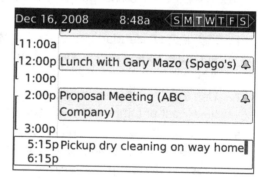

2. If you need to change the **start time**, press the **ALT** key (up/down arrow in lower left corner) while rolling the trackpad up/down.

3. To change the **ending time**, just glide the trackpad by itself. When you're done, click the trackpad or press the **Enter** key.

> **TIP: Quick Scheduling** is so fast that you can even use your **Calendar** app for reminders such as "Pick up the dry cleaning," "Pick up Chinese food," or "Pick up dog food."

Using Detailed Scheduling

1. Click on the **Calendar** icon.

2. If you are in **Day View** you can simply click the trackpad on an hour closest to when your appointment starts.

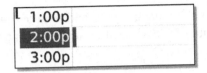

3. Or, in any view or press the **Menu** key and select **New** to get into the **New Appointment** Screen.

4. Type the **Subject** and optional **Location**. The **Location** will appear in parentheses in your calendar day view, for example this event would appear as: **Staff Meeting (Conf. Rm. A-103)**.

5. Click **All Day Event** if it will last all day, like an all day conference.

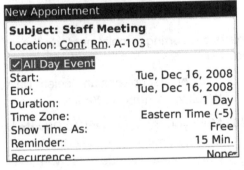

6. Click on the field you need to change (if any) and put in the correct information. Scroll down to where it reads **Start** and use the trackpad to highlight the date, year, or time.

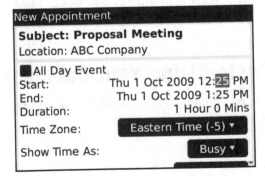

> **TIP:** Use your **number keys (1, 2, 3...)** to enter specific dates, years, and times. For example, type in "45" to change the minutes to 45. See the Quick Reference pages for how to quickly set dates and times (starting on page 169).

7. You can skip changing the end time of the appointment, and instead just change the length of the appointment by scrolling to **Duration** and putting in the correct amount of time.

8. Set a reminder alarm by clicking on **Reminder** and setting the reminder time for the alarm from five minutes prior to nine hours prior.

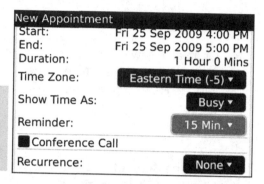

> **TIP:** The default reminder time is usually 15 minutes, but you can change this by going into your Calendar Options screen (see page 302).

If this is a recurring appointment, do the following:

9. Click on Recurrence and select Daily, Weekly, Monthly, or Yearly.

10. Mark your appointment as **Private** by clicking on the checkbox. If you would like to include notes with the appointment, simply input them at the bottom of the screen.

11. Press the **Menu** key and select **Save**.

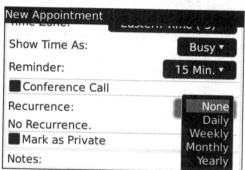

Customizing Your Calendar with Options

You can change a number of things to make your **Calendar** app work exactly as you need it to (see Figure 15-3).

 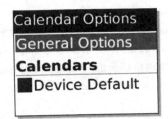

Figure 15-3. *The Calendar Options menu*

Before you can make any of the changes that follow, you need to get into your **Calendar Options** screen. To get there, first open the **Calendar** app, press the **Menu** key, and select **Options** from the menu.

Next, click **General Options** at the top of the screen.

Changing Your Initial View

If you prefer the **Agenda**, **Week**, or **Month** view instead of the default **Day** view when you open your **Calendar** app, you can set your preferred view in the options screen. Click the drop down list next to **Initial View** to select your preferred option.

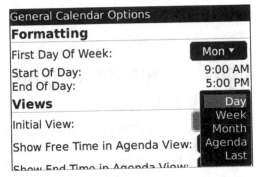

Changing the Start and End of Day Time in Day View

If you're using the Day view, and you are someone who has early morning or evening appointments, the default 9 AM – 5 PM calendar will not work well. You will need to adjust the **Start of Day** and **End of Day** hours in the **General Calendar Options** screen. These options are located at the top of the screen, under the **Formatting** section.

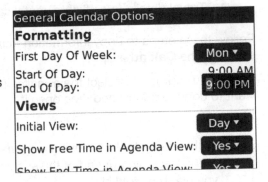

TIP: You can use the number keys on your keypad to type in the correct hours (e.g., type **7** for 7:00 and **10** for 10:00), glide over to the AM/PM setting, and press the **Space** key if you need to change it. It's faster to do this than to click the Trackpad and glide to an hour.

Changing the Default Reminder (Alarm) and Snooze Times

If you need a little more advanced warning than the default **15 minutes**, or a little more **Snooze** time than the default **5 minutes**, you can also change those values in the **General Calendar Options** screen.

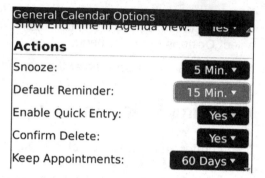

Copying and Pasting Information into Your Calendar or Any Icon

The beauty of the BlackBerry is how simple it is to use. Let's say that you want to copy part of some text in an e-mail and paste it into your **Calendar** app. For example, you might want to copy the text like the following:

- Conference call information via e-mail

- Driving directions via e-mail

- Travel details (e.g., flights, rental cars, and hotel) via e-mail

Follow these steps to copy information from an e-mail to the **Calendar** app:

Glide the Trackpad to select the e-mail you want to copy text from and then open it.

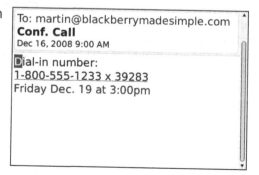

1. Highlight the text by moving the cursor to the beginning or end of the section you want to highlight.

2. Press the **Shift** key to start selecting text to copy. You can also press the **Menu** key and the **Select** menu item.

3. Glide the trackpad to move the cursor to the end (or beginning) of the section you want to highlight.

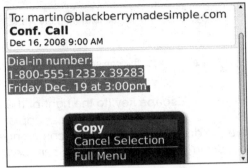

The text that you just highlighted will turn blue. Press the Trackpad and select **Copy**.

4. Press the **Red Phone** key to jump back to your **Home** screen and leave this e-mail open in the background.

Glide to and click the **Calendar** icon  to open it.

5. Schedule a new appointment by clicking the Trackpad in **Day** view.

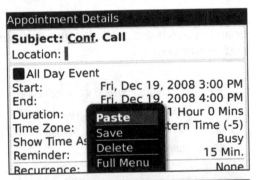

6. Move the cursor to the field to which you want to insert the text that is in the clipboard.

7. Click the Trackpad or press the **Menu** key and select **Paste**. Finally, you will see your information pasted into the calendar appointment.

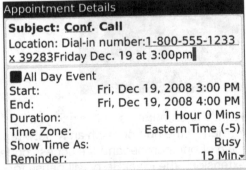

TIP: The following shortcuts enable you to copy-and-paste on your BlackBerry:

Select: Press the **Shift** key (to right of the **Space** key) to start the **Select** mode.

Copy: To copy selected text, hold the **Alt** key (the lower leftmost key – up/down arrow) and click the Trackpad.

Paste: To paste the copied (or cut) text, click the Trackpad and select **Paste**.

Press the **Escape** key (to the right of the Trackpad) and select **Save** when prompted. Now your text is in your **Calendar** app and it's available exactly when you need it. Gone are the days of hunting for the conference call numbers, searching for driving directions, or asking yourself: *"What rental car company did I book?"*

Dialing the Phone from a Ringing Calendar Alarm

What is really great is that if you put a phone number into a **Calendar** item (as you did in the preceding copy-and-paste example), you can actually dial the phone right from the ringing **Calendar** alarm!

All you need to do to initiate the call is to open the event and then click the underlined phone number.

> **TIP:** This is a great way to instantly call someone at a specified time, without ever having to hunt around for the person's phone number!

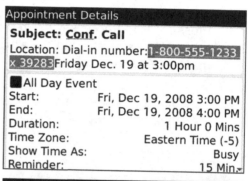

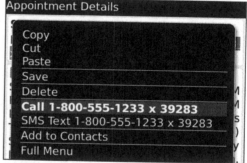

What's even better is that, since you formatted the number with an **X** between the main phone number and the access code (or extension), the BlackBerry will pause for three seconds and automatically dial the access code!

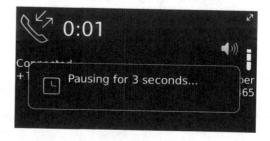

Setting up Alarms and Recurring Appointments

Some appointments occur every week, month, or year. Others are easy to forget, so setting an alarm is helpful to remind you where to be or where to go.

Scheduling an Alarm

It requires only a few steps to schedule an alarm:

1. Navigate to the **Calendar** icon and click it.

2. Begin the process of scheduling an appointment, as detailed previously.

3. In the **New Appointment** screen, scroll down to **Reminder**.

4. The default reminder is **15 minutes** – click the highlighted field and change the reminder to any of the options listed.

5. Press the **Escape** key or the **Menu** key and select **Save**.

6. When the **Calendar** alarm rings, you can glide down and open either **Dismiss** or **Snooze** from the **Alarm Popup** window.

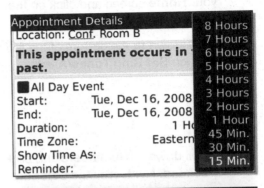

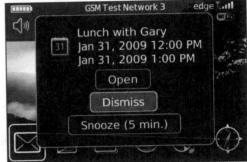

Adjusting Your Calendar and Task Alarms in Sound Profiles (For OS 5.0+)

Most BlackBerry smartphones ship with the **Calendar** alarm profile set to silent and not vibrate when your **Calendar** app's alarm rings and your BlackBerry is **Out of Holster** (e.g., sitting on your desk)! If you are an avid user of the **Calendar** app, you will definitely want to adjust this profile setting.

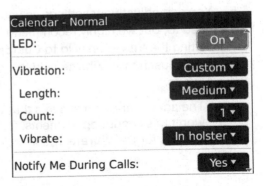

Here is how to change your **Calendar** profile so that it will ring and/or vibrate when the alarm rings and your BlackBerry is sitting on your desk.

1. Scroll to the upper left-hand corner of your **Home** screen and click on the **Speaker** icon.

2. Glide down to the bottom of the list and click on **Set Ring Tones/Alerts**.

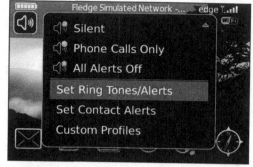

3. Scroll down to **Reminders** and click the Trackpad. Next, click the **Calendar** submenu.

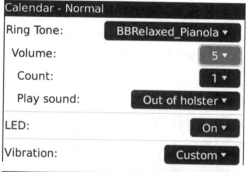

4. Glide down and click any of the fields to change those settings.

> **NOTE:** The default **Task** alarms work the same way; if you use **Task** alarms, you will want to change **Tasks**, as well.

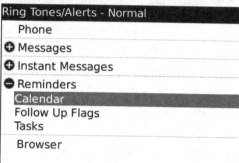

5. You can adjust your settings as you need to, but we highly recommend setting the **Vibration** field to **Custom** and adjusting the **Vibrate** field to **Always**.

   The added vibration ensures that you won't miss your appointments. Other options for the **Vibrate** option include:

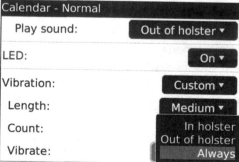

- **Out of Holster:** Your BlackBerry is sitting on your desk or in your hand (out of the approved holster)

- **In Holster:** Your BlackBerry is inside the approved holster (plastic or leather).

6. Navigate through the tunes on your BlackBerry, either in the Device memory or on your MicroSD card, and select the tune you wish to use for reminders. The **Number of Beeps** option sets the number of times the tone rings.

7. Press the **Menu** key and save your settings.

8. Finally, press the **Escape** key a few times to get back to your **Home** screen.

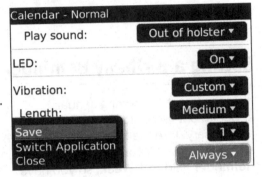

Setting a Recurring Appointment

Recurring appointments can occur daily, weekly, monthly, or yearly. Follow these steps to set a recurring appointment:

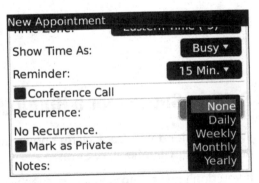

1. Click your **Calendar** icon.

2. Click an empty slot or on an existing **Calendar** event in **Day** view to bring up the appointment scheduling screen.

3. Scroll down to **Recurrence** and click the highlighted field. Select from **None**, **Daily**, **Weekly**, **Monthly**, or **Yearly**.

4. Press the **Escape** or **Menu** key, and select **Save**.

TIP: If your meeting is every two weeks, and it ends on 12/31/2008, then your settings should look like this.

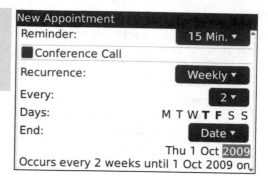

Setting a Birthday Reminder

It's easy to set a recurring annual appointment for a birthday or an anniversary. Use the **Recurrence** field to set an interval of **Yearly** and set the **Reminder** field to **1 Week**, so you have time to buy the present or send a card.

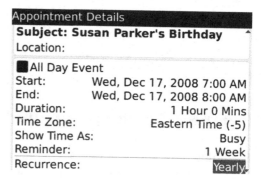

Setting Snooze for a Ringing Calendar or Task Alarm

When a **Calendar** or **Task** alarm rings, you can **Open** it, **Dismiss** it, or **Snooze** it.

If you don't see a **Snooze** option, then you need to change your options in your **Calendar** app from **None** to some other value.

Click **Snooze** to have the alarm ring in the specified number of minutes.

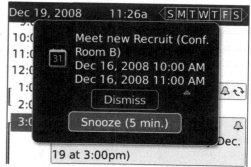

Do the following to make sure you have the **Snooze** option active:

1. Open the **Calendar** application.

2. Push the **Menu** key and glide down to **Options**.

3. Click **General Options**.

4. Look under the **Actions** subheading and set the field next to **Snooze** to something other than **None**.

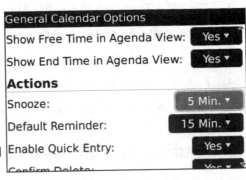

Increasing the Snooze Interval

It's possible you will want to increase the time until the **Snooze** alarm goes off. If so, follow these steps:

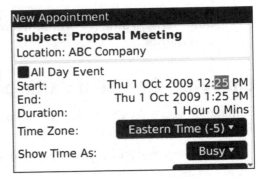

1. Open and scroll down to the scheduled time and change that.

2. Use the number key**s** on your BlackBerry to change the date or time. For example, typing **25** in the **Minutes** field would change the time to **:25**. Or, you can change the hours or days by highlighting them and pressing the **Space** key.

Inviting Attendees and Working with Meeting Invitations

With your BlackBerry, you can invite people to meetings and reply to meeting invitations. If your BlackBerry is connected to a BlackBerry Enterprise Server (BES), you may also be able to check your invitees' availability for specific times, as well.

Inviting Someone to Attend this Meeting

Follow these steps to create a new appointment in your **Calendar** app or to open an existing meeting by clicking it with your Trackpad:

1. Click the Trackpad to see the **Short** menu.

2. Click **Invite Attendee** and follow the prompts to find a contact.

3. Click that contact to invite the person.

4. Follow the same procedure to invite more people to your meeting.

5. Click the Trackpad and select **Save**.

Responding to a Meeting Invitation

When you receive a meeting invitation, you will see it in your **Messages** (**E-mail** inbox). Follow these steps to respond to the invitation:

1. Open the invitation by clicking it with the Trackpad and then pressing the **Menu** key.

2. Several options will become available to you. Choose from **Accept, Accept with Comments, Tentative, Tentative with Comments, Decline,** or **Decline with Comments.**

Changing the List of Participants for a Meeting

Sometimes you will want to change the list of participants for a meeting you've set. Follow these steps to do so:

1. Click the meeting in your **Calendar** application.

2. Navigate to the **Accepted** or **Declined** field and click the contact you wish to change.

3. You will see several options: **Invite Attendee, Change Attendee,** or **Remove Attendee.** Just click the correct option.

Contacting Your Meeting Participants

Contacting one of the participants at your meeting is also straightforward. Simply follow these steps:

1. Open up the meeting, your meeting invitation, or even one of the responses from the participants.

2. Highlight the person you want to contact and press the **Menu** key.

3. Scroll through the various ways you can reach that contact and choose the one that works best for you, whether it's e-mail, PIN message, SMS message, or simply to call the contact directly.

E-mailing All Meeting Attendees

Finally, you can choose to send a message to all others who are attending the same meeting. Follow these steps to do so:

1. Navigate to the meeting in your **Calendar** and click the Trackpad.

2. Click **E-mail all Attendees** and compose your e-mail.

3. Click the Trackpad and select **Send**.

Using Google Sync

The great thing about using **Google Sync** for BlackBerry is that it provides you full two-way wireless synchronization of your BlackBerry **Calendar & Contacts** with and your **Google Calendar** and **Address Book**.

> **NOTE:** You can sync your **Google Contacts** using the BlackBerry Internet Service when you set up your e-mail (see page 47). We strongly suggest not trying to sync **Google Contacts** with **Google Sync**, as well as with the BlackBerry Internet Service – you are just asking for trouble if you do so. Instead, use **Google Sync** for your **Google Calendar** only.

This means anything you type on your **Google Calendar** or **Address Book** *magically* (wirelessly and automatically) appears on your BlackBerry **Calendar** or **Contacts** app in minutes! The same thing goes for **Contacts** or **Calendar** events you add or change on your BlackBerry – they are transmitted wirelessly, and they automatically show up on your **Google Calendar** or **Address Book**.

> **NOTE:** The only exceptions occur with those **Calendar** events you have added on your BlackBerry prior to installing the **Google Sync** application – those old events don't get synced. However, contacts on your BlackBerry prior to the install are synced.

This wireless **Calendar Update** function has previously only been available with a BlackBerry Enterprise Server.

Getting Started with Gmail and Google Calendar on your Computer

To leverage **Gmail** and **Google Calendar**, you need to set them up on your computer. If you haven't done so already, you must sign up for a free **Google Mail** (**Gmail**) account at www.gmail.com.

Next, follow the great help and instructions on Google to start adding **Address Book** entries and creating **Calendar** events on **Gmail** and **Google Calendar** on your computer.

Installing the Google Sync Program on Your BlackBerry

Next, you need to install the Google Sync program on your BlackBerry. Follow these steps to do so:

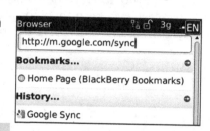

1. Click your **Browser** icon to start it.

2. Type this address into the address bar at the top: http://m.google.com/sync.

> **TIP:** Clicking **Shift** + the **Space** key will type the forward slash "/" in the web address.

3. Click the **Install Now** link on the page that comes up.

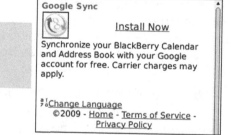

> **NOTE:** This page may look slightly different when you see it.

4. Click the **Download** button.

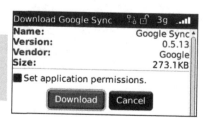

> **NOTE:** The version numbers and size will probably be different when you see this page.

After you download and install the **Google Sync** program, you can run it or just click **OK**. If you clicked **OK** and exited the browser, you may need to check in your **Downloads** folder for the new **Google Sync** icon.

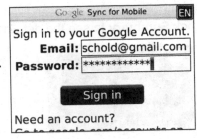

After you successfully log in, you will see a page similar to this one describing what **Google Sync** will sync to and from on your BlackBerry.

Notice the bottom of this screen, where you will see details on which fields (or pieces of information) from your BlackBerry will be shared or synchronized with your **Google Address Book**.

Next, click **Sync Now** at the bottom of this page.

You will also see some sync status screens.

Finally, you will see a screen like the one that follows. Click **Summary** to see the details of what was synced.

From this point forward, the **Google Sync** program should run automatically in the background. It will sync every time you make changes on your BlackBerry or at a minimum of every two hours. From both the BlackBerry **Calendar** and **Contacts** icons, you will see a new **Google Sync** menu item. Select that to see the status of the most recent sync. You can also press the **Menu** key from the **Sync status** screen to **Sync Now** or go into **Options** menu for the sync. If you are having trouble with the sync, check out the "Fixing Problems" section on page 533 or view Google's extensive online help.

Viewing the Results of a Successful Google Sync

You're now ready to view the results of synching your BlackBerry **Calendar** app with **Google Calendar** on your computer.

Google Calendar on the computer:

The BlackBerry Calendar app:

Notice that the **Calendar** events from **Google Calendar** are now on your BlackBerry. Anything you add or change on your BlackBerry or **Google Calendar** will be shared both ways going forward. Automatically!

Google Address Book on your computer:

The BlackBerry Contact list:

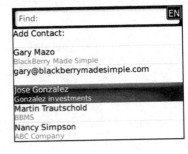

Chapter 16

Getting Tasks Done

Our lives are busy. One of the reasons we use a BlackBerry in the first place is to simply keep track of what we need to do and when we need to do it. The BlackBerry helps us multitask and the **Tasks** app helps us keep track of specific tasks.

Your BlackBerry provides robust task-management functionality in the form of a **Tasks** list program. In this chapter, you'll learn how to use this application to manage **Tasks** in your life, as well as to synchronize the **Tasks** on your BlackBerry with your computer.

We will also show you how to view your tasks, categorize them, filter them and then check them off when they are completed.

Exploring the Tasks App

Like your **Contacts, Calendar**, and **MemoPad** app, your **Tasks** app becomes more powerful when you share or synchronize it with your computer. Since the BlackBerry is so easy to carry around, you can update, check off, and even create new tasks anytime and anywhere they come to mind. Gone are the days of writing down a **Task** on a sticky note and hoping to find it later when you need it.

Getting Tasks from Your Computer to Your BlackBerry

You can also mass load or sync up your computer's **Tasks** list with your BlackBerry **Tasks** app.

If your BlackBerry is tied to a BlackBerry Enterprise Server, the synchronization is wireless and automatic. Otherwise, you will use either a USB cable or Bluetooth wireless to connect your BlackBerry to your computer to keep it up to date. If you use a Windows PC, see page 67; if you use an Apple Mac computer, see page 125.

Viewing Tasks on Your BlackBerry

Press the hotkey letter **T** to start the **Tasks** utility (see page 548 for help on using hotkeys). Or, you can locate and click the **Tasks** icon.

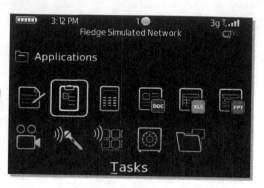

You may need to press the **Menu** key to bring up all your applications on the **Home** screen; you may also need to click the **Applications** folder.

You can find the icon that says **Tasks** when you glide over it. You may need to press the **Menu** key to the left of the Trackpad to see all your icons.

The first time you start the **Tasks** program on your BlackBerry, you may see an empty **Tasks** list if you have not yet synchronized your BlackBerry with your computer.

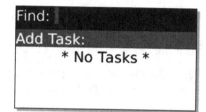

Adding a New Task

Your next goal is to add a new **Task** to your **Tasks** list. Press the **Menu** key and select **New**. From here, you can enter information for your new **Task** (see Figure 16-1).

> **TIP:** Keep in mind the way the **Find:** feature works as you name your **Task**. For example, all **Tasks** for a particular *Project Red* should have *Red* in the name for easy retrieval.

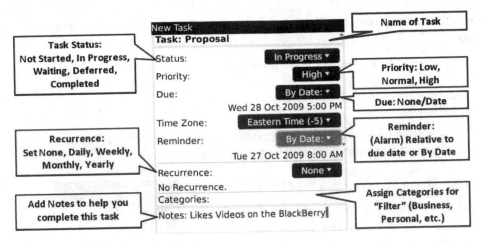

Figure 16-1. *New Task menu options*

Categorizing Your Tasks

As with **Address Book** entries, you can group your **Tasks** into **Categories**. You can also share or synchronize these **Categories** with your computer.

Assigning a Task to a Category

It's easy to assign a **Task** to a **Category** (see Figure 16-2); simply follow these steps:

1. Highlight the **Task**, click the Trackpad, and open it.

2. Press the **Menu** key and select **Categories**.

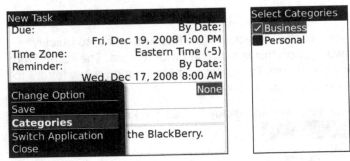

Figure 16-2. *Assigning Tasks to Categories*

3. Select as many **Categories** as you like by checking them with the Trackpad or pressing the **Space** key.

4. You may even add new **Categories** by pressing the **Menu** key and selecting **New**.

5. Once you're done, press the **Menu** key and select **Save** to save your **Category** settings.

6. Press the **Menu** key and select **Save** again.

Filtering Tasks

Once you assign a **Task** to a **Category**, you can filter or show only those **Tasks** assigned to a particular **Category**. To do this, follow these steps:

1. View your **Tasks** list and press the **Menu** key.

2. Select **Filter**, then check off a particular **Category** for the filter by tapping the **Space** key on the appropriate check box.

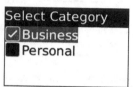

Immediately, you will see a black line at the top of the window with the **Category** name showing; this indicates that the **Tasks** list is filtered by the specified **Category**.

Here is the filtered **Tasks** list:

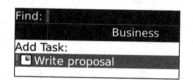

To un-filter your **Tasks** list, you need to repeat the steps just described, but uncheck the selected **Task**. Pressing the **Escape** key to exit the **Tasks** list and re-enter information will not unfilter your **Tasks**.

Finding Tasks

Once you have a few **Tasks** in your **Tasks** list, you will want to know how to quickly locate them. One of the fastest ways to do this is with the **Find:** feature. The same **Find:** feature from the **Address Book** works in the **Tasks** list; just start typing a few letters to view only those **Tasks** that contain the letters you type.

The example that follows assumes you want to quickly find all **Tasks** that have any word

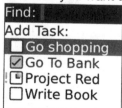

starting with the letter **G**.

Typing the letter **G** filters the list of **Tasks** you see to only those that start with the letter **G**.

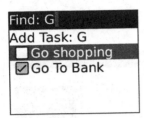

Checking off or Completing Tasks

You can mark **Tasks** complete by pressing the **Menu** key and selecting **Mark Completed** or, more easily, by highlighting the **Task** in the full list and pressing the **Space** key.

> **TIP:** Press the **Space** key again to uncheck a **Task** (mark it as incomplete).

Handling a Task Alarm

When a **Task** alarm rings, you will see a popup window similar to the one shown to the right. At this point, you have three options:

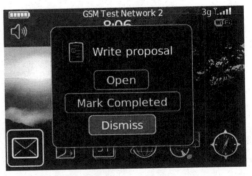

1. Open the **Task** to change the due date, add notes, or edit anything else you want to.

2. Click **Mark Completed** if you completed this **Task**.

3. Click **Dismiss** to ignore this ringing **Task** alarm.

Adjusting the Way Task Alarms Notify You

Please see the "Calendar and Task Alarms" section on page 305 to learn how to make sure your **Task** alarms notify you by vibrating or vibrating and playing a tone when your BlackBerry is sitting on your desk (**Out of Holster**).

Sorting Your Tasks and Task Options

You may sort your **Tasks** by the following methods in your **Task Options** screen: **Subject (default)**, **Priority**, **Due Date**, or **Status**.

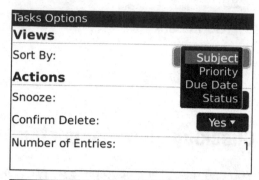

You may also change the value of **Snooze** from **None** to **30 Min** or the value of **Confirm Delete** to **No** (the default value is **Yes**).

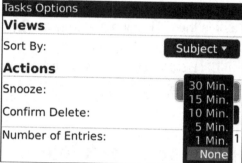

Chapter 17

MemoPad: Using Sticky Notes

One of the simplest, most useful programs on your BlackBerry is the **MemoPad**. Its uses are truly limitless. There is nothing flashy about this program – just type your memo or your notes and keep them with you at all times.

Using the **MemoPad** program is easy and intuitive. The following steps will guide you through the basic process of inputting a memo and saving it on your BlackBerry. There are two basic ways of setting up Memos on the BlackBerry, either compose the note on your computer organizer application and then synchronize (or transfer) that note to the BlackBerry or compose the Memo on the BlackBerry itself.

Transferring Your Computer's MemoPad Items to Your BlackBerry

You can synchronize or share your computer's **MemoPad** notes list with your BlackBerry **MemoPad** icon.

If your BlackBerry is tied to a BlackBerry Enterprise Server, the synchronization is wireless and automatic. Otherwise, you will use either a USB cable or Bluetooth wireless to connect your BlackBerry to your computer to keep it up-to-date. If you use a Windows PC, see page 67; if you use an Apple Mac computer, see page 125.

The sync works both ways, which extends the power of your desktop computer to your BlackBerry. You can add or edit notes anywhere and at anytime on your BlackBerry – and be certain these changes will be synced back with your computer (and backed up) after the next sync.

1,001 Uses for the MemoPad (Notes) Feature

OK, so maybe we won't list 1,001 uses here, but we could. Anything that occupies space on a sticky note on your desk, in your calendar, or on your refrigerator could be written neatly and organized simply by using the **MemoPad** app.

Finding Common Uses for the MemoPad

There are many **Tasks** you can use your BlackBerry's **MemoPad** for that you could also use sticky notes for in real life. For example, you might use **MemoPad** or sticky notes for the following:

- A grocery list

- A hardware store list

- A shopping list for any store

- A meeting agenda

- A training log, whether for running, biking, or swimming)

- A packing list for you next ski or sun vacation

- BlackBerry Made Simple videos you want to watch

- Movies you want to rent next time at the video store

- Your parking space at the airport, mall, or theme park

Adding or Editing Memos on the BlackBerry

To locate the **MemoPad** app, look for an icon like this one. Your icon may look different, but look for **MemoPad** to be shown when you highlight it.

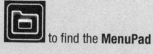

NOTE: You may need to first click the **Applications** folder to find the **MenuPad** program.

If you have no memos in the list, then you can add a new memo by pressing the Trackpad and starting to type.

If you have memos in the list and want to add a new one, you just click **Add Memo**.

To open an existing memo, just glide to it and click it. You will probably be in **Edit** mode, where you can change the memo. If not, click the Trackpad again and select **Edit**.

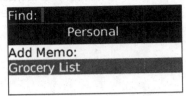

When typing a new memo, you will want to enter a title that will be easy to locate using the Find: feature later, simply by typing a few matching letters. Follow these steps to create a new memo:

1. Type your memo into the Body section.

2. Press the Enter key to go down to the next line.

3. When you're done, click the Trackpad to select Save.

If you have copied something from another program, such as E-mail, you can paste it into your memo (see page 22 for details on using copy-and-paste functionality.)

TIP: When you pick up an item in the store, check it off by putting a Space character in front of the item; this helps you make sure you get everything, even when you have a long list.

Locating or Finding Memos Quickly

Like the **Contacts** and **Tasks** programs, the **MemoPad** program includes a **Find** feature you can use to locate memos quickly by typing the first few letters of words that match the title of your memos. Example, typing **gr** would immediately show you only memos matching those three letters in the first part of any word, such as *grocery*.

Ordering Frequently Used Memos

For frequently used memos, you can type numbers (e.g., **01, 02,** and **03**) at the beginning of the title to force those memos to be listed in order at the top of the list. (The reason you start with **0** is to keep your memos in order after the number 10.)

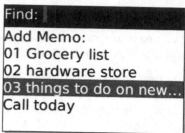

Viewing Your Memos

Once you've created some memos, you'll want to view them at some point. Follow these steps to view a memo:

1. Glide the Trackpad down to a memo or type a few letters to find the memo you want to view.

2. Click the Trackpad to instantly view the memo.

> **TIP:** You might find it useful to time stamp your memos. Typing **ld** (which stands for *Long Date*) and pressing the **Space** key will insert this date: **Tue, 28 Aug 2007**. Similarly, typing **lt** (which stand for *Long Time*) and pressing the **Space** key will enter this time: **8:51:40 PM**. Note that this value will be in the local date/time format you have set on your BlackBerry.

See page 166 to learn how to create a customized time stamp.

Organizing Your Memos with Categories

Similar to the **Address Book** program and the **Tasks** list, the **MemoPad** program allows you to organize and filter memos using **Categories**.

> **TIP: Categories** are shared between your **Address Book, Tasks** list, and **MemoPad**. They are even synchronized or shared with your desktop computer.

Note that you must assign your memos to **Categories** before you filter them.

One way to be extra organized with your **MemoPad** application is to utilize **Categories** so all your memos are filed neatly away.

The two default **Categories** are **Personal** and **Business**; however, you can easily change or add to these **Categories**.

TIP: **Categories** are shared between your **Address Book**, **Tasks** list, and **MemoPad**. They are even synchronized or shared with your computer.

Filing a Memo in a New or Existing Category

Just as with the **Contact** list (from the **Address Book** program) and the **Tasks** list, you can organize your **MemoPad** items with **Categories**:

1. Start the **MemoPad** icon by clicking it.

2. Locate the memo you want to assign to one or more **Categories** by gliding to and clicking it, or by typing a few letters and using the **Find:** feature at the top of the app.

3. Press the **Menu** key again and select **Categories.**

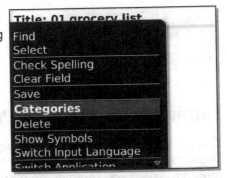

4. Now you will see a screen similar to the one at the right. Glide the Trackpad to a **Category** and click to check or uncheck it. You can add a new **Category** by pressing the **Menu** key and selecting **New**.

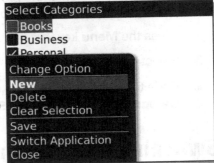

5. Click the **Save** option to save your **Categories** settings, and then click the **Save** option to save the memo.

To filter memos using the **Categories** option or to see only memos in a specific **Category**, follow these steps:

1. Start the **MemoPad** program by clicking it.

2. Press the **Menu** key and select **Filter**.

3. Now glide to and click (or press the **Space** key) on the **Category** you would like to use to filter the list of memos. You can tell a **Category** is filtered because it is shown with a black line at the top of the window, under the **Find:** heading.

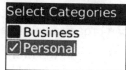

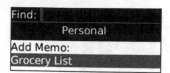

Turning off the Filter on Your MemoPad

You've probably noticed that pressing the **Escape** key (which clears out the **Find:** characters typed) will do nothing for the Filter; doing this just exits the **MemoPad** program. When you re-enter the program, you still see the filtered list. To unfilter, or turn off the filter, you need to do the following:

1. Press the **Menu** key.

2. Select **Filter**.

3. Glide to and uncheck a checked **Category** by clicking the Trackpad on that **Category** or by pressing the **Space** key.

Switching Applications and Multitasking

From almost every program on your BlackBerry, the **MemoPad** included, pressing the **Menu** key and selecting **Switch Application** allows you to *multitask* by leaving your current open program and jumping to any other program on your BlackBerry. This is especially useful when you want to copy-and-paste information between icons.

> **TIP:** The shortcut for switching applications is **Alt + Escape**; or you can press and hold the **Menu** key. Give it a try!

Here's how you jump or switch applications from the menu (see Figure 17-1):

1. Press the **Menu** key and select **Switch Application**.

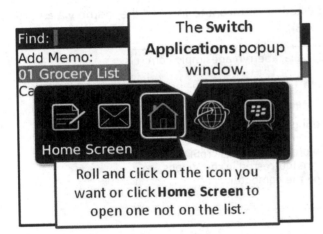

Figure 17-1. *Multitasking on the BlackBerry*

2. You will now see the **Switch Application** popup window, which shows you the icon for every application that is currently running. If you see the icon for the program you want to switch to, just glide to and click it.

3. If you don't see the icon you want, then click the **Home** screen icon. From here, you can locate and click the right icon.

4. You can then jump back to the **MemoPad** or the application you just left by selecting the **Switch Application** menu item from the program you jumped to (see Figure 17-2).

Figure 17-2. *Switching applications*

TIP: Pressing and holding the **Alt** key and then tapping the **Escape** key is the shortcut to bring up the **Switch Application** popup window. You can also just press and hold the **Menu** key to activate the popup window.

Forwarding Memos

Say you just took some great notes at a meeting, and now you want to send them to your colleague. You can send a memo via e-mail, BlackBerry PIN message, or SMS text message to other people. Follow these steps to accomplish that **Task**:

1. Highlight the memo you want to send and press the **Menu** key.

2. Select **Forward As**, then select whether you want to forward the memo via **E-mail**, **PIN**, or **SMS** (see Figure 17-3).

 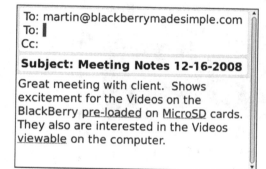

Figure 17-3. *Forwarding a memo*

3. Finish composing your message, click the Trackpad, and select **Send**.

Using Other Memo Menu Commands

There may be a few other things you want to do with your memos. You can find some of these options in the more advanced **Menu** commands, which you access by clicking the **MemoPad** icon.

Some of these advanced **Menu** items can only be seen when you are either writing a new memo or editing an existing one. So, you can access these items either by selecting **New** and working on a new memo or selecting **Edit** and editing an existing memo.

From the **Editing** screen, press the **Menu** key to bring up the options shown in the table that follows:

Option	Description
Find	If you are in a memo item, then this option will allow you to find any text inside the memo.
Paste	Suppose you have copied text from another program and want to paste it into a memo. Select and copy the text (from the **Calendar** app, **Address Book**, or another application), and then select **Paste** from this menu. The text is now in your memo.
Select	This option allows you to click and select text from the memo, then press the **Menu** key again and select **Copy**. Now use the **Switch Application** menu item to navigate to another application, press the **Menu** key, and select **Paste** to put the text in that application.
Check Spelling	This option runs the BlackBerry spell checker on the currently open memo item.
Clear Field	This option clears all contents of the entire memo item – use this option with caution!
Save	This option saves the changes in the open memo.
Categories	This option allows you to file the open memo into either the **Business** or **Personal** categories. After selecting the **Categories** option, you can press the **Menu** key again and select **New** to create yet another **Category** for this memo.
Delete	This option deletes the current memo.
Show Symbols	This option brings up the list of character symbols.

> **TIP:** You can also just press the SYM key to see the list of character symbols.

Switch Application	This option brings up the **Multitasking** window, so you can jump to another application icon (see page 22).
Close	This option lets you exit the current application; using it is the same as pressing the **Escape** key.

Simplifying Memo Tips and Tricks

There are a few cool tips and tricks you can use to make filing, locating, and using your memos even easier. These include adding separate items for each store you need to shop from; placing numbers in front of your memo names, and adding a space in front of list items to indicate they are "checked off."

Adding Separate Items for Each Store

It's not uncommon to go to a hardware or grocery store for a particular item, purchase several additional items while you are there, yet also forget to pick up the one item you actually went to that store to buy. Adding separate items for each store you need to shop from to a memo can help you avoid forgetting that one particular item you are supposed to get, saving you time and gas money!

Putting Numbers in Front of Your Memo Names

Another handy trick is to place numbers in front of your memo names. This lets you order them numerically on your BlackBerry, and it gives you a great way to prioritize your memos and keep the most important ones always at the top of the list.

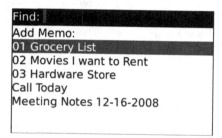

Finally, see page 162 for information on how to add a **time stamp** to your memos.

Using the Space Key to Check Off Items

When you are checking off items you have purchased in a grocery or other type of store from your memo list, roll the cursor up to the beginning of the item and press the **Space** key to move the item over one space.

Each item moved over one space has been placed in your shopping cart, so now you know what you still have left to buy.

In the image to the right, we have already placed the swirl bread, mini wheats, and oat squares into the shopping basket. Each space serves as a checkmark.

This is especially helpful when you have a long list, or your list is not in the order of the aisles in the store. It helps you make sure you have not forgotten anything.

Title: 01 Groceries

Peanut butter
 Swirl bread
Apples
 Miniwheats
 Oat squares
Milk
Dog food

Chapter 18

SMS Text and MMS Messaging

As you may be aware, a key strength of all BlackBerry devices is their ability to send various kinds of messages. We have covered e-mail extensively; in this chapter, we now turn to *Short Messaging Service* (SMS) and *Multi-Media Messaging* (MMS) messaging. Specifically, we will show you how to send and view both text messages (i.e. SMS) and multi-media messages (i.e. MMS). We will also show the various apps from which you can send a message and offer some advice on how to keep your messages organized.

Using Text and Multi-Media Messaging

MMS is a short way to say that you have included pictures, sounds, video, or some other form of media right inside your e-mail – be careful not to confuse MMS with regular e-mail, where media is an attachment to an e-mail message. The BlackBerry is beautifully equipped to use both of these services – learning them will make you more productive and make your BlackBerry that much more fun to use.

> **TIP:** Watch out! Many phone companies charge extra for SMS text messaging and MMS multi-media messaging, even if you have an unlimited BlackBerry data plan. Typical charges can be $0.10 to $0.25 per message. This adds up quickly!
>
> The solution to this is to check with your carrier about bundled SMS/MMS plans. For just $5 or $10 per month, you might be able to receive several hundred, thousands, or even unlimited monthly SMS/MMS text messages.

Using SMS Text Messaging

Text messaging has become one of the most popular services on cell phones today. While it is still used more extensively in Europe and Asia, it is growing in popularity in North America.

The concept is very simple; instead of placing a phone call, you send a short message to someone's handset. It is less disruptive than a phone call, and you may have friends, colleagues, or co-workers who do not own a BlackBerry – so e-mail is not an option.

One of this book's authors uses text messaging with his children all the time – this is how their generation communicates:

Author: "R u coming home 4 dinner?"

Child: "Yup."

There you have it: meaningful dialogue with a seventeen year old! It's short, instant and easy.

Composing SMS Text Messages

Composing an SMS message works much like sending an e-mail. The beauty of an SMS message is that it arrives on virtually any handset, and it is so easy to respond to. You have two basic options for sending an SMS message: from the **Messages** list and from the **Contact** list. We'll cover how to do both options next.

Option #1: Sending an SMS Message from the Messages list

1. Use the Trackpad to navigate to your Messages list and press the Menu key. Or, you can try this shortcut: Glide to a date row separator – such as **Mon, July 6, 2009** – and click the Trackpad.

2. Select **Compose SMS Text**.

3. Begin typing in a contact name (as you did when selecting an e-mail recipient in Chapter 7).

4. When you find the contact, click the Trackpad.

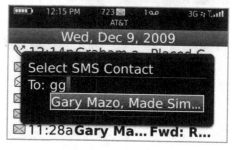

5. If the contact has multiple phone numbers, the BlackBerry will ask you to choose a number. Click the number you desire to use.

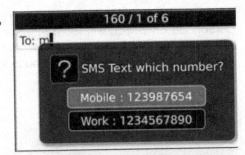

6. After you select a recipient, you can easily add more by typing a phone number or a name (to find matching contact entries).

7. In the main body (where the cursor is), just type your message as if you were sending an e-mail. Remember: SMS messages are **limited to 160 characters** by most carriers. If you go over that number in the BlackBerry, two separate text messages will be sent.

8. When you are done typing, click the Trackpad and choose **Send**. That's all there is to it.

TIP: Roll over the **Smiley Face** icon

and click it to see a list of icons (aka *emoticons*) you can add to enhance your message! You can also create an emoticon using a keyboard shortcut. In the image shown, typing **:D** would create a **Big Smile** icon.

As you carry on a conversation with another person via SMS, you will see a threaded discussion with different colors for your replies and those of the person you are communicating with.

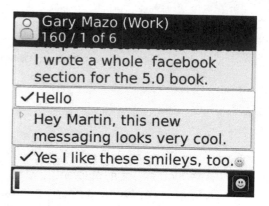

Option #2: Sending an SMS Message from the Contact List

Your second option for sending an SMS message is to do so from the **Contact** list. You can accomplish this by following these steps:

1. Click your **Address Book** icon (it may say **Contacts**, instead).

2. Type a few letters to find the person to whom you want to send your SMS message.

3. With the desired contact highlighted from the list, press the **Menu** key, and you will see one of your menu options is **SMS Text**, followed by the contact name.

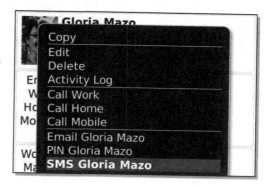

4. Select this option and follow the steps described in the previous section to send your message.

Leveraging Basic SMS Menu Commands

As with the BlackBerry's **E-mail** feature, you can find many options available via the menu commands when sending SMS messages. These are covered in Table 18-1.

Table 18-1. *Menu Command Options*

Option	Description
Help	This option gives you contextual help with SMS messaging (see page 159 for more tips on using the **Help** feature).
Paste	Suppose you have copied text from another program and want to paste it into your SMS message. This option lets you select and copy the text (from the **Calendar** app, **Address Book**, or another application) and select **Paste** from this menu. The text is now in your SMS message.
Select	Click **Select** (or just use the shortcut: the **Shift** key) to begin selecting text from the SMS message, then press the **Menu** key or the Trackpad again to choose the **Copy** or **Cut** option. Now use the **Switch Application** menu item to navigate to another application, and then press the **Menu** key and select **Paste** to put the text into that application.
Add Smiley	This option inserts a smiley or emoticon (such as a happy, sad, or angry face).
Mark Unopened	This option marks the selected message as unopened.
Check Spelling	This option runs the BlackBerry spell checker on the message.
Clear Chat	This option clears all messages from the entire chat session.
Delete Chat	This option deletes all messages from the entire chat session.
Show Recipients	This option shows every recipient of an SMS message you are about to send.
Send	This option sends the current SMS message.
Save Draft	This option saves the current message as a Draft, which you can later edit and send.
Add To:	This option adds a second line for putting in another recipient.
Edit AutoText	This option allows you to add or edit **AutoText** entries.
Show Symbols	This option brings up the list of character symbols.

> **TIP:** You can also just press the **Sym** key to see the list of character symbols.

Switch Input Language	This option changes the language used for typing, as well as the spell checker.
Switch Application	This option brings up the **Multitasking** window, so you can jump to another application (see page 22).
Close	This option exits the current application; using it is the same as pressing the **Escape** key.

Using Advanced SMS Menu Commands and Options

There are several ways to personalize and customize your SMS messages; you can access these settings by clicking the **Options** icon. Follow these steps to customize an SMS message:

1. Click your **Options** icon; it may be inside the **Applications**, **Settings**, or another folder, if you don't see it from your **Home** screen.

2. Scroll down to **SMS Text** or **SMS** and click it with the Trackpad.

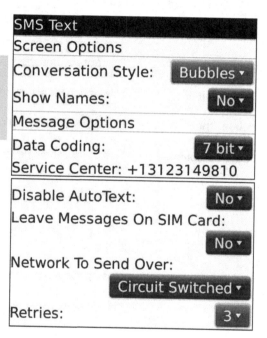

> **TIP:** Press the letter S on your keyboard a few times to jump down to this entry – it's usually faster than scrolling.

Usually, the options shown are available for you to adjust; however, some BlackBerry phones are more limited, so this isn't always true. (The options available to adjust depend on your BlackBerry phone software version and your wireless carrier.)

You have the following customizable **Screen** options when using a BlackBerry:

- **Conversation Style:** Choose from **Bubbles** or **Lines** to control the look-and-feel of threaded conversations.
- **Show Names:** Show or hide the names of the people in the conversation.

- **Message Options:** Indicates data coding, which is generally kept at 7-bit.

- **Service Center:** Shows the phone number of the SMS text service center for your wireless carrier. This will probably be different from what is shown.

- **Disable AutoText:** Turns the **AutoText** feature off. Generally, this is set to **No**, indicating you want to use the **AutoText** feature when typing SMS messages.

- **Leave messages on SIM card:** Change this option to **Yes** if you want to keep copies of your messages on the SIM card and not have them deleted. Watch out: Your SIM card will get filled pretty quickly if you use SMS a lot!

- **Delivery reports:** Change this feature to **On** if you want delivery confirmation for your SMS messages.

- **Network to Send Over:** Choose between **Circuit Switched**, **Packet Switched**, **Circuit Preferred**, or **Packet Preferred**.

  Packet Switching is a more modern way of delivering data – but it may not work in all coverage areas. Your BlackBerry usually does a good job of choosing the correct method; however, you can try switching these settings if you have problems.

- **Retries: 3** retries is the default, but you can adjust this option up or down (**0** to **5**) to meet your needs. Some networks may need more retries.

Opening and Replying to SMS Messages

Opening your SMS messages couldn't be easier – the BlackBerry makes it simple to quickly keep in touch and respond to your messages.

Navigate to your waiting messages by clicking the **Messages** icon on the **Home** screen; or, you can click the **SMS Messages** icon and then click the new SMS message.

If you are in the midst of a dialogue with someone, your messages will appear in a threaded message format, which looks like a running discussion (see Figure 18-1). Follow these steps to reply to and compose a message:

1. Click on the SMS message to which you wish to reply with your trackpad.

2. The cursor appears in a blank field – type in your reply, click the Trackpad, and select **Send**.

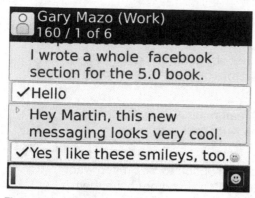

Figure 18-1. *Threaded text messaging on the BlackBerry*

Finding an SMS or MMS Message

You find an SMS or MMS message just as you find any other message; go to page 259 to learn how to search for specific messages. Or, if you need to search for information contained in other types of apps, such as your BlackBerry **Messenger**, **Calendar**, **Contacts**, or **Tasks** programs, go to page 521.

> **TIP:** Pressing **Alt + S** will show you only the SMS text messages in your **Inbox**.

Cleaning up an SMS Mailbox

It is possible for your SMS mailbox to get a little unwieldy; however, if that happens, just follow these suggestions to view and clean up a particular SMS folder (see Figure 18-2):

1. Click your **Messages** icon and press the **Menu** key.

2. Scroll down to **View Folder** and click it. You will then see a list of your available message folders.

3. To clean up your **Inbox**, click the **SMS** inbox, and only your SMS inbox messages will now be displayed.

4. Highlight the date row separator (e.g., **Mon, Sep 4, 2007**) under the most recent message you desire to keep, press the **Menu** key, and select **Delete Prior**.

5. All older messages will then be deleted. To delete an individual message, just click the message, press the **Menu** key, and choose **Delete**.

6. Choose the **SMS Outbox** folder and repeat the steps just described to clean up your sent messages, as well.

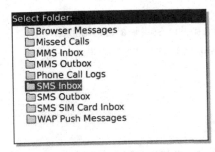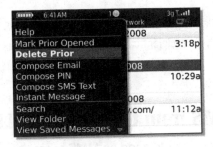

Figure 18-2. *Deleting messages from an SMS inbox*

SMS Tips and Tricks

Here are some quick keystrokes you can use to navigate quickly through your messages. You enter these shortcuts when you're in the **Messages** list:

- Press the **C** key to compose a message from the **Messages** list.

- Press the **R** key to reply to a message.

- Press the **L** key to reply to all senders.

- Press the **F** key to forward a message.

- Push and hold the **Alt** key and press **I** to view **Incoming** (received) messages.

- Push and hold the **Alt** key and press the **S** key to view all SMS text messages.

- Press the **Escape** key to view your entire **Messages** list once more (i.e., unfilter it).

TIP: Most of these shortcuts work for e-mail messages, as well.

MMS Messaging on Your BlackBerry

MMS stands for *Multi-Media Messaging*. MMS includes pictures, video, and audio in the body of the message. The fact that the media is included in the body of the message makes it different than regular e-mail, which can include media as attachments. The other key difference with MMS compared to e-mail is that you can send MMS to phones that do not have e-mail capabilities. This might be useful if not all your colleagues, friends, and family have BlackBerry smartphones!

> **NOTE:** Not all BlackBerry devices or carriers support MMS messaging, so it is a good idea to make sure that your recipient can receive these messages before you send them such messages.

Sending MMS from the Messages List

Perhaps the easiest way to send an MMS message is to start the process just like you started the SMS process earlier:

1. Click on the **Messages** icon and press the **Menu** key.

2. Scroll down to **Compose MMS** and click the trackpad.

3. Press the **Menu** key and select **Attach Picture.**

4. Locate and click on a picture to attach. Depending on the phone company that supplied your BlackBerry, you may be prompted to locate the MMS file, which is often stored in your **mms/pictures** folder.

Some BlackBerry devices have a pre-loaded Birthday.mms in this folder. Click on the **Birthday MMS**, if you have it.

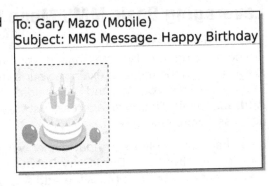

To: Gary Mazo (Mobile)
Subject: MMS Message- Happy Birthday

5. Then type in the recipient in the **To:** field, scroll to the appropriate contact, and click.

6. You can add a subject and text in the body of the MMS.

7. When finished, just click the trackpad and select **Send**.

There are lots of template MMS files you can download from the web and put into this folder to be selected in the future.

Sending a Media File As an MMS from the Media Icon

This might be the more common and easier way for you to send media files as MMS messages.

1. Use the Trackpad to navigate to your **Media** icon and click it. You will be brought to the **Media** screen.

2. Click **Pictures** and find the picture either on your device or media card that you wish to send.

3. Highlight the picture you want (there's no need to click it) and press the **Menu** key.

4. Scroll down to **Send as MMS** and click it. You will then be directed to choose a recipient from your contacts.

5. Find the contact you desire and click it.

> **NOTE:** If you do not have an MMS or SMS Text Messaging service plan from your phone company, you can usually **Send as E-mail** for no additional cost.
>
> You need to know whether you have an unlimited BlackBerry data plan. If you don't have such a plan, then you will want to send pictures only very rarely because they can eat up your data much faster than a plain-text e-mail.

6. Enter a subject and any text into the message, click the Trackpad, and send your message.

Leveraging Basic MMS Menu Commands

You can use the **MMS** menu to personalize your MMS message even more. When you are composing the MMS message, press the **Menu** key to view these options, then scroll through the menu to examine your options. For example, you can easily add more recipients to the **To:**, **Cc:**, and **Bcc:** fields. You can also attach addresses from your **Address Book**. To add an address, just click **Attach Address** and find the appropriate address on the next screen.

If you have scheduled a birthday dinner with a contact, then you might want add an appointment from your BlackBerry **Calendar** app (e.g., "Dinner at the Fancy French Restaurant for Two") and click the **Add Appointment** option.

You could even attach one of your recorded voice notes by selecting **Attach Voice Note** to personalize your message. Follow these steps to add an audio file to accompany a picture:

1. Choose **Attach Audio** and then navigate to the folder that contains the audio file (see Figure 18-3).

 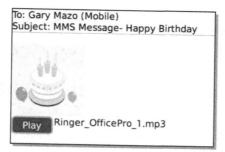

Figure 18-3. *Attach an audio file to an MMS message.*

2. At this point, you can also attach other items by pressing the **Menu** key and selecting any other items you want to attach.

Using Advanced MMS Commands

While you are composing your MMS message, press the **Menu** key and scroll down to **Options**.

In the **Current Message Options** screen, you will see the estimated size of the MMS. This is important because, if the file is too big, your recipient may not be able to download it onto her device.

You can also set the importance of this MMS, as well as set the delivery confirmation options.

To access additional advanced MMS commands, follow these steps:

MMS	
Multimedia Reception:	Always ▾
Automatic Retrieval:	Always ▾
	Never
Notifications:	
☑ Allow Delivery Confirmation	
☑ Allow Read Confirmation	
☐ Confirm Delivery	
☐ Confirm Read	
Message Filtering:	
☐ Reject Anonymous Messages	

1. Navigate from the **Home** screen to **Options** and click it.

2. Scroll to the **MMS** option and click it.

3. From this screen, you can set your phone to always receive multimedia files by setting the first line to say **Always**.

4. You can also set your automatic retrieval to occur **Always** or **Never**.

5. You can check each check box to set your notification and message filtering options, as well. Your filtering options include the following:

- **Allow Delivery Confirmation:** This option allows your BlackBerry to send delivery confirmation messages when you receive MMS messages from others.

- **Allow Read Confirmation:** This option allows your BlackBerry to send a confirmation message when you have opened an MMS message you received.

- **Confirm Delivery**: This option requests a delivery confirmation from people to whom you send MMS messages.

- **Confirm Read**: This option requests a *read receipt* message when your MMS recipient opens the MMS message you sent.

We recommend leaving the default filtering options checked.

Troubleshooting Messages

Sometimes you encounter problems when sending messages. If that happens, the following troubleshooting tip can help you resolve issues for MMS, SMS, e-mail, and web browsing – in short, for anything that requires a wireless radio connection.

Registering With the Host Routing Table

Specifically, you might it helpful to register with the Host Routing Table. Follow these steps to do so:

Host Routing Table—Register Now

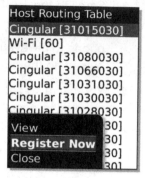

1. From your **Home** screen, click the **Options** icon.

2. Click **Advanced Options** and then scroll to **Host Routing Table** to see a screen similar to the one shown to the right. (You will see different carrier names if you are not on the carrier shown.)

3. Press the **Menu** key and then click **Register Now**.

4. While the BlackBerry is still on, do a *battery pull* – that is, take off the back of the casing, remove the battery, wait 30 seconds, and then re-install it. Once the BlackBerry reboots, you should be all set for SMS Text and MMS messaging.

Chapter 19

Even More Messaging

You already know that your BlackBerry is an amazing messaging device. What you may not realize is that there are so many more ways to use messaging on the BlackBerry. In this chapter, we will look at PIN messaging (using the unique identifying PIN for each BlackBerry), BlackBerry messaging (BBM), as well as voice notes and other forms of instant messaging.

PIN Messaging

BlackBerry handhelds have a unique feature called PIN-to-PIN, also known as **PIN Messaging** or **Peer-to-Peer Messaging**. This allows one BlackBerry user to communicate directly with another BlackBerry user as long as you know that user's BlackBerry PIN. We'll show you an easy way to find your PIN and send it in an e-mail to your colleague.

> **Gary Mazo**
> *gg*
> Made Simple Learning
> Vice President
>
> Email: gary@madesimplelearning.com
> Work: 386-555-1299
> Home: 386-555-1109
> Mobile: 386-555-1183
> PIN: 1903A309

Sending Your PIN number via e-mail with the Mypin Shortcut

1. Compose an e-mail to your colleague. In the body of the e-mail, type something like This is my BlackBerry PIN number

2. Type the code letters **mypin.**

> To: Martin Trautschold
> To:
> Cc:
> **Subject: PIN**
> This is my PIN number
> Mypin

3. Press the **Space** key to see your own BlackBerry PIN number inserted right in the text replacing the **mypin** text.

4. Click the trackpad and select **Send**.

> **TIP:** Store your friends' PINs in your **Contact** List for easy access.

Replying to a PIN Message

Once you receive your PIN message, you will see that it is highlighted in red text in your **Inbox**.

To reply to a PIN message, click the Trackpad to open it, and then click the Trackpad again and select **Reply,** just as you do with e-mail and other types of messages.

Adding Someone's PIN to Your Contacts

Once you receive an e-mail containing a PIN number from a colleague or family member, then you should put this PIN number into your **Contact** list.

If you *do not* already have this person in your **Contact** list, follow these steps (see Figure 19-1):

1. Highlight the PIN number and press the **Menu** key to select the **Add to Contacts** option.

2. Enter this new contact's name, phone number, e-mail address, and other information.

Press the **Menu** key

Figure 19-1. *Adding a PIN to contact information*

If you *do* already have this person in your **Contact** list, then you should copy-and-paste this contact's PIN into the associated contact record. Do so by following these steps:

1. Highlight the PIN number.

2. Click the Trackpad and select **Copy**.

3. Press the **Menu** key and select **Switch Application**. Or, you can press the **Alt + Escape** multitasking hot-key combination.

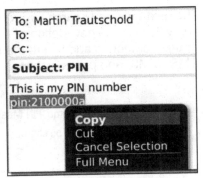

4. Locate and click your **Contact** list, if it is visible in the popup window. Otherwise, click the **Home** screen icon and launch your **Contact** list by clicking the **Contact** list icon.

5. Type a few letters of the person's first, last, or company name to find him, and then press the **Menu** key and select **Edit**.

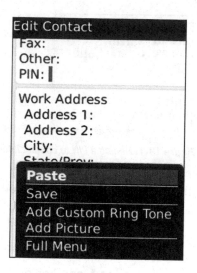

6. Glide down to the contact's **PIN number**, click the Trackpad, and select **Paste**.

7. Press the **Menu** key and select **Save**.

The next time you search through your **Contact** list, you will have the new option of sending a PIN message to this contact, in addition to the standard e-mail, SMS, MMS, and phone options.

> **TIP:** As of publishing time, PIN Messages are still free. Contrast this with SMS text, and MMS messages, which may be charged as extra services by your phone company.

Using BlackBerry Messenger (BBM)

So far, we have covered e-mail, SMS text, MMS, and BlackBerry PIN-to-PIN messaging. If you need still other ways of communicating with friends, family, and colleagues, you can try **BlackBerry Messenger** or any one of the most popular instant messaging (IM) programs, such as **AIM (AOL Instant Messenger)**, **Yahoo**, or **GoogleTalk**. **BlackBerry Messenger** is really the ultimate communication tool for communicating with other BlackBerry users.

BlackBerry Messenger (known as BBM by those who use it) is instantaneous messaging based on your BlackBerry's unique PIN number. It travels over the BlackBerry secure network, so it is also private.

> **TIP:** If you don't see the **BlackBerry Messenger** icon, try looking in your **Instant Messaging, Messaging, or Applications** folders (see Figure 19-2). If you don't still don't see it, then download and install the BlackBerry Messenger program. Go to mobile.blackberry.com from your BlackBerry web browser or click your **BlackBerry App World** icon and follow the directions you see there.

Figure 19-2. *The BlackBerry Messenger icon*

Many users have IM programs on their PCs and even on their mobile phones. BlackBerry includes a messaging program just for fellow BlackBerry users called **BlackBerry Messenger**. You will find the **BlackBerry Messenger** icon in your **Applications** menu or in your **Instant Messaging** folder.

> **NOTE:** There is a brand new version of **BlackBerry Messenger**, – version 5.0 – that offers many great enhancements. Go to the BlackBerry App World site (see Page 441 for instructions on how to do so) and download it.

Setting up BlackBerry Messenger

BlackBerry Messenger offers you a little more secure way of keeping in touch quickly with fellow BlackBerry users. Setting it up is very easy.

If you don't see the **BlackBerry Messenger** icon, then press the **Menu** key (to the left of the Trackpad) and glide up or down to find its icon. Follow these steps to set up the program:

1. Click the **BlackBerry Messenger** icon. You will be prompted to set your **User Name**.

2. Type in your **User Name** and click **OK**.

3. You will then be asked to set a **BlackBerry Messenger** password. Type in and confirm your password, and then click **OK**.

4. To change your **Display Name** or **Picture**, just press the **Menu** button and select **My Profile**. Next, move the cursor next to your **Display Name** to make changes.

5. When you are done, press the **Escape** key and save your changes.

Add Contacts to Your BlackBerry Messenger Group

Once your set up your **User Name**, you need to add appropriate contacts to your **BlackBerry Messenger Group**. In **BlackBerry Messenger**, your contacts are fellow BlackBerry users who have the **BlackBerry Messenger** program installed on their handhelds.

Follow these steps to add appropriate contacts:

1. Navigate to the main **BlackBerry Messenger** screen and press the **Menu** key.

2. Scroll to **Invite Contact** and click it.

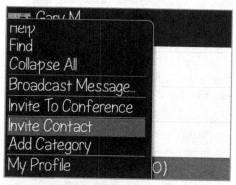

3. Begin typing the name of the desired contact. When the desired contact appears, click the Trackpad.

4. Choose whether to invite the contact by PIN or e-mail.

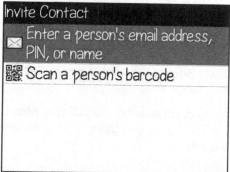

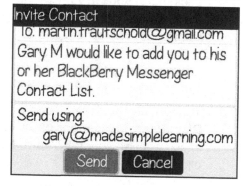

Your BlackBerry generates a message stating: "(Name) would like to add you to his/her BlackBerry Messenger." Click **OK** to send the message to your contact.

The message request shows up in your **Pending** group, under **Contacts**; the contact will be listed under **Pending** until the recipient responds to your invitation.

If you do not get a response, then click the contact's name and use another communications method (e.g., phone, e-mail, SMS, and text) to ask your colleague to hurry up and accept.

Joining a Fellow User's BlackBerry Messenger Group

You may be invited to join another BlackBerry user's messaging group. You can either **Accept** or **Decline** this invitation. You will receive your invitations via e-mail, or you can see them directly in **BlackBerry Messenger**. Follow these steps to respond to a request:

1. Click your **BlackBerry Messenger** icon.

2. Scroll to your **Requests** group, highlight the invitation, and click it.

3. A menu pops up with three options: **Accept**, **Decline**, or **Remove**.

4. Click **Accept**, and you will now be part of that messaging group. Click **Decline** to refuse the invitation or **Remove** to no longer show the invitation on your BlackBerry.

Exploring BlackBerry Messenger Menu Commands

To see BlackBerry Messenger's available menu commands, click the program's icon, get to your **Main** screen, and press the **Menu** key. You will see the following options available to you:

- **Help:** Launches the built-in **Help** menu.

- **Find:** Allows you to type in a contact name to search for a contact in **BlackBerry Messenger**.

- **Collapse All:** Hides all group members.

- **Broadcast Message:** Allows you to send one message to as many of your **BlackBerry Messenger Contacts** as you wish.

- **Invite to Conference:** Allows you to invite **BlackBerry Messenger Buddies** to a **BlackBerry Messenger Conference**.

- **Add Category:** Adds a new messaging **Category**, such as **Work**, **Family**, or **Friends**.

- **My Profile:** Allows you to make yourself **Available** or **Unavailable** to your **BlackBerry Messenger Buddies** or to change your **Picture** or **Display name**.

- **Options:** Brings up an expanded **Options** screen (you will learn more details about these options momentarily).

- **Backup/Restore Contact List:** New to **BlackBerry Messenger 5.0**, this option lets you create a wireless backup of your **BlackBerry Messenger Contacts** and restore them if you lose them or need to change your phone.

- **Create New Group:** Allows you to create new **BlackBerry Messenger Groups** to facilitate quick communication with more people.

- **Scan a Group Barcode:** Allows you to use your camera to scan a unique barcode that is part of the display profile of all **BlackBerry Messenger** users – scanning the barcode essentially invites a contact to your **BlackBerry Messenger** group.

- **Switch Application:** Allows you to multitask or jump to another application while leaving the **BlackBerry Messenger** application running.

- **Close:** Exits the **BlackBerry Messenger** application.

Options Screen

Below, we show you the entire **Options** screen to give you a feel for those items you can customize in your BlackBerry Messenger. We do not describe every option in detail as some are self-explanatory.

To see your BBM options, press the **Menu** key and select **Options** to see the screens shown in Figure 19-3.

- The default for **Press Enter key to Send** is **checked**. If you want to turn this off, **uncheck** the box. If this is **unchecked**, you will have to click the trackpad and select **Send** to send your BBM message.
- The default is a **checkmark** in the **Show Chats in Messages Application** box. This will show your BBM messages in your **Messages** (e-mail Inbox).
- You can also choose to have the BlackBerry vibrate when someone **pings** you (the default is Yes — a **checkmark** in the box).
- To save a copy of your contact list—just click on **Backup**.

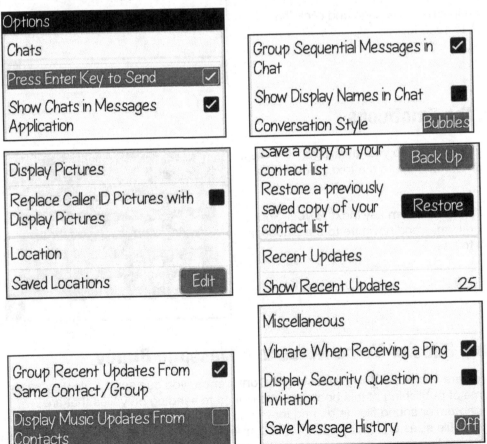

Figure 19-3. *BlackBerry Messenger's numerous options*

> **NOTE:** There are far more options to adjust in version 5 than in previous versions of BlackBerry Messenger. On the Messenger Options screen, you can set the following (and much more)

Starting or Continuing Conversations

Instant messaging works a lot like text messaging, but you actually have more options for personal expression, as well as the ability to see a complete conversation with the **BlackBerry Messaging** program.

Your **Conversations** list is in your **Main** screen. Just highlight the individual with whom you are conversing and click the Trackpad to open the **Conversation** screen.

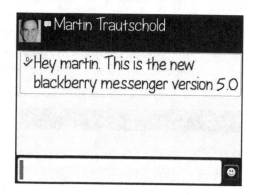

Next, type in a new message and click the Trackpad to send it.

Using the Emoticons

To add an emoticon to your message, click the **Emoticon** button next to the text input window

or press the **Sym** key (next to your **Space** key) several times and navigate to the emoticon you wish to use.

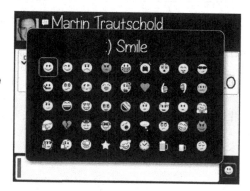

Sending Files or Voice Notes to a Message Buddy

Unless you are in a **BlackBerry Messenger Conference**, you can send a file very easily (At the time of publishing of this book, you are limited to sending only files that are images, photos, or sound files (e.g., ring tones and music). Also, sound files are limited to very small file sizes of 15KB – a ring tone). Larger image files, such as photos that are 400KB or even larger, can be sent because they are compressed to less than 15KB. Follow these steps to send a picture file:

1. Click the contact in your **Conversation** screen and open a dialogue with that individual.

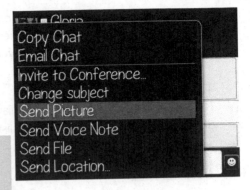

2. Press the **Menu** key and scroll and click **Send a Picture**.

> **NOTE:** You can also choose to select **Send a Voice Note**, **Send a File**, or **Send Location** to a **BlackBerry Messenger** contact, as well. With version 5.0, you can send up to a 6GB file or picture.

3. Using the Trackpad, navigate to where the image or audio file is stored on your BlackBerry and click it.

4. Selecting the file will automatically send it to your BlackBerry Messenger Buddy.

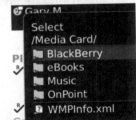

5. Click the folder that contains your music and pictures – this is usually the **BlackBerry** folder.

6. Then select music, pictures, or ringtones.

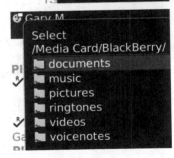

7. If you are viewing pictures, you can see either **List** view or **Thumbnail** view. **List** view shows the file names and very small pictures.

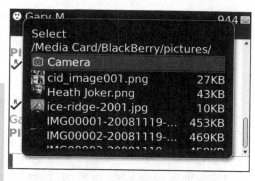

> **TIP:** To snap a picture and send it immediately, click the **Camera** option at the top of the list!

8. To see the **Thumbnail** view, press the **Menu** key and select the **View Thumbnails** option.

The cool thing about sending voice notes is that you can use them to send a highly personalized a message with your own voice. You can see what a voice note looks like for the person who receives it in the window to the right.

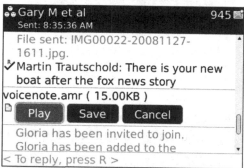

The receiver can either play or save the voice note on her own BlackBerry. When a user presses **Play**, the **Media Player** program pops up to play the voice note.

Receiving a New Messenger Item or Ping Notification

As when receiving an e-mail, you will see new BlackBerry Messenger items on your home screen with a red asterisk at the very top of the screen next  to the time, as well as on the **BlackBerry Messenger** icon itself.

> **NOTE:** That is **Pixie,** Martin's family Labradoodle, pulling on her leash.

Pinging a Contact

Let's say that you want to reach a **BlackBerry Messenger** contact quickly. One option available to you is to **Ping** that contact (see Figure 19-4). When you **Ping** a BlackBerry user, his/her device will vibrate once to let him/her know that he/she is wanted/needed immediately.

> **TIP:** You can set your BlackBerry to vibrate or not vibrate when you receive a **Ping** in your **BlackBerry Messenger Options** screen.

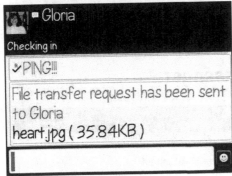

Figure 19-4. *Pinging a contact and sending a file in BlackBerry Messenger*

And you will also see the **Ping** in your **Messages** inbox.

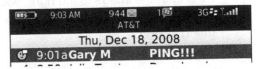

Adjusting the My Status Options

Sometimes, you might now want to be disrupted with instant messages. If so, you can change your status to **Unavailable**, and you won't be disturbed. Conversely, one of your contacts might be **Offline**, so to speak, and you will want to know when that person becomes **Available**. You can even set an alert to notify you of that person's availability. Follow these steps to change your availability:

1. Navigate to your main **Messaging** screen and press the **Menu** key.

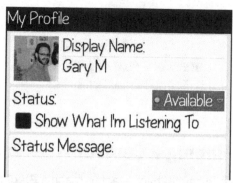

2. Scroll to **My Profile** and click it.

3. Highlight the bar next to **Status** and click the Trackpad.

4. Choose either **Available** or **Busy**.

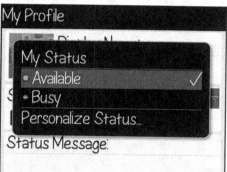

You can also personalize your status by selecting **Personalize Status** and then typing in a description and even selecting a new **Status** icon.

Conferencing with BlackBerry Messenger

One great new feature on BlackBerry Messenger is the ability to have a **Conference** chat with two or more of your Messenger contacts.

1. Just start up a conversation as you did before. In the image to the right, you can see that I am in a conversation with my friend Martin.

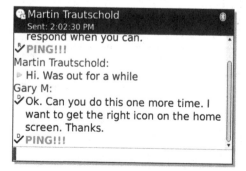

2. Now, let's say I wanted to invite Gloria to join a conversation; I press the **Menu** button and scroll to **Invite to Conference** and click the trackpad.

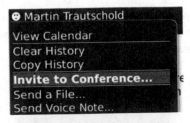

3. Then I find the contact from my Messenger list to invite Gloria.

4. An invitation is sent for her to join the conference. When she accepts, it will be noted on the Messenger screen and all three of us can have our conversation.

   Notice the 3 face icons in the top left corner, showing we are in a group

conversation.

Using Groups in BlackBerry Messenger

One of the new features in version 5.0 of **BlackBerry Messenger** is the ability to create and use **Groups**. This is very useful when you don't need to send a **Broadcast Message** to everyone, but just want to target a small group of colleagues. Follow these steps to create a new group:

1. From your main **BlackBerry Messenger** screen, click the **BlackBerry Groups** tab.

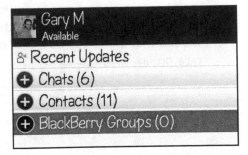

2. If you don't have any existing **BlackBerry Groups**, you will see only the **Create a New Group** tab.

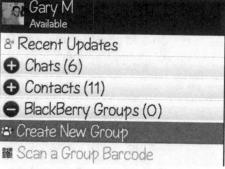

3. Fill in the **Name** and **Description** fields, and you can even choose a new **Group** icon if you wish.

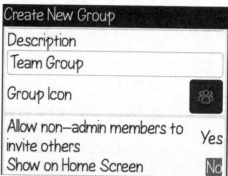

4. Click the **Create Group** option, and you will see your new group displayed.

5. Click **Members** and begin choosing members for your group.

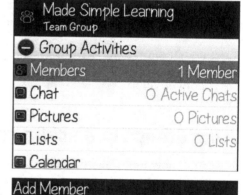

6. You can add a someone's e-mail address or scan a BlackBerry user's barcode (which we'll discuss momentarily) to add a member to your new group; or, you can simply choose an existing **BlackBerry Messenger** contact to be a part of the new group.

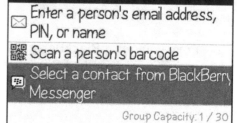

7. In the next example, I want to invite Martin and Evan to be a part of the **Made Simple Learning** team group, and they are existing **BlackBerry Messenger** contacts. So, I choose to **Select** a contact from **BlackBerry Messenger**, and then I place checkmarks next to their names.

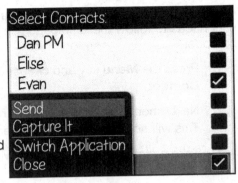

8. When I am done, I press the **Menu** key and select **Send**.

Using BBM Barcodes

Perhaps the most innovative feature of the new **BlackBerry Messenger** is the ability to use a unique barcode as a means of connecting to someone as a **BlackBerry Messenger** contact.

Each BlackBerry can generate its own unique barcode. Follow these steps to find your unique barcode:

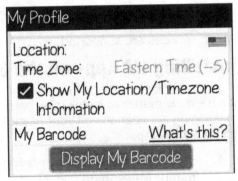

1. Start up the **BlackBerry Messenger** application, press the **Menu** key, and select **My Profile**.

2. Scroll down to **Display My Barcode** and click the Trackpad. The screen will now show your unique barcode.

Any other BlackBerry user (with **BlackBerry Messenger 5.0** installed *and* a BlackBerry with a camera) can now snap a picture of your barcode.

At this point, another **BlackBerry Messenger** user needs to follow these steps to use your barcode:

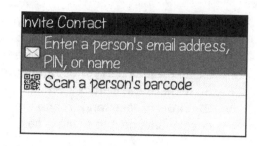

1. Press the **Menu** key and choose **Invite Contact.**

2. Next, choose **Scan person's barcode**. This will activate the user's camera.

3. Take a picture of your barcode with the buil

Using AIM, Yahoo, and Google Talk Messaging

As you get used to **BlackBerry Messenger**, you will begin to see that it is a powerful way of quickly keeping in touch with friends, family, and colleagues. Realizing that many people are still not in the BlackBerry world, you can also access and use popular IM programs such as **AOL Instant Messenger** (**AIM**), **Yahoo Messenger**, and **Google Talk Messenger** right out-of-the-box on the BlackBerry. Individual carriers do have some restrictions, however, and you will need to check your carrier's web site to see which services are supported.

Installing IM Apps on the BlackBerry

It's a simple matter to install third-party instant messaging applications on your BlackBerry. Simply follow these steps:

1. First see whether your carrier has placed an **IM** or **Instant Messaging** folder icon in your **Applications** directory.

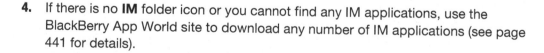

2. If so, navigate to the **Applications** directory and scroll for an icon that is called **IM**.

3. If you have an **IM** folder icon, click and follow the on-screen prompts to install the desired applications.

4. If there is no **IM** folder icon or you cannot find any IM applications, use the BlackBerry App World site to download any number of IM applications (see page 441 for details).

Chapter 20

Adding Memory with a Media Card

As we have shown you in this book, your BlackBerry is a very capable media device. Eventually, you will need additional space to hold all those pictures, songs and videos that you will be downloading and transferring onto your BlackBerry.

Your BlackBerry comes with about 0.25GB (Gigabyte) of main memory, but all of that won't be available to you. Operating system and installed software takes up some of that room and so will all your personal information. (The image of the SanDisk MicroSD card and the SanDisk logo are copyrights owned by SanDisk Corporation.)

You will find yourself quickly wishing you had more room to store things like music files, videos, ringtones, and pictures. In this chapter, we'll walk you through how you can expand the amount of available memory on your BlackBerry by installing a media card. We will show you how to verify and use your additional memory to store the files that are important to you.

Boosting Your Memory with a Media Card

You can expand on your BlackBerry's built-in memory by using a specialized MicroSD memory card comes in. You can purchase MicroSD memory cards of 2GB, 4GB, and even higher capacities. At the time of publishing, the maximum allowable capacity for a BlackBerry running Operating System Software version 5.0 is 32GB; however, it is likely that this value will increase over time.

Installing your Memory Card / Media Card

The BlackBerry's MicroSD card slot is actually under its battery door – next to the battery. To insert a MicroSD card, follow these steps:

1. Access the MicroSD card slot by pressing on the release latch at the bottom of the BlackBerry's cover to remove it.

2. Insert the card with the metal contacts facing down, and then slide the card towards the bottom of the BlackBerry, with the printed label facing up (see Figure 20-1).

3. Replace the back cover of the BlackBerry.

Media Card Slot
(Inside the back door)
(MicroSD format)
Place the card with metal contacts facing down and slide it into the slot to the left of the battery.

NOTE: You do not need to remove the battery to insert the Media Card.

Slide Micro SD Card into the Media Card Slot

Figure 20-1. *A BlackBerry Curve with the back off*

You don't even need to power off the BlackBerry; you can insert the card with the BlackBerry on. When the card is correctly inserted you should see **Media Card Inserted** text appear on the screen.

Verifying the Media Card Installation and Free Memory

Once the card is installed, it is a good idea to double-check that the card is installed correctly and to see how much free space is available (see Figure 20-2). Follow these steps to do so:

1. Use the Trackpad to glide to the **Options** icon and click it. You may need to press the **Menu** key to the left of the Trackpad to see this icon if it is not visible. You can also press the letter **O** if you have your hotkeys turned on.

Options
About
Advanced Options
Auto On/Off
AutoText
CellData
Date/Time
GPS Extended Ephemeris
Language
Memory
Mobile Network

2. Scroll down, select **Memory**, and click it.

> **TIP:** Pressing the first letter of an entry in the **Options** screen (or in menus) will jump to the first entry in the list, starting with that letter. So pressing **M** will jump to the first entry starting with **M**, while pressing it a second time will jump to the next entry that starts with **M**.

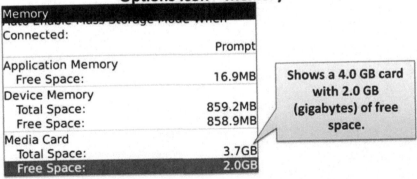

Media Card
Verify it is Installed Correctly and
Amount of Free Space
Options Icon > Memory

Memory	
Connected:	
	Prompt
Application Memory	
Free Space:	16.9MB
Device Memory	
Total Space:	859.2MB
Free Space:	858.9MB
Media Card	
Total Space:	3.7GB
Free Space:	2.0GB

Shows a 4.0 GB card with 2.0 GB (gigabytes) of free space.

Figure 20-2. *The free space available on the media card*

Look at the **Total Space** value listed at the bottom of the screen. A 4GB card will read about 3.7MB (1GB equals about 1,000 MB). If you see that number, all is good.

Chapter 21

Exploring Your Music Player

Your BlackBerry is more than your personal digital assistant, your e-mail machine, and your **Address Book**. Today's BlackBerry is also a very capable **Media Player** program, letting you carry your music, playlists, podcasts, and more. You can transfer playlists from iTunes and other media programs, as well.

In this chapter we will show you how to locate and listen to your music on your BlackBerry. You will learn how to use the media-centric keys on the device.

We will also show you how to use playlists on the BlackBerry and how to control every aspect of your music playing experience.

Listening to Your Music

You may be amazed at how great a music player your BlackBerry can be! For example, you can even use it listen to free streaming Internet radio with software such as **Slacker** and **Pandora** – see page 384 for more information. A good-sized media card and the BlackBerry's built-in the media capabilities might even have you suggest the following: "Why do I need an iPhone or iPod? I've got a BlackBerry!"

Important Media Player Keys

Your BlackBerry includes several dedicated keys that you use manipulate media on your device (see Figure 21-1).

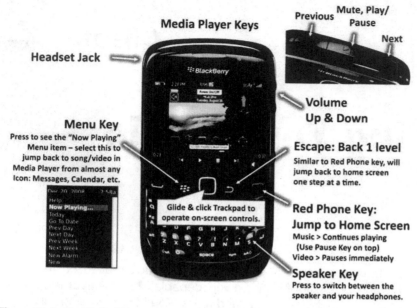

Figure 21-1. *The Media Player's buttons and keys*

Media Player Hotkeys, Tips, and Tricks

See page 553 for a list of many important hot keys, tips, and tricks.

Getting Music and Playlists onto Your BlackBerry

The BlackBerry comes with internal memory, but the operating system (OS) and other pre-loaded programs take up some of that space , what's left over is usually not enough to store all your music. For that reason, we highly recommend you buy and insert a media card to boost the memory available to store your favorite music – see page 22 for more information on how to do this.

NOTE: Some BlackBerry smartphones come pre-installed with media cards.

If you are Windows PC user, please refer to page 105 for information on how to transfer music and playlists onto your BlackBerry. If you are an Apple Mac user, please refer to page 141. In addition to the approaches outlined on the pages just cited, you can also use these approaches to get music and videos onto your computer:

- Save music or video files from a web site to your BlackBerry.
- Receive music or video using a Bluetooth file transfer.

The next couple sections will walk you through how to accomplish these **Tasks**.

Acquiring Music or Videos from the Web

Some web sites offer you videos or music to download to your BlackBerry. You usually are given two options for playing media: streaming it (i.e., opening and playing the file in real time) or downloading and saving it for future playback.

You may see this question to the right when you try to access a file. If so, you must select **OK** if you want to stream the video on your BlackBerry. Check the **Don't ask this again** option to avoid seeing this question again.

Finally, after a little time during which you may see a loading or buffering message, the video will start playing.

NOTE: When you choose to stream videos, you will not be able to save the video on your BlackBerry. If you want to save a file, you should select the **Download** option instead of **Open** or **Play**.

Is that the Terminator?

No, it's the Governor.

Playing Your Music

Once your music is in the right place, you are ready to start enjoying the benefit of having your music on your BlackBerry at all times.

The fastest way to get to your music is by clicking the **Music** icon . You may first

need to click your **Media** folder icon,  and then select **Music**.

Inside the **Music** program, you see various preset options to find and play your favorite music, including the following:

All Songs: Shows you every song on your BlackBerry.

Artists: Shows you all artists; you can click artists to see all their songs.

Albums: Shows a list of all albums.

Genres: Shows a list of all genres on your BlackBerry, such as pop, rock, jazz, and so on.

Playlists: Shows all playlists or allows you to create new ones.

Sample Songs: Shows one or more sample songs preloaded on your device.

Shuffle Songs: Plays all your music in a shuffle mode or random order.

Finding and Playing an Individual Song

One you have your music on your BlackBerry, you're ready to listen to it. Follow these steps to do so:

1. If you know the name of the song, then just type a few letters of any word in the song's name into the **Find:** field at the top of the device to instantly locate all matching songs.

2. In the example to the right, typing **Love** shows all matching songs on my device.

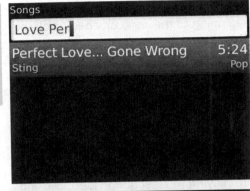

TIP: To narrow the list, press the **Space** key and type a few more letters of another word. Notice that after I type **Love Per**, only "Perfect Love... Gone Wrong" shows in the list.

3. Click a song to bring up the **Media Player**. Once the **Music Player** program opens, your song will begin to play.

4. Clicking the Trackpad will pause the player or continue playback.

TIP: Pressing the **Mute** key on the top of your BlackBerry will also pause or resume playback of songs and videos.

The volume keys on the side of the BlackBerry control the song volume.

Controlling Your Song or Video

There are a few ways to move around to a different section of song or video. First, if the song or video is playing, you need to click the Trackpad once (or the **Mute** key on the top of the BlackBerry) to stop the current media from playing.

To stop the playback and go to the beginning of the song or video, click the **Stop** icon.

To go to the beginning of the song or video, click the **Back** button shown to the right. To jump to the previous song/video in the list, click the button again.

To go to next song/video in the list / playlist, click the **Forward** button. If you are playing the last song/video, clicking this button will take you to the end of the current item.

To move around to a specific location in a song or video, follow these steps:

Click the slider to start moving it.

1. Pause the media as described previously.

2. Glide the Trackpad up to highlight the slider bar and then click it.

Glide the Trackpad to move the slider.

3. Glide the Trackpad left or right to move to a different location. When done, click the Trackpad again to complete the move.

Click the Trackpad to complete the move.

4. Click the **Play** button again to resume playback.

Getting Back to Your Video or Song

If you have pressed the **Escape** key a few times or the **Red Phone** key to leave your music playing or video paused, then you will see a new menu item on most of your icons near the top: the **Now Playing...** item (see Figure 21-2). Just select this option to jump right back into the **Media Player** program where you left off, and you can continue playing your video or song.

Figure 21-2. *Using the Now Playing option in the Music menu*

Getting the Most from Your Music

The **Music Player** program offers quite a few nifty options for playing back your music in interesting ways. For example, you can choose to just play songs in your library, shuffle the order you play them, repeat a song, and so on.

Playing All Your Music and Selecting Shuffle

Sometimes you just want to play the songs in your library; other times you want to have songs play randomly. In this section, we will cover how to do both of these things. Navigate to your music as described previously and highlight the first song in the folder or playlist you wish to play. If you have not set up individual folders or playlists, just highlight the first song – and then click the Trackpad to begin playing the highlighted song. At this point, the **Music Player** will begin to play all the songs in that particular folder or playlist. (You can also select **Play** from the menu.)

To **Shuffle** the order in which your BlackBerry plays the songs in a particular folder, follow these steps.

1. Navigate to the first song in your folder.

2. Press the **Menu** key and click **Shuffle**.

> **TIP:** If there is a checkmark next to **Shuffle** in the menu, the feature is already on; clicking it again will turn the feature off.

The Shuffle icon: Two crossed, bolded arrows

Repeating a Song or Video

When a song or video is playing, you can also choose to have that song or video (or the library or folder it comes from) keep playing indefinitely. To do so, press the **Menu** key and select **Repeat**.

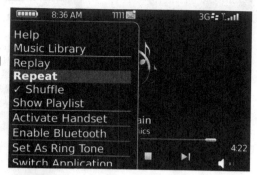

Now you will see the **Repeat** icon in the lower left corner of your device.

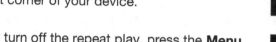

To turn off the repeat play, press the **Menu** key again and select the **Repeat** option – this will turn off the checkmark next to the menu item, and stop the track from playing continuously.

Finding Your Music When You Use a Memory Card

Assuming you have followed the steps recommended previously about how to store your music files, your music is now on a MicroSD media card. Assume you want to play your music from the card –what do you do?

From your **Home** screen of icons, you have two ways to view and listen to music:

Option 1: Click the **Music** icon.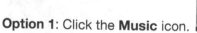

Option 2: Click the **Media** folder, and then click the **Music** icon.

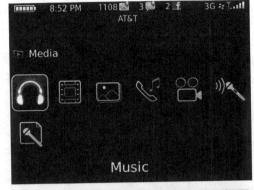

The available music folders are now displayed.

Click the appropriate folder (if your music is on a media card, click that folder), and all of your music will now be displayed. Click any song to start playing it.

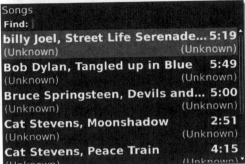

Playing One of Your Playlists

To see the playlists on the BlackBerry, follow these steps:

1. Glide to the **Media Player** icon and click it.

2. Find the **Music** icon and click it. Or, just click the **Music** icon from the **Home** page.

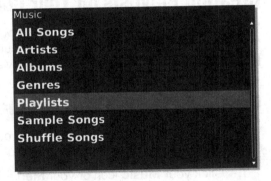

3. Scroll down to **Playlists** and click the Trackpad.

You can see playlists synced from iTunes are now listed right on the BlackBerry.

4. Now simply click the **Bike Riding** playlist to begin playing the songs in that list.

5. To see the list of songs in a playlist, press the **Menu** key and select **Show Playlist.**

Many MP3 players utilize playlists to organize music, enabling you to create a unique mix of songs.

NOTE: See page 354 for information on what types of music the BlackBerry supports.

Creating Playlists on Your Computer

You can use the supported computer software on your computer to create playlists and then sync them to your BlackBerry. If you use a Windows PC, please refer to page 105 for more information; if you use an Apple Mac, please refer to page 141.

Creating Playlists on Your BlackBerry

You don't have to create playlists on your computer; you can also create them directly on your BlackBerry by following these steps:

1. Click your **Music** icon or your **Media** icon, and then click **Music**.

2. Click **Playlists** to get into the **Playlists** section, as shown to the right.

3. Next, you can either click [**New Playlist**] at the top of the screen... or you can press the **Menu** key and select **New Playlist** from the menu.

4. Now you need to select **Standard Playlist** or **Automatic Playlist**. Select **Standard Playlist** to select and add any songs already stored on your BlackBerry.

5. Now give your new playlist a name next to the **Name:** field at the top, press the **Menu** key, and select **Add Songs** to begin adding new songs.

TIP: To find your songs, you can just scroll up or down the list or type a few letters you know are in the title of the song, such as **love**. Doing this instantly shows all matching songs.

6.   When you find the song you want, just click it to add it to your playlist.

TIP: You can remove songs from the playlist by selecting a song, pressing the **Menu** key, and then selecting **Remove**.

TIP: The **Automatic Playlist** feature allows you to create some general parameters for your playlists, based on artists, songs, or genres.

BlackBerry's Supported Music Types

The BlackBerry will play most types of music files. If you are an iPod user, all music except the music that you purchased on iTunes should be able to play on the BlackBerry.

Sometimes you can use software to help play music your BlackBerry couldn't otherwise play out-of-the-box. For example, if you burn your iTunes tracks to a CD (make a new playlist in iTunes, copy your iTunes tracks, and then burn that playlist), **Roxio Media Manager** can convert these tracks to play on the BlackBerry.

The most common audio/music formats supported on the BlackBerry include the following:

- **ACC:** Audio compression formats AAC

- **AAC+ and EAAC+ AMR:** Adaptive Multi Rate-Narrow Band (AMR-NB) speech coder standard

- **MIDI:** Polyphonic MIDI

- **MP3:** Encoded using MPEG

- **WAV:** Supports sample rates of 8 kHz, 16 kHz, 22.05 kHz, 32 kHz, 44.1 kHz, and 48 kHz with 8-bit and 16-bit depths in mono or stereo

NOTE: Some WAV file formats may not be supported by your BlackBerry.

Exploring Your Media Player Options

To adjust your media options, press the **Menu** key and select **Options** to see the options screen (see Figure 21-3). You can then toggle the equalizer for your headset on or off. You can also enable the **Audio Boost** option, which is disabled by default, as well as turn on **Auto Backlighting** or adjust **Closed Captions** (options include **Enable**, **Change Style**, and **Change Position**).

TIP: You can pause (and instantly silence) any song or video playing on your BlackBerry by pressing the **Mute** key on the top of your BlackBerry. Press **Mute** again to resume playback.

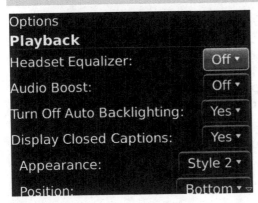

Figure 21-3. *The Media Player options*

Music Player Tips and Tricks

The **Music Player** program includes quite a number of helpful tips and tricks you can use to enhance your enjoyment of music on your blackberry:

- To pause a song or video, press the **Mute** key on the top of the BlackBerry.

- To resume playing a track, press the **Mute** key again.

- To move to the next item, press **N** (this also works for pictures).

- To move to the next track, press and hold the **Volume Up** key.

- To move to a previous item (in your playlist or Video library), press **P**.

- To move to the previous track, press and hold the **Volume Down** key.

> **TIP:** Check out our list of the **Media Player** program's hotkeys on page 169.

Streaming Music

One of the amazing things about the BlackBerry is just how powerful it can be as a media center. Using a Bluetooth stereo in your car, you can stream your music via Bluetooth right through your car stereo.

To stream stereo music via Bluetooth, just pair your BlackBerry with a Bluetooth music source, as described on Page 451. Also, ensure that the Bluetooth device supports the **Bluetooth Stereo Audio** format (sometimes called **A2DP**). You should also ensure that your BlackBerry is connected to a stereo music player or use the BlackBerry **Remote Stereo Gateway** utility mentioned on page 459. If you meet these criteria, you can simply follow the steps for playing your music described earlier in this chapter.

Streaming Free Internet Radio

Internet radio is a great way to listen to music on the go. There are several applications that allow you to set up and listen to streaming Internet radio, including several great free applications for the BlackBerry. All these applications work well. The two most popular are **Pandora** and **Slacker Radio**, both of which you can find on the BlackBerry App World site.

Just set up your account, specify the type of music you like and you should be **Streaming** Internet Radio in minutes.

Pandora Internet Radio

Pandora is an outgrowth of the Music Genome project. Essentially, **Pandora** is streaming Internet radio where you shape the playlists by building radio stations based around your favorite artists.

Downloading Pandora

The easiest way to download **Pandora** is to go to the BlackBerry App World site (see page 441) and download the **Pandora** app. If **Pandora** is not part of the **Featured Apps** section, you can find it in the **Music** section or by doing a simple search for **Pandora**.

You can also visit www.pandora.com and download the app from the company's web site right to your BlackBerry – just agree to the company's terms and select **Download** when the download screen appears.

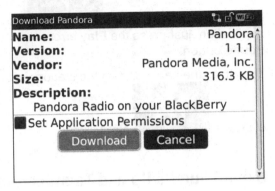

Starting Pandora for the First Time

When **Pandora** starts for the first time, you will be asked if you have an existing account or if you would like to create a new one.

If you have an account, just type in your e-mail and your password; and if you don't have an account, just type in your e-mail and a password – a new account will be created for you. The best thing about **Pandora** is that it is absolutely free!

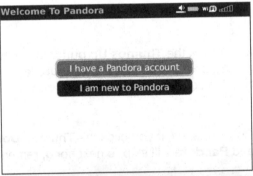

If this is your first time using **Pandora**, you will be asked to **Create a New Station**. If you have an existing **Pandora** account, you will see all your stations on the front page, along with the **Create a New Station** option.

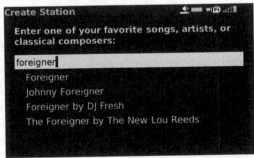

NOTE: Pandora also works on your PC or Mac. You can create your stations and listen to them on your computer. To listen on your BlackBerry instead, just log in, and all the stations you created on your computer will appear.

Using Pandora's Controls and Options

The interface of **Pandora** is very clean and intuitive. To play or pause the application, just press the **Play** arrow or **Pause** button.

To skip to the next song on the station, just click the  **Next** arrow.

Using Thumbs Up and Thumbs Down

You can also click the **Thumbs Up** and **Thumbs Down** buttons.

If you click the **Thumbs Up** button, a checkmark is placed on the song, letting **Pandora** know that you like this song, and it can be used again.

Consequently, if you click the **Thumbs Down** button, a very quick checkmark appears, and **Pandora** will skip to next song, remembering to never play that song again.

Listening to Slacker Radio

Conceptually, **Slacker Radio** is similar to **Pandora**. This application lets you build stations around your favorite artists or choose from hundreds of existing stations to listen to.

Like **Pandora**, **Slacker Radio** works on both your PC or Mac, as well as your BlackBerry.

Downloading and Installing Slacker Radio

As you did for **Pandora**, you have two options for downloading **Slacker**. You can find **Slacker** in the BlackBerry App World site, or you can also go to the company's web site at www.slacker.com and download the latest build for BlackBerry. Follow the on screen instructions you find on the site to download and install the application. Accept the license agreement, and you will be *Slacking* in no time!

Creating or Logging into Slacker

As with **Pandora**, your first screen for **Slacker** will ask whether you have an existing **Slacker** account or you wish to create one. Either log in or create a new account by clicking the button at the bottom of the screen. Like **Pandora**, **Slacker** can also run on your computer!

If you have an existing **Slacker** account, you will see a screen with your favorite stations displayed.

If you are signing on for the first time, you have two options:

- **Option 1:** Scroll down to check out stations by genre.

- **Option 2:** Click **Search** at the top of the app and build a new station with music created from your favorite artists, just as you did with **Pandora**.

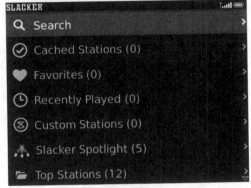

In the example shown to the right, we are creating a new station based on music by Peter Gabriel.

Choosing Your Station

Once you have some created stations, **Slacker** will present you with a couple options each time you log in. You can choose to listen to one of your favorite stations, or you can listen to other spotlight stations or genres in the **Slacker** library of music stations.

Using Controls in Slacker

Slacker offers a few more controls and options than **Pandora** does. You can access the controls via the dock of buttons at the bottom. The **Home** button takes you back to the app's **Home** screen, where you can choose your station.

The **Next** arrow takes you to the next song in the station's lineup. Notice that **Slacker** displays a picture of the next song or artist that will play to the right of the album cover of the current song.

If you like the current artist or song, click the **Heart** button to instruct **Slacker** to remember that.

If you don't want to hear the current artist or song again, click the **Do Not Play** (or **Ban**)

button.

Leveraging Slacker's Menu Commands and Shortcut Keys

Slacker offers some very cool commands in its basic menu. Just press the **Menu** button on your BlackBerry, and you can see a list of significant options: **Stations**, **Lyrics** (to the current song), **Artist Bio**, **Album Review**, **Ban This Artist**, **Filter Explicit Content**, **Enable Bluetooth** (see page 459 for more information on **A2DP Stereo Bluetooth**), and many more.

Using Slacker's One-Key Shortcuts for Slacker

Slacker includes quite a few one-key shortcuts you can use to improve your listening experience. Key shortcuts include the following:

- **N** = Skip to Next Song

NOTE: The free version of **Slacker** limits you to six skips per hour.

- **Space** = Play / Pause Song

- **H** = Heart; this option indicates you like the song playing, so play more songs like it

- **B** = Ban Song; this option indicates you don't like the song, so don't ever play it again

Chapter 22

Snapping Pictures

Many BlackBerry devices sold today come with a built-in camera – which makes the device perfect for snapping a quick picture. Some BlackBerry devices issued by companies might not have a camera for security reasons. Your device's camera – and the photos you take – can easily be shared with others via e-mail or MMS messaging. They can even uploaded to Facebook and other social media programs.

Using the Camera

Your BlackBerry includes a feature-rich camera. This gives you the option of snapping a picture anywhere you might be. You can then send the picture to friends and family, sharing the moment.

You can get as involved as you want in taking pictures with your BlackBerry, not least because options that ship with the camera give you a lot of control over the pictures you take. Before we get to that, however, let's familiarize ourselves with the camera's main buttons and features.

Starting the Camera Application

The **Camera** application can be started in one of two ways: by pushing the **Convenience** key on the right-side of the device or by clicking the **Camera** icon (see Figure 22-1).

Figure 22-1. *Using the Camera app on the BlackBerry*

Starting the Camera with the Convenience Key

Unless you have re-programmed your **Convenience** key (see page 187 for details on how to do that), then pressing the right-side key – the one directly below the volume control buttons – will start your camera.

Push this button once, and the **Camera** app should start.

Starting the Camera with the Camera Icon

Alternatively, you can start the **Camera** app in only a couple steps using the **Camera** icon:

1. Press the **Menu** key to see all your icons.

2. Scroll to the **Camera** icon and click the Trackpad.

Using the Normal Viewfinder Mode

The BlackBerry has one standard **Viewfinder** mode.

If you use the **Viewfinder**, you will see a picture in the background with the status bar at the bottom.

If you don't do anything, then the status bar disappears.

As soon as you click a picture or touch any key, then the status bar reappears.

Taking Action Shots

Once you start the Camera and are in viewfinder mode. You can press the Right Convenience key to focus the camera. You will see the little box in the middle of the screen go from white to green. Green shows that the BlackBerry thinks it has focused.

This allows you to snap the picture immediately when you click the trackpad.

If you do not use the Convenience key to focus the camera, when you click the trackpad, the camera will first focus, then take the picture. This may cause you to miss an action shot.

Using the Camera Zoom

Like many cameras, the camera on your BlackBerry lets you zoom in and out relative to your subject. Zooming could not be easier.

Simply frame your picture and gently glide up the Trackpad; the **Camera** app will zoom in on the subject.

> **TIP:** You can also use the Volume Up/Down keys to zoom.

The digital **Zoom** level will be displayed to the right of the **Camera** icon, in the middle of the bottom status bar. This **Zoom**-level indicator will show a range of **1.0x – 5.0x**, indicating the power of zoom chosen.

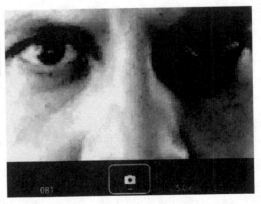

To Zoom back out, just glide the Trackpad down.

Exploring the Camera Screen's Icons

You will usually see one of two things when you open the **Camera** application: the last picture you took or what the camera lens currently sees. You can see five icons underneath the picture window, four of which are detailed in the following table (the fifth, the **E-mail Envelope** icon, will be covered later in this chapter):

IMG 00112-2008 1219 -08 16

 **The Take a Picture** icon

Click this icon to take another picture.

 **The Trash Can** icon

Sometimes, the picture you take might not be what you want. If this happens, simply scroll to the **Trash Can** icon and click it. The last picture taken will then be deleted.

 **The Rename / Folder** icon

With a picture you desire to save on the screen, click the **Folder** icon to specify a new location or file name. We recommend renaming important pictures to a more meaningful name than what the Camera app assigns by default. For example, you might change the default name **IMG00008-20100314-1855** to **Martha Birthday**.

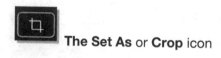 **The Set As** or **Crop** icon

You can click the **Set As** icon to use the picture in the main window as either the **Home** screen wallpaper or as a picture-based caller ID for someone in your **Address Book**.

 **The E-mail as** icon

You can also set that picture as a background image for your **Home** screen, just as you might set the desktop background image on your computer. Follow these steps to set the background image:

1. Open a picture from the **My Pictures** folder.

2. Press the **Menu** key and select **Set As...**

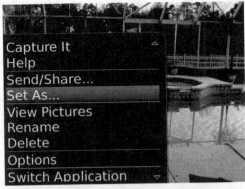

3. Select the **Wallpaper** option to use the image as your background image.

Sending Pictures with the Envelope Icon

 The BlackBerry gives you several ways to send your pictures via e-mail. For example, the **Camera** application contains the handy **Envelope** icon, which lets you e-mail the picture on your screen quickly to one of your contacts.

Clicking the **Envelope** icon brings up the **Send As** dialog box.

From here, you can click one of the following options:

- **MMS:** Sends a file via Multi Media Message (as the body of an e-mail); you can learn all about MMS on page 343.

- **Send to Messenger Contact:** Sends a file via **BlackBerry Messenger**, the BlackBerry's instant messaging app. This option may not be available if you have not yet set up **BlackBerry Messenger** – see page 352 to learn more).

- **E-mail:** Sends a file via e-mail, where the file is attached to the e-mail as an image file.

- **Send to Facebook:** Sends the file to Facebook. You must have Facebook installed to use this feature.

- **Send to Flikr:** Sends the file to Flikr. You must have Flikr installed to use this feature.

- You may see additional options in this list, depending on what other apps you have installed.

After choosing a method to deliver your picture, navigate to the contact you want to send the file to, and click the Trackpad to finish sending your picture.

Fine-Tuning Your Camera Settings

You can fine tune your Curve camera to fit your needs with flash, zoom, white balance, picture quality and size.

Setting the Flash Mode and Zoom

One of the nice features of the BlackBerry camera is the fact it includes a flash. As with most digital cameras, you can adjust the properties of the camera's flash. The BlackBerry includes two option for customizing its flash:

- Adjust Flash Mode: Tap the **Space** key to change the Flash mode.

- Adjust Zoom: Glide the Trackpad up/down or use the Volume keys on the right side to adjust the Zoom level (see Figure 22-2).

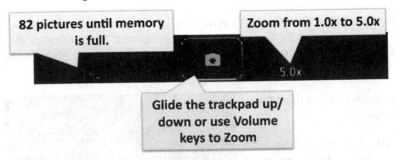

82 pictures until memory is full.

Zoom from 1.0x to 5.0x

Glide the trackpad up/down or use Volume keys to Zoom

Figure 22-2. *Adjust the Camera app's Flash and Zoom settings*

Changing the Default Flash Settings

Setting your camera's default flash setting is simple enough. Simply follow these steps:

1. With your subject framed in the camera window, press the **Space** key.

2. Look in the lower right-hand corner of the screen to see the current flash mode of the camera displayed. You will see three available **Flash** modes:

   - **Automatic:** Indicated by the **Flash** symbol with the **A** next to it.

   - **On:** Indicated by the Flash symbol (this will use more battery power)

   - **Off:** Indicated by the **No Flash** symbol

3. The next step is to change the default **Flash** mode. When using the **Camera** app, press the **Menu** key and select **Options**.

4. Use the Trackpad and highlight the **Default Flash Settings** in the upper right-hand corner.

5. Select from **Off**, **On**, or **Automatic** (the default).

6. Press the **Menu** key and save your settings.

Adjusting the Size of the Picture

The size of your pictures corresponds to the number of pixels or dots used to render the image. If you tend to transfer your BlackBerry pictures to your desktop for printing or e-mailing, you might want a bigger or smaller picture to work with. Follow these steps to adjust the camera's picture size:

1. From the Camera screen, press the **Menu** key and select **Options.**

2. Scroll down to **Picture Size** and select the size of your picture: **Small**, **Medium**, or **Large**.

3. Press the **Menu** key and then select **Save** to keep your settings.

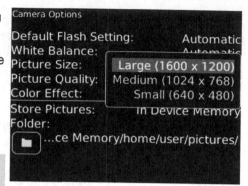

> **TIP:** If you like to e-mail your pictures, you will send them faster if you set your **Picture Size** option to **Small**.

Adjusting the White Balance

Usually the automatic white balance works fairly well. However, there may be times when you want to manually control it.

In this case, you would select from the manual options for the **White Balance** setting in the aforementioned **Camera Options** screen.

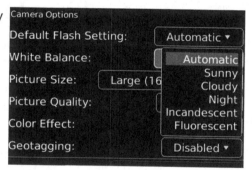

Adjusting the Picture Quality

While the BlackBerry is not meant to replace a 7- or 8-mega pixel camera, it is a very capable photo device. There are times when you might need or desire to change the picture quality. For example, perhaps you are using your BlackBerry camera for work, and you need to capture an important image. Fortunately, it is quite easy to adjust the quality of your photos, but this does affect how much space is required to save a picture.

CAUTION: Increasing the quality or the size of your pictures will also increase the memory requirements for that particular picture.

In one non-scientific test, changing the picture quality resulted in the following changes to the file size of the picture at a fixed-size setting of **Large (1600 x 1200)**:

- **Normal**: The image's file size is approximately 80k (for an indoors picture).

- **Fine**: The image's file size is approximately 250% larger than for the Normal setting.

- **Superfine**: The image's file size is approximately 400% larger than for the **Normal** setting.

NOTE: Pictures taken outdoors usually are larger than those taken indoors.

Follow these steps to adjust your **Picture Quality** setting:

1. Press the **Menu** key and select **Options**.

2. Scroll to **Picture Quality** and click one of these three options to choose your preferred quality: **Normal**, **Fine**, or **Superfine**.

3. Press the **Menu** key and save your settings.

Geotagging - Adding GPS Location to Pictures

One fun feature available on some BlackBerry devices is **geotagging**, where you assign the current GPS (Global Positioning System) longitude and latitude location (if available) to each picture taken on your BlackBerry camera.

NOTE: Geotagging is only available if you have built-in BlackBerry GPS (e.g. 8530 model) or you have paired up your BlackBerry with a Bluetooth GPS receiver.

Of course, you might wonder why would you want to enable geotagging. Some online sites, such as **Flickr** (photo sharing) and **Google Earth** (mapping), can put your geotagged photo on a map to show exactly where you took the picture (see Figure 22-3).

TIP: To install **Flickr** on your BlackBerry, go to `http://mobile.blackberry.com` and click the **Social Networking** link.

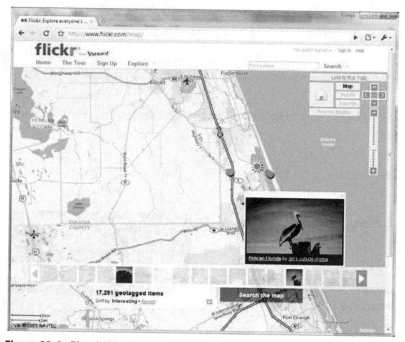

Figure 22-3. *Pinpointing where you took a picture with Flickr*

This preceding map from the **www.flickr.com** site shows what geotagging your photos can accomplish – essentially, this feature will allow you to see exactly where you snapped your photos and help you organize them.

Other programs you can purchase for your computer can organize all your photos by showing their location on a map. To find such software, do a web search for the following phrase: **geotag photo software (mac or windows)**.

To turn **Geotagging** feature on or off, follow these steps from the **Camera** screen:

1. Press the **Menu** key and select **Options**.

2. Glide down to **Geotagging** and set it to **Enabled**.

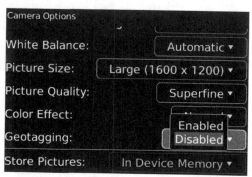

3. You will then see the warning message displayed to the right. Make sure you glide down to the **Don't ask this again** check box, and then check it by clicking the Trackpad or pressing the **Space** key.

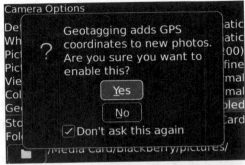

You know the **Geotagging** feature is turned on if you see the white plus sign with circle around it and the three waves to the right of it in the lower right of your **Camera** screen.

If the **Geotagging** feature is turned on, but your BlackBerry does not have a GPS signal to tag the pictures with, you will see a red plus sign with a circle around it right next to a red **X** in the lower right-hand corner.

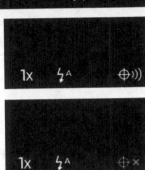

Managing Picture Storage

We, the authors, strongly recommend buying a MicroSD Media Card for use in your BlackBerry. Prices for such cards have dipped below US $20 for a 2GB card, which is very low when compared to the price of your BlackBerry. For more information on inserting the media card, please see page 367. You will learn more about storing pictures on the media card later in this chapter.

If you do not have a media card, then you will want to carefully manage the amount of your BlackBerry's main **Device Memory**, which is used for pictures.

Selecting Where Pictures Are Stored

The default setting is for the BlackBerry to store pictures in main Device Memory; however, if you have a media card inserted, we recommend selecting that location instead.

To confirm the default picture storage location, follow these steps:

1. Press the **Menu** key from the main **Camera** screen, scroll to **Options**, and click that selection.

2. Scroll down to the **Store Pictures** and select **On Media Card** (if you have one) or **In Device Memory** (if you do not have a media card).

3. Look at the **Folder** icon at the bottom and make sure the folder name ends with this word: **/pictures**. Doing this will help keep pictures together with pictures, videos with videos, and music with music. This general approach will make it easier on you when you want to transfer pictures to and from your computer.

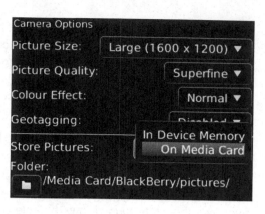

Using the Optional Media Card

At publishing time, your BlackBerry can support up to a 32GB MicroSD media card. To give you some perspective, a 4GB card can store many times the volume of information that ships with the BlackBerry's internal device memory. This is equivalent to the space required for several full-length feature films or thousands of songs. You can learn how to install a media card in the chapter beginning on page 22. Program files can only be stored in **Main** memory, so recommend putting as much of your media files on the MicroSD card as possible.

Viewing Pictures

Your BlackBerry gives you two primary ways of viewing stored pictures: from the **Camera** program or from the **Media Player** program. Next, you'll learn how to use each approach.

Option #1: From the Camera

Follow these steps to use the built-in **Camera** program to view pictures on your BlackBerry:

1. Open up the **Camera** application and press the **Menu** key.

2. Scroll down to **View Pictures** and navigate to the appropriate folder to view your pictures (see Figure 22-4).

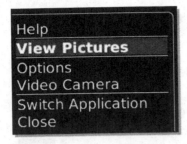 

Figure 22-4. *Viewing pictures from the Pictures folder*

Option #2: From the Media Player

Your second option is to use the **Media Player** menu to view pictures on your BlackBerry. Follow these steps to do so:

1. Navigate to the **Media** icon and click it.

2. Scroll to the **Pictures** selection and click it. Your initial choices will be **All Pictures** or **Picture Folders**.

3. Click the appropriate folder and navigate to your pictures to view them.

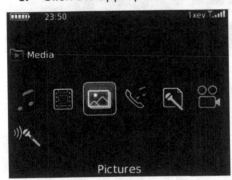 

Viewing a Slide Show

Next, let's look at how to view a slide show of pictures on your BlackBerry. Follow this pair of steps to do so:

1. Follow the steps just described to navigate to your pictures, and then press the **Menu** key when you are in your picture directory.

2. Scroll to the **View Slideshow** option and click it.

Taking a Picture to Set as Caller ID or Home Screen Wallpaper

As discussed previously, you can assign a picture as a Caller ID for your contacts. Follow these steps to do so:

1. If you want to take a picture of someone and use it right away as caller ID for that person, then press the **Crop** button at the bottom of the **Camera** screen.

2. Next, select **Caller ID** or **Wallpaper**.

3. If the picture is the wrong size (whether it's too small or too big) for the frame showing in the middle, then click the Trackpad or the **Menu** key and select **Zoom** to change its size.

4. Finally, you can re-center the image by gliding the Trackpad. Once you get it centered, click the Trackpad and select **Crop and Save**.

5. If you were using the picture to set the **Wallpaper**, then you are done. However, if you selected **Caller ID** originally, then select the contact you want to associate the picture with from your **Address Book** program (or **Contact** list).

6. Next, type a few letters to find the contact and click the Trackpad to select the person.

Find: Ma Trau
Trautschold (Florida), Martin
Trautschold, Martin
Trautschold, Martin
Trautschold, Martin Cmt publications PP
Trautschold, Martin Handheld Contact

Now, every time that person calls or you call him, you will see his picture in addition to his name on the phone screen.

Transferring Pictures To or from Your BlackBerry

There are a few ways to transfer pictures you have taken on your BlackBerry to another device. For example, you can send or share them individually; transfer them using Bluetooth; transfer them using BlackBerry's built-in software, or transfer them using BlackBerry's **Mass Storage** mode. We've covered all of these approaches at one point or another in this book, so we'll explain where you learn how to implement each of these approaches.

Method 1: Using Send/Share Command (Individual)

1. Take a picture and click on the **Envelope** or **Send/Share...** icon.

2. Select where you want to send or share the picture. Depending on which apps you have installed you may see Facebook, Messenger Contact, Fliker, E-mail, MMS and more.

3. After choosing the method, follow the onscreen prompts to complete the send or share command.

You may also send pictures when you are viewing them in your **Pictures** application.

1. From **Pictures**, highlight the picture you want to send.

2. Press the **Menu** key and select **Send/Share...**

3. Follow the steps to send or share the image.

Method 2: Using Bluetooth

If you want to transfer pictures to or from your computer (assuming it has Bluetooth capabilities), you can do that, as well. We explain exactly how to get this done in the Bluetooth chapter on page 458.

Method 3: Using Computer Software

Transferring pictures and other media to your computer is handled using the **Media** section of your desktop software. You would use the **BlackBerry Desktop Manager** or the **BlackBerry Media Sync** program to do this. If you use a Windows PC, see page 105; if you use an Apple Mac, see page 141.

Method 4: Using Mass Storage Mode

This approach assumes you have stored your pictures on a media card (see page 367 for more information on media cards).

The first time you connect your BlackBerry to your computer, you will probably see this question: **Turn on Mass Storage Mode?**

> **NOTE:** If your BlackBerry was supplied to you by your workplace, this **Mass Storage Mode** feature may be disabled for security reasons by your BlackBerry Administrator. If this feature does not appear to work, contact your help desk for assistance.

If you answer **Yes**, then your media card looks just like another hard disk to your computer (similar to a USB flash drive). At this point, you can drag-and-drop pictures to and from your BlackBerry and computer. We show you how to do this on page 144.

Chapter 23

Fun with Videos

We have already covered how to get the most out of music and pictures on your BlackBerry; however, your BlackBerry can handle even more media than what we have discussed so far. For example, your BlackBerry can also handle videos – from short videos you shoot on the BlackBerry to full length movies you watch on the device.

Recording and Playing Back Videos

In addition to a camera, your BlackBerry also comes with a built-in video recorder, which you can use to catch your world in full motion video and sound when a simple picture won't suffice. Your **Media** app can play all videos you record or help you transfer videos to your BlackBerry from your computer.

Adding Videos to Your BlackBerry

If you use a Windows PC, then check out the built-in media transfer and sync capabilities of the **BlackBerry Desktop Manger** software described on page 105. If you use an Apple Mac, please refer to page 141.

Using Your Video Recorder

One of the new features of your BlackBerry is the inclusion of a video recorder. The video recorder is perfect for capturing parts of a business presentation or your child's soccer game. Videos can be e-mailed or stored on your PC for later use – just like pictures. Follow these steps to start and use the built-in video recorder:

1. Push the **Menu** key, scroll down to the **Applications** folder, and click it.

2. Glide to the **Video Camera** icon and click it.

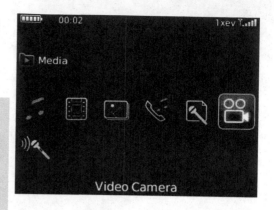

> **TIP:** You can also start the camera, press the **Menu** key, and then select **Video Camera**.

3. If this is your first time in the camera after installing a media card, your BlackBerry should ask whether you always want to save videos to the media card – we recommend answering **Yes** to this question.

4. Use the screen of the BlackBerry as your viewfinder to frame your video.

5. When you are ready to record your video, click the Trackpad. This causes the light in the center to change to a **Pause** button, as shown in the figure to the right.

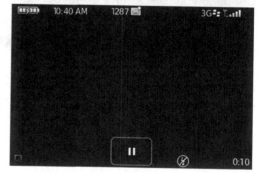

6. When you're ready to stop recording, click the Trackpad again to see the screen to the right. To continue recording, click the white circle in the left corner.

7. To stop recording, glide over and click the white **Stop** square or press the **Escape** key.

8. To play back the video you just recorded, glide over and click the **Play** triangle button.

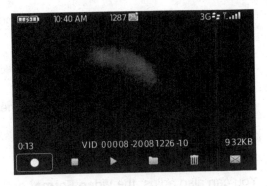

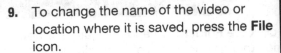

(Yes – that probably is Martin's fingertip.)

To send the video via e-mail or MMS (if available), click the **Envelope** icon.

9. To change the name of the video or location where it is saved, press the **File** icon.

10. 10. To delete the video, click the **Trash Can** icon.

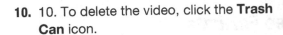

Changing Your Video Recording Options

Like the BlackBerry's built-in camera, the device's video camera lets you set a number of options for controlling the recording process. To access these options, press the **Menu** key and select **Options**.

For example, you can use this menu to choose from the following **Color Effect** options:

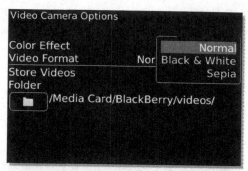

- Normal (color)
- Black and White
- Sepia (a quasi-brown, old-fashioned tinting)

You can also adjust the **Video Format** option to select for **Normal** video storage or **MMS Mode.**

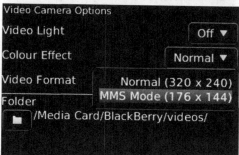

NOTE: MMS mode uses a much smaller screen and file size that is suitable for sending wirelessly; however, it will be of lower quality than Normal mode.

To choose where your videos are stored, click the **Folder** icon and navigate to a new folder. Remember, we strongly recommend storing your videos on a media card. This way, you don't fill up your main BlackBerry device memory.

BlackBerry's Supported Video Formats

Your BlackBerry supports many different video formats. The following tables list the video formats supported by the BlackBerry 8500 series in particular.

Supported Formats (Source: www.blackberry.com)

File Format / Extension	Component	Codec	Notes	RTSP Streaming
MP4 M4A		H.264	Baseline Profile, 320x240 pixels, up to 1500 kbps, 24 frames per second	Supported
MOV 3GP	Video	MPEG4	Simple and Advance Simple Profile, 320x240 pixels, up to 1500 kbps, 24 frames per second	Supported
		H.263	Profile 0 and 3, Level 45	Supported

File Format / Extension	Component	Codec	Notes	RTSP Streaming
	Audio	AAC-LC, AAC+, eAAC+		Supported
		AMR-NB		Supported
AVI	Video	MPEG4	Simple and Advance Simple Profile, 320x240 pixels, up to 1500 kbps, 24 frames per second	Supported
	Audio	MP3		
ASF	Video	Windows Media Video 9	WMV3, Simple and Main Profile, 320x240 pixels, 24 frames per second	
WMV		Windows Media Audio 9 Standard/Professional		
WMA	Audio	Windows Media 10 Standard/Professional		
MP3	Audio	MP3		

Recommended video format for local playback

File Format / Extension	Component	Codec	Notes
MP4	Video	MPEG4	Advance Simple Profile, 320x240 pixels, up to 1500 kbps, 24 frames per second
	Audio	AAC-LC	

*** We recommend searching the online BlackBerry Knowledge Base for the most up-to-date listing. View this at: http://na.blackberry.com/eng/devices/blackberryCurve 8520/Curve_specifications.jsp.

Viewing Videos on the BlackBerry

The BlackBerry contains a very sharp screen that is perfect for watching short videos. Fortunately, the BlackBerry's **Video Player** program is as easy to use as its **Audio Player** program.

Playing a Video

Follow these steps to play a video on your BlackBerry:

1. Click your **Media** folder.

2. Click the **Video** icon and choose the folder where your video is stored.

3. The **Video Player** screen looks very similar to the **Audio Player** screen – just click the Trackpad to pause or play a file, and use the volume controls on the side of the BlackBerry.

4. Next, glide up and down to click and select a video; or, you can type a few letters to quickly locate the video you want to watch. For example, typing the word **Address** would locate all videos with the word **Address** in the title.

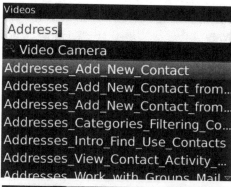

5. Just click the video to start playing it.

TIP: Press the **Menu** key and select **Full Screen** to see the video without the top and bottom status bars.

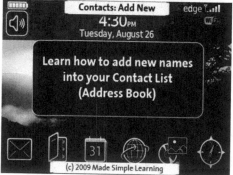

6. Click the Trackpad again or the **Mute** key on the top of the BlackBerry to pause the video.

You can access the **Video Player** program's menu options by pressing the **Menu** key from **List** view. That brings up the following options:

Help: Displays contextual help with video player.

Now Playing…: Switches back to the currently playing song or video.

Media Home: Displays the **Media** folder.

Play: Plays selected item.

Delete: Erases selected item.

Rename: Changes name of selected item.

Properties: Displays properties such as **Location**, **File Size**, **Date Created**, and **Modified Date**.

You see the **Activate XPLOD** option because this BlackBerry has an **XPLOD** Bluetooth device attached to it. You would see your Bluetooth devices (headsets) listed here, too.

Learn about Bluetooth on page 451.

Here are some other options you may see when you are viewing songs:

Replay: Replays the last viewed video.

Repeat: Repeats the last video.

Show Playlist: Displays all items in a playlist.

Activate Handset: Plays the audio of the video through your headset.

Switch Application: Allows you to go to any other open application.

Close: Closes the application.

Chapter 24

Social Networking

BlackBerry smartphones aren't just for business executives anymore—but you already know that. Your BlackBerry can keep you in touch in many ways beyond the messaging features shown earlier in this book.

Your BlackBerry can keep you in touch in many ways beyond e-mail and the Web.

Some of the most popular places to "connect" these days are those sites that are often called social networking sites—places that allow you to create your own page and connect with friends and family to see what is going in their lives. Some of the most popular web sites for social networking are Facebook, Twitter, and LinkedIn.

In this chapter, we will show you how to access these various sites. You will learn how to update your status, "tweet," and keep track of those who are both important or simply of interest to you.

Downloading the Apps

In order to find these apps, use the **Search** feature in App World and simply type the name of the app—**Facebook**, **MySpace** , **LinkedIn**, or **Flickr**—to quickly find each of these apps.

Follow the steps we show you in Chapter 25 to get each app downloaded and installed.

As of publishing time, BlackBerry had just released its own Twitter client. There are also more than half a dozen pretty good Twitter clients, many of them free. Try out UberTwitter or one of the others.

Logging into the Apps

In order to connect to your account on Facebook, Flickr, and MySpace , you will need to locate the icon you just installed and click on it. We use the example of Facebook here, but the process is very similar for the rest of the apps.

Once Facebook is successfully downloaded, the icon in your **Downloads** folder should look something like this.

> **NOTE:** You might find your **Facebook** icon in your **Social Networking** folder—depending on your carrier.

There is a lot to like about having Facebook and these other social networking apps on your Blackberry. You can always stay in touch. Just log in as you do on your computer and you are ready to go. Anytime, anywhere from your BlackBerry.

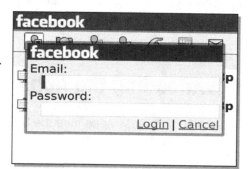

Facebook

Facebook was founded in February of 2004. Since that time, it has served as the premier site for users to connect, re-connect, and share information with friends, co-workers, and family. Today, over 400 million people use Facebook as their primary source of "catching up" with the people who matter most to them.

Using Facebook for BlackBerry

Now that Facebook is a full stand-alone app for BlackBerry, you can do pretty much everything you can do with your computer Facebook account right on your BlackBerry.

Once you have downloaded and installed Facebook, the first thing you will see is the Login screen. Input your account information—your e-mail and password.

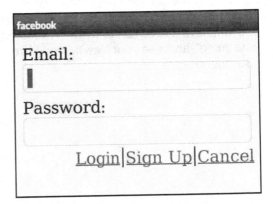

Account Integration

The next screens help you set up your facebook account on your BlackBerry. You can integrate your Facebook friends with your BlackBerry contacts as well as integrate any Facebook calendar events with your BlackBerry calendar.

Just place a check in the box for those actions you wish to take.

You can also have every Facebook message sent to you or any status update, Pokes, or any action by your friends show up as a Facebook message in your BlackBerry Message Application.

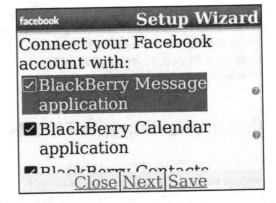

Status Update/News Feed

Once you log on to Facebook for BlackBerry, you will have the option to write "What's on your mind" and see your News Feed from your friends.

Top Bar Icons

Along the top bar are icons for some of the most-used features of Facebook. You will see icons for the **News Feed**, **Notifications**, **Upload a Photo**, **Friends**, **Add a Friend**, **Write on a Wall**, or **Send a Message**.

Communicating with Friends

Click on the **Friends** icon and your list of friends is displayed. If you have contact information in your BlackBerry address book and/or phone numbers stored in your BlackBerry, the icons next to your friends' names will show that.

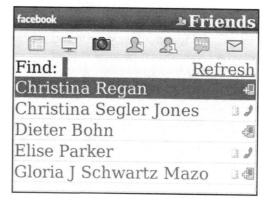

Click on the friend you wish to communicate with to see all the options available to you.

In this example, I clicked on my wife Gloria's name and now I can Poke her, see her profile, write on her wall, or see her BlackBerry contact information.

Uploading Pictures

An easy and fun thing to do with Facebook is to upload pictures. You can upload pictures by either clicking on the small **Camera** icon in the **Facebook** app, or by uploading any picture right after you take it or from your Pictures Application.

1. Just locate the picture in your Photo album and press the **Menu** key. Select **Send to Facebook** and this screen will pop up, allowing you to put a caption for the photo and to also select which **Album** you wish the picture to go into. I chose a picture of our book *CrackBerry: True Tales of BlackBerry Use and Abuse* (BookSurge Publishing, 2008).

2. Write a caption if you desire, and then click **Upload**.

3. To view the picture, from your Facebook account page, press the **Menu** key, select **My Albums,** and navigate to the album into which you put the picture (in my case, that's Mobile Uploads).

MySpace and Flickr

You will find the process of downloading and installing the apps for MySpace , Flickr, and other social networking programs to be virtually identical to the Facebook process described previously. Go to http://mobile.blackberry.com on your BlackBerry Browser for all the core BlackBerry applications such as Facebook, MySpace , Flikr, and more. Twitter, the ultra-popular micro-blogging site is handled separately because of its popularity.

Twitter

Twitter was started in 2006. Twitter is essentially an SMS (text message)-based social networking site. It is often referred to as a "Micro-Blogging" site where the famous and not-so-famous share what's on their mind. The catch is that you only have 140 characters to get your point across.

With Twitter, you subscribe to "follow" someone who "tweets" messages. You might also find that people will start to follow you. If you want to follow us, we are: @garymadesimple on Twitter.

Creating a Twitter Account

Creating a Twitter account is very easy. We do recommend that you first establish your Twitter account on the Twitter web site, www.twitter.com. When you establish your account, you will be asked to choose a unique user name—we use @garymadesimple— and to choose a password.

You will then be sent an e-mail confirmation. Click on the link in your e-mail and you will be taken back to the Twitter web site. You can choose people to follow or make tweets on the web site and also read tweets from your friends.

Download the **Twitter** App

There is a proprietary **Twitter** app for the Blackberry, just as there was a proprietary **Facebook** app. The best way to find the **Twitter** app is to go to the BlackBerry App World and search for "Twitter."

Once the Twitter app is installed, App World will let you know that the installation is complete. You can then choose **OK** to close or **Run** to start the **Twitter** app.

NOTE: The **Twitter** app is often listed in the **Featured Items** at the very top of the App World. Just scroll through the featured items and you should see the **Twitter** app.

Using Twitter for BlackBerry

The first time you use Twitter for BlackBerry, you will be asked to log into your Twitter account. Just input your Twitter username and password.

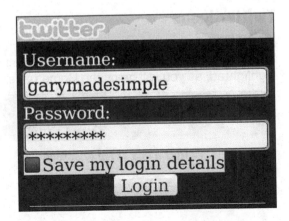

Once your account information is put in, just click on the **Login** button and the BlackBerry will sign into your Twitter account. The initial view in Twitter has a small box at the top of the screen where you can tweet your message to those who are following you. Under that are the tweets from those you are following.

Just scroll through the list of tweets to catch up on all the important news of the day!

Update your Tweets

At the very top of the Twitter home screen is a box, in which is written the words **What's happening?**. That is your space to tweet about what is important (in 140 characters.)

Type your message and then click on the **Update** button to post your tweet.

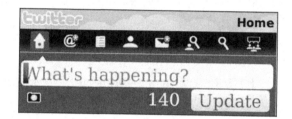

Twitter Icons

Along the top of the Twitter screen are eight icons; these are the quick links to the basic Twitter functions (Figure 24-1). When you first start Twitter, you will see the Home icon highlighted, as you will be on the Home page.

Figure 24-1. Twitter icons at top of screen

Mentions

A *mention* in Twitter speak is a tweet that mentions your @username somewhere in the body of the tweet. These are collected and stored in your **Mentions** section of your Twitter account.

My Lists

You can create a custom list so that your followers cannot only follow everything you say, they can choose to follow a specific topic (a list) that you create. In this example, I created a list so that users can choose to only follow our special announcements if they choose.

My Profile

Just as it sounds, the **My Profile** icon will take you to your Twitter profile. You can see your followers, your tweets, and your bio. Just click on any field in your profile and a short menu comes us. To edit your information, just choose **Edit Profile** from the menu.

Direct Messages

Direct messages are messages between you and another user on Twitter. Click the **Direct Messages** icon to see your direct messages. To compose a direct message to a Twitter user:

1. Click on the **Compose Message** icon.

2. Fill in the **to** field with the Twitter user name.

3. Type your 140 character message in the box.

4. When you are done, just click on the **Send** button.

Find People

The **Find People** icon takes you to a
search window where you can type in a
username, business name, or last name
to search for someone who might be on
Twitter.

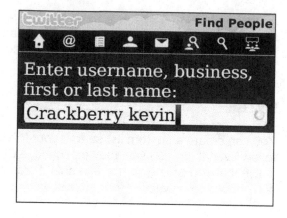

1. Type in the name and your query
   will be processed.

2. Scroll through the results to see if
   you find what you are looking for. If
   so, just click on the entry that
   matches your search and scroll
   down.

You will be able to see the statistics of how many followers there are and if they have
particular Lists to follow. You can also choose the select **Follow** or **Block** to either
follow this contact on Twitter or block all tweets.

Search

The **Search** icon takes you to another
search window. Here, you can type in any
keyword to find opportunities to follow a
topic or individual. For example, if you
were to type in the word **golf**, you might
find popular golf courses, golfers, or
driving ranges that all use Twitter. You
also might find thousands of individuals
who just want to brag about their golf
score.

TIP: Be very specific in your search to help narrow down the search results.

Popular Topics

The **Popular Topics** icon will simply lists those topics that are currently popular on Twitter. So, if you wanted to scroll through, you might find everything from the current playoff series to the President's visit overseas—on Twitter, someone always has something to say about everything.

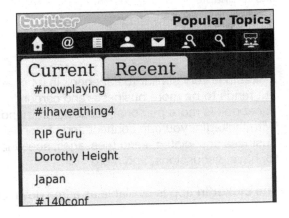

Twitter Options

From your **Twitter** home screen, press the **Menu** key, scroll down, and click **Options**. You will notice several boxes in which you can click to place or remove a check mark.

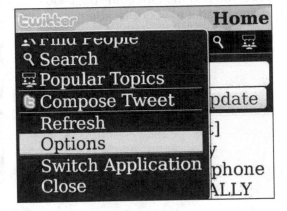

The available options are:

- Integrate in Messages application
- Tweet refresh in background
- Notify on new tweets
- Notify on replies and mentions
- Specify number of tweets per refresh
- Spell-check before sending
- Show navigation bar
- Show tweet box on home screen

Just click to put a check box into the corresponding box next to the option you would like to enable.

LinkedIn

LinkedIn is very similar to Facebook in its core functionality, but tends to be more business- and career-focused, whereas Facebook is more personal, focusing on friends and game. With LinkedIn, you can connect and re-connect with past business associates, send messages, see what people are up to, have discussions, and more.

The **LinkedIn** app is available as a free download from the BlackBerry App World.

Download the App

Once you find the **LinkedIn** app, choose to download it to your BlackBerry.

Once the app is downloaded, go to your **Downloads** folder to launch the app.

Login to LinkedIn App

Once the App is installed, click on the **LinkedIn** icon and enter your login information.

Navigating Around the LinkedIn App

LinkedIn has icon-based navigation that is similar to Facebook. The top of the home screen has a box for posting your profile update (similar to a status update on Facebook.)

Just type your message and then click on the **Post** button.

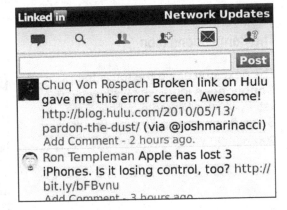

The LinkedIn Icons

At the top of the LinkedIn home screen are six icons. The first one is the **Home Page** icon that will return you to the Home page with profile updates and the ability to update your own LinkedIn status.

The Search Icon

Click in the **Search** box and LinkedIn will try to first match your search with contacts in your LinkedIn directory. Next, the **Search** field will show individuals who match the search criteria who may be part of your Network.

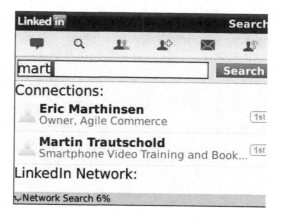

NOTE: LinkedIn uses a Network system. Someone who is a direct contact is considered a 1st degree connection in your network. Someone who is connected to one of your contacts (but not you) is considered a 2nd degree contact, and so on.

The Connections Icon

The next icon along the top is the **Connections** icon, which shows you a listing of your LinkedIn connections. Scroll down and find the particular connection you are looking for.

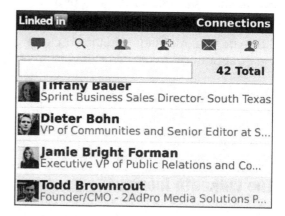

TIP: Press the **Menu** key on your BlackBerry when a connection is highlighted and scroll and click on **Link to BlackBerry Contact** in the menu. This will attach all contact information (including the LinkedIn picture) to your BlackBerry contact for that individual.

The Invitation Icon

Click on the Invitations icon to see if you have any pending invitations for connections. You can also press the **Menu** key and select **Compose New Invitation**.

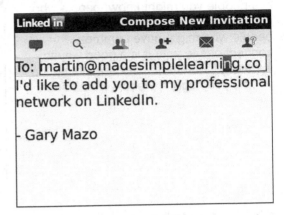

1. Type in the e-mail address of the individual you would like to add to your LinkedIn network.

2. Edit the text below the e-mail field.

3. Press the **Menu** key and select **Send**.

NOTE: Unlike the LinkedIn desktop application, you don't have to say how you know the individual with whom you would like to connect. This makes it much easier to send an invitation from the mobile application.

The Messages Icon

The **Messages** icon is where you go for direct messages to your contacts. You can read messages that are sent to you here. You can also press the **Menu** key and select **Compose Message** to send a direct message to any of your LinkedIn contacts.

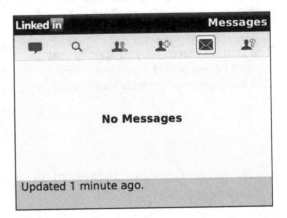

The Reconnect Icon

The **Reconnect** icon is where you click to
see people you might know, people who
might be in groups you belong to, or
people who might have common
connections to you. It is a good way to
expand your network and see interesting
people you might have forgotten about.

LinkedIn Options

Press the **Menu** key from any section of the **LinkedIn** app, scroll to **Options**, and click.
You will notice a selection of check boxes that you can check or uncheck, depending on
your needs and desires.

Select **BlackBerry Mail** to have LinkedIn
messages displayed in your BlackBerry
message list. Select **BlackBerry
Contacts** to have your LinkedIn contacts
displayed as part of your **Contact**
directory.

The bottom boxes let you specify your
type of network and if you want BES or
BIS integration of your LinkedIn account.

Gary Mazo's Options
☑BlackBerry Mail
☑BlackBerry Contacts
LinkedIn Network Updates
☑Show Connection Updates
Network Settings
Current Selection : BIS
☑Auto
☐BES (Not Available)
☑BIS
☑TCP

NOTE: Some options like BES, WiFi, and WAP are only available if your BlackBerry is connected
to those networks.

YouTube

One of the most fun sites to visit on the computer is YouTube for viewing short video clips on just about everything. Your new BlackBerry is able to view YouTube videos without doing anything special.

Just navigate to the YouTube web site (m.youtube.com) and it will detect that you are on a mobile device.

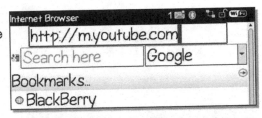

Search just like you do on your computer for any video you might want to watch. The video will load in your media player and you can control it just like you do any other video.

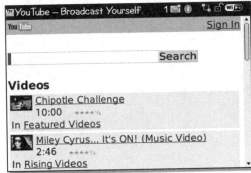

Chapter 25

Connect With Wi-Fi

We live in a Wi-Fi world today. It is difficult to go anywhere and not hear about Wi-Fi. Wi-Fi, according to some, stands for Wireless Fidelity (IEEE 802.11 wireless networking.) Others say that the term is a wireless technology brand owned by the Wi-Fi Alliance.

In this chapter, we will show you how to connect your BlackBerry to available Wi-Fi networks, how to prioritize and organize your networks, and how to diagnose wireless problems.

Understanding Wi-Fi on Your BlackBerry

What is important to know is that your Internet signal can be transmitted wirelessly (using a wireless router) to computers, game consoles, printers, and now to your BlackBerry. If your BlackBerry is Wi-Fi equipped, you can take advantage of must faster web browsing and file downloading speeds via your home or office wireless network. You can also access millions of Wi-Fi hotspots in all sorts of places such as coffee shops and hotels, some of which are free!

The Wi-Fi Advantage

Wi-Fi is a great advantage to BlackBerry users around the globe. The advantages to using a Wi-Fi connection as opposed to the carrier data connection (1X, 1XEV, GPRS, or EDGE) are many:

- Web Browsing speeds are much faster.

- You are not using up data from your data plan.

- Most file downloads will be faster.

- You can get great Wi-Fi signals sometimes when you cannot get any regular cell coverage (1X / 1XEV / GPRS / EDGE / 3G), such as in the bottom floors of a thick-walled building.

Setting up Wi-Fi on Your BlackBerry

Before you can take advantage of the speed and convenience of using Wi-Fi on your BlackBerry, you will need to set up and configure your wireless connection.

1. Press the **Menu** key to see all your icons. Scroll down and click on the **Set Up** or **Settings** folder.

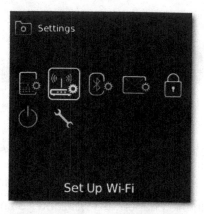

2. Click on **Set up Wi-Fi**.

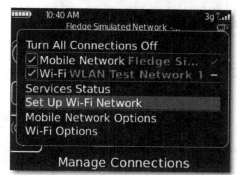

3. The **Welcome to Wi-Fi Setup** screen appears. Scroll down to read the introduction to Wi-Fi.

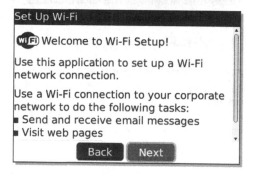

TIP: To skip seeing this Introduction message, scroll to the bottom and click on the "Don't show this introduction again" before clicking the **Next** button.

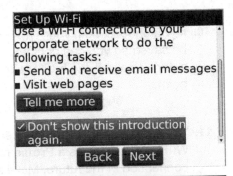

4. When you are done, click Next at the bottom of the screen.

5. You have two options before you—we would suggest to first **Scan for Networks.** In setting up our own BlackBerry Smartphones, we never had to **Manually Add Networks.** Click on **Scan for Networks.**

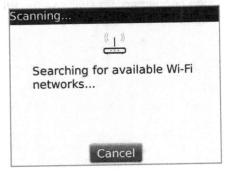

6. Next you will see a status message telling you that your BlackBerry will then automatically scan for available Wi-Fi networks.

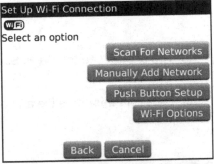

7. If Wi-Fi is not yet turned on, you will be prompted to **Turn on Wi-Fi**. Click on that option to turn on your Wi-Fi radio.

8. You will then see a list of available networks. When you see the correct network name, just click on the trackpad.

9. If your network uses a pre-shared key (PSK) you must type it in at the prompt. Then scroll to and click **Connect**. You might also be asked if you want to perform a WPS setup.

10. If you choose **Yes**, your Wi-Fi Profile will be saved so you can connect automatically in the future to this access point.

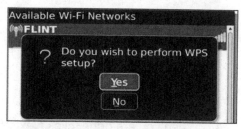

11. You will then be prompted to save your Wi-Fi connection as a **Profile** for easy connection in the future. Make sure **Yes** is shown, and click **Next**.

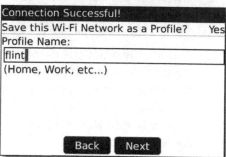

12. You should see the **Wi-Fi Success** message.

13. Click on **Finish** to save and exit the setup process.

Once connected, you will see the **Wi-Fi** logo in the top right-hand corner of your screen

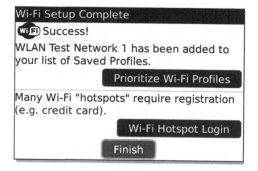

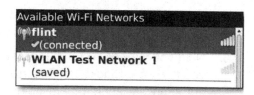

Single Profile Scanning

New in version 5.0 of the BlackBerry operating system is the ability to have your Wi-Fi enabled BlackBerry have a single profile to scan or prompt you for a manual login.

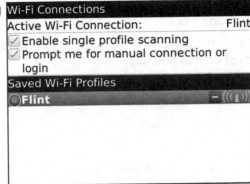

A Manual Connection Prompt is more secure and your BlackBerry will never just connect to an available network (which could pose a security risk).

Putting a check in the Enable single profile scanning check box coupled with selecting the radio button under **Saved WiFi Profiles** will allow your BlackBerry to connect automatically to preferred networks you select.

Connecting to a Wireless Hotspot

1. Get to your Wi-Fi setup screen as shown previously and then press the **Menu** key. One of the options will be **Wi-Fi Hotspot Login**. (See Figure 25-1)

2. Click on **Wi-Fi Hotspot Login**.

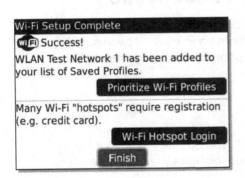

Figure 25-1. *Using Wi-Fi Hotspot Login*

3. You should then be taken to the carrier/store specific logon screen for that particular hotspot. Type the required information and a **You are Successfully Connected to the Internet** message should be displayed.

4. If you are already connected to one wireless network and want to change networks, do the following:

From your **Home** screen, go to your **Options** by pressing the letter **O** if you have hotkeys enabled (see page 548), or click on the **Options** icon.

Press the letter **W** to jump down to **Wi-Fi** and click on it to see this screen.

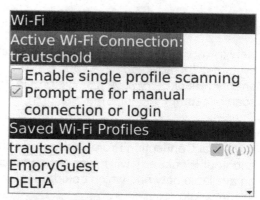

5. You will see the **Active** Wi-Fi connection highlighted.

6. Click in the trackpad and select **New** from the **Menu**.

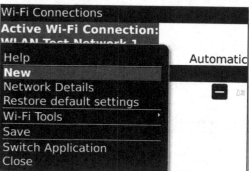

Follow the instructions in the "Setting up Wi-Fi on Your BlackBerry" section earlier in the chapter.

Changing/Prioritizing Your Wi-Fi Connection

One of the nice things about Wi-Fi is that you can connect to a wireless network just about anywhere. While you may have saved your home and work networks in the previous section, there may be times you want to prioritize or change networks altogether.

Prioritizing Your Networks

Let's say that 90% of the time, the wireless network you connect to is your home network. You want to make sure that your home network is at the top of the list of networks your BlackBerry searches for.

To **Prioritize your Networks**—just do the following:

1. Follow the steps shown previously to get into your Wi-Fi settings.

2. Scroll down to **Saved Wi-Fi Profiles** at the bottom of the screen and highlight the top network.

3. Press the **Menu** key and then select **Move**.

4. The blue highlighted network then becomes grey. Just scroll with the trackpad and **Move** the network into the priority you desire.

Using Wi-Fi Diagnostics

There may be times when your Wi-Fi Connection doesn't seem to work for you. Thankfully, your BlackBerry has a very powerful diagnostics program built-in to help you in those instances.

To launch the **Wi-Fi Diagnostics**, just follow steps 1 and 2 from the previous section.

Press the **Menu** button and scroll to and click **Wi-Fi tools**. Then, select **Wi-Fi Diagnostics**.

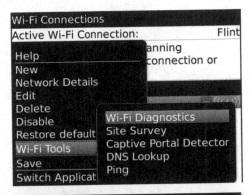

The available wireless networks and detailed connection information will now be displayed. If you are an advanced user with experience in wireless networking, click on the trackpad for access point details.

After the diagnosis, you can press the **Menu** key and select **E-mail Report**, copy the details into an e-mail, and send it to your Help Desk for assistance.

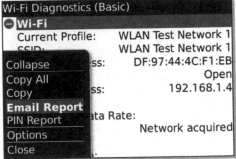

Chapter 26

BlackBerry App World

You can find software applications inside the App World, but since the App World is a relatively new addition to the BlackBerry environment, you will also find many applications outside of App World. Check out our chapter on **Adding and Removing Software** starting on page 485 for more information.

The App World Concept

Application stores are all the rage in the world of smartphones these days. One of the great things about a BlackBerry is that you can find applications in lots of places—not just the sanctioned App Store. BlackBerry App World is a new concept for BlackBerry and deserves some explanation. Remember that you can always go to the other locations mentioned on page 485 to find additional applications for your BlackBerry as well.

Downloading the App World Program

BlackBerry App World is a free download for all BlackBerry users and it works particularly well on your new BlackBerry Curve. If the **App World** icon was not already on your BlackBerry when you received it, you will need to download and install it.

Start your Web Browser by clicking on the
Browser icon or press the letter **B** if you
enabled the **Home** screen HotKeys. (Page 548)

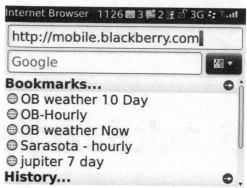

In the **Address bar** of the Browser, type
mobile.blackberry.com. It is possible that the
Home page of your Browser is already set to
the mobile BlackBerry site.

At the top of the Mobile BlackBerry page, you should see and link for the **BlackBerry
App World**. Just glide to the link and click the trackpad. You will then be taken to the
Download page for the application (Figure 26-1). Accept any terms and conditions and
click on the **Download** button.

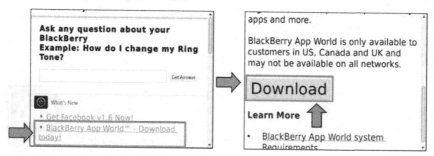

Figure 26-1. *Download BlackBerry App World*

Starting App World for the First Time

The **App World** icon will probably be in your
Downloads folder. If you want to move it to your
home screen, just follow the directions on page
170.

Find the **App World** icon and click on the
trackpad to start it. The first time you start the
App World, it might take a little while to load—
this is normal.

NOTE: We have detailed instructions in our "Personalize Your BlackBerry" chapter on page 181.

Featured Programs

Highlighted in the App World program are large icons for the **Featured Programs**. Many of these are free; others need to be purchased (which we will discuss in the "download and purchase an app" section below.) Glide the trackpad through the featured programs to find one that interests you. To gain more information about the program, click the trackpad to be taken to the next screen.

Categories, Top Downloads, and Search

Along the bottom of the App World screen, you will see five small icons: **Categories**, **Top Free**, **Top Paid**, **Search**, and **My World** (Figure 26-2). Each gives you a different way to look for, download, or manage **Apps** on your BlackBerry. In order to activate these soft keys, you need to glide the trackpad down.

Figure 26-2. *Layout of BlackBerry App World*

Categories

Categories

Just like it sounds, the **Categories** icon, when clicked, gives you all the categories of applications in the new **BlackBerry App World**. At publication time, there were over a dozen categories ranging from **Games** to **Sports** to **Finance** to **Reference** and much more.

Just click on a category and find more information about a particular application that may interest you. Once you click a category, the icons for the available programs will show on your screen. Glide your trackpad through the options and click. You can usually read reviews or see screen shots for most applications before you decide to download.

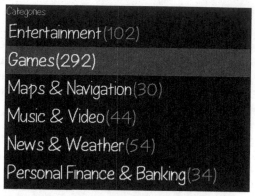

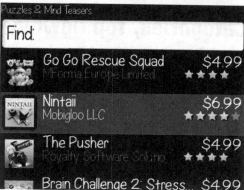

Top Free Downloads

Top Free Downloads

As the name implies, the **Top Free** icon will show you the most downloaded free applications from the App World. Click on any program to see screen shots or read reviews or to download the app to your BlackBerry.

Top Paid Downloads

Top Paid Downloads

As the name implies, the **Top Paid** icon will show you the most downloaded paid applications ($0.99 or higher) from the App World. Click on any program to see screen shots or read reviews or to download the app to your BlackBerry.

Search

Search

The App World has a very good, built-in Search tool. If you have an idea of what you might be looking for, but don't know the exact name, just type a word into the **Search** bar. In this example, we want to find music applications that are currently available, so we type in **music** into the **Search** bar and all the available music apps are displayed. (Figure 26-3)

Figure 26-3. *Search BlackBerry App World*

TIP: You can sort the search results by clicking the icon in the upper right corner: The results are shown in Figure 26-4.

Figure 26-4. *Sort search results*

After you select a different sort criteria, you can reverse the sort order (highest to lowest, A–Z, Z–A) by clicking the same icon again.

Downloading Apps

As of publishing time, the BlackBerry App World only accepts PayPal for purchase. (This may change in the future.) If you have a PayPal account, all you need to do is input your PayPal username and password when you purchase an application. If you do not have a PayPal account, go to www.paypal.com from your computer and follow the instructions to set up your account. Generally, setting up a PayPal Personal account is fine for most users.

Download and Purchase an App

Scroll through the applications to find what interests you. When you find an App that you want to download, click the **Download** button from the **Details** screen.

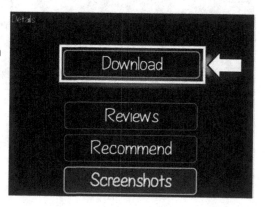

If the application is not a free download, the **Download** button will be replaced by a **Purchase** button. Click **Purchase** and input your PayPal information.

> **NOTE:** For future purchases, your PayPal information will be stored to make purchases easier. (Figure 26-5)

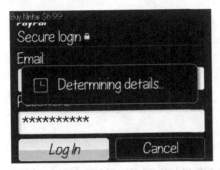

Figure 26-5. *Purchase an app using PayPal*

You will see the progress bar of the application as it downloads, prepares to install, and then installs on your BlackBerry.

Using the My World Feature

My World

All the apps that you purchase or download are listed in your **My World** area of the App World.

Glide and click on the **My World** icon (in the lower right-hand corner of the **App World**) and all the programs you have downloaded or purchased are recorded there.

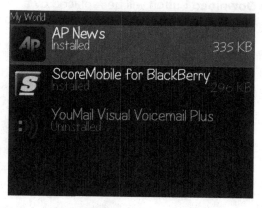

NOTE: If you restart your BlackBerry or do a battery pull, you will be logged out of your account and you will be asked to re-enter your PayPal password.

My World Menu Commands

Highlight any **App** in your **World** and press the **Menu** Key.

From the menu, you can **Log in** to your account, **Run** the selected program, **Review** the program and **Recommend** the program or **Uninstall** the program.

NOTE: If Application **Updates** are available, that will also be indicated in **My World**.

Deleting or Uninstalling Programs

After you start to download lots of new apps to your BlackBerry, you may decide that you do not want to use some of them or simply want to free up space for new apps.

1. In order to delete an app, you need to be in the **My World** section of App World.

2. Highlight the app you wish to remove and press the **Menu** key.

3. Select **Delete** to remove that program from your BlackBerry.

4. On the next screen, you will be asked to confirm your selection to remove the program.

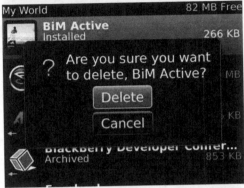

Most programs will require you to reboot (reset) your BlackBerry to complete the uninstall process.

TIP: If you are removing more than one application, select **Reset Later** or **Reboot Later** until you have selected and uninstalled all the apps you want to remove. Then, at the end, select **Reset Now** to remove all at once—this will save you a lot of waiting time!

Chapter 27

Connect with Bluetooth

Bluetooth allows your BlackBerry to communicate with such things as headsets, GPS devices, and other hands-free systems with the freedom of wireless. Bluetooth is a small radio that transmits from each device. The BlackBerry gets paired—connected to the peripheral. You can use many Bluetooth devices up to 30 feet away from the BlackBerry.

In this chapter, we will show you how to connect (pair) to a Bluetooth headset, how to connect to a Bluetooth stereo device, and how to prioritize your Bluetooth connections.

History of Bluetooth

The BlackBerry ships with Bluetooth 2.0 technology. Think of Bluetooth as a short-range, wireless technology that allows your BlackBerry to connect to various peripheral devices (headset, speakers, computer) without wires.

Bluetooth is believed to be named after a Danish Viking and king, Harald Blåtand (which has been translated as *Bluetooth* in English.) King Blåtand lived in the 10th century and is famous for uniting Denmark and Norway. Similarly, Bluetooth technology unites computers and telecom. His name, according to legend, is from his very dark hair, which was unusual for Vikings. Blåtand means dark complexion. A more popular story states that the king loved to eat Blueberries, so much so his teeth became stained with the color blue. Believe what you choose!

Sources:

http://cp.literature.agilent.com/litweb/pdf/5980-3032EN.pdf
http://www.cs.utk.edu/~dasgupta/bluetooth/history.htm
http://www.britannica.com/eb/topic-254809/Harald-I

Using Bluetooth on Your BlackBerry

In order to use Bluetooth on your BlackBerry, you must first turn it on. This is done through the **Setup** folder and the **Setup Bluetooth** icon.

Setup Folder:

> **TIP:** You should also be able to get here from the **Manage Connections** icon.

Setup Bluetooth:

Setup Bluetooth

When Bluetooth is on, you will see this small **Bluetooth** icon in the upper part of your **Home** screen. Depending on your **Theme**, it may be on the left or right side.

If you don't see a **Turn On Bluetooth** or **Setup Bluetooth** icon, then click on the **Manage Connections** icon. Make sure that there is a check mark in the box next to **Bluetooth**. You should now see the **Bluetooth** icon appear on the screen.

.

Once Bluetooth is enabled, you will want to use the steps that follow to take full advantage of the Bluetooth capabilities of the BlackBerry.

There can sometimes be two or three ways to get into the Bluetooth **Setup** and **Options** screens. This depends a bit on your BlackBerry software version and BlackBerry carrier (cell phone) company. We will just show you one way.

1. Click on the **Setup** folder.

2. Scroll to and click **Set Up Bluetooth**.

3. If you see the window asking you to either search or be discovered, press the **Escape** key.

4. Press the **Menu** key and scroll down to **Options** and click**.**

5. If you have already paired your BlackBerry with Bluetooth devices, you will see those devices listed (we cover pairing later in this chapter.)

6. To change your device name (the way other Bluetooth devices will see your BlackBerry), click where it says **Device Name** and type a new name.

7. To make your BlackBerry discoverable to other devices, click next to **Discoverable** and select **Yes** (the default is **No**), As we note in a bit, you should set this back to **No** after you finish pairing for increased security.

8. Make sure that it says **Always** or **If Unlocked** after **Allow Outgoing Calls**.

9. Set **Address Book Transfer** to **Enable** (depending on your software version, you may see the options of **All Entries**—same as **Enable**, **Hotlist Only**, or **Selected Categories Only**—depending on your preferences). This option allows your Address Book data to be transferred to another device or computer using Bluetooth.

10. To see a blue flashing LED when connected to a Bluetooth device, make sure the **LED Connection Indicator** is set to **On**.

Bluetooth Security Tips

Here are a few security tips from a recent BlackBerry IT Newsletter. These tips will help prevent hackers from getting access to your BlackBerry via Bluetooth:

- Never pair your BlackBerry when you are in a crowded public area.

- **Disable** the **Discoverable** setting after you are done with pairing your BlackBerry.

- **Do not accept** any pairing requests with unknown Bluetooth devices, only accept connections from devices with names you recognize.

- **Change the name of your BlackBerry** to something other than the default "BlackBerry"—this will help deter hackers from easily finding your BlackBerry.

Source: http://www.blackberry.com/newsletters/connection/it/jan-2007/managing-bluetooth-security.shtml?CPID=NLC-41

Supported Devices

Your BlackBerry should work with most Bluetooth headsets, car kits, hands-free kits, keyboards, and GPS receivers that are compliant with Bluetooth 2.0 and earlier versions. At publishing time, Bluetooth 2.1 was just coming on the scene; you will need to check with the device manufacturer of newer devices to make sure they are compatible with your BlackBerry.

How to Pair Your BlackBerry with a Bluetooth Device

Think of "pairing" as establishing a connection between your BlackBerry and a peripheral (headset, global positioning device (GPS), external keyboard, Windows or Mac computer, and so forth) without wires. Pairing is dependent on entering a required passkey—, which locks your BlackBerry into a secure connection with the peripheral. Similar to getting into the Bluetooth **Options** screens, there could be several ways to get into the Bluetooth **Setup** screen to pair your BlackBerry and establish this connection.

First, put your Bluetooth device in **Pairing** mode as recommended by the manufacturer. Also, have the passkey ready to enter.

Navigate to the Bluetooth **Setup** screen with one of the following methods:

- **Method 1:** Click on the **Options** icon (may be inside the **Settings** icon). Then scroll to and click **Bluetooth**.

- **Method 2:** Scroll to the **Set Up Bluetooth** icon and click on it.

- **Method 3:** Scroll to the **Manage Connections** icon, click on it, then select **Setup Bluetooth**.

The BlackBerry will ask you to search for devices from here or allow another device to fine you. Choose the option you desire and then click **OK**.

CAUTION: If you are pairing your BlackBerry with your computer, then you need to make sure that both your BlackBerry and your computer are in **Discoverable** mode. Set this on the **Bluetooth Options** screen by setting **Discoverable** to **Yes** or **Ask**. (The default setting is **No**, which will prevent you from pairing.)

When the device is found, the BlackBerry will display the device name on the screen. Click on the device name to select it.

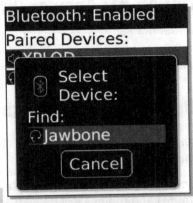

You will then be prompted to enter the four-digit **passkey** provided by the manufacturer of the Bluetooth peripheral. Enter in the **passkey** and then click the trackpad (many default passkeys are just "0000" or "1234").

You will then be prompted to accept the connection from the new device.

> **TIP:** If you check the box next to "**Don't ask this again**," you will only have to do this once.

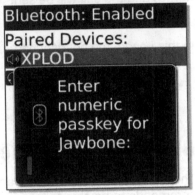

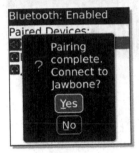

Your device should now be connected, paired, and ready to use.

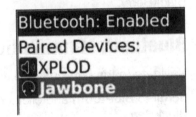

Answering and Making Calls with the Headset

Some Bluetooth headsets support an **Auto Answer** protocol, which will, as it sounds, automatically answer incoming calls and send them right to the headset. This is very helpful when driving or in other situations where you should not be looking at your BlackBerry to answer the call. Sometimes, you will need to push a button—usually just one—to answer your call from the headset.

Option #1: Answer Directly From the Headset Itself

When the call comes into your BlackBerry, you should hear an audible beep in the headset. Just press the **Multi-function** button on your headset to answer the call. Press the **Multi- function** button when the call ends to disconnect.

Option #2: Transfer the Caller to the Headset

When a phone call comes into your BlackBerry, press the **Menu** key.

Scroll and then click to **Activate (*your Bluetooth headset name*)** and the call will be sent to the selected headset.

In this image, the headset name is Jawbone.

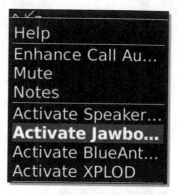

Bluetooth Setup Menu Commands

There are several options available to you from the **Bluetooth** menu. Learn these commands to be able to take full advantage of Bluetooth wireless technology on your BlackBerry.

Bluetooth Menu Options

Navigate to the **Options** icon and click.

Scroll to **Bluetooth** and click. You will now see the list of paired devices with your BlackBerry.

Highlight one of the devices listed and press the **Menu** key. The following options become available to you (See Figure 27-1):

- **Disable Bluetooth**—Another way to turn off the Bluetooth radio; this will help to save battery life if you don't need Bluetooth active

- **Connect /Disconnect**—Clicking this will immediately connect/disconnect you to/from the highlighted Bluetooth device

- **Add Device**—To connect to a new Bluetooth peripheral

- **Delete Device**—Removes the highlighted device from the BlackBerry

- **Device Properties**—To check whether the device is trusted, encrypted, and if the **Echo** control is activated

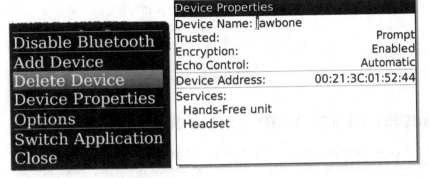

Figure 27-1. *Bluetooth device properties*

You should change your device name to something other than "**BlackBerry 8500**" for security reasons. Use something that is not easily recognizable.

> **NOTE:** Some images in this section might use a different model number for the BlackBerry than your Curve. These screens apply to all BlackBerry models.

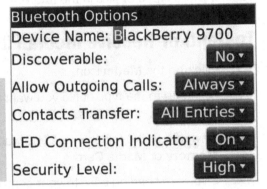

Also, make sure **Discoverable** is set to **No** after you are done pairing.

You can set **Contacts Transfer** to **Disabled**, **All Entries** (default), **Hotlist Only**, or **Selected Categories Only**.

Select the categories by pressing the **Menu** key and select (check-off) the categories you wish to be able to transfer.

The **Services** can be enabled or disabled for security purposes. Press the **Space** key to check or uncheck any services.

☑ Desktop Connectivity
☑ Wireless Bypass
☑ Data Transfer
☑ SIM Access Profile
☑ Dial-Up Networking
☑ Audio Source
☑ A/V Remote Control Target

Send and Receive Files with Bluetooth

Once you have paired your BlackBerry with your computer, you can use Bluetooth to send and receive files. At publishing time, these files were limited to media files (videos, music, pictures) and address book entries, but we suspect that you will be able to transfer more types of files in the future.

To Send or Receive Media Files on Your BlackBerry:

1. Click on the **Media** icon.

2. Navigate to the type of file you want to send or receive—**Music**, **Video**, **Ringtones**, or **Pictures**.

3. Navigate to the folder where you want to send or receive the file – either **Device Memory** or **Media Card**.

4. If you are sending a file to your computer, then glide to and highlight the file and select **Send using Bluetooth**. Then you will need to follow the prompts on your computer to receive the file.

NOTE: You may need to set your computer to be able to **Receive via Bluetooth**.

5. If you are receiving a file (or files) on your BlackBerry, then you need to select **Receive via Bluetooth**. Go to your computer, select the file or files, and follow the commands to **Send via Bluetooth**. You may be asked on the BlackBerry to confirm the folder that is receiving the files.

NOTE: You can send (transfer) only media files that you have put onto your BlackBerry yourself. You cannot transfer the pre-Loaded media files via Bluetooth.

Streaming Bluetooth Stereo

Devices such as the BlackBerry Remote Stereo Gateway allow you to stream any music source via Bluetooth, or stream music from your BlackBerry to your home stereo. Just pair and connect the Bluetooth device with your BlackBerry and begin playing music. The music from your BlackBerry will then be sent to your home stereo or even your car stereo.

Bluetooth Troubleshooting

Bluetooth is still an emergent technology and, sometimes, it doesn't work as well as we might hope. If you are having difficulty, perhaps one of these suggestions will help.

My passkey is not being accepted by the device.

It is possible that you have the incorrect passkey. Most Bluetooth devices use either "0000" or "1234"—but some have unique passkeys.

If you lost your manual for the Bluetooth device, many times you can use a web search engine such as Google or Yahoo to find the manufacturer's web site and locate the product manual.

I have the right passkey, but I still cannot pair the device.

It is possible that the device is not compatible with the BlackBerry. One thing you can try is to turn off encryption.

Click **Options**, then **Bluetooth,** highlight the problem device, and click. In **Device Properties**, disable **Encryption** for that device and try to connect again.

I can't share my Address Book.

Inside the **Bluetooth Setup** screen, press the **Menu** key and select **Options**. Make sure that you have enabled the **Address Book Transfer** field.

NOTE: Many Bluetooth headsets and car kits do not fully support address book transfers—double check the documentation that came with your Bluetooth device.

Chapter 28

Connect as Tethered Modem

Tethering is the process of connecting your BlackBerry to your computer and using the BlackBerry as a "Modem" to access the Internet. This is particularly useful if you are in an airport or a hotel with no Internet connection on your notebook and need more than the capabilities of your BlackBerry.

Connecting Your Laptop to the Internet Using Your BlackBerry

Depending on your wireless carrier (phone company) and the type of software you use, you should be able to use your BlackBerry to connect your laptop (PC or Mac) to the Internet. This is called Tethered Modem (or Tethering), or sometimes IP Modem. You need the USB cable for PCs and sometimes you can use Bluetooth for Mac.

Tethering Usually Costs Extra

Most, but not all, wireless carriers charge an extra fee to allow you to use your BlackBerry as a Tethered Modem. You may not be able to connect using your BlackBerry as a modem, however, unless you have specifically signed up for the "BlackBerry as Modem" or similar data plan. We have heard of users getting a surprise phone bill in the hundreds of dollars, *even when they had an "unlimited BlackBerry data plan"* (this particular carrier did not include BlackBerry modem data in the unlimited plan).

Some carriers allow you to turn this **BlackBerry As Modem Extra Service** on and off as needed. Check with your particular carrier. Also, beware that turning this modem service on and off might extend or renew your two-year commitment period. Ask your phone company for their policies.

Assuming there are no extra hidden costs or commitments, you could just enable it for a scheduled trip and then turn it off when you return home.

We also want to thank Research In Motion, Ltd. and BlackBerry.com for valuable information contained in their extensive BlackBerry Technical Solution Center. We strongly encourage you to visit this site for the latest information on using your BlackBerry as a modem and anything else! Visit: http://www.blackberry.com/btsc/supportcentral/supportcentral.do?id=m1 and search for "modem how to."

Searching Tidbits

When searching the knowledgebase, do not enter your specific BlackBerry model, but instead enter the series. For example, if you have a Curve 8520 or 8530, then enter Curve 8500 or 8500 series, or just leave that out of the search.

To locate the modem instructions for your particular BlackBerry, you will need to know the network—EDGE, GPRS, CDMA, EVDO—on which your BlackBerry operates. The Curve 8520 runs on the EDGE/GPRS networks and the Curve 8530 runs on the CDMA/EVDO networks. Not every BlackBerry wireless carrier supports using your BlackBerry as a modem. Please check with your carrier if you have trouble.

This Feature Changes Often

The steps and software to use your BlackBerry as a modem have changed and continues to change frequently, almost on a monthly basis. Therefore, some of the software and information contained in this chapter may be slightly different when you are reading it than when the book was published.

So, How Can You Find the Latest Information?

Please do a web search using terms like these: **BlackBerry as Modem**, **BlackBerry Tethered Modem**, or **BlackBerry IP Modem**.

Understanding the Options for Getting This Done

You have a few options to use your BlackBerry as a Tethered Modem for your laptop (PC or Mac).

- **Option 1:** Purchase third-party software
- **Option 2:** Use your wireless carrier's software (contact them to ask if something is available)

■   **Option 3:** Use BlackBerry Desktop Manager software (this is usually only an option for you if Option 2 is not available)

Option 1: Purchase Third-Party Software

Tether is a popular option here and now works for both Windows and Mac computers. Check out their site at www.tether.com. (Figure 28-1) The bonus claimed by Tether is that you do not need to pay for a separate modem plan from your carrier and you may be able to save a lot on monthly connection charges. Cost for Tether was about USD $30 at publishing time, but they offer a 7-day free trial so you can give it a try before you buy.

Figure 28-1. *Tether—third-party tethering software setup*

Option 2: Use Your Wireless Carrier's Software

Contact your wireless carrier's technical support to find out if they offer software and service plans for this option. Tell them you want to use your BlackBerry as a modem for your laptop. AT&T (USA), Sprint/Nextel (USA), and Verizon (USA) have simple software (such as Communication Manager or Verizon Access Manager) that you can download and install.

Option 3: Use Desktop Manager to Connect to the Internet

This works for both Windows and Mac computers. Windows computer users see the following section. Mac users, skip ahead to the section called Using Desktop Manager for Mac.

Using Desktop Manager for Windows

If you have confirmed with your carrier that you can use the IP Modem feature in BlackBerry Desktop Manager (Figure 28-2,) then follow the steps shown here. Learn how to download and install Desktop Manager for Windows on page 67.

1. Start **Desktop Manager** by going to Start → BlackBerry → Desktop Manager.

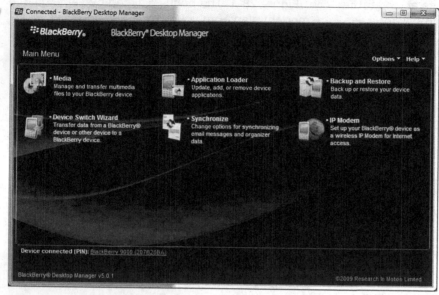

Figure 28-2. *Configure IP modem in Desktop Manager for Windows.*

2. Click on the **IP Modem** icon. (If you don't see this icon, then you will need to confirm with your carrier that you can use it. Sometimes, you can re-enable this icon by editing a specific file—see page 22.)

3. Configure the IP Modem by clicking the **Configure...** button, as shown in Figure 28-3.

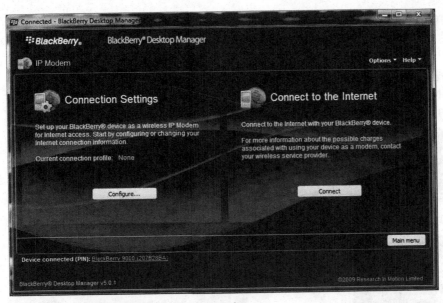

Figure 28-3. *Click **Configure** in connection settings*

4. Now, try the drop-down list next to **Connection Profile** to see if your carrier is listed (Figure 28-4).

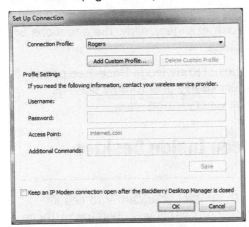

Figure 28-4. *Look for your carrier in the drop-down menu*

If not, then select **Add Custom Profile** and follow the steps to enter the information. Most likely, you will need to contact your wireless carrier for the setup information.

5. Make sure to check the box at the bottom of the **Set Up Connection** screen if you want your Internet connection to remain active even after you close out of Desktop Manager. Click **OK** and save your settings.

6. Make sure your BlackBerry is connected to your computer and recognized by Desktop Manager. You can tell if Desktop Manager sees your BlackBerry by looking in the lower left corner.

Now, you are ready to connect.

7. Click the **Connect** button. If you see any error messages, follow the directions or contact your wireless carrier for setup assistance.

For help, also consider visiting the BlackBerry Technical Knowledge Base (see page 543). Or, you can ask your question at one of the BlackBerry user forums such as www.crackberry.com, www.pinstack.com, or www.blackberryforums.com.

How to Re-Enable the IP Modem Icon Inside Desktop Manager for Windows

Before you follow these steps, you should be sure to contact your carrier to see if you can use Desktop Manager's IP Modem feature. If their answer is yes, then follow these steps to edit this file: **ip_modem_configuration.xml.** If your carrier says no, then following these steps will likely not work; in that case, use the software recommended by your carrier.

1. Open the file using a text-only editor, such as Windows Notepad or WordPad.

2. Locate your wireless carrier name. Take note that carrier names with ampersands such as AT&T will be listed as "**AT&T**"

3. Change the **enabled="false"** to **enabled="true"** as shown in Figure 28-5.

```
ip_modem_configuration.xml*                                        ×
       <password>web</password>
571  </carrier>
572  <carrier uid="101" id="Indosat" enabled="true">
573    <vendorid>240</vendorid>
574    <supportednetwork>GSM</supportednetwork>
575    <apn>indosatgprs</apn>
576  </carrier>
577  <carrier uid="102" id="AT&amp;T" enabled="true">
578    <vendorid>102</vendorid>
579    <supportednetwork>GSM</supportednetwork>
580    <apn>isp.cingular</apn>
581  </carrier>
582  <carrier uid="103" id="Starhub" enabled="true">
583    <vendorid>128</vendorid>
584    <supportednetwork>GSM</supportednetwork>
585    <apn>shwap</apn>
586  </carrier>
```

Figure 28-5 *Use text-based editor to edit connection string*

4. Save your changes and re-start Desktop Manager. The icon should re-appear. If it does not, then re-start your computer and try again.

It is probably best to use the Windows search feature or Google Desktop to find this file, but you may find it in one of these places:

- Vista: C:\ProgramData\Research In Motion\BlackBerry

- Windows XP: C:\Documents and Settings\All Users\Application Data\Research in Motion\BlackBerry

Using Desktop Manager for Mac

First, download and install the latest version of Desktop Manager for Mac from www.blackberry.com. Learn how on page 125.

Now, connect your BlackBerry to your Mac. Go to **Settings → Network** on your Mac, to see the window shown in Figure 28-6.

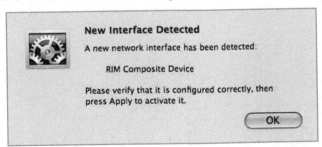

New Interface Detected

A new network interface has been detected:

RIM Composite Device

Please verify that it is configured correctly, then press Apply to activate it.

OK

Figure 28-6. *Configure BlackBerry as modem on a Mac*

Your Mac now sees your BlackBerry as a new network interface and will attempt to configure it as a dial-up modem for tethering.

If you have a Tethering or BlackBerry as a Modem service plan with your carrier, you can continue with the setup and choose **Network Preferences....** (Figure 28-7)

NOTE: Most, but not all, carriers charge extra for using your BlackBerry as a modem for your Mac to connect to the Internet. Contact your carrier for pricing.

Many carriers will allow you to turn on and off this extra service—say you were taking a trip and needed to use the modem feature for three weeks, then turn it off again when you return home.

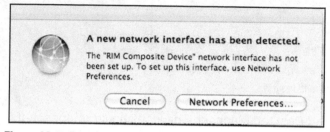

Figure 28-7. *Pop-up window advising you to use Newtwork Preferences to configure BlackBerry as modem*

Network Preferences

NOTE: Only proceed with these steps if have all the necessary carrier setup strings provided by your wireless carrier.

1. Click the **Default** next to the **Configuration**: field and select **New Connection**. Type a connection name—in this image (Figure 28-8), we used *BlackBerry 8900*, but you might want to choose **BlackBerry 8500** or **Curve 8500**.

2. Fill in your phone number, account name, and password in the appropriate boxes to begin the configuration process.

Figure 28-8. *Configuration settings on a Mac*

3. If you need to access more settings, click the **Advanced...** button in the lower right corner. The advanced options screen will have tabs along the top for **Modem**, **DNS**, **WINS**, **Proxies**, and **PPP** settings (Figure 28-9).

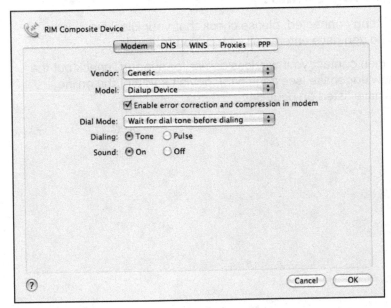

Figure 28-9. *Advanced configuration settings on a Mac.*

4. When you are done, click OK to close the advanced settings screen.

5. Then, click **Connect** from the main screen (Figure 28-10).

Figure 28-10. *Click* **Connect** *to go online*

Having Trouble Getting Online?

If you have any trouble getting connected, please check that your BlackBerry is connected to your Mac and you have entered all information correctly.

If everything looks okay, then contact your wireless carrier for support, check out the BlackBerry Technical Knowledgebase (see page 543), or visit some of the online BlackBerry forums as we have listed on page 544.

Chapter 29

Web Browser

A prerequisite for any smartphone today is the ability to get online and browse the web. Now, smartphone web browsing will never be a substitute for desktop browsing, but you will be surprised by all the features available on your BlackBerry.

In this chapter, we will show you how to get online, how to set Browser bookmarks, how to use your browsing history, and how to use some *hotkeys* to get around the Browser quickly.

Web Browsing on Your BlackBerry

One of the amazing features of smartphones like the BlackBerry is the ability to browse the web right from your handheld. More and more web sites are now supporting mobile browser formatting. These sites "sense" you are viewing them from a small mobile browser and automatically reconfigure themselves for your BlackBerry so they load quickly—some, even quicker than a desktop browser.

Using Alternative Web Browsers

The native Web Browser may seem slow to some people, so vendors have appeared that are creating alternative web browsers for your BlackBerry.

We have seen several alternatives to the native BlackBerry Web Browser appear on the market. A couple of the more notable ones recently have been Opera Mini and Bolt Browser. We have not extensively tested them, but they do keep improving the look, feel, and performance of the overall web browsing experience. You can locate these browsers and other alternatives by performing a web search for "blackberry 8500 web browser" or "blackberry web browser."

Current links to the two alternative web browsers are:

- Opera Mini Browser: www.opera.com/mini or m.opera.com
- Bolt Web Browser: www.boltbrowser.com

> **NOTE:** The rest of this chapter focuses on the primary or native Web Browser that is included with every BlackBerry.

Locating the Web Browser from the Home Screen (HotKeys: B or W)

Web browsing can actually start with a few of the icons on your **Home** screen. The easiest way to get started is to hit the hotkey **B** for the Internet Browser or **W** for the WAP Browser. (For help with hotkeys, see page 548) Or, you can find the **Browser** icon—it looks like a globe.

Most of the screen shots in this book are from the Internet Browser, not the WAP Browser.

Use the trackpad and navigate to the **Browser** icon and click. It might say **Browser**, **BlackBerry Browser**, or **Internet Browser**, or even something different such as **mLife** or **T-Zone**.

You will either be taken directly to the **Home** screen of your particular carrier or to your list of Bookmarks.

The **Start** page—this is nice because on a single screen, it allows you to:

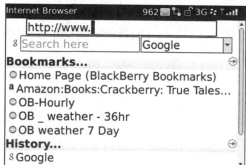

- Type a web address (URL)
- Do a web search
- See your popular bookmarks
- See your web history.

The Bookmarks List page:

Learn how to add bookmarks on page 477.

> **TIP:** Type a few letters of the bookmark's name to instantly find it. (Just like finding names in your Contact list.)

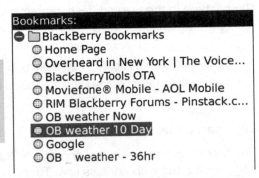

Your customized **Home** page (set to anything you want, such as www.google.com as it is here—see page 22.)

Speed up your Browser by Clearing the Browser Cache

You can really speed up your Web Browser by periodically clearing out the cache. See page 535.

Web Browser Shortcut Keys

We have put many of the hotkeys and shortcuts in the beginning of the book for easy access and to keep them all together. Please go to page 169 to see the complete list of Web Browser hotkeys.

Go To a Web Page: Your Start Page or the Go To Page

In order to get to any web page, you can either type it on your **Start** page or press the **Menu** key and select **Go To**… from the menu.

The Address bar comes up with the "**http://www.**" in place waiting for you to type the rest of the address.

> **TIP:** Pressing the **Delete** key will quickly erase the www.

Simply type in the web address (remember, pressing the **Space** bar will put in the dot (.)).

> **TIP:** Pressing **Shift+Space** is the shortcut to type a "/" slash, as in `www.google.com/gmm` (the address to download Google Maps application at time of publishing this book).

The Start page:

The first thing you see on the top of the **Start** page will be the web address line. Then you will see your **Bookmarks** and then your **History** of recently visited pages below. Click on any bookmark or history entry to instantly jump to it.

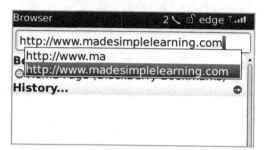

> **TIP:** As you start typing a web address, any similar addresses instantly are shown beneath it.

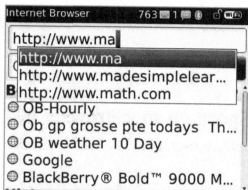

To save time, glide down and click on the address you want as soon as you see it in the list.

Type a few more letters to narrow the list of web addresses shown.

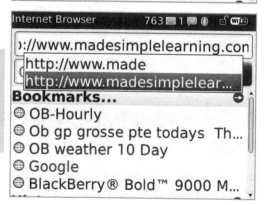

> **TIP:** To edit the address in the drop-down list, glide down to it and then glide to the right with the trackpad to change it in the top window.

Press the **Enter** key or click the trackpad to go to the selected web page or history item.

Browser Menu Options

While in the **Browser** application, press the **Menu** key

The following options are available to you (See page 169 for All the Browser HotKeys/Shortcuts):

- **Help**—See on-screen text help for the Web Browser, useful when you forget something and need quick help.

- **Column View/Page View**—Toggles between the two views. Column view offers are more zoomed-in view, Page view gives you a view of the entire page (more like a PC web browser.) (HotKey: **Z**)

- **Zoom In**—Allows you to zoom in multiple times to see text more clearly. (HotKey: **I**)

- **Zoom Out**—Allows you to zoom out to see more of the page. (HotKey: **O**)

- **Find**—Lets you search for text on a web page. (HotKey: **F / V**)

- **Find Next**—Searches for the next occurrence of the last **Find**.

- **Home**—Takes you to the Browser **Home** page. You can set or change the **Home** page inside the Browser →Options screen. (HotKey: **H**)

- **Go To...**—Allows you to type in a specific web address for browsing (see page 22 for details). (Hotkey: **G**)

- **Recent Pages**—Allows you to view the most recent web pages browsed.

- **History**—Shows your entire web browsing history. (HotKey: **Y**)

- **Refresh**—Updates the current web page. (HotKey: **R**)

- **Set Encoding**—This is an advanced feature to change character encoding of web browsing. (You probably won't need to change this).

- **Add Bookmark**—Sets the current page as a favorite or bookmark, which is extremely useful (see page 477 for details). (HotKey: **A**)

- **Bookmarks**—Lists all your bookmarks, which is also extremely useful) (see page 22 for details on using bookmarks, and page 22 for details on organizing bookmarks with folders). (HotKey: **K**)

- **Page Address**—Shows you the full web address of the current page. (HotKey: **P**)

- **Send Address**—Sends the current page address to a contact.

- **Options**—Set Browser Configuration, Properties, and Cache settings here. (HotKey: **S**)

- **Save Page**—Saves the page as a file and puts it in your **Messages** icon (your e-mail inbox).

- **Switch Application**—Lets you jump or multitask over to other applications while leaving the current web page open. (Hotkey: **D** jumps to **Home** screen)

- **Close**—Closes the Web Browser and exit to the **Home** screen. (HotKey: Press and hold **Escape** key)

> **NOTE:** These hotkeys work only while you are viewing a web page and only if the cursor is not in an input (typing) field. If the cursor is in the Google search field, for example, typing these hotkey letters will only show you the letters—not perform the command.

To Copy or Send the Web Page You are Viewing

1. Open the **Browser** icon and press the **Menu** key.

2. Scroll down to **Page Address** and click.

3. The web address is displayed in the window. Scroll down with the trackpad for options.

4. Scroll to **Copy Address** and click. This will copy the web address to the clipboard and can easily be pasted into a contact, an e-mail, a memo, or your calendar.

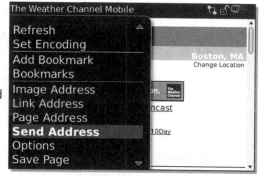

5. Alternatively, scroll to **Send Address** and click. This will allow you to send the particular web address information via e-mail, MMS, SMS, or PIN messaging. Just select the form and then the contact.

Setting and Naming Bookmarks (Such as Local Weather)

> **TIP:** You can instantly find bookmarks by typing a few letters of the bookmark name—just like you look up contacts in your Address Book. Keep this in mind as you add new bookmarks.

One of the keys to great web browsing on your BlackBerry is the liberal use of bookmarks. Your BlackBerry will come with a couple of bookmarks already set. It is very easy to customize your bookmarks to include all your web favorites for easy browsing.

Adding and Naming Bookmarks to Easily Find Them

Let's set up a bookmark to find our local weather instantly.

1. Open the Browser and use the **Go To...** command (or "." Shortcut key) to input a favorite web page. In this example, we will type www.weather.com

2. Type in your ZIP code or city name to see your current weather.

3. Once the page loads with your own local weather, press the **Menu** key and select **Add Bookmark** (or use the **A** shortcut key).

4. The Full name of the web address is displayed. In this case, you will probably see TWC Weather—you may want to re-name it (see the following).

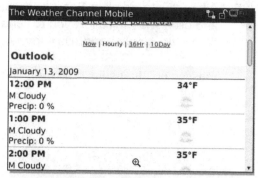

5. In this case (and most cases), we recommend changing the bookmark name to something short and unique.

> **NOTE:** If you bookmarked four different weather forecasts, the default bookmark names would all show up as "The Weather Channel"—sort of useless if you want to get right to the ten-day forecast.

Keep these things in mind as you name your bookmarks:

(a) **Make all bookmark names fairly short.** You will only see about the first 10-15 characters of the name in your list (because the screen is small).

(b) **Make all bookmark names similar but unique.** For example, if you were adding four bookmarks for the weather in New York or your area, you might want to name them:

- ▪ NY – Now
- ▪ NY – 10 day
- ▪ NY – 36 hour
- ▪ NY – Hourly

This way you can instantly locate all your forecasts by typing the letters **NY** in your bookmark list. Only those bookmarks with the letters **NY** will show up.

TIP: You can save time by editing a bookmark. If you want to enter a web address that is similar to a bookmark, you should highlight the previously entered address, press the **Menu** key, and select Edit Bookmark

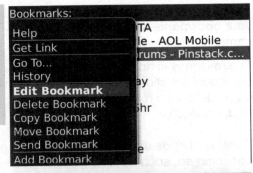

Then type your changes, glide to the bottom, and click **Accept** to save your changes or **Cancel** to stop editing and not save any changes.

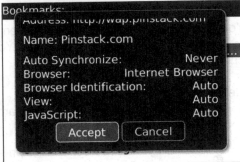

Setting Your Browser Start Page (Bookmarks/Home/Start)

You might prefer to see the bookmark list rather than the **Start** page, or you might prefer to see your **Home** page when you open the Browser.

One reason to set your bookmark list as your **Start** page when you open the Browser is that it gives you a very fast way to get to your favorite web pages.

If you have **Home** screen hotkeys turned on (see page 548), and your **Browser Bookmarks** as the startup page, then you could type the letters **BNY** to instantly see all your Weather bookmarks for New York City.

Pressing the **Home** screen hotkey **B** opens the Browser, showing you your bookmarks (assuming you have set your bookmarks to be your startup page in Browser options).

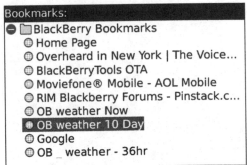

Typing **NY** shows you all matching entries in your bookmarks with the letters **NY** in the name.

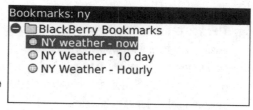

The reason is simple: typing letters in the bookmark list allows you to instantly locate the bookmarks with matching letters (like the Address Book).

Benefits: It ends up being much faster to get to favorite web pages that are bookmarked, such as local weather (hourly, 7 day) or your favorite search engine (Google).

Your BlackBerry may automatically open up to your bookmarks list, but you may prefer to see a selected **Home** page instead. You can use these instructions to make that change as well.

Here's how to set your bookmarks (or something else) to appear when you start your browser:

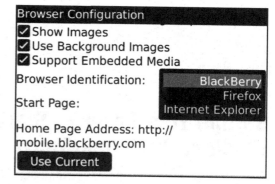

1. Click on your **Browser** icon or press the hotkey **B**.

2. Press the **Menu** key and select **Options** (or press **S**).

3. Click on **Browser Configuration**.

4. Glide all the way down to the **Start Page** near the bottom and click on the options. You will most likely see three options: **Bookmarks Page** (list of bookmarks), **Home Page** (the web site you have listed as your home page, which you do on this screen), or **Last Page Loaded** (keeps the last web page in memory and brings it back up when you re-enter your Browser).

5. To select bookmark list, choose **Bookmarks Page** and make sure to save your settings.

Using Your Bookmarks to Browse the Web

1. Click on your **Browser** icon or press the hotkey **B** to start it.

2. If you don't see your bookmark list automatically when you start your Browser, press the **Menu** key and scroll down to **Bookmarks** and click.

3. All of your bookmarks will be listed, including any default bookmarks that were put there automatically by your phone company.

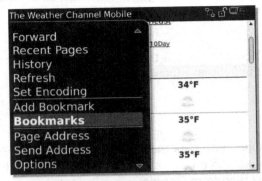

You might want to click on a particular folder to open all the bookmarks contained within or if you see the bookmark you need, just click on it.

However, if you have a lot of bookmarks, then you should use the **Find** feature and type a few letters matching the bookmark you want to find.

See the previous image—typing the letters **ny** will immediately find all bookmarks with **ny** in the bookmark name.

Search with Google

Google also has a mobile version that loads quickly and is quite useful on your BlackBerry. To get there, just go to www.google.com in your BlackBerry Web Browser.

Example: To find all the pizza places in the ZIP code 32174, just type **pizza 32174** in the Google search field.

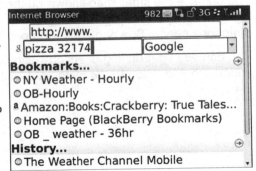

You can set this search bar for Google or other built-in search engines. Just click on the drop-down arrow to the right of the search bar.

You can change the default search provider on the Options → Browser Configuration screen.

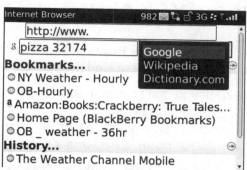

Once you click the **Enter** key or trackpad, your web search starts. Shown here is the results screen from Google.

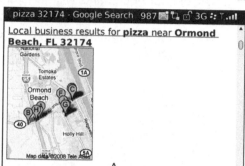

Scroll down a little to see all the local pizza establishments. What's great is that since your BlackBerry is a phone, you can just click on any underlined phone number and call for your pizza order immediately.

To Find a Quick Map of Your Search

You can see the small map shown on the regular Google search results screen, but we highly recommend using the Google Maps application for all your mapping and directions needs. See page 504 for more on using this feature.

You can even get driving directions using Google Maps to find the quickest path from your current location to the restaurant—all on your BlackBerry!

To Copy or Send the Web Page You are Viewing

1. While you are viewing the web page, hit the hotkey **P** or press the **Menu** key to select **Page Address**.

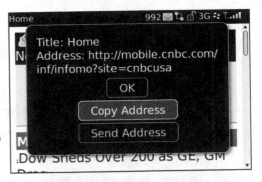

2. Scroll to **Copy Address** and click. This will copy the web address to the clipboard and then you can easily paste it into a contact, an e-mail, a memo, or your Calendar.

3. Alternatively, scroll to **Send Address** and click. This will allow you to send the particular web address information via e-mail, PIN messaging, SMS Text, MMS multimedia message, or BlackBerry Messenger.

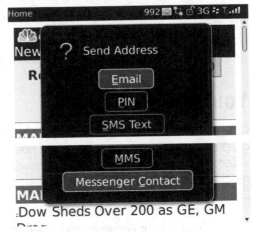

4. Just select the desired method and enter the contact information, type your message, and send!

Search with Yahoo! Mobile

Yahoo!, like most of the other big search engines, does have a mobile version of its search site. The web site senses you are viewing it from your small BlackBerry Browser and adjusts to a scaled-down version that gives you most of the functionality on a smaller screen.

How to get access? Go to www.yahoomobile.com from your BlackBerry Web Browser. It's free!

Finding Things Using Google Maps

In this book, we describe in detail how to obtain and use Google Maps on your BlackBerry. Please go to page 504.

Web Browser Tips and Tricks

There are some helpful shortcuts to help you navigate the Web faster and easier. We have included a few for you here:

- To insert a **period "."** in the web address, in the **Go To...** dialog box, press the **Space** key**.**

- To insert a **forward "/" slash**, in the **Go To...** dialog box, hold the **Shift** key and press the **Space** key.

- To open the **Bookmark List** from a web page, press **K**.

- To **Add a Bookmark** from a web page, press the **A** Key.

- To stop loading a web page, press the **Escape** key.

- To access the **Go To...** command to go to a specific web page, press the **G** key.

- To close a Browser, press and hold the **Escape** key.

YouTube

One of the most fun sites to visit on the computer is YouTube for viewing short video clips on just about everything. Your new BlackBerry is able to view most YouTube videos without any problems. You may notice that some videos are not formatted for mobile viewing and will see that message if the video cannot be played on your BlackBerry.

1. Open your Browser and navigate to the YouTube web site (m.youtube.com) and it will detect that you are on a mobile device.

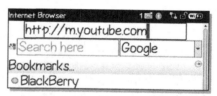

2. Search just like you do on your computer for any video you might want to watch. The video will load in your media player and you can control it just like you do any other video.

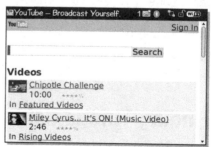

Chapter 30

Add or Remove Apps

Your BlackBerry comes with most of the major apps you would need already installed. However, there are literally thousands of third-party apps available in virtually any category you can think of to help you get the most out of your BlackBerry.

There are apps for productivity, reference, music, and fun—like lots of great games. One nice thing about the BlackBerry platform is that while there is an official **App World**, there are also lots of ways to find and download apps. In this chapter, we will show you how to navigate **BlackBerry App World** and how to download and install apps onto your BlackBerry.

Downloading and Adding New Software

One of the very cool things about your BlackBerry is that, just like on your computer, you can go on the Web and find software to download. You can download everything from ring tones to games to content that is "pushed" like your e-mail to your BlackBerry on a regular basis.

Today, there are hundreds of software applications and services to help extend the capabilities of your BlackBerry. The authors have used or are currently using the programs or applications listed in the next section. Find many more programs using **BlackBerry App World** on page 441.

Selected Apps Used By the Authors

There are thousands of apps available for the BlackBerry. While we can't review and comment on all of them, the apps listed in Table 30-1 are ones we have used and found to be well implemented for the BlackBerry.

Table 30-1. *Selected apps recommended by authors.*

App Name	What it does	Where to get it
AP Mobile News	Associated Press reader	http://ap.mwap.at/
CrackBerry & Shop CrackBerry	CrackBerry Blogs CrackBerry Store	http://wap.crackberry.com
ESPN	ESPN web site	www.espn.com
Facebook	Facebook Mobile	http://mobile.blackberry.com
Flycast	Internet streaming radio	www.flycast.fm
Google Maps	Mapping & search software	http://google.com/gmm
Google Mobile App	Voice-activated search and access to all Google apps	http://m.google.com
Kindle	Read your kindle books on your BlackBerry	www.amazon.com/kindlebb
Newsweek	Newsweek Mobile	http://mobile.blackberry.com
NY Times	New York Times web site	www.nytimes.com
Pinstack	Pinstack BlackBerry Forum	www.pinstack.com
Slacker	Internet streaming radio	www.slacker.com
Viigo	RSS news reader	www.viigo.com
Wall St. Journal	Wall St. Journal Mobile	http://mobile.blackberry.com
YouTube	YouTube Mobile	http://m.youtube.com

Ways to Install New Software

There are several ways to install software on your BlackBerry.

Option 1: Browse mobile.blackberry.com or another web site to locate software designed for your BlackBerry. Then click on a link and download wirelessly or Over the Air (also called OTA). You can also have the link e-mailed to you after entering your address into a web form on the software vendor's or web store's site. Another way is to type a web address directly into your BlackBerry Web Browser.

TIP: You may need to use the **Go To...** menu command in your Browser to type a web address.

Some sites ask you to enter your mobile phone number—this is your BlackBerry phone number—in order to send you an SMS text message with the download link.

Option 2: Download a file to your computer, then connect your BlackBerry to your computer and install it via USB cable connection or sometimes Bluetooth connection. For Apple Mac users, see the chapter starting on page 125. For Windows PC users, see the chapter starting on page 67.

Option 3: (Only if your BlackBerry is connected to a BlackBerry Enterprise Server.) Your BlackBerry server administrator can push new software directly to your BlackBerry device. Using this option is both wireless and automatic from the user's perspective.

We will describe options 1 and 2 in this book.

Wirelessly Installing Software Directly from Your BlackBerry Over-the-Air (OTA)

The beauty of the wireless OTA software installation process is that you do not need a computer, CD, or even a USB cable to install new software. It is really quite easy to install software OTA on the BlackBerry.

NOTE: Software installation used to be a much more painful process in older BlackBerry models; thank goodness for Research In Motion's continuous technical advances!

To Install Software Wirelessly OTA

To install software on your BlackBerry, as we described earlier, you need to either click a link you received in your e-mail or SMS text message or start the Web Browser and **Go To...** a web address where the software download files are located. In this example, we will use www.mobile.blackberry.com.

1. Navigate around the web site and click on a link for the software title you want to install.

2. Usually, a **License Agreement** screen pops up. You must click **Accept** to continue with the download.

3. The next screen to appear is the standard **Download** screen. This screen shows the name, version, the vendor (software company), and size of the program. Beneath all this information, you see a **Download** button to click on.

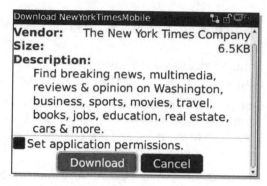

4. The progress of the download will be displayed in the center of the screen.

NOTE: You may see a warning message that says something like:

"**WARNING: Application is not digitally signed. Do you want to continue? Yes or No**"

5. If you get the warning message, you must click **Yes** to continue, but make sure this is software from a vendor that you recognize or have confidence that it is not malicious.

6. Once the application is completely downloaded, a dialogue box pops up notifying you the download was successful. You may be given an option to run the program.

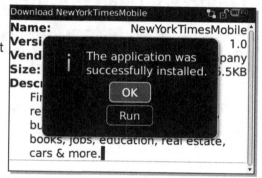

7. Finally, if you clicked on **Run**, you would start the newly installed software; clicking **OK** brings you back to the original web page where you downloaded the file. To exit to your **Home** screen, press the **Escape** key a few times.

8. You will then see the new icon either on your **Home** screen of icons, in the **Applications** sub-folder, or after you press the **Menu** key to see all your icons.

Downloading and Installing Games and Other Apps on your BlackBerry

The BlackBerry can truly be a multimedia entertainment device. Sometimes, you might want to play a new game on your BlackBerry. While your BlackBerry may have come with a few games, there are many places on the Web where you can find others.

BlackBerry App World (see page 441) is a great place to find new games!

One place to start looking for additional games is the Mobile BlackBerry site listed previously: http://mobile.blackberry.com.

Another good site is www.shopcrackberry.com—they also have an Applications store that you can access from your device.

See the Web Browser section on page 473 to learn how to get to these web pages on your BlackBerry.

Scroll through the choices and find a game that you want to try and then just select the **Download** link.

Another site to look at is www.bplay.com, where you can also find some of the most popular games available for BlackBerry entertainment.

Usually, you can just add the game to a shopping cart and either have it billed to your mobile number or pay online with a credit card or PayPal.

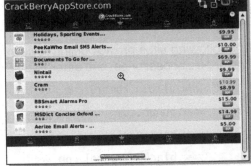

Then, just download and install exactly as you did previously when installing the **Web Push** app. Initially, the program file will go into your **Downloads** folder. You can always move the icon for the game into your **Games** folder—just take a look back at page 169 to see how to do that.

BlackBerry App World Store

Earlier in 2009, BlackBerry launched the on-the-BlackBerry mobile software store called **BlackBerry App World**. This will compete with the Apple iPhone **AppStore**. We have an entire chapter dedicated to getting the most out of **BlackBerry App World** (see page 441).

Other Places to Get BlackBerry Software

Since your BlackBerry is not locked to only use the BlackBerry App World, you really do have a myriad of possibilities as to where you can find quality software for your BlackBerry. We mention some web sites in this section, but you can also do a simple web search for **BlackBerry Software** and see if other options come up.

Web Stores

You can usually purchase software from these stores:

- www.crackberry.com
- www.shopcrackbery.com
- www.bberry.com
- www.handango.com
- www.mobihand.com

Additional Resources

The following sites provide online reviews of software, services, ringtones, themes, wallpaper, accessories, and other BlackBerry-related news and technical support:

- www.allblackberry.com
- www.bbhub.com
- www.berryreview.com
- www.blackberrycool.com
- www.blackberryforums.com
- www.boygeniusreport.com
- www.howardforums.com (The RIM-Research In Motion Section)

- www.pinstack.com
- www.RIMarkable.com

BlackBerry Solutions Catalog

The software and services you will find in the Solutions Catalog will be more focused toward business users than individuals:

http://www.blackberrysolutionscatalog.com/

BlackBerry App World Online

You can browse BlackBerry App World from your computer's web browser by going to: http://appworld.blackberry.com/webstore/

Removing Software Directly From Your BlackBerry

There will be times when you wish to remove a software icon from the BlackBerry and you are not connected to your computer. Fortunately, it is very easy and intuitive to remove programs from the BlackBerry itself.

> **TIP:** If you have installed software using the BlackBerry App World, you can also remove it from the **My World** section (please see page 448 for help).

Deleting an App or Icon from the Home Screen

Probably the easiest way to delete an app is to highlight the icon, then press the **Menu** key and select **Delete**.

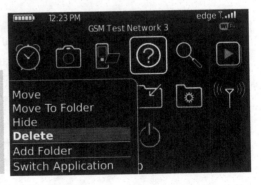

> **NOTE:** You cannot delete some core icons such as **Messages**, **Calendar**, and **Contacts**, so you won't see the **Delete** option on the menu item.

Using the Options Icon

To remove software directly from the BlackBerry, do the following:

1. Press the **Menu** key and click on the

   Options icon.

2. Click on **Advanced Options**.

3. Scroll to the top of the list and click on **Applications**.

4. The screen will now display all the programs installed on your BlackBerry. Scroll to the application you want to delete to highlight it, then press the **Menu** key and select **Delete**.

5. Then you will need to confirm that you want to delete the program and it will be removed.

Options
About
Advanced Options
Auto On/Off
AutoText
CellData
Date/Time
GPS Extended Ephemeris
Language

Advanced Options
Accessibility
Applications
Browser
Browser Push
Cell Broadcast Settings
Default Services
Enterprise Activation

Applications	
BlackBerry 4.6 Core Applications	4.6
BlackBerry Sample Content	4.6.0
BlackBerry 4.6 System Software	4.6
Help	4.6.0
View Properties	4.6.0
Delete	4.6.0
Modules	4.6.0
Edit Default Permissions	1.001.145
Switch Application	4.6.0
Close	2.3.1

NOTE: Sometimes, your BlackBerry will need to reboot itself in order to complete the program deletion process. It will tell you if it needs to reboot and ask you to confirm.

Troubleshooting: If the software is not completely removed from your BlackBerry after following the preceding steps, then try this:

1. Go back into the **Options** icon.

2. Select **Advanced Options**.

3. Select **Applications**.

4. Press the **Menu** key and select **Modules**.

Applications
BlackBerry 4.6 Core Applications   4.6
BlackBerry Sample Content   4.6.0
BlackBerry 4.6 System Software   4.6
Help   e   4.6.0
View Properties   4.6.0
Delete   4.6.0
Modules   4.6.0
Edit Default Permissions   1.001.145
Switch Application   4.6.0
Close   2.3.1

5. Now scroll down the list of modules and make sure to delete every module with a name that is related to the software you are trying to remove. (Highlight a module, press the **Menu** key, and select **Delete** from the menu).

NOTE: If you have a Windows computer, you can also use the **Application Loader** icon built into BlackBerry Desktop Manager software to remove icons (see page 90).

Chapter 31

Traveling: Maps and More

Depending on whether or not you are leaving the country with your BlackBerry, there are a few things you should know how to do. There are plenty of mapping applications that use the Global Positioning System (GPS) location in the BlackBerry to help you find your destination and provide you with turn-by-turn directions.

If you are going to another country, there are some definite things to do before you take off so you do not get surprised with a huge data roaming phone bill. We'll cover this and more in this chapter.

International Travel—Things to Do Before You Go

Some BlackBerry smartphones are equipped for international travel, and some are more of a challenge. Networks in the US, such as Verizon and Sprint, use CDMA technology—widely available in North America, but not in other places.

BlackBerry smartphones that use SIM cards (AT&T and T-Mobile) in the US are more common throughout the world.

We always recommend that you call your cell provider well in advance of your trip to see if there is an **international** feature you can turn on.

How to Avoid a Surprisingly Large Data or Voice Roaming Phone Bill

We have heard of people who traveled to another country being surprised with $300 or $400 monthly data or voice roaming charges after their trip. You can avoid these by taking a few easy steps before and during your trip.

Before Your Trip

There are a few simple steps you can take to ensure that your BlackBerry will always be working – no matter where you might be in the world.

Step 1: Check to see if you have a SIM card inserted.

If you are traveling to a country where you will need to connect to a GSM network, then you will need to have a SIM card in your BlackBerry. Most times, with an 8520 Curve, you will already have a SIM card pre-inserted by the phone company.

You can check that you have a SIM card by clicking on the **Options** Icon. Then select **Advanced Options**. Finally, tap the letter **S** a couple times to jump down to **SIM Card** and click on it. If you see a screen that says: **SIM Card: No Valid SIM Card**, then you do not have a SIM card or your SIM card is not inserted correctly.

You can also quickly check if you have a SIM Card, by removing the back cover of your BlackBerry and taking a look. (See page 4 for a picture of where the SIM Card Slot is located.)

Step 2: Call your BlackBerry phone company—You may need to turn on a temporary International Rate Plan.

Check with your wireless carrier about any voice and data roaming charges—you can try searching on your phone company's web site, but usually you will have to call the help desk and specifically ask what the voice roaming and data roaming charges are for the country or countries you are visiting. If you use e-mail, SMS Text, MMS messaging, web browsing, or any other data services, you will want to specifically ask about whether or not any of these services are charged separately.

Some phone companies offer an **International Rate Plan** that you will need to activate. In some cases, you must activate such a plan to use your BlackBerry at all; in other cases, activating such a plan will allow you to save some money on the standard data and voice roaming charges. Check out these plans to see if they can save you some money while you are on your trip, especially if you need to have access to data while you are away.

Unlocking Your BlackBerry to Use a Foreign SIM Card

In some cases, your BlackBerry phone company does not offer special deals on international data roaming plans or their rates are unreasonably high. In these cases, you may want to ask your phone company to unlock your BlackBerry so that you can insert a SIM card you purchase in the foreign country. Many times, inserting a local SIM card will eliminate or greatly reduce data and voice roaming charges. However, you should check carefully the cost of placing and receiving international calls on that foreign SIM card. Using a foreign SIM card may save you hundreds of dollars, but it's best to do some web research or try to talk to someone who has recently traveled to the same country for advice.

Airplane Travel—How to Get into Airplane Mode

See page 14 to learn how to turn off the wireless radio and other connections on your BlackBerry. Some airlines force you to completely power-down your electronic devices during take-off and landing, but then allow use of "approved electronic devices" (read: BlackBerry with the radio turned off) while in flight.

International Travel—Things to Do While You Are Abroad

Once you've done everything so far and have prepared for your trip, there are still some things to do once you get to your destination.

After You Get There

Once you arrive at your destination, there are just a couple of thing to do to make sure your BlackBerry is ready to use.

Step 1: Adjust your time zone to the local time zone.

See page 37 for help with setting the time zone.

Step 2: If data roaming charges are unknown or too high, turn off data roaming.

If you were unable to find out about data roaming charges from your local phone company, try to contact the phone company in the country where you are traveling to find out about any data roaming or voice roaming charges.

Worst case, if you are worried about the data roaming charges, and can do without your e-mail and web while away, then you should disable data services when you are roaming:

1. Start the **Options** icon or you can click the **Manage Connections** icon.

2. Highlight **Mobile Network** and click on it.

3. Your **Data Services** will most likely say **On**; there is a secondary tab for **While Roaming.** We recommend setting the switch to **Off** in the **While Roaming** field so that you can continue to receive data in your **Home Network**.

4. Press the **Escape** key—your settings are saved automatically.

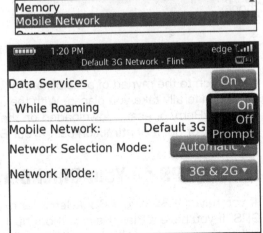

Setting this to **Off While Roaming** should help you avoid any potentially exorbitant data roaming charges. (You still need to worry about voice roaming charges, but at least you can control those by watching how much you talk on your phone).

Remember, with the **Off While Roaming** setting, when you return to your home network, all data services (e-mail, web, and so forth) will work automatically.

Step 3: Register with the local network.

If you are having trouble connecting to the local wireless network, you may need to register your BlackBerry on the local network. See the Host Routing Table (Register Now) on page 22.

International Travel—Arriving Home

As you did when you arrived at your destination, there are a few changes to make once you arrive back home.

Step 1: Make sure to adjust your time zone back to your local time zone.

See page 37 for help with setting the time zone.

Step 2: If you have turned Data Services to Off, then you will need to make sure to turn them back **On** or **Off When Roaming** so you can receive data when you return home.

Step 3: You may need to register your BlackBerry on the local network.

See the Host Routing Table (Register Now) on page 22.

Step 4: Turn Off Special International Plans, if not needed.

(Optional) If you have activated some sort of special international roaming rate plan with your BlackBerry phone company and do not need it any more, turn it off to save some money.

BlackBerry Maps, Google Maps, Bluetooth GPS

In addition to the myriad of possibilities in which your BlackBerry can manage your life, it can also literally take you places. With the aid of software that is either pre-loaded on the BlackBerry or easily downloaded on the web, you can find just about any location, business, or point of attraction using your BlackBerry.

Enable GPS on Your BlackBerry

If you have GPS on your BlackBerry (for example, Curve 8530), then you can enable GPS. If you have a BlackBerry without built-in GPS, such as the Curve 8520, then you will have to acquire a Bluetooth GPS puck to have GPS available to your mapping applications. Google Maps does give you a general fix on your position (usually within about 1,000 meters or so) using the cellular towers.

For BlackBerry devices with built-in GPS:

In order to get the maximum benefit out of any mapping software on your BlackBerry, you need to make sure your GPS receiver is enabled or turned on.

1. To turn on your GPS receiver, go into your **Options** icon. Select **Advanced Options**, and finally, click on **GPS**.

2. Make sure **GPS Services** is set to **Location ON** as shown, then press the **Menu** key and select **Save**.

GPS	
GPS Services	Location ON ▾
GPS Location:	Location Off
Latitude:	N 0° 0.00'
Longitude:	W 0° 0.00'
Fix Time:	None
Number of Satellites:	0
Accuracy:	0.0 m
Geolocation Service:	Enabled ▾
Location Aiding:	Enabled ▾

Using BlackBerry Maps

The BlackBerry ships with the BlackBerry Maps software—a very good application for determining your current location and tracking your progress via the built-in GPS receiver on your BlackBerry.

> **NOTE:** For GPS to work, you first have to turn on or enable GPS on your BlackBerry, see the preceding section.

To enable GPS use on BlackBerry Maps (using either Bluetooth GPS receiver or a built-in GPS)

1. Click the **Maps** icon in the **Applications** folder to launch the app and then press the **Menu** key.

2. Click on **Options**.

3. Under **GPS Source**, select either **Internal GPS** or an external GPS unit if you have one.

4. 4. Press the **Escape** key and save your choices.

To Start GPS Navigation

1. From the **Map** icon, press the **Menu** key from the main **Map** screen and select **Find Location.**

2. On the Mapping screen, press the **Menu** key and select **Start GPS Navigation**.

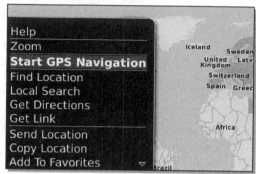

The BlackBerry Map software will now search for your current location.

To view a particular map from a contact

1. From the **Map** icon, press the **Menu** key from the main **Map** screen and select **Find Location**.

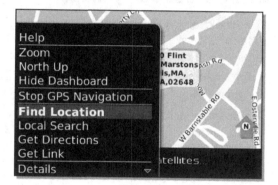

2. You can search based on your current location or you can enter an address, search from contacts, or look at recent searches.

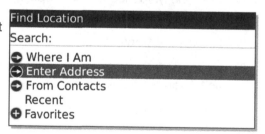

3. On the next screen, scroll down to **From Contacts**.

4. Select and click the contact.

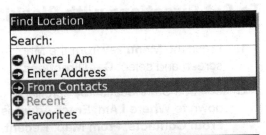

5. Then a map of their location will appear on the screen.

To Get Directions with BlackBerry Maps

1. Press the **Menu** key from the **Map** screen and select **Get Directions**.

2. Select a Start location by scrolling down to **Where I Am**, **Enter Address**, **From Contacts**, **From Map**, **Recent**, or **Favorites**.

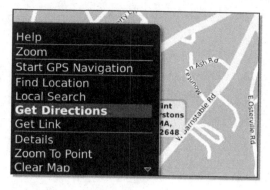

3. Repeat the steps now for the End location.

4. When done, click on the trackpad and the BlackBerry Map program will create a route for your trip.

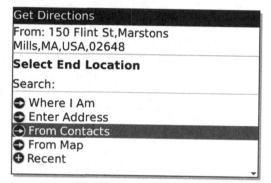

You can choose whether you want the **Fastest** or **Shortest** route and whether you want to avoid highways or tolls. Then, just click on **Search** to have your route displayed for you. If you click **View on Map** you will see a Map View of the route.

If you have enabled GPS use, the GPS will track you along the route but it will not give you voice prompts or turn-by-turn voice directions.

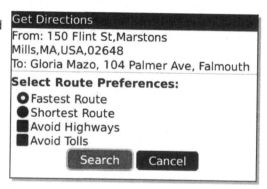

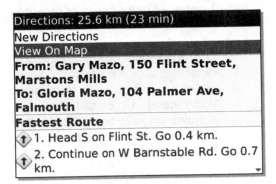

BlackBerry Maps Menu Commands

There is a great deal you can do with the BlackBerry Map application. Pressing the **Menu** key offers you many options with just a scroll and a click. From the menu, you can do the following:

- **Zoom**—Takes you from street level to the stratosphere (keyboard shortcut keys: **L** = Zoom In, **O** = Zoom Out).

- **North Up**—Places the North Arrow straight up and keeps the map oriented so up is always north (only with GPS enabled).

- **Hide Dashboard**—Simply puts the map into full screen mode without the bottom border.

- **Stop GPS Navigation**—This option ends GPS tracking (only with GPS enabled).

- **Find Location**—Type in an address to jump to that address.

- **Local Search**—Search for restaurants, stores, or places of interest near your current location.

- **New Directions**—Find directions by using your location history or typing in new addresses.

- **View Directions**—If you are in **Map** mode, this switches to text.

- **Zoom to Point**—Shows the map detail around the currently selected point in the directions (only when viewing directions).

- **Send Location**—Sends your map location via e-mail.

- **Copy Location**—Adds your current location to your Address Book or another application.

- **Add to Favorites**—Adds your current location as a Favorite for easy retrieval on the Map.

■ **Layers**—Shows layers of recent searches, favorites, or links on the map.

■ **Options**—Changes GPS Bluetooth device, disables backlight timeout settings, changes units from metric (kilometers) to imperial (miles), enables or disables tracking with GPS, and enables you to show or hide the title bar when starting.

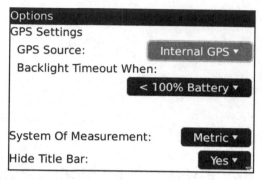

■ **About**—Shows information about the current provider of the mapping data and software.

■ **Cell Data**—Allows you to control whether you can be tracked or not.

■ **Switch Application**—Jumps over to any other application (multitask).

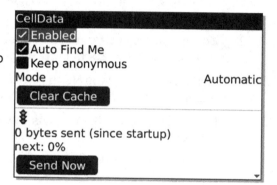

Google Maps: Downloading & Installing

If you have ever used Google Earth, you have seen the power of satellite technology in mapping and rendering terrain. Google Maps Mobile brings that same technology to handheld devices, including the BlackBerry.

With Google Maps, you can view 3-D rendered satellite shots of any address, anywhere in the world. To get started with this amazing application, you need to first download it onto your BlackBerry.

1. Click on the **Browser** icon from your **Applications** screen .

2. Press the **Menu** key and scroll to the **Go To...** command and click.

TIP: Use the shortcut hotkey of "." (period) for **Go To**.

3. Enter in the address to perform an OTA download right onto the BlackBerry: `http://www.google.com/gmm`.

4. Click on **Download Google Maps** and the installation program will begin.

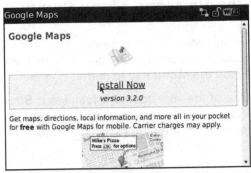

5. Click the **Download** button on the next screen.

6. Finally, you will see a screen indicating that the application was successfully installed. Select **OK** to close the window or **Run** to start Google Maps right away, or click on the icon on the BlackBerry, which should be in the **Downloads** folder.

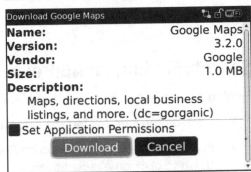

7. You might get prompted to reboot your device; if so, just click on **Reboot** and then try to run the program.

The first time you start up Google Maps Mobile, just click the icon (usually in your **Downloads** folder). Then read the terms and conditions, push in the trackpad, and select **Accept**.

Google Maps Menu Commands

Google Maps is full of great features, most of which you can access right from the menu. Press the **Menu** key to see it.

One of the very cool new features is **Street View**, which shows you actual photos of your location on the map (where available).

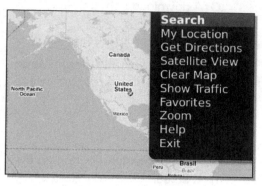

Search/Finding an Address (Location) or Business

Finding an address or business is very easy with Google Maps.

1. Click on the icon to start the Google Maps application.

2. Press the **Menu** key and choose **Search**. Click on **Enter new search** or glide down to click on a recent search.

> **TIP:** You can edit saved (recent) searches by rolling the trackpad down to the search and then rolling it to the right.

3. Just type about anything in the search string—an address, type of business and ZIP code, business name and city/state, and so forth. If we wanted to find bike stores in Winter Park, Florida, we would enter "**bike stores winter park fl**" or "**bike stores 32789**" (if you know the ZIP code).

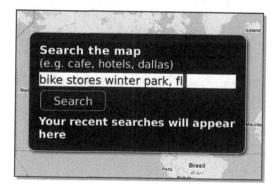

4. Your search results will show a number of matching entries; just glide the trackpad up/down to select an entry and click the trackpad to see details.

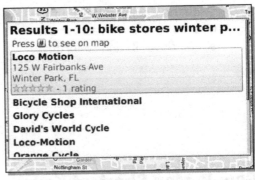

5. Press the # key to see the search results on the map.

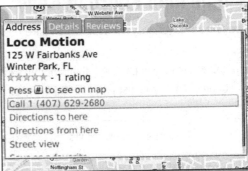

6. To see the new **Street** view, just click on **Street View** from the menu:

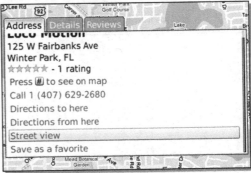

7. Glide the trackpad left/right to change your view—across the street, down it, and so forth.

Google Map Shortcut Keys

Use these keys on your BlackBerry keyboard to control Google Maps.

> **NOTE:** Just press the key with the number without holding ALT—for example, to press the #4 in Google Maps, you just press the **S** (**4**) key by itself.

4	Previous search results
6	Next search results
#	Toggle between Map view and Search Results List
2	Toggle between Satellite and Map views
1 / "O"	Zoom out
3 / "I"	Zoom in
*	Favorites list/Add a new favorite location
9	More search options & search tips
0	Show/hide location (if available)

Switching Views in Google Maps

Google Maps give you the option of looking at a conventional map grid or looking at real satellite images.

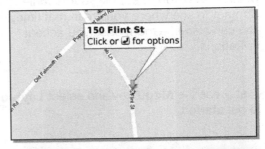

To Switch between views (shortcut key = **2**)

1. Press the **Menu** key and select **Satellite View** (or **2**).

2. Press the **Menu** key and select **Map View** (or press **2**).

See Your Current Location—the Little Blue Dot

Version 3.0 and higher of Google Maps allows you to show your location as a little blue dot, which is pinpointed by the GPS receiver, built into your BlackBerry.

> **NOTE:** When your GPS cannot get a satellite lock, or for your friends without GPS built-in to their BlackBerry, the approximate location is determined by triangulation using cell phone towers. When cell towers are used, there is a shaded circle around the blue dot to show that the location is approximate.

This is a great feature and very easy to access using the shortcut key of zero **0**. Pressing **0** or selecting **My location** from the menu will show you the blue dot.

Another new feature is **Google Latitude**, which allows you to enable your Google Contact to see where you are in real time; you can also see them once you accept invitations.

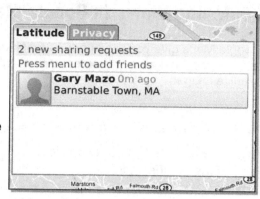

Just press the **Menu** key and select **Latitude** to get started.

Once set up, your location on the map is sent to whomever you choose, to share your location.

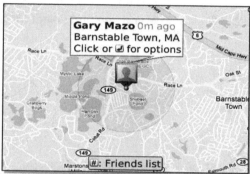

NOTE: In some places, the software cannot find enough information to show your location, so it will tell you.

Layers—Finding More Things Nearby

In the newest version of Google Maps (version 4.02 at the writing of this book,) there is a new feature called **Layers** (Figure 31-1.) Essentially, Layers will show you Wikipedia entries for things nearby, traffic conditions, transit lines, or personal maps. The data will be overlaid on the current map.

In this example, I have used Latitude to locate Martin in Florida; I then used Layers to find things nearby.

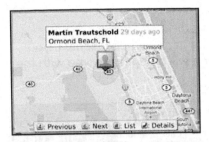
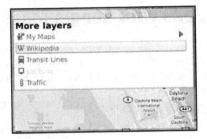

Figure 31-1. *Using **Layers** in Google Maps*

In the Wikipedia entries, I see that the Granada Bridge is near to him, so I click on it. I can now find more details—even see a picture of the bridge (Figure 31-2).

Figure 31-2. *Viewing the street view of a Wikipedia entry using **Layers***

See Current Traffic in Google Maps

One other useful thing you can do in major metropolitan areas or on major highways (this does not work everywhere) is to view current traffic with Google Maps. First, map the location you want to view traffic for.

Press the **Menu** key and select **Show Traffic** (Figure 31-33).

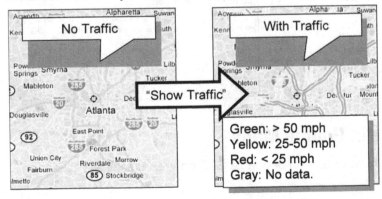

Figure 31-3. *Using the **Show Traffic** feature of Google Maps*

Getting Directions with Google Maps

One of the things you will most likely use Google Maps for is getting directions. If you are familiar with mapping software on your computer, you will be right at home with the directions features of Google Maps on your BlackBerry.

1. Press the **Menu** key and select **Get Directions**.

2. Set your **Start Point** (the default will be **My Location** (blue dot)), and then set your **End Point**.

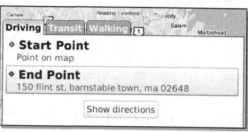

3. Click on the **Show Directions** button at the bottom to display turn-by-turn directions to your destination.

4. Press the number key **(#)** to see the map with your directions.

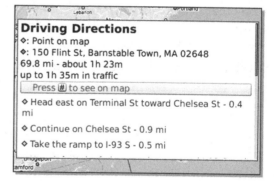

To Enable GPS Use in Google Maps

For GPS to work, you first have to turn on or enable GPS on your BlackBerry (see the section on page 498).

1. Start Google Maps and press the **Menu** key. Then select **Bluetooth GPS** or **Enable GPS**, depending on how you are accessing the GPS signal in your BlackBerry.

2. On the next screen, select the GPS device that you paired with your BlackBerry and the GPS commands will now be available to you.

Once GPS is enabled, your location will be shown with a little blue dot. If you press the **Space** key (**0**), then the map will move and follow your location.

Chapter 32

Other Applications

As if your BlackBerry doesn't do enough for you, RIM was very thoughtful and included even more utilities and programs to help keep you organized and to help manage your busy life. Most of these additional programs will be found in the **Applications** folder.

In this chapter we will show you how to use your BlackBerry as a calculator, a full functioning alarm clock, a voice note recorder and a password keeper.

Calculator (HotKey U)

There are many times when having a calculator nearby is handy. Gary usually likes to have his 15-year-old math genius daughter nearby when he has a math problem, but sometimes she's in school and not available to help.

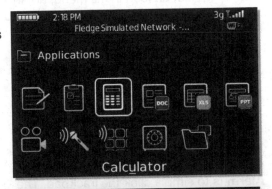

1. To start the **Calculator** program, click the **Applications** folder.

2. One of the icons should say **Calculator** (hotkey U).

3. Input your equation as you would on any calculator program.

One handy tool in the **Calculator** program is that it can easily convert amounts to metric. Press the **Menu** key and scroll to **To Metric**.

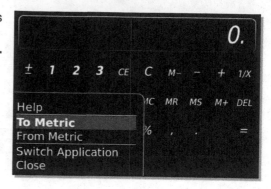

Clock and Alarm Clock

While having a clock is nothing new for a BlackBerry, the features and the ability to customize the clock, especially when the BlackBerry is on your bedside table, is new and appreciated.

To start the **Clock** application, go once again to the **Applications** folder and find and click the **Clock** icon. On some devices, the **Clock** icon might just an icon in the menu, not in a folder. By default, the clock is initially set to an analog face, but you can change that.

The first feature to look at is the **Alarm**. The easiest way to bring up the settings for the **Alarm** is to simply click the trackpad. The **Alarm** menu will appear on the bottom.

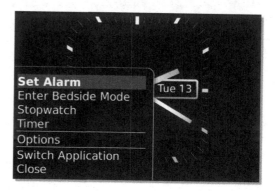

Glide the trackpad to the desired field and then glide up or down in that highlighted field to change the option. In the farthest field to the right, after it is highlighted, glide and select **Off**, **On**, or **Weekdays** for the alarm setting. Press the **Escape** key to save your changes.

Also built into the **Clock** application are a stopwatch and a timer, which you can start by selecting them from the menu.

> **TIP:** The clock can be changed to a Digital Clock, a Flip Clock, or an LCD Digital face by selecting the clock face from the **Options** menu.

Want to stop your clock from being displayed when you connect your BlackBerry to your computer?

By default, you will see your clock every time you connect your BlackBerry to your computer (when it is plugged in) or when you connect your BlackBerry to the power charger.

You can turn off this feature in the **Clock Options**. Inside the **Clock**, press the **Menu** key and select **Options**. Glide down and click next to **When Charging** and set it to **Do Nothing**.

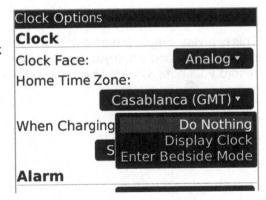

Bedside Mode

One of the nice new features of the **Clock** application is the **Bedside Mode** setting. For those of us who keep our BlackBerry by the side of our bed, we now have the option of telling our BlackBerry not to flash, ring, or buzz in the middle of the night. We just have to activate **Bedside Mode** by pressing the **Menu** key and selecting **Enter Bedside Mode.**

To configure the **Bedside Mode Options**, press the **Menu** key in the **Clock** application and scroll down to **Options**. Down towards the bottom of the **Options** menu are the specific **Bedside Mode** options. You can disable the LED and the radio and dim the screen when **Bedside Mode** is set.

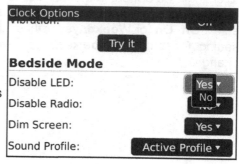

Voice Notes Recorder

Another useful program in your **Media** folder is the **Voice Notes Recorder**. Say you need to dictate something you need to remember at a later time. Or, perhaps you would rather speak a note instead of composing an e-mail. Your BlackBerry makes that very easy for you.

This is a very simple program to use—just click the trackpad when you are ready to record your note. Click it again when you are done.

You will then see options along the lower part of the program that will allow you to: **continue recording**, **stop**, **play**, **resume**, **delete**, or **e-mail** the voice note.

Just click on the corresponding icon to perform the desired action.

Password Keeper

It can be very hard in today's web world with different passwords and different password rules on so many different sites. Fortunately, your BlackBerry has a very effective and safe way for you to manage all your passwords—the **Password Keeper** program.

Go back to your **Applications** folder and navigate to the **Password Keeper** icon and click. The first thing you will need to do is set a program password—pick something you will remember!

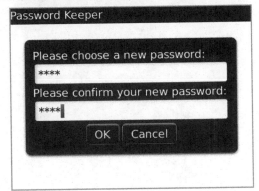

Once your password is set, you can add new passwords for just about anything or any web site.

Press the **Menu** key and select **New**. Here, you can add passwords, usernames, and web addresses to help you remember all your various login information.

New Password
Title:
Made Simple Learning
Username:
martin.trautschold
Password:
12345678
Website:
http://www.madesimplelearning.com
Notes:
BlackBerry Training Site

Chapter 33

Searching for Lost Stuff

Your BlackBerry can hold so much information—so much different information – that it can sometimes be difficult to keep track of where everything is. Thankfully, BlackBerry comes with a very comprehensive search program to help you find exactly what you are looking for.

In this chapter, we will show you how to search across applications, messages and contacts and how to filter your search information to show just what you want.

> **TIP:** With the Search feature, you can find calendar events and even answer such questions as:
>
> When is my next meeting with Sarah?
>
> When did I last meet with her?
>
> *(For this to work, you need to type people's names in your calendar events like Meet with Sarah or Lunch with Tom Wallis).*

Understanding How Search Works

Once you get used to your BlackBerry, you will begin to rely on it more and more. The more you use it, the more information you will store within it. It is truly amazing how much information you can place in this little device.

At some point, you will want to retrieve something—a name or a word or phrase—but you may not be exactly sure of where you placed that particular piece of information. This is where the **Search** feature can be invaluable.

> **NOTE:** There is also a nice search program built right into your Messages (E-mail) icon that allows you to search for Names, Subjects, and has many options. Learn how to use this built-in Messages Search on page 259.

Finding the Search Icon (HotKey: S)

In your **Applications** there is a **Search** Icon. If you have enabled hotkeys (see page 548), pressing the letter **S** will start the **Search** feature. From your **Home** screen of icons, use the trackpad to find the **Search** icon. It may be located within the **Applications** folder.

> **NOTE:** The application menu and application folder are two separate things. When you press the menu key, that gives you the menu of applications. In that menu, there are some folders as well - one of them is the Applications folder.

Search Several Apps at Once

It is possible that the desired text or name could be in one or several different places on your BlackBerry. The **Search** tool is quite powerful and flexible. It allows you to narrow down or expand the icons you want to search. If you are sure your information is in the **Calendar**, then just check that box; if not, you can easily check all the boxes using **Select All** from the menu. (Figure 33-1)

Click on the **Search** icon (or press the hotkey **S**) and the main **Search** screen opens.

By default, only the **Messages** field is checked.

Figure 33-1. *Search several apps at once*

To search all the icons for your name or text, press the **Menu** key, scroll to **Select All**, and click.

Searching for Names or Text

In the **Name** field, you can search for a name or an e-mail address. The **Text** field enables you to search for any other text that might be found in the body of an e-mail, inside a calendar event, in an address book entry, in a memo, or in a task.

If you decide to search for a name, then you can either type a few letters of a name, such as **Martin**, or press the **Menu** key and choose **Select Name**.

Type the name…

Or press the **Menu** key and **Select Name**.

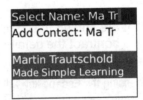

Then type a few letters to select the name from your contact list. Click on the highlighted name.

If you are looking for a specific text, such as a word, phrase, or even phone number that is not in an e-mail address field, then you would type it into the **Text** field.

When you are ready to start the search, click the trackpad and select **Search**.

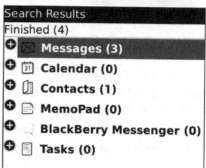

The results of the search are displayed with the number of found entries. The image to the right shows that there were four total matches found, three in the Messages (E-mail) and one in the Contacts.

To expand your search results, click on one of the items that are shown to see more details. Click again to contract the details.

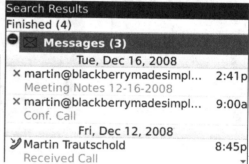

NOTE: Pressing the **Escape** key will clear your search results and bring you back to the **Search** screen.

Search Tips and Tricks

You can see that the more information you enter on your BlackBerry (or enter on your desktop computer and sync to your BlackBerry), the more useful it becomes. When you combine a great deal of useful information with this **Search** tool, you truly have a very powerful handheld computer.

As your BlackBerry fills up, the possible places where your information is stored increases. Also, the search might not turn up the exact information you are looking for due to inconsistencies in the way you store the information.

TIP: You can even search notes added to calendar events.

Remember to add notes to your calendar events and the notes field at the bottom of your contacts. You can do this right on your BlackBerry or on your computer and sync them. Use the **Search** app to find key notes on your BlackBerry right when you need them.

Try to be consistent in the way you type someone's name; for example, always use **Martin** instead of **Marty** or **M** or any other variation. This way, the **Search** will always find what you need.

Occasionally, check your address book for doubles of contact information. It is easy to wind up with two or three entries for one contact if you add an e-mail one time, a phone number another, and an address another—try to keep one entry per contact. It is usually easier to do this cleanup work on your computer, and then sync the changes or deletions back to your BlackBerry.

If you are not sure whether you are looking for Mark or Martin, just type in **Mar** and then search. This way, you will find both names.

Remember, if you want to find an exact name, then glide to the **Name** field, press the **Menu** key, and choose **Select Name** to select a name from your address book.

Do your best to put consistent information into calendar events. For example, if you wanted to find when the next dentist appointment for Gary was, you could search for **Gary Dentist** in your calendar and find it. But only if you made sure to put the full words **Gary** and **dentist** in your calendar entry. It would be better to just search for just **dentist**.

If you wanted to find a phone number and just remembered the area code, then you would type that area code into the **Text** field and search the Address Book.

If you wanted to find when the name Gary was in the body of an e-mail, not an e-mail address field (To:, Cc:, From:, Bcc:), then you would enter the name in the **Text** field, not the **Name** field on the Search screen.

TIP: Traveling and want to find local contacts? Let's say you are traveling to New York City and want to find everyone in your BlackBerry address book with a 212 area code. Type in **212** in the **Text** field, check the **Address Book**, and then click **Search** to immediately find everyone who has a 212 area code.

Chapter 34

Securing Your Data

In this chapter, we talk all about security and securing your BlackBerry data. Most of us keep very important information on our devices and would want to be prepared, just in case.

What if Your BlackBerry was Lost or Stolen?

Would you be uncomfortable if someone found and easily accessed all the information on your device?

For most of us the answer would be **YES!**

On many of our BlackBerry smartphones, we store friends' and colleagues' names, addresses, phone numbers, confidential e-mails, and notes. Some of our devices may even contain Social Security numbers, passwords, and other important information in your contact notes or your **MemoPad**.

In that case, you will want to enable or turn on the **Password Security** feature. When you turn this on, you will need to enter your own password in order to access and use the BlackBerry. In many larger organizations, you do not have an option to turn off your password security; it is automatically turned on by your BlackBerry Enterprise Server Administrator.

Prepare for the Worst-Case Scenario

There are a few things you can do to make this worst-case scenario less painful.

- **Step 1**: Back up your BlackBerry to your computer.
- **Step 2**: Turn on (enable) BlackBerry **Password Security**.
- **Step 3**: Set your Owner Information with an incentive for returning your BlackBerry.

Step 1: Back up or Sync Your Basic BlackBerry Data

For Windows users, check out our full description of how to back up and restore your BlackBerry data using Desktop Manager software on page 96. Mac users, use the backup feature in Desktop Manager for Mac shown on page 137.

> **CAUTION:** If you have important media (personal pictures, videos, music, and so forth) stored on your media card (what's a media card? see page 367), then you will have to copy your media card information separately from the sync or backup process. See our Media Sync/Transfer chapters for Windows users on page 105 and Mac users on page 141.

Step 2: Turn On (Enable) Password Security

Make sure you turn on (enable) the **Password Security** feature. This is really your plan B to safeguard all your data should you happen to lose your BlackBerry.

1. Click on your **Options** icon on your **Home** screen. Hit the letter **P** to jump down to **Password** and click on it.

2. Then, select **General Settings** to see this screen.

3. Click on the **Disabled** setting next to **Password** and change it to **Enabled**.

4. Click on **Set Password** to create your password. You can adjust the other settings unless they are locked out by your BlackBerry Administrator.

5. Save your settings.

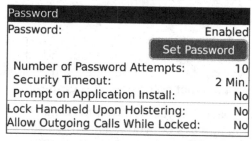

> **CAUTION:** If you cannot remember your password, then you will lose all the data (e-mails, addresses, calendar, tasks, everything) from your BlackBerry. Once you enter more than the set number of password attempts (default is ten attempts), the BlackBerry will automatically **Wipe** or **erase all data**.

Step 3: Set Your Owner Information

We recommend including something to the effect of "Reward offered for safe return" in your owner information, which would show up when someone found your BlackBerry in a locked mode. You may have already set your owner information in the **Setup Wizard**, however you can also set it by going to the **Options** icon and selecting **Owner Information**.

1. Click on your **Options** icon on your **Home** screen. Hit the letter **O** to jump down to **Owner** in the list of **Options Settings**, and click the trackpad to open it.

2. In the **Owner Information** settings screen, put yourself into the mind of the person who might find your BlackBerry and give them both the information and an incentive to return your BlackBerry safely to you.

3. Press the **Menu** key and save your settings.

Options
Mobile Network
Owner
Password

Owner
Name: Gary Mazo
Information:
Call 1-508-555-1210 to claim a REWARD
for returning my BlackBerry

TIP: Shortcuts to Lock

From your **Home** screen, quickly tapping the **K** key or pressing & holding the **A** key will **Lock** your BlackBerry. (Assumes you have turned on **Home Screen HotKeys**—see page 548). You can also press the **Lock** button on the top of your device.

Test what you've entered by locking your device. Tap the **Lock** button on the top of your BlackBerry or click on the **Lock** icon.

Keyboard Lock

Now you will see your owner information:

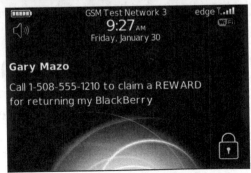

E-mail Security Tips

Never send personal information or credit card information via e-mail. Examples of information not to send are: credit card numbers, Social Security number, date of birth, mother's maiden name, or sensitive passwords / PIN numbers (such as for your bank account ATM card). If you have to transmit this information, it's best to call the trusted source or, if possible, visit them in person.

Web Browsing Security Tips

Like e-mail, if you are in an organization with a BlackBerry Enterprise Server, then when you use the BlackBerry Browser that is secured by the encryption from the Server, your communications will be secure as long as you are browsing sites within your organization's Intranet. Once you go outside to the Internet and are not using HTTPS connection, your web traffic is no longer secure.

Anyone that visits a site with HTTPS (Secure Socket Layer) connection will also have a secure connection from your BlackBerry to the web site, just like with your computer's web browser.

Whenever you are browsing a regular HTTP web site on the Internet (not your organization's secure Intranet), then be aware that your connection is not secure (even if are using a BlackBerry Enterprise Server). In this case, please make sure not to type or enter any confidential, financial, or personal information.

If You Lose Your BlackBerry

If you work at an organization with a BlackBerry Enterprise Server or use a Hosted BlackBerry Enterprise Server, immediately call your Help Desk and let them know what has happened. Most Help Desks can send an immediate command to wipe or erase all data stored on your BlackBerry device. You or the Help Desk should also contact the cell phone company to disable the BlackBerry phone.

If you are not at an organization that has a BlackBerry Enterprise Server, then you should immediately contact the cell phone company that supplied your BlackBerry and let them know what happened. Hopefully, a good Samaritan will find your BlackBerry and return it to you.

How to Turn Off (Disable) Password Security

NOTE: If you work at an organization with a BlackBerry Enterprise Server, you may not be allowed to turn off your password.

To turn off **Password Security**, go into the **Options** icon. Then click on **Password** and change it to **Disabled**. Save your settings. you will be required to enter your password one last time in order to turn it off for security purposes.

SIM Card Security Options

With any GSM phone, such as the BlackBerry 8520, if your phone was ever lost or stolen, your SIM card could be removed and used to activate another phone.

1. Click on Options and then Advanced Options.

2. Click on SIM card.

3. Press the **Menu** key and select **Enable** Security. The PIN code locks your SIM card to your BlackBerry.

4. Also change the PIN2 code for added security.

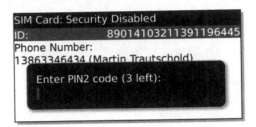

Chapter 35

Fixing Problems

Your BlackBerry is virtually a complete computer in the palm of your hand. Like your desktop computer, sometimes it needs a little tweaking or maybe even a reboot to keep it in top running order. This chapter has some of the most valuable tips and tricks to fix problems and keep your BlackBerry running smoothly.

BlackBerry Running Slowly? Clear Out the Event Log

Your BlackBerry tracks absolutely everything it does in order to help with debugging and troubleshooting in what is called an **Event Log**. It helps your BlackBerry run smoother and faster if you periodically clear out this log.

1. From your **Home** screen of icons, press and hold the **ALT** key and type **LGLG** (*Do not* press the **Shift** key at the same time) to bring up the **Event Log** screen, as shown.

2. Press the **Menu** key and select **Clear Log**.

3. Select **Delete** when it asks you to confirm.

4. Finally, press the **Escape** key to get back to your **Home** screen.

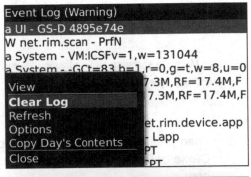

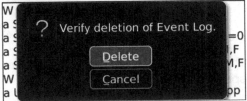

BlackBerry Running Slowly? Close Unused Icons Running in the Background

If you have been using the **Switch Application** menu item, the **Red Phone** key, or the **Alt+Escape** trick to multitask (see page 22), you may have many icons running in the background and slowing down your BlackBerry.

Periodically, you should verify that you have closed out all unnecessary application icons.

1. First, bring up the **Switch Applications** pop-up window to see what is running. Press and hold the **Menu** key or press and hold the **Alt** key and tap the **Escape** key.

> **NOTE:** These five icons cannot be closed: **BlackBerry Messenger** (which you will not see until it's installed), **Messages**, **Browser**, **Phone Call Logs**, **Home** (Home screen).

2. Now, glide the trackpad to the left/right to look for icons that you may not be using, such as **BlackBerry Maps**.

> **TIP:** Mapping software can really slow down your BlackBerry and reduce battery life as it tries to keep your current location mapped.

3. Then press the **Menu** key and select **Close** or **Exit**, usually the last menu item.

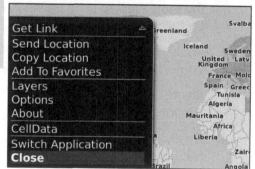

Then, repeat this procedure for every unneeded icon that is running. This should help speed up your BlackBerry.

> **TIP:** In the future, when you are done using an icon, press the **Menu** key and select **Close** or **Exit** to make sure that that icon is actually exiting out and freeing up memory and other resources on your BlackBerry.

Web Browser Running Slowly? – Clear out the Cache

You can make a dramatic improvement in the speed of your Web Browser by clearing out the cache. Start your Browser by clicking on the icon.

1. Inside the Browser, click the **Menu** key and select **Options**.

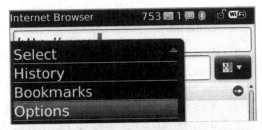

2. Select **Cache Operations**.

3. Click **Clear History**, then click all the **Clear** buttons below.

4. Answer **Yes** when it asked about clearing pushed content.

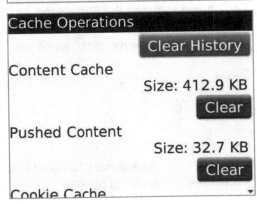

5. When done, press the **Escape** key a few times to return to the browser. This will usually improve your browsing speed significantly.

Automatic Memory Cleaning—Keep it Running Smoothly

One thing that may help keep your BlackBerry running smoothly is to utilize the automatic **Memory Cleaner** feature. Although your BlackBerry has lots of built-in memory, all smartphones are prone to *memory leaks*, which can cause the device to really slow down, and programs to hang or not work properly.

1. Start your **Options** icon and click on **Security Options**.

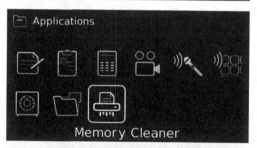

2. Glide down and click on **Memory Cleaning**.

3. Change the **Status** to **Enabled**. Once enabled, you will see more options. We recommend leaving the first two as **Yes** and adjusting the **Idle Timeout** down from **5** minutes to **1** or **2** minutes.

4. Finally, if you want, you can select **Show Icon on Home Screen**. Save your changes.

5. If you selected the **Show Icon on Home Screen** option, you will see it in the **Applications** folder, as shown.

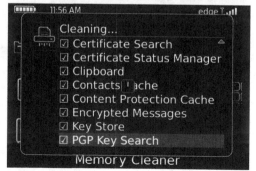

When you click the **Memory Cleaner** icon, you will see the cleaning happen.

Understanding Your Wireless Data Connection

Normally, you never have to think about your wireless signal, it just works. There may be times, however, when you realize that e-mails and SMS messages are not coming through.

If you see an hourglass or X instead of a check mark when you try to send an e-mail, you know something is wrong. The BlackBerry makers were nice enough to give you a wireless signal status meter at the top of your BlackBerry screen (or it might be on the bottom, depending on your particular BlackBerry wireless carrier or Theme).

There are two components to your wireless status meter: The **Signal Strength Meter** and the **Data Connection Letters** that are usually right next to the signal strength.

Data Connection Letters (Vary by Network Type)

CDMA Networks:

1XEV, 1X, 1xev, 1x

GSM Networks:

3G (logo), EDGE, GPRS, GSM, edge, gprs, 3G (no logo)

Your **data connection** is what allows you to send/receive e-mail, browse the Web, and send/receive data (addresses, calendar, and more). The confusing thing is that you may have very strong signal strength (for example, four-five bars), but still not be able to send/receive e-mail. The three or four letters (and maybe numbers) that are shown next to the **Signal Strength Meter** will vary based on the type of wireless network to which you are connected.

If you are connected to a CDMA Network (for example, Verizon/Sprint-USA, Telus, or Bell-Canada), then you will see 1XEV, 1X, 1xev, 1x.

If you are connected to a GSM Network (for example, AT&T/T-Mobile-USA, ROGERS-Canada,and so forth), then you will see these letters/symbols: 3G (with /without logo), EDGE, GPRS, edge, gprs, and GSM.

Take a look at Table 35-1 to understand whether or not you have a data connection.

Table 35-1: *Data connection letters, what they mean and what you need to do*

If you see ...	It means that...	What you should do...
OFF	Your radio is turned off	Turn your radio back on: Click on **Manage Connections → Restore Connections**.
GSM (no logo)	No data connection, only phone & SMS work	See the following section called **Turn Your Radio Off & On** and other sections in this chapter.
1XEV, 3G with logo	Highest-speed data, phone & SMS text are working	If e-mail and Web are not working, then see the **Register Now** section on page 22 and other sections in this chapter.
1X, EDGE	High-speed data, phone & SMS are working	If e-mail and Web are not working, then see the **Register Now** section on page 22 and other sections in this chapter.
GPRS	Low-speed data, phone & SMS are working	If e-mail and Web are not working, then see the **Register Now** section on page 22 and other sections in this chapter.
3G (no logo), 1xev, 1x, edge, gprs	No data connection, phone & SMS work only	See the following section called **Turn Your Radio Off & On** and other sections in this chapter.

Trouble with E-mail, Web, or Phone? Turn Your Radio Off &

Many times, the simple act of turning your radio off and back on will restore your wireless connectivity.

1. To do this, first go to your **Home** screen. From your **Home** screen, and click the **Manage Connections** icon, then and click on **Turn all Connections off**. (Figure 35-1)

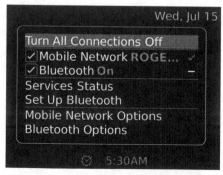

Figure 35-1. *Manage Connections screen*

2. Wait until you see the word OFF next to the wireless signal strength icon on your **Home** screen and then click on **Restore Connections** to turn your radio on again.

3. Look for your wireless signal meter and upper case **1XEV**, **1X,3G (with logo), EDGE or GPRS**. Check to see if your e-mail and Web are working. If not, try some more troubleshooting tips in the next few sections.

Trouble with E-mail, Web, or Phone? Host Routing >Register Now

If you try all the steps we just discussed and you still have trouble with sending/receiving e-mails or other problems involving your wireless connection, there is another option. Registering with the Host Routing Table can connect you to your network provider's data connection. Just follow these steps.

1. From your **Home** screen, click on your the **Options** icon or press the hotkey letter **O**.

2. Click on **Advanced Options.**

3. Now, click on **Host Routing Table.** (Figure 35-2)

TIP: Press **H** to jump down there.

Advanced Options
Browser Push
Cell Broadcast Settings
Default Services
Enterprise Activation
GPS
Host Routing Table
Maps
Service Book
SIM Card
TCP

Host Routing Table
* No Entries *

Register Now
Close

Registration message sent!
OK

Figure 35-2. *Register BlackBerry with the Host Routing Table*

4. On the **Host Routing Table** screen, you will see many entries related to your BlackBerry phone company.

5. Press the **Menu** key and select **Register Now.** If you see the **Registration message sent!** alert, then you should be okay. If you see a message like **Request queued and will be send when data connection is established**, then try some more troubleshooting steps in the following sections.

Trouble with E-mail, or Web? Send Service Books

This step will work for you only if you have **Setup Internet E-mail** or **Setup Personal E-mail.** (What is Internet/Personal E-mail? See page 37.)

1. From your **Home** screen, click on the **Setup** folder then on the **Manage Personal E-mail** or **Set Up Internet Mail** icon (each carrier is a bit different.)

2. If this is your first time, you may be asked to create an account or log in to get to **Personal E-mail Set Up**.

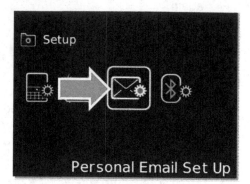

3. Press the Menu key and select the Service Books menu item and click.

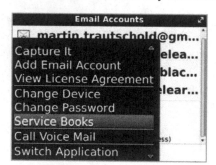 

Figure 35-3. *Send Service Books*

4. On the next screen (on the right, above), roll to the bottom of the screen and click on **Send Service Books** (Figure 35-3)

5. You should see a **Successfully Sent** message and then in your **Messages** icon, see a number of **Activation** messages—one per e-mail account (Figure 35-4).

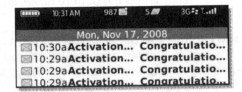

Figure 35-4. *Service Books successfully sent*

If you see any other message indicating the message was not sent, then you may want to verify that you have good coverage at your current location. You may also want to repeat some of other the troubleshooting steps in this chapter or contact your Help Desk or wireless carrier support.

Trouble with General Slowness of E-mail/Web? Try a Soft Reset

Sometimes, like on your computer, you simply need to try a reset or reboot (much like Ctrl+Alt+Del on a Window computer). You can do a similar soft reset on your BlackBerry by pressing and holding three keys simultaneously: ALT+CAP+DEL. (Figure 35-5)

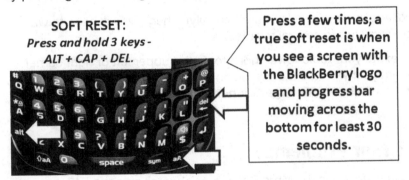

Figure 35-5. *How to perfrom a soft reset*

When You Really Need to Start Over... Hard Reset (Remove Battery)

Check out more images and help with opening your BlackBerry on page 4. Turn off your BlackBerry by pressing and holding the power button (the **Red Phone** key).

Remove the battery cover. After your BlackBerry is off, then turn it over and press the cover release button on the bottom of your BlackBerry. Then gently lift up the battery cover from the bottom of the device.

Gently pry out and remove the battery. You will have to put your fingernail in the top right or left edge next to the printed gray semi-circle and pry the battery out from the top side. It has a few small tabs holding it in at the bottom of the BlackBerry.

Using your fingernail, gently pry the battery up and out

Wait about 10-20 seconds.

Replace the battery. Make sure to slide in the bottom of the battery first, and then press down from the top.

Replace the battery door by aligning the tabs at the top and then sliding it so it clicks in and is flat.

Power-on your BlackBerry (it may come on automatically). Then you will need to wait a little for the timer to go away (up to several minutes).

Now, if you see **OFF** next to your radio tower indicator in the upper left or right corner, then you will need to turn your wireless radio back on. To do this, tap the **Menu** key and click the **radio tower** icon that says **Manage Connections**, and then **Restore Connections.**

Still Cannot Fix Your Problems?

Check out all the resources found in the More Resources chapter on page 543.

Chapter 36

More Resources

One of the great things about owning a BlackBerry is that you immediately become a part of a large, worldwide camaraderie of BlackBerry owners.

Many BlackBerry owners would be classified as enthusiasts and are part of any number of BlackBerry user groups. These user groups, along with various forums and web sites, serve as great resources for BlackBerry users.

Many of these resources are available right from your BlackBerry, and others are web sites that you might want to visit on your computer.

Sometimes, you might just want to connect with other BlackBerry enthusiasts, ask a technical question, or keep up with the latest and greatest rumors, apps, and accessories. This chapter gives you some great resources.

BlackBerry Technical Solution Center

Where to go for more help for anything to do with your BlackBerry:

Do a web search for **BlackBerry Technical Knowledge Base** or **BlackBerry Technical Solution Center.** One of the top links will usually get you to this page on www.blackberry.com.

You may also be able to get directly to the Solution Center by typing in this web address: www.blackberry.com/btsc/.

Just type your question in as few words as possible in the **Search** box in the middle of the screen. The Solution Center may look similar to the image in Figure 36-1.

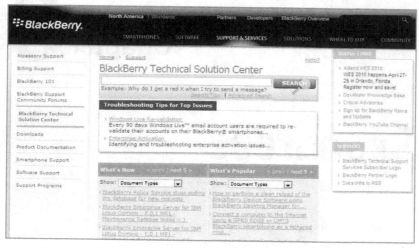

Figure 36-1. *BlackBerry Technical Solution Center web page*

Resources to Access from the BlackBerry Itself

The first place to start is the **Help** item found on most of the Menus. Learn all about how to use BlackBerry built-in **Help** on page 159.

Some of the resources actually have software icons to install right on your BlackBerry **Home** screen. Others, you will want to set as bookmarks in your BlackBerry Web Browser (learn about bookmarks on page 22).

The official BlackBerry mobile web site: Start your BlackBerry Web Browser.

Press the **Menu** key and select **Go To...**. Type in `mobile.blackberry.com`.

The page is organized with a **Help Directory**, a **What's Hot** section, **Fun and Games**, **Great Sites**, **Messaging**, **Maps & GPS**, and a **BlackBerry** page.

Click on any link to download software or visit the linked web site.

BlackBerry Forums and Discussion Groups

There are many of these discussion groups such as CrackBerry, BerryReview, BlackBerry Rocks, and BlackBerry Forums. A forum is an organized discussion about anything and everything BlackBerry. On each of these sites, you can discuss your BlackBerry, find tips and tricks, as well as post questions and read answers to other user's questions.

At the time of publishing, here are a few of these more popular forums.

- www.boygeniusreport.com
- www.blackberrycool.com
- www.blackberryforums.com
- www.crackberry.com
- www.berryreview.com
- www.blackberryrocks.com

Some sites even provide you a way to install an icon in your BlackBerry **Applications** menu for one-click access to participate in the discussion right from your BlackBerry.

Navigate through the forums or use the **Search** tool to find a particular topic of interest. One of the forums will be specific to your particular BlackBerry. Look for forums that match your BlackBerry model or series. For example, **BlackBerry Curve 8530** or **BlackBerry Curve 8520**.

> **TIP:** Try your best to enter your question under the correct forum topic; you are much more likely to find people answering you if you are in the correct topic area.

There are many, many other web sites to visit for more information and helpful resources that offer news, information, and discussion forums.

Made Simple Learning Free BlackBerry Tips

The authors host a web site at www.madesimplelearning.com that provides free BlackBerry tips via e-mail and free sample video tutorials. We also have a **Contact Us** page. Please drop us a line and let us know what is on your mind.

Thanks Again!

We sincerely thank you for purchasing this book and hope it has helped you really learn how to get every last drop of productivity and fun out of your BlackBerry!

Hotkeys – Open Almost any App with One Key!

You have learned the basics and can now navigate around your BlackBerry, but sometimes, you just want to get somewhere even more quickly. You may not use all the following information on a daily basis, but if you take the time to learn the hotkeys – you will save time doing thing things you do most often.

Throughout this book, we have shown you how to get the most out of your BlackBerry, where to find key information, and even suggested lots of tips and tricks to help along the way.

BlackBerry's built-in **hotkeys** to quickly take you to an app or through a menu without needless scrolling and searching.

For example, let's say you want to go to your **Messages** app – once **hotkeys** are enabled, just hit the letter **M**. No scrolling, searching, or fumbling. These hotkeys can be very useful.

Home Screen Hotkeys

Hotkeys can get you around your BlackBerry home screen, but there are also hotkeys inside of each of the core apps. We will show you how to not only launch programs quickly, but how to jump around inside of your apps and menus.

Once you enable your **Home Screen Hotkeys**, you will be able to launch most of the built-in applications with just one letter. This is extremely useful when you have lots of programs and you don't exactly remember where the launch icons are located.

> **NOTE:** Depending on the version of the operating system software installed on your BlackBerry smartphone, some of these Home screen hotkeys or key combinations may not work.

Enable Home Screen HotKeys

Use these steps to turn on the Blackberry **Home Screen** HotKeys (listed in the following table).

1. Access your **Phone call logs** by tapping the **Green Phone** key once.

2. Press the **Menu** key.

3. Select **Options** from the **Phone Logs** menu.

4. Click **General Options**, as shown in the screen to the right.

5. Glide to **Dial from Home Screen** and change it to **No** by pressing the **Space** key.

6. Press the **Menu** key and save your **Options** settings.

General Options	
Auto End Calls:	Into Holster
Auto Answer Calls:	Never
Confirm Delete:	Yes
Restrict My Identity:	Network Determined
Phone List View:	Call Log
Dial From Home Screen:	No
Show "My Number":	Yes
Default Call Volume:	Previous
Enhance Handset Call Audio	Previous
Enhance Headset Call Audio	Previous
Ringtone Lighting:	Off

List of Home Screen HotKeys

Below are the list of one key shortcuts to start most of your major icons.

M	Messages (Email)	**H**	Help
L	Calendar	**K**	Keyboard Lock
C	Contact or **A** = Address Book	**O**	Options Icon
V	Saved Messages	**U**	Calculator
N	BlackBerry Messenger	**S**	Search Icon
T	Tasks	**D**	MemoPad
B	Web Browser	**P**	Phone (Call Logs)
W	WAP Browser		

Once turned on, the hotkeys are denoted by the underlined letter. For example, highlight the **Options** icon and see that the hotkey O is underlined, as shown on the right.

CAUTION: Don't press and hold any of these hotkeys, otherwise you will start Speed Dialing (page 224)

E-mail Messages HotKeys

Not only are hotkeys helpful to launch apps, they are also very useful from inside an app to take you to a specific menu command. The following are the hotkeys that can get you around your **BlackBerry Mail** app.

NOTE: There is nothing you need to do to activate the hotkeys in the **Mail** app.

T Top of Inbox **B** Bottom of Inbox **U** Go to next newest Unread Message	**Space** key - Page Down **ALT + Glide trackpad** - Page Up/Down ENTER - Open Item (or compose new message when on date row separator)	**C** Compose new e-mail **R** Reply to selected message **L** Reply All to selected message **F** Forward selected
N Next day **P** Previous day **ALT + U** Toggle read / unread message	**E** Find Delivery Error(s) **V** Go to Saved Messages Folder **Q** (When highlighting e-mail/name) Show/Hide E-mail Address Or Friendly Name	**K** Search for next message in thread (Replies, Forward, etc.) **S** Search
Shift + Glide trackpad - Select messages **DEL** Delete selected message(s) CAUTION: If wireless e-mail synchronization is on, this will also delete e-mail from your inbox.	**ALT + O** – Filter for Outgoing Messages **ALT + I** – Filter for Incoming Messages	**ALT + M** – Filter for MMS Messages **ALT + S** – Filter for SMS Messages

Web Browser HotKeys

Just like in your **E-mail** app, you can quickly launch certain commands or jump to specific places in your **Browser** menu by using certain hotkeys, such as the ones in the following table.

TIP: When typing a web address, try these handy shortcuts:

- Use **Space** key for the "." (dots) in the web address.

- Press **Shift + Space** key to get the "/" (slash) (for example, in www.google.com/gmm).

- Press the **Escape** key to stop loading a web page and back up one level; or press and hold the **Escape** key to close the Browser.

T/X Top of Web Page	**Enter** – Select (click-on) highlighted link	**I** Zoom into web page
B Bottom of Web Page		**O** Zoom out of web page
Space key – Page Down	**Y** View history of web pages	**U** Show/hide top status bar
Shift + Space key – Page Up	**R** Refresh the current web page	**F/V** Search for text on the current web page
G Go to your Start page where you can type in a web address	**P** View the address for the page you are viewing with an option to copy or send the address (via e-mail, PIN, or SMS).	**Z** Switch between column and page view
H Go to your Home page (Set in **Browser** menu → Options → Browser Configuration)	**L** View the web page address the clickable link that is currently highlighted	**A** Add new bookmark
		K View your Bookmark List
Escape key/**DEL** key Go back 1 page		**S** View Browser Options screens
D Jump out of Browser, go to Home screen of icons	**J** Turn on JavaScript support	
C View connection information (bytes sent/received, security)		

NOTE: These hotkeys do not work in your Bookmark List or **Start** page; only when you are actually viewing a web page. In the Bookmark List, typing letters will find your bookmarks that match the typed letters.

Calendar HotKeys

You can turn on the **Calendar** hotkeys listed in the following table on your BlackBerry using these steps:

1. Start your **Calendar**.

2. Press the **Menu** key.

3. Select **Options** from the **Calendar** Menu.

4. In the **General Calendar Options** scree glide to **Enable Quick Entry** and change to **No** by pressing the **Space** key.

5. Save your **Options** settings.

General Calendar Options	
Initial View:	Day
Show Free Time in Agenda View:	Yes
Show End Time in Agenda View:	Yes
Actions	
Snooze:	5 Min.
Default Reminder:	15 Min.
Enable Quick Entry:	Yes
Confirm Delete:	No
Keep Appointments:	60 Days
Show Tasks:	No

D	Day View
W	Week View
M	Month View
A	Agenda View
N	Next day
P	Previous day
G	Go To Date
T	Jump to Today (Now)
C	Schedule new event (detail view)
Space key	Next Day (day view)
DEL	Delete selected event

Shift + glide trackpad – select several hours – example if you wanted to quickly schedule a 3 hour meeting you would highlight the 3 hours and press **Enter**.

Enter – (in Day View – not on a scheduled event) Start Quick Scheduling

Enter – (in Day View – on a scheduled event) Opens it.

Quick Scheduling New Events in Day View:

Enter key   Begin Quick Scheduling, then type Subject of Appointment on Day View screen.

4:00p Quick scheduling │
4:15p

ALT + Glide trackpad down – Change **Start** time

4:30p Quick scheduling │
4:45p

Glidetrackpad up/down – Change **Ending** time

4:30p Quick scheduling │
5:30p

Enter or click **trackpad** – Save new event

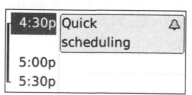

Enter or click **trackpad** – Open the event you just scheduled to change details such as Recurring, Notes, Alarms, and so forth.

Moving Around: Glide **trackpad** left/right to move a day-at-a-time (Day or Week View)

Media Player HotKeys

The hotkeys and tips below will help you enjoy media on your BlackBerry by performing many of the common functions with a single keystroke or special key combinations.

You also have dedicated media control keys— **Previous Track**, **Play/Pause**, **Next Track**—on the top of your BlackBerry Curve.

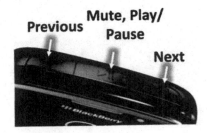

These keys work only inside the Media Player App	These keys work anytime (Whether inside the Media App or not)
N Next track/video	Press & hold **Volume Up** key – Next track/video
P Previous track/video	Press & hold **Volume Down** key – Previous track/video
Space key Play / pause	**Mute** Key on top – Play/pause
Enter key Selects highlighted button (same as clicking trackpad / clicking trackball)	**$/Speaker** key – Switch between speaker and handset/headset (including Bluetooth headset)
DEL Delete selected media item (song, video, and so forth, when in list or icon view)	
Jumping Out of the Media Player: Press the **Red Phone** key to jump back to the Home screen.	Jumping Back into the Media Player and currently playing song/video: Tap the **Menu** key and select **Now Playing**… from the top of the menu. Press and hold the **Menu** key, then select the **Media** icon from the pop-up.

Index

3GP format, 410

 A

C

N

O

■S